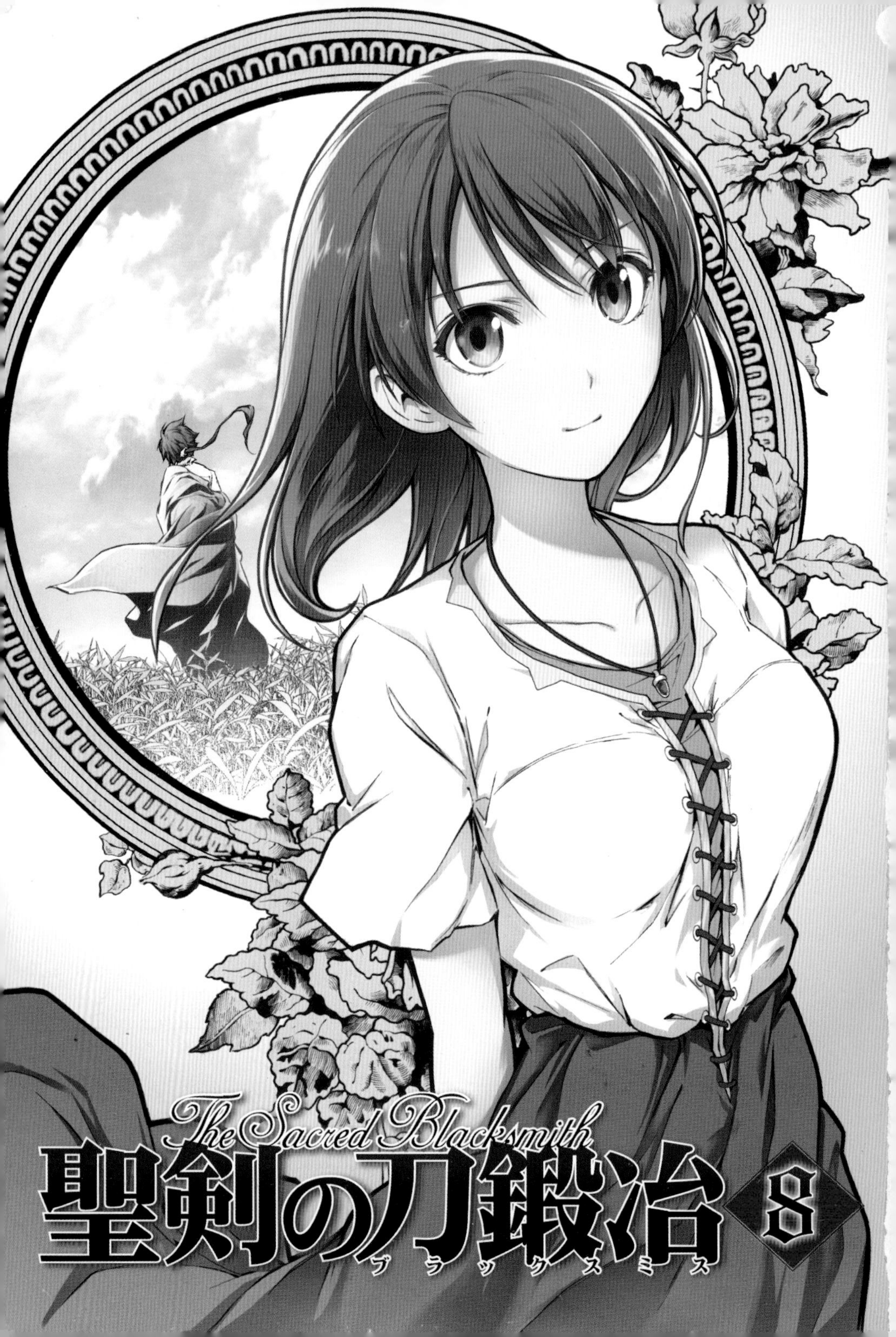
The Sacred Blacksmith
聖剣の刀鍛冶
ブラックスミス
8

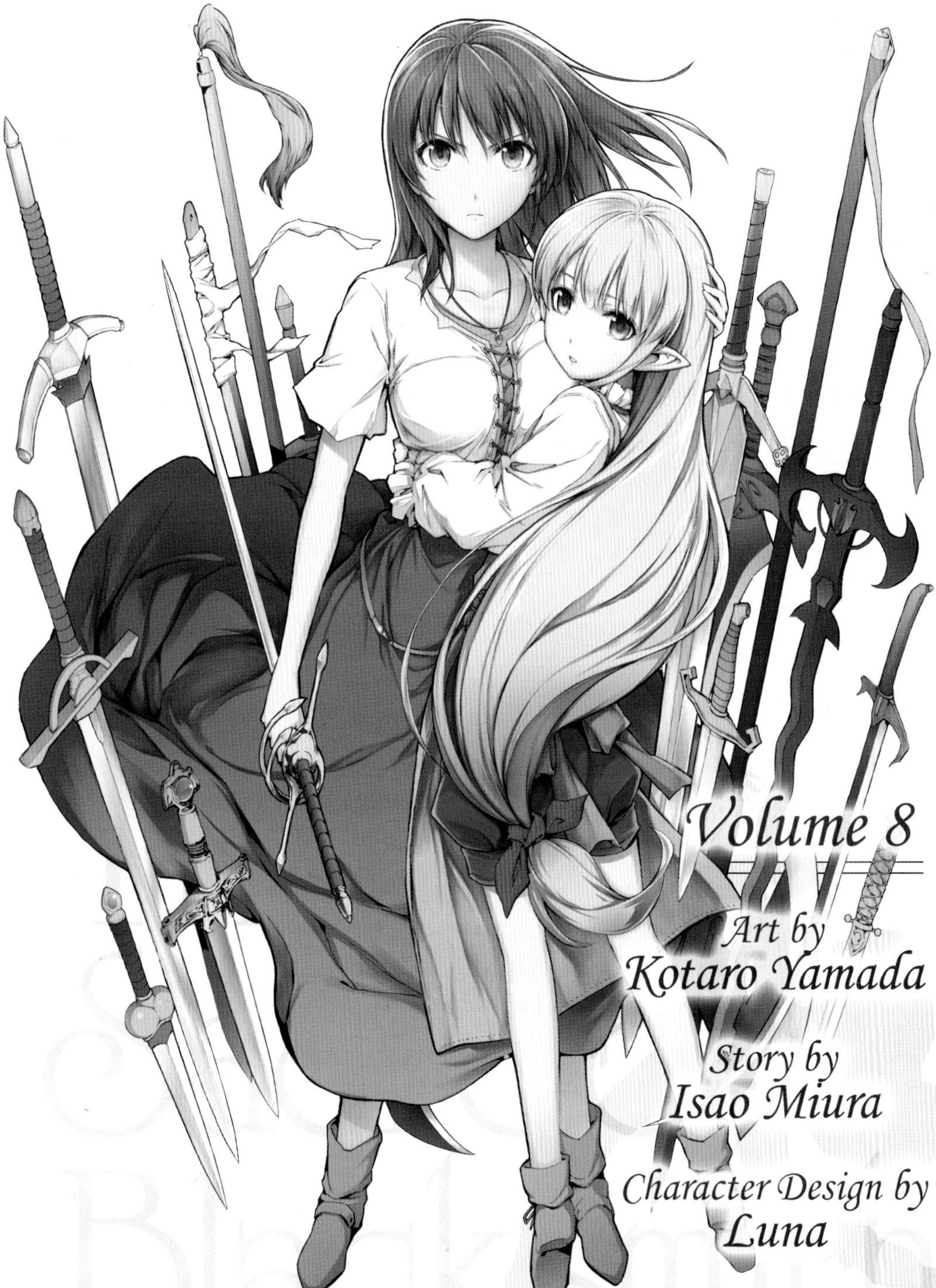

Volume 8

Art by
Kotaro Yamada

Story by
Isao Miura

Character Design by
Luna

登場人物紹介 Character

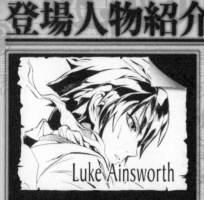

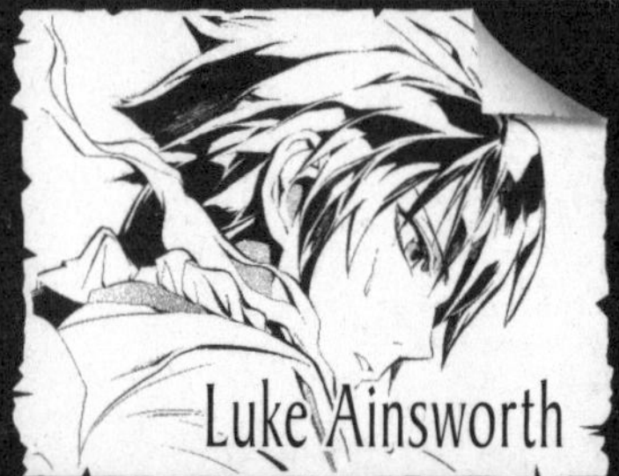
Luke Ainsworth

A proficient swordsman who uses an unusual blade called a "katana." Pessimistic and world-weary, he runs his own smithy.

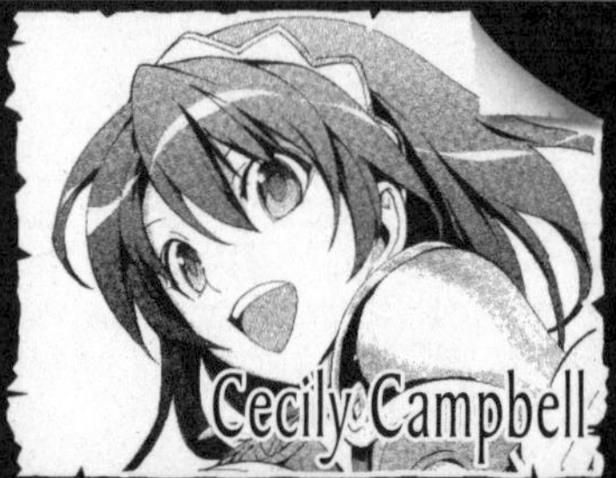
Cecily Campbell

A young lady knight who is part of the Knight Guard, charged with defending the independent trade city of Housman. Ex-nobility, she has a strong sense of justice.

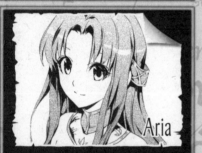

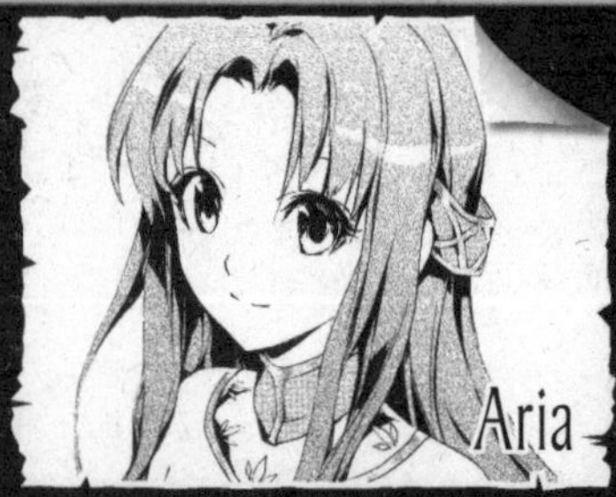
Aria

The "Demon Blade" of wind. A demon "born" at the end of the Valbanill War, she normally walks about as a human woman. However, she can turn into a rapier at will.

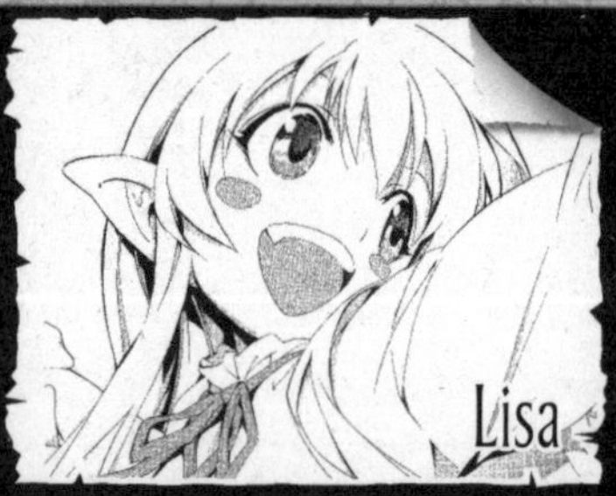
Lisa

The assistant who lives and works at Luke's smithy. Innocent and carefree, she loves talking with everyone. She says she is only three years old.

Other Characters

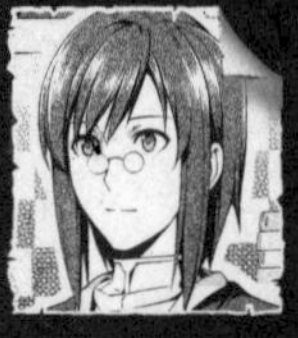

Ewain Benjamin
An archaeologist from the Militant Nation, he and Luke went to Blair Volcano, where they got lost. He is fascinated with Aria.

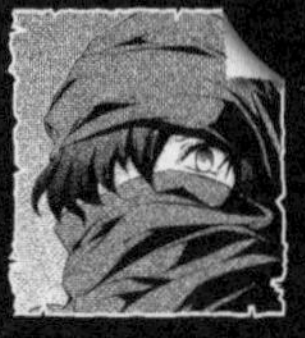

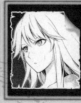

Hilda
An assassin from the former Crowd Powers, she was once rescued by Cecily and now feels a debt of gratitude to her.

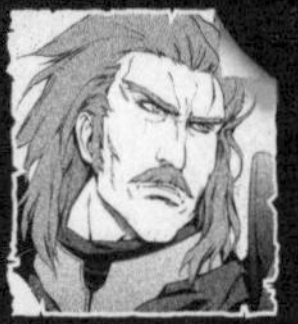

Horatio Disraeli
An elite in the Imperial Crowd Power Army, he wields the Demon Blade Francesca.

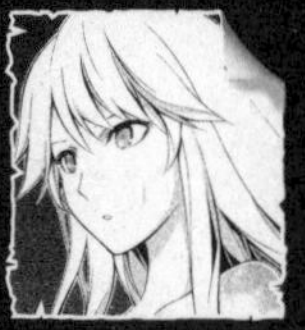

Nameless
A Demon Blade owned by the Imperial Crowd Power. She tells Aria the secret to transforming into a sword one last time.

Decades ago, a great war raged across the continent. Called the "Valbanill War," it saw the widespread use of powerful Demon Pacts. Forty-four years later, a young lady knight named Cecily Campbell meets a mysterious blacksmith named Luke Ainsworth and asks him to forge for her a sword.

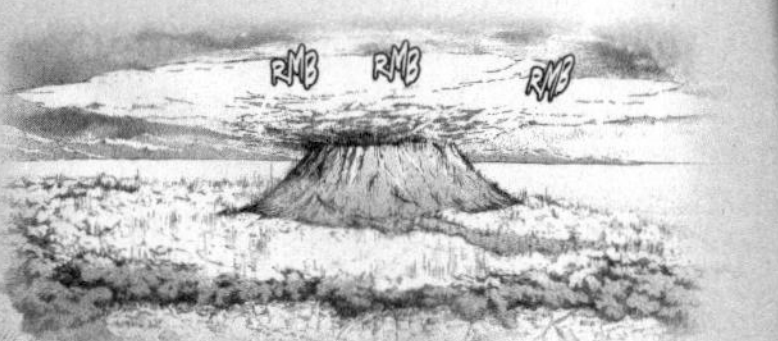
RMB
RMB
RMB

Out of nowhere, an earthquake shook the Independent Trade City. Realizing that the tremor is a sign of Valbanill's impending awakening, Luke rushed off to Blair Volcano to view the original Sacred Blade, in the hope that it would help him speed up the forging of a new Sacred Blade.

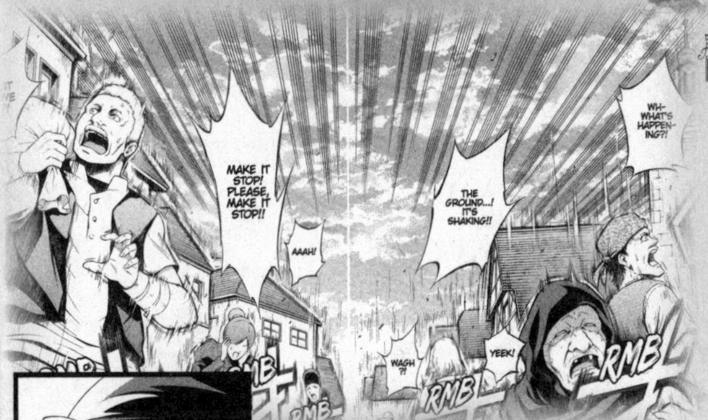
WH-WHAT'S HAPPENING?!
THE GROUND...! IT'S SHAKING!!
MAKE IT STOP! PLEASE, MAKE IT STOP!!
AAAH!
YEEK!
RMB
WAGH?!
RMB
RMB
RMB

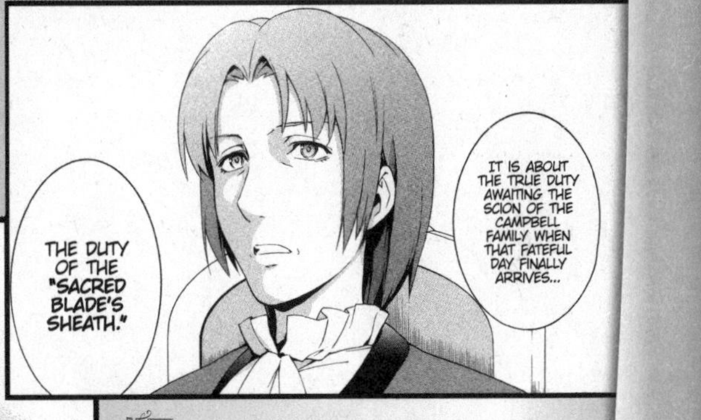
IT IS ABOUT THE TRUE DUTY AWAITING THE SCION OF THE CAMPBELL FAMILY WHEN THAT FATEFUL DAY FINALLY ARRIVES...
THE DUTY OF THE "SACRED BLADE'S SHEATH."

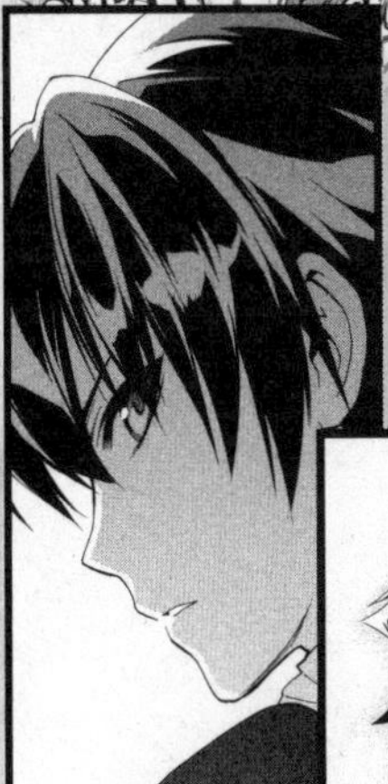

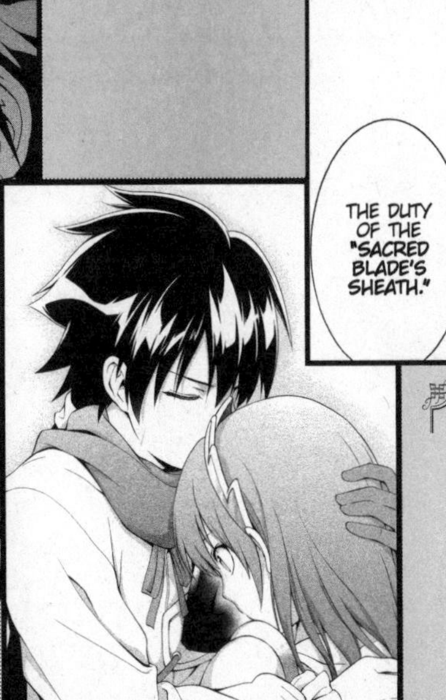

Meanwhile, Cecily's mother finally revealed to her the duty of becoming "The Sacred Blade's Sheath," which falls to all of the scions of the Campbell family. Though she knows it is her duty to become a "replacement" Sacred Blade, Cecily still believes that Luke will finish the true one in time.

あらすじ Story

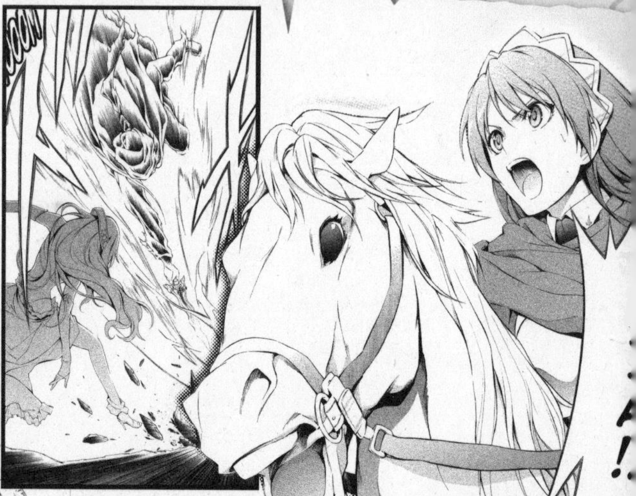

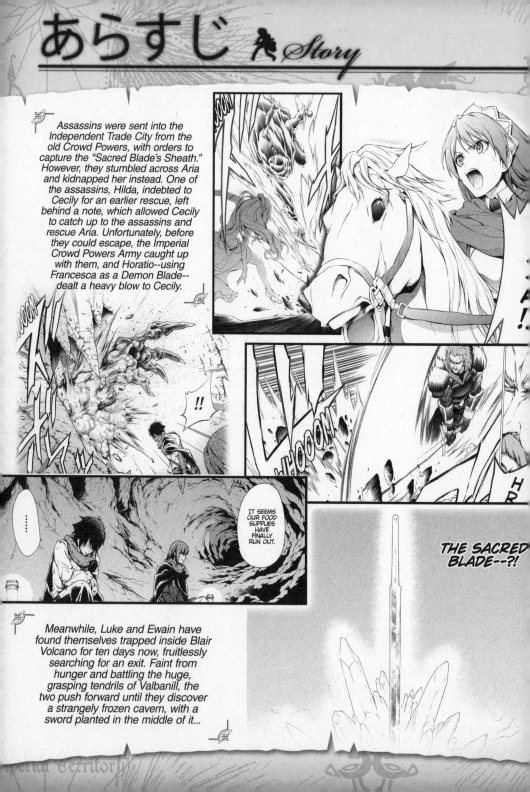

Assassins were sent into the Independent Trade City from the old Crowd Powers, with orders to capture the "Sacred Blade's Sheath." However, they stumbled across Aria and kidnapped her instead. One of the assassins, Hilda, indebted to Cecily for an earlier rescue, left behind a note, which allowed Cecily to catch up to the assassins and rescue Aria. Unfortunately, before they could escape, the Imperial Crowd Powers Army caught up with them, and Horatio--using Francesca as a Demon Blade--dealt a heavy blow to Cecily.

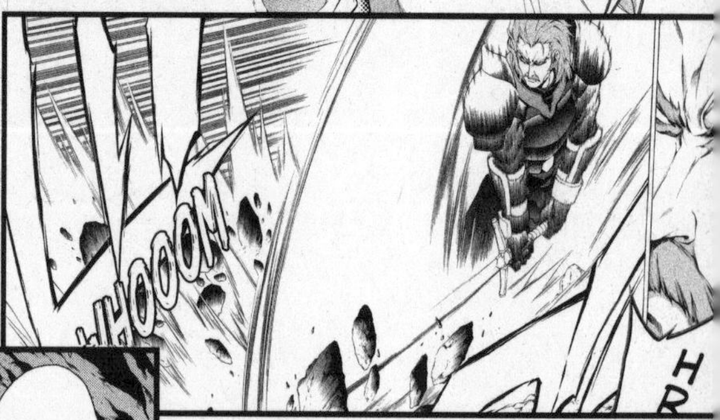

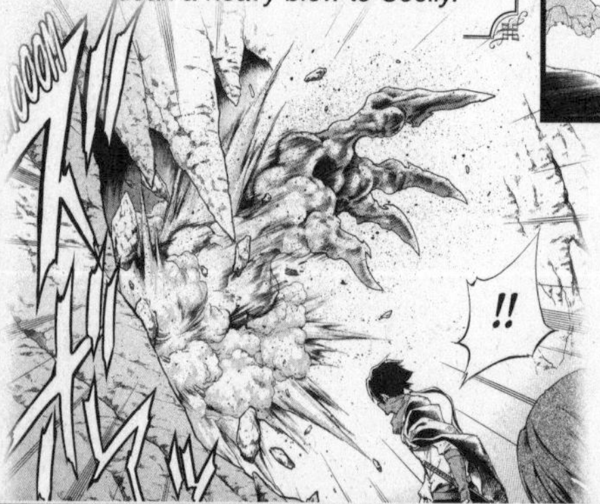
!!

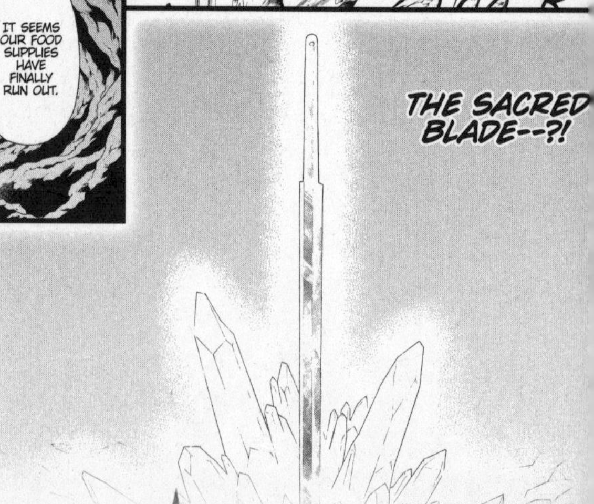
THE SACRED BLADE--?!

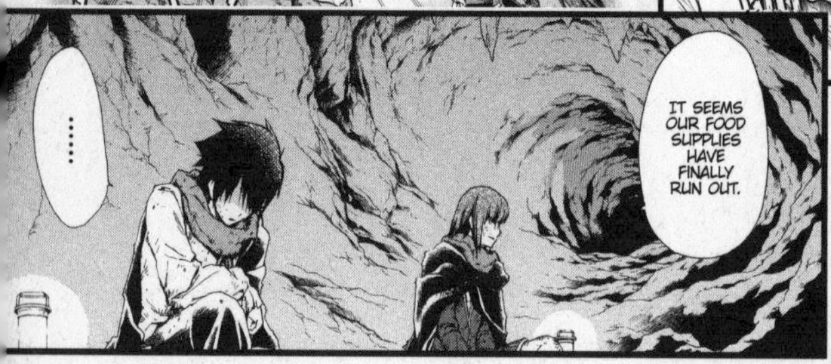
IT SEEMS OUR FOOD SUPPLIES HAVE FINALLY RUN OUT.
......

Meanwhile, Luke and Ewain have found themselves trapped inside Blair Volcano for ten days now, fruitlessly searching for an exit. Faint from hunger and battling the huge, grasping tendrils of Valbanill, the two push forward until they discover a strangely frozen cavern, with a sword planted in the middle of it...

The Sacred Blacksmith

聖剣の刀鍛冶

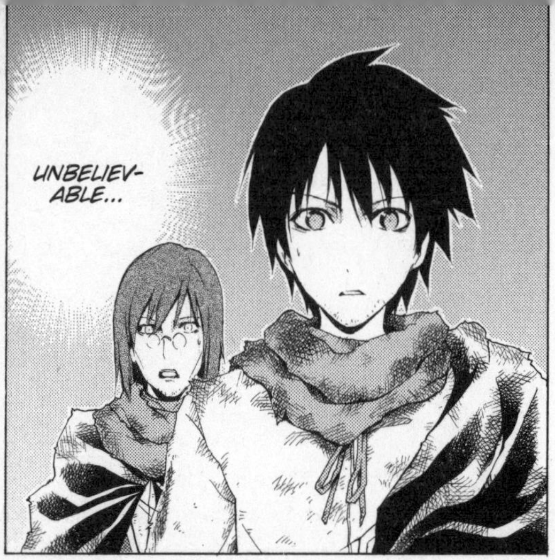
UNBELIEV-
ABLE...

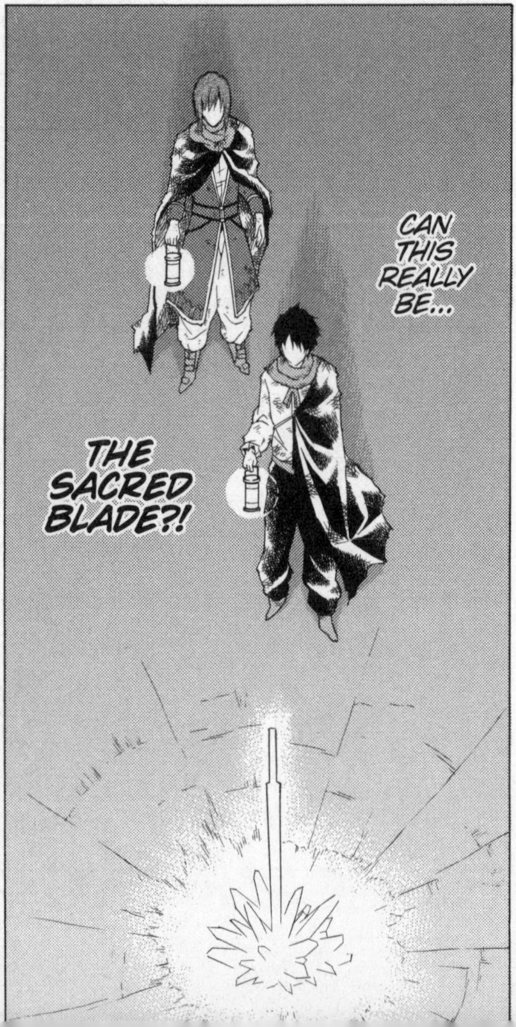
CAN THIS REALLY BE...
THE SACRED BLADE?!

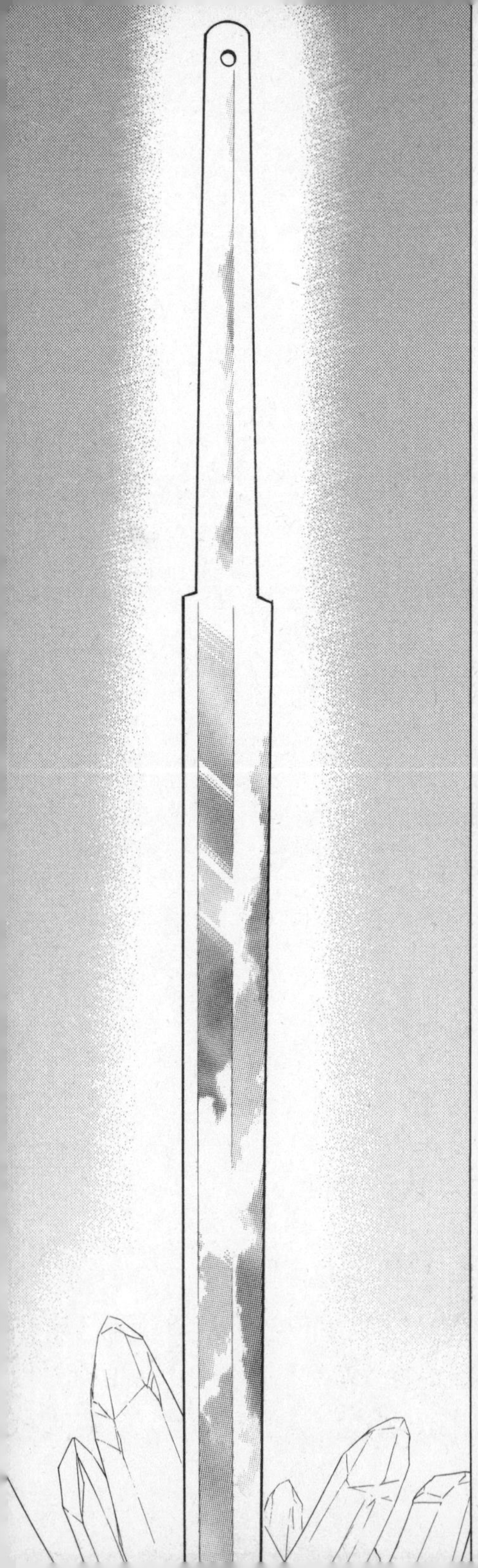

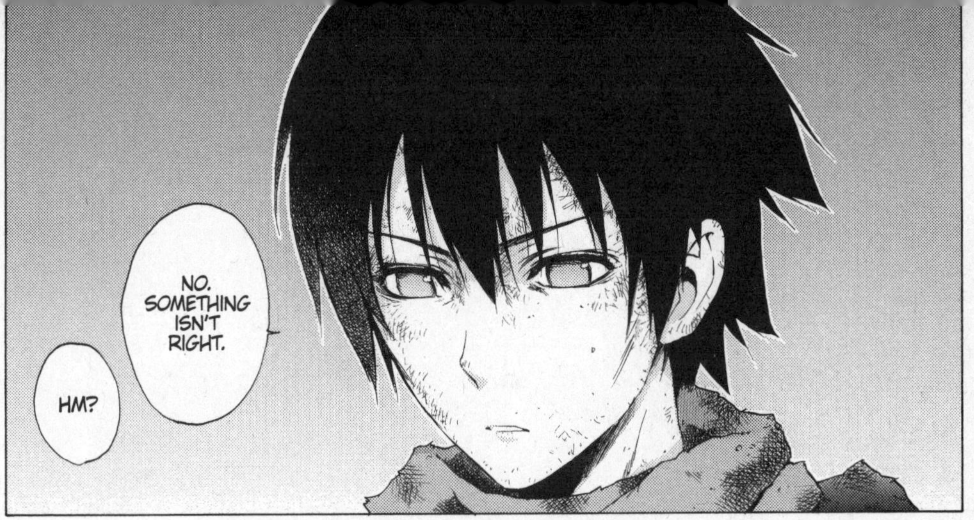
NO. SOMETHING ISN'T RIGHT.
HM?

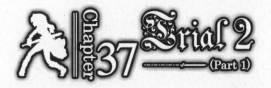

Chapter 37 Trial 2 (Part 1)

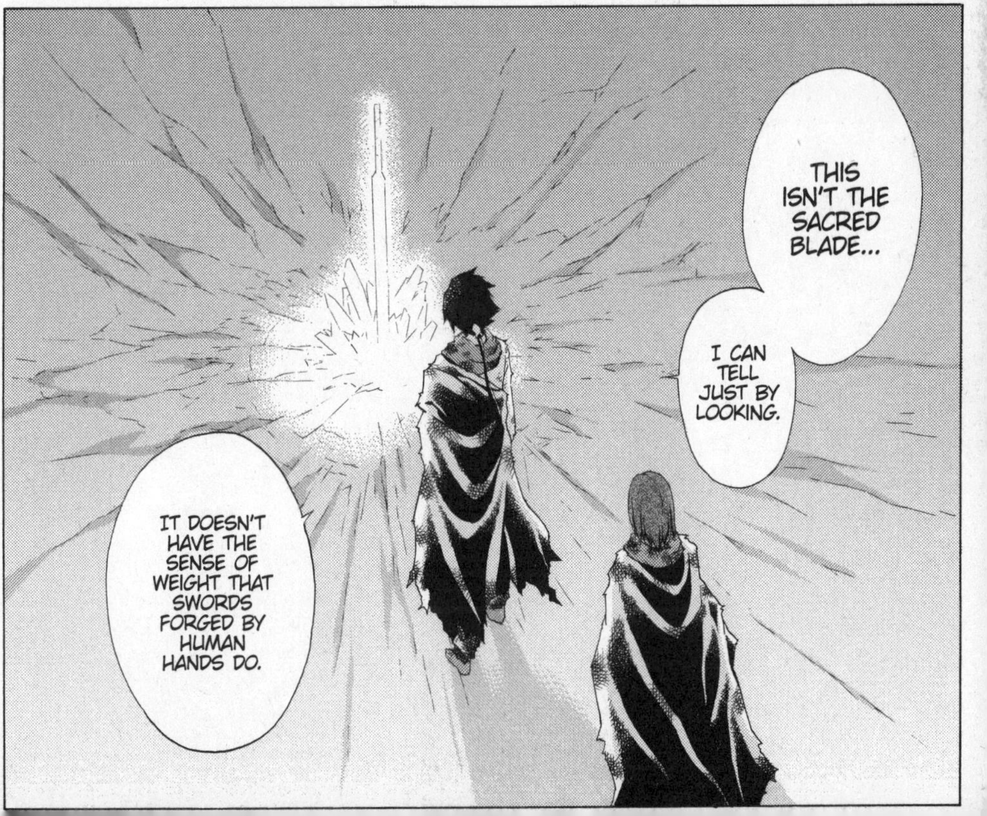
THIS ISN'T THE SACRED BLADE...
I CAN TELL JUST BY LOOKING.
IT DOESN'T HAVE THE SENSE OF WEIGHT THAT SWORDS FORGED BY HUMAN HANDS DO.

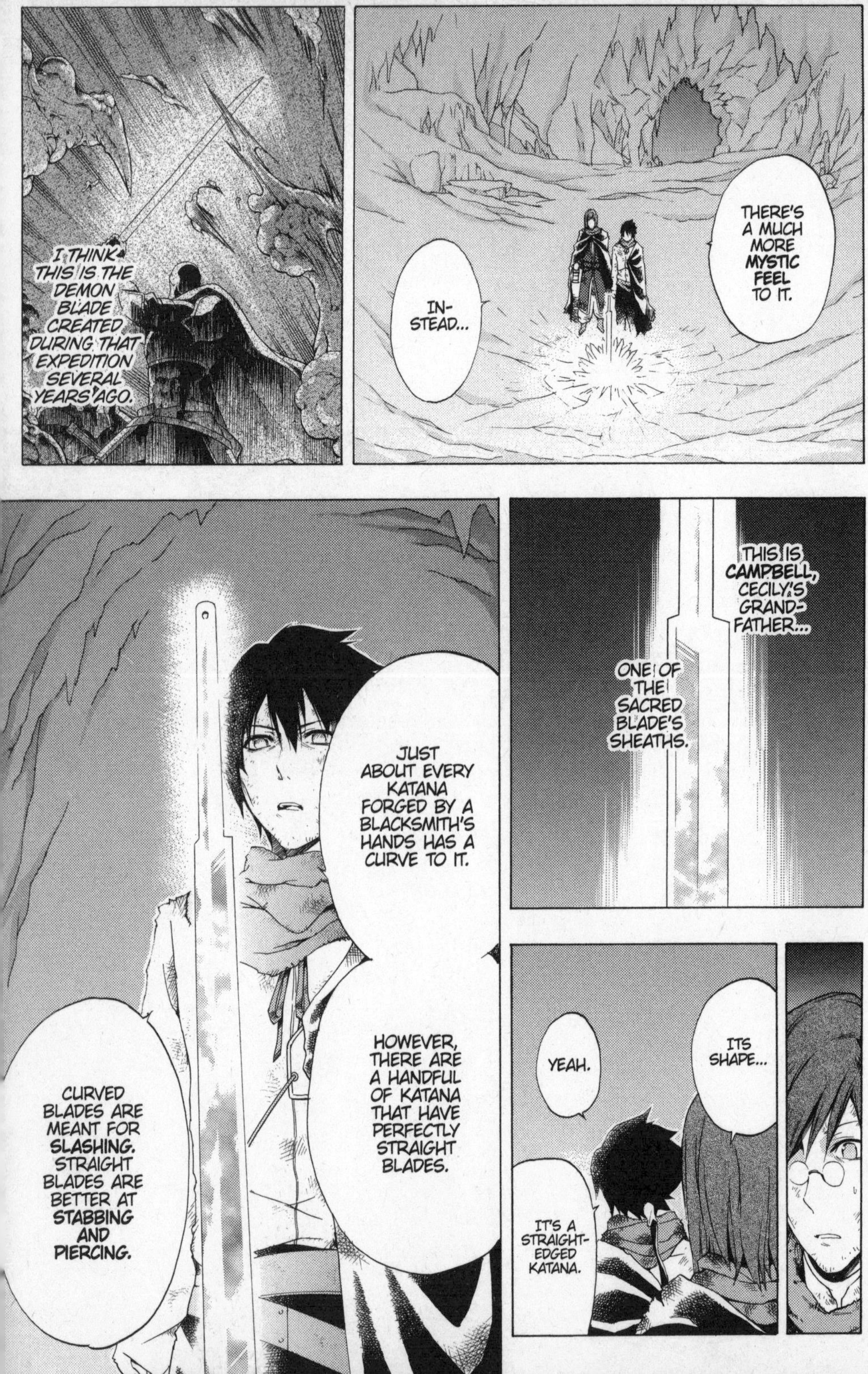
THERE'S A MUCH MORE MYSTIC FEEL TO IT.
IN-STEAD...
I THINK THIS IS THE DEMON BLADE CREATED DURING THAT EXPEDITION SEVERAL YEARS AGO.
THIS IS CAMPBELL, CECILY'S GRAND-FATHER...
ONE OF THE SACRED BLADE'S SHEATHS.
ITS SHAPE...
YEAH.
IT'S A STRAIGHT-EDGED KATANA.
JUST ABOUT EVERY KATANA FORGED BY A BLACKSMITH'S HANDS HAS A CURVE TO IT.
HOWEVER, THERE ARE A HANDFUL OF KATANA THAT HAVE PERFECTLY STRAIGHT BLADES.
CURVED BLADES ARE MEANT FOR SLASHING. STRAIGHT BLADES ARE BETTER AT STABBING AND PIERCING.

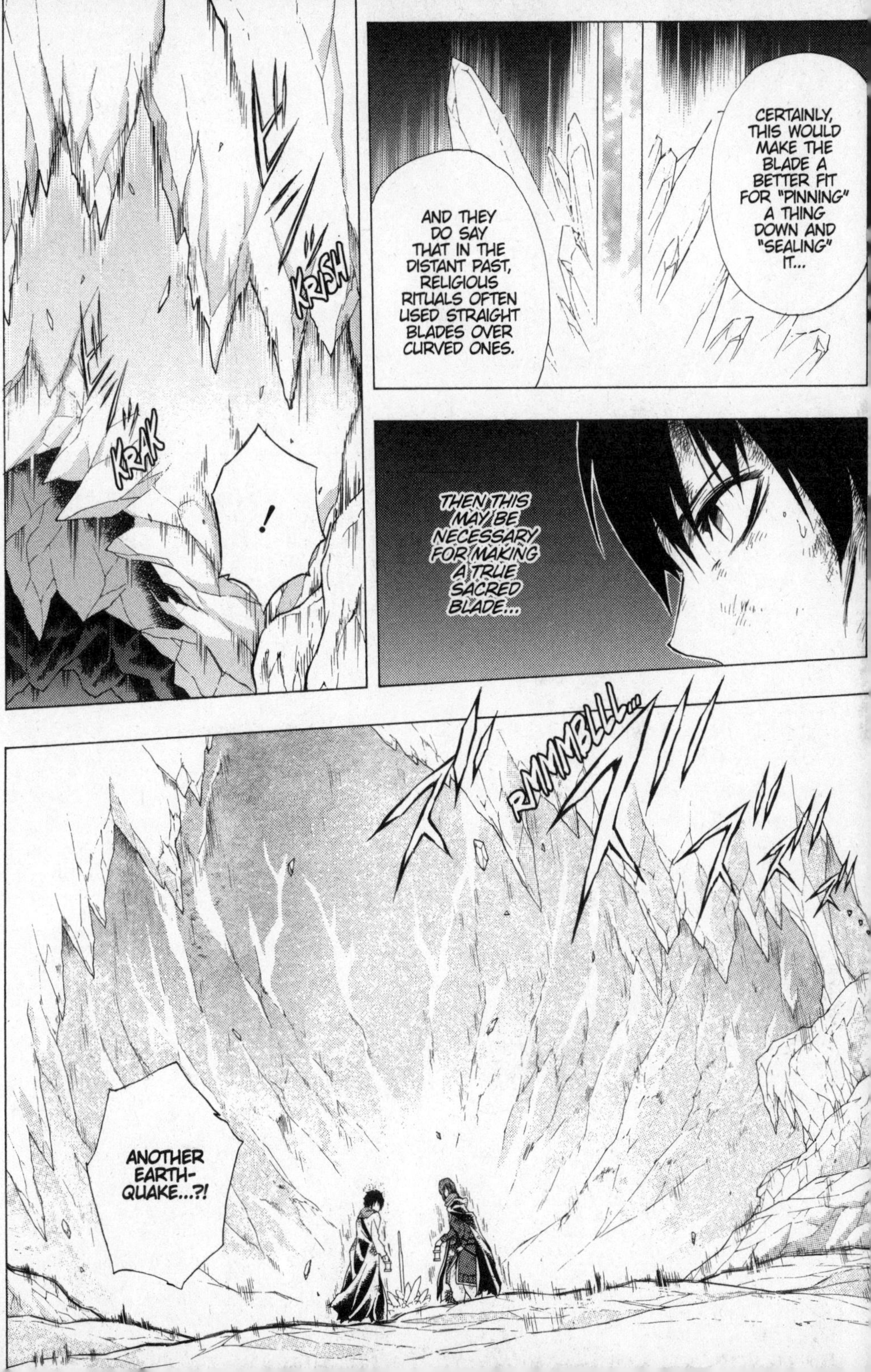
CERTAINLY, THIS WOULD MAKE THE BLADE A BETTER FIT FOR "PINNING" A THING DOWN AND "SEALING" IT...
AND THEY DO SAY THAT IN THE DISTANT PAST, RELIGIOUS RITUALS OFTEN USED STRAIGHT BLADES OVER CURVED ONES.
THEN THIS MAY BE NECESSARY FOR MAKING A TRUE SACRED BLADE...
KRISH
KRAK
!
RMMMBLLL...
ANOTHER EARTH-QUAKE...?!

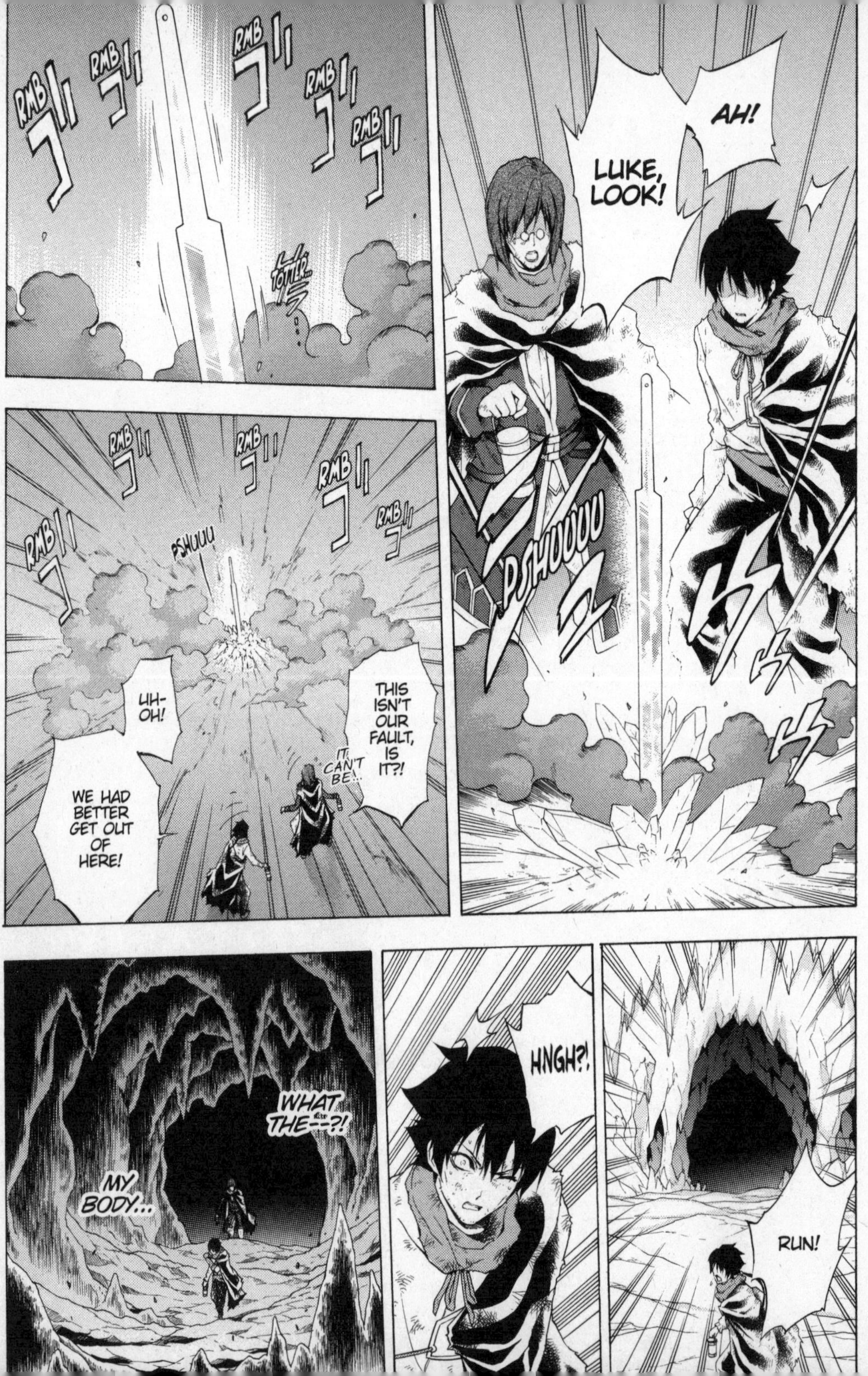
AH!
LUKE, LOOK!
PSHUUUU
RMB
RMB
RMB
RMB
RMB
TOTTER...
RMB
RMB
RMB
RMB
RMB
PSHUUU
THIS ISN'T OUR FAULT, IS IT?!
IT CAN'T BE...
UH-OH!
WE HAD BETTER GET OUT OF HERE!
RUN!
HNGH?!
WHAT THE--?!
MY BODY...

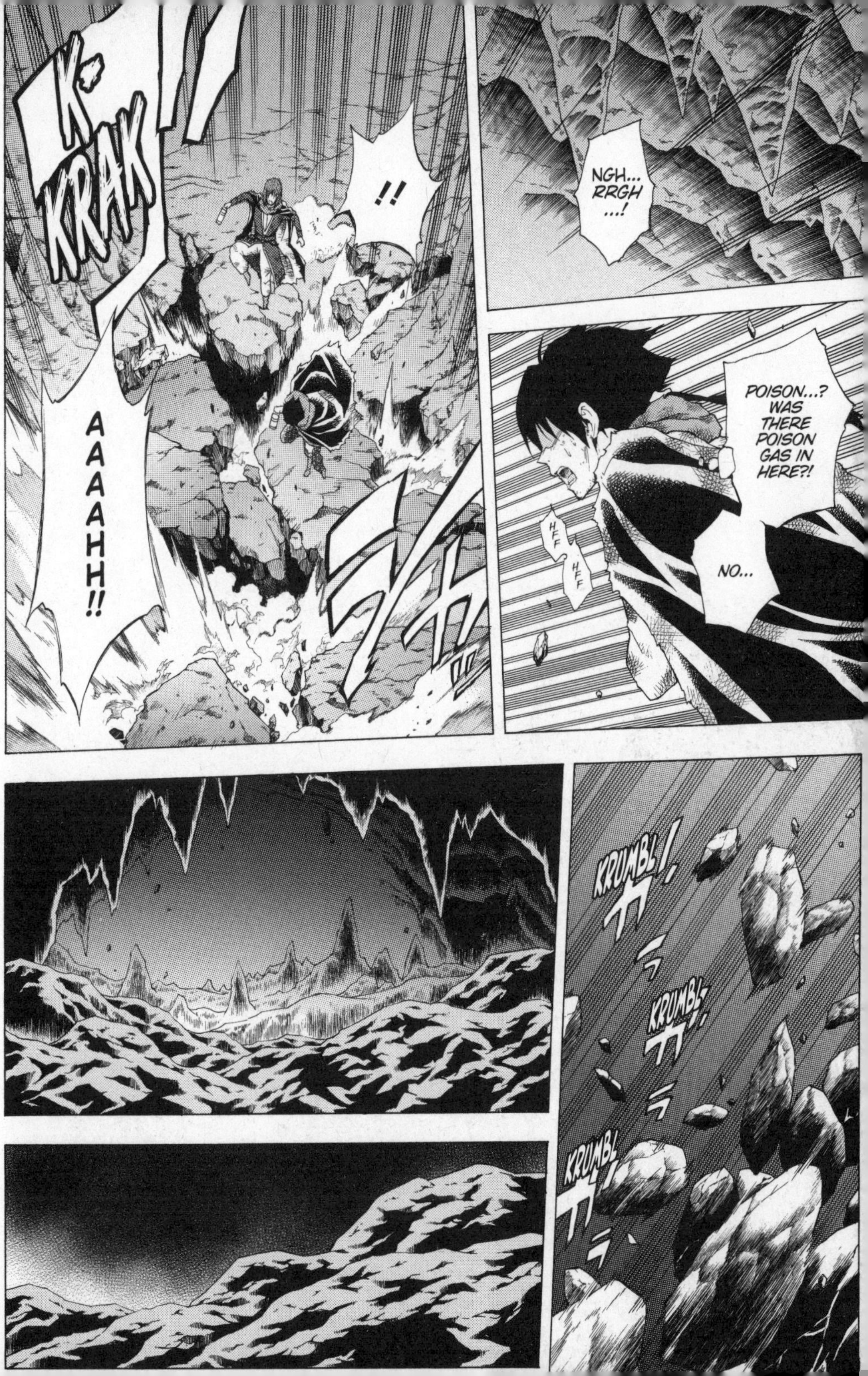
NGH... RRGH ...!
POISON...? WAS THERE POISON GAS IN HERE?!
HFF HFF
NO...
K-KRAK
!!
AAAAAHH!!
KRUMBL
KRUMBL
KRUMBL

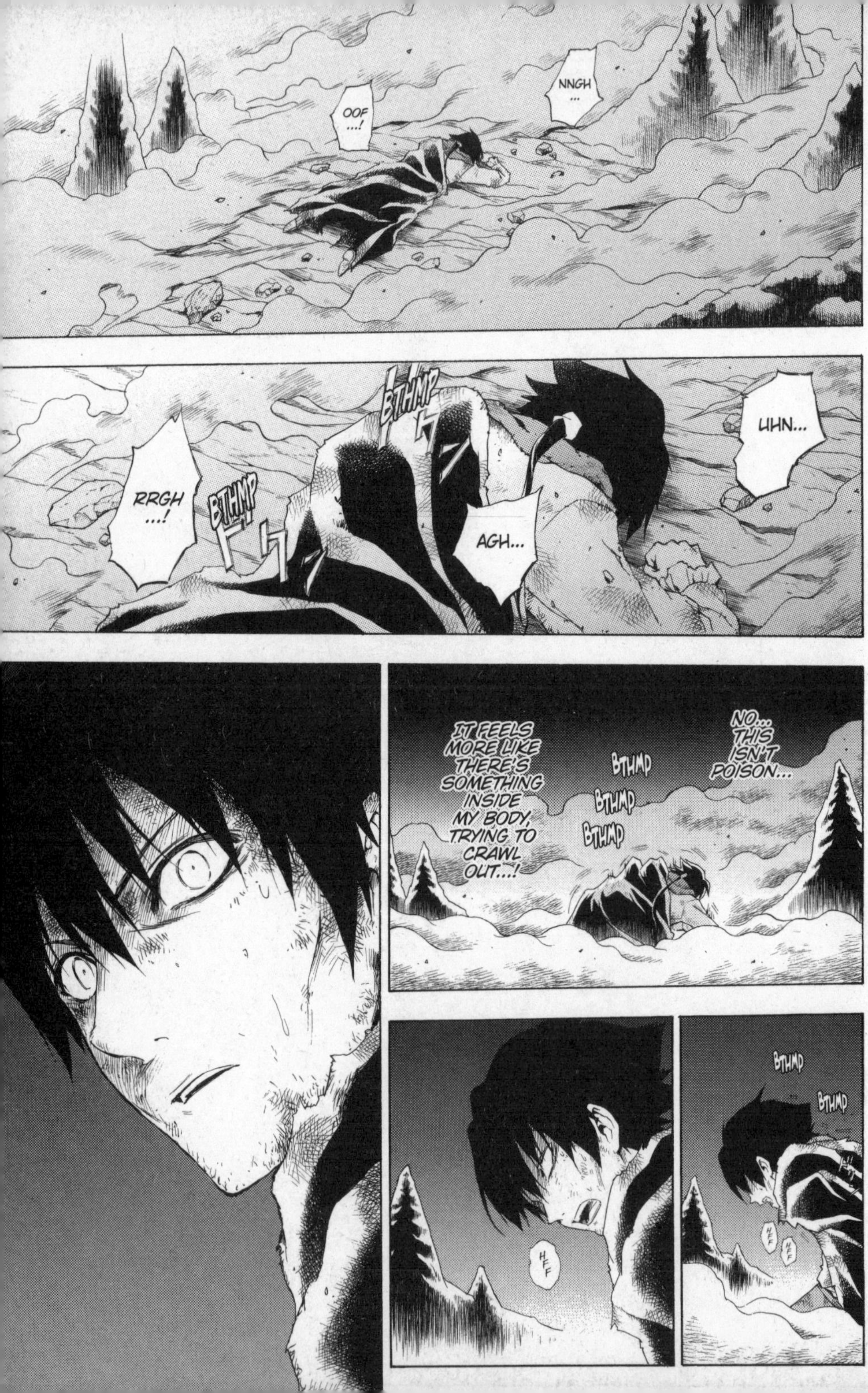
NNGH ...
OOF ...!
UHN...
BTHMP
AGH...
RRGH ...!
BTHMP
NO... THIS ISN'T POISON...
BTHMP
BTHMP
BTHMP
IT FEELS MORE LIKE THERE'S SOMETHING INSIDE MY BODY, TRYING TO CRAWL OUT...!
BTHMP
BTHMP
HFF
HFF
HFF

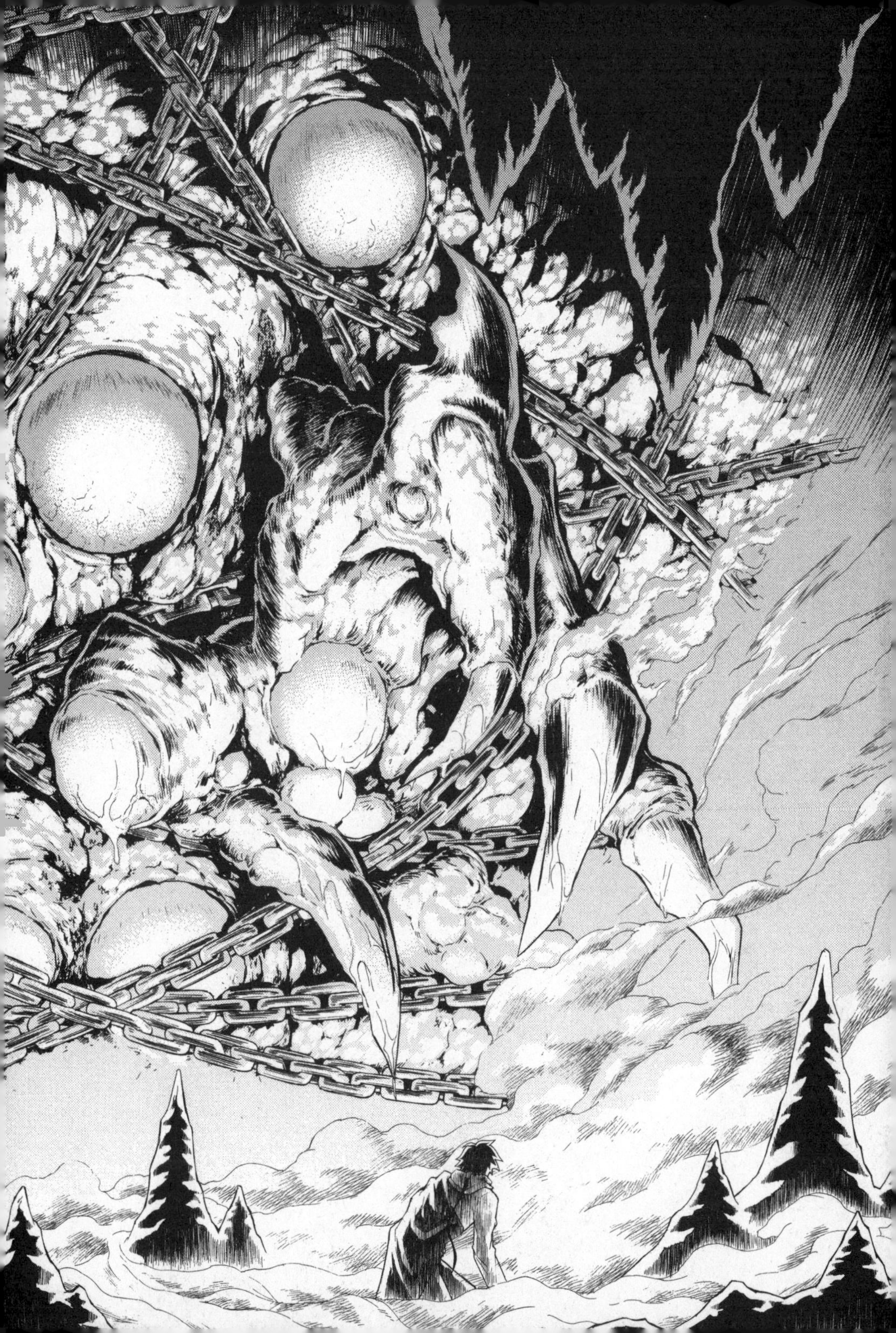

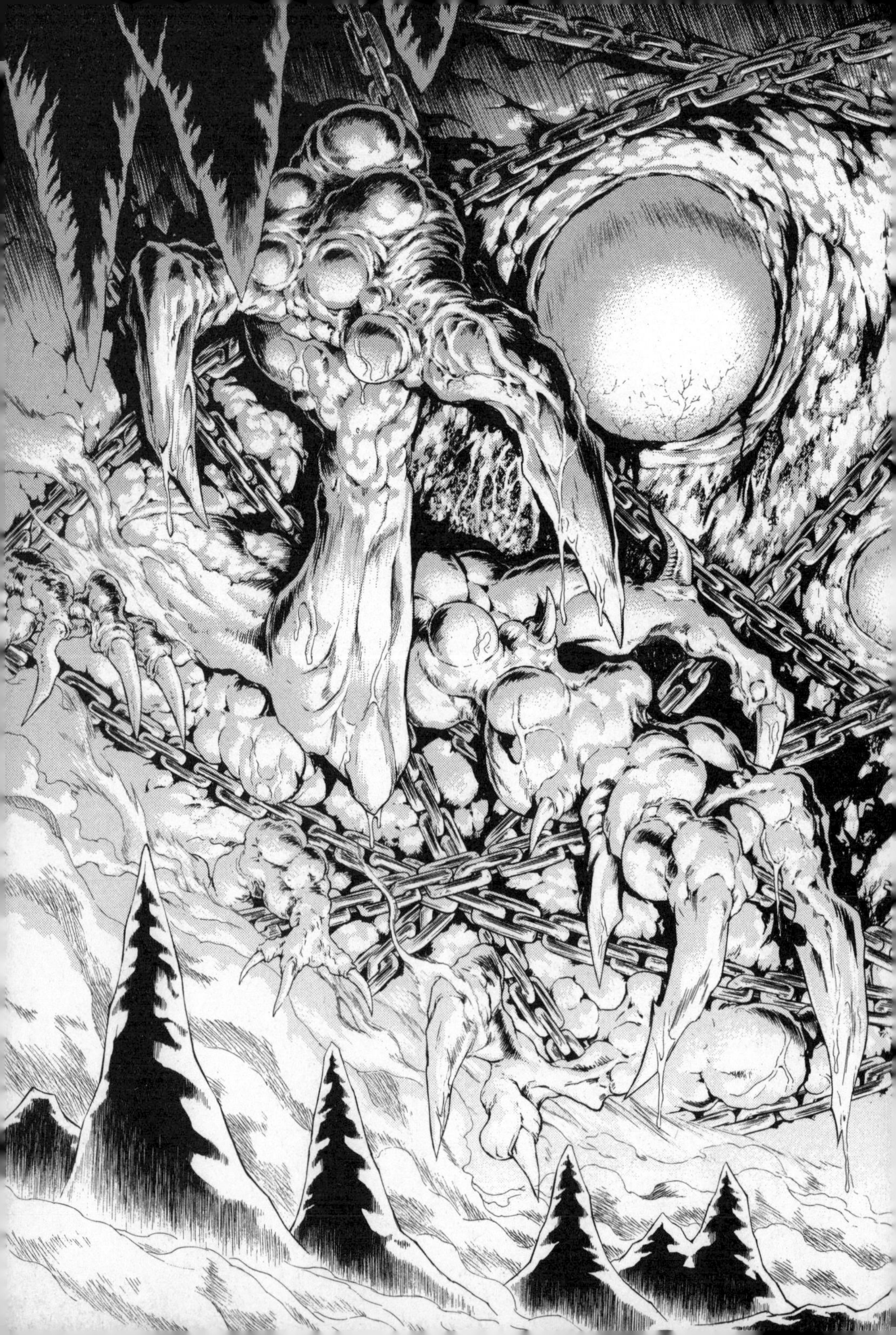

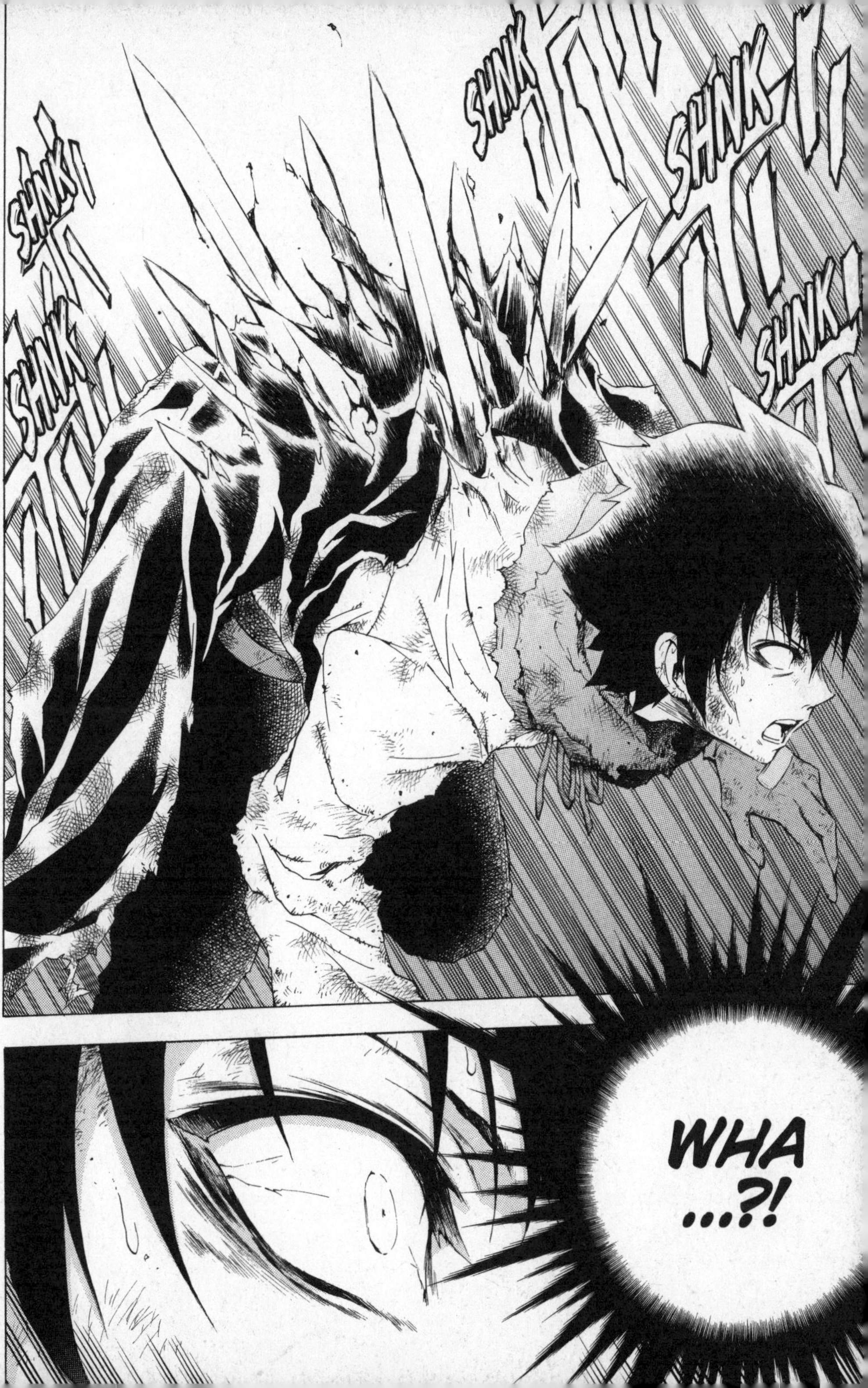

SHNK!
SHNK
SHNK!
SHNK!
SHNK
WHA ...?!

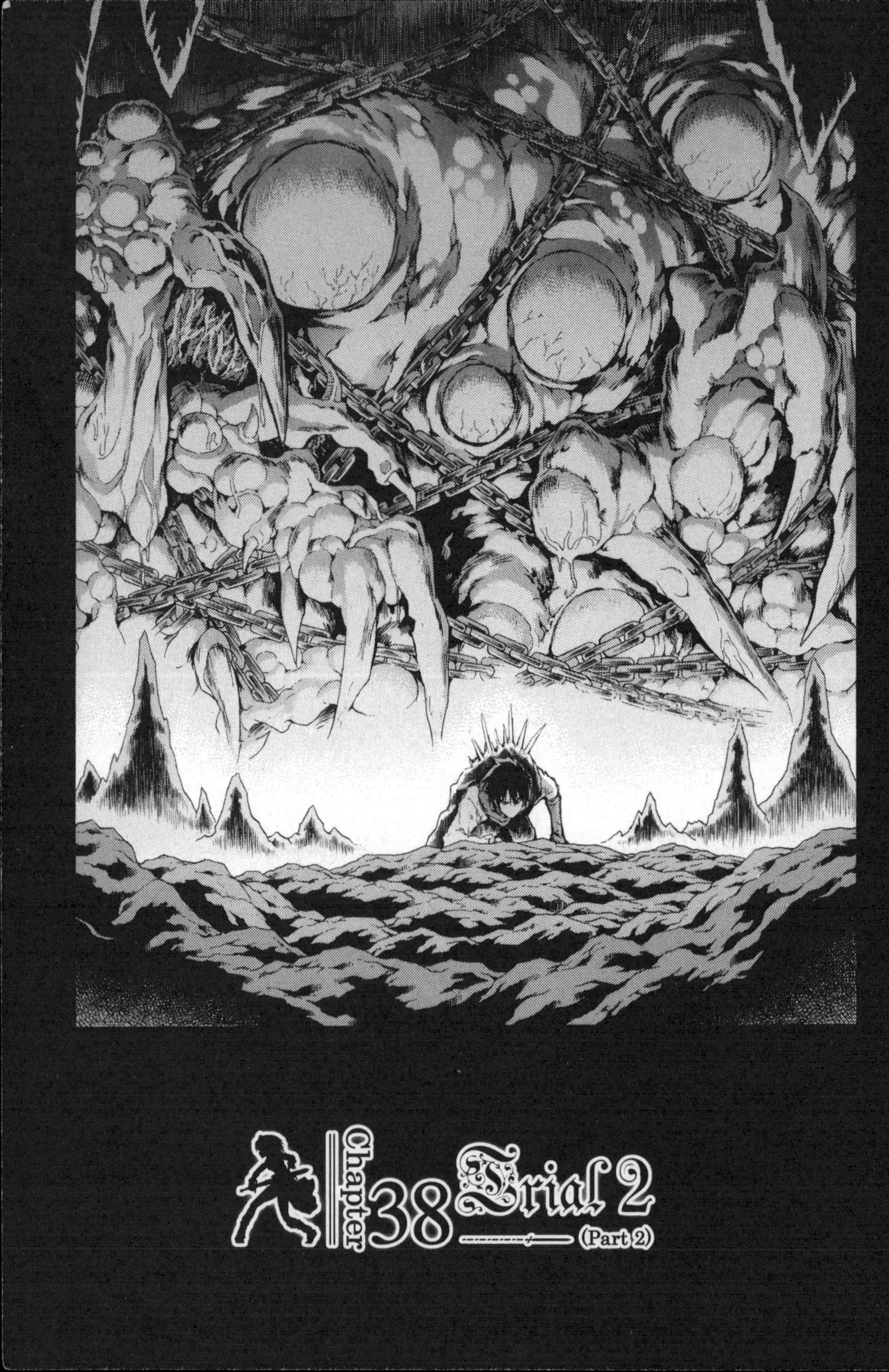

Chapter 38 Trial 2 (Part 2)

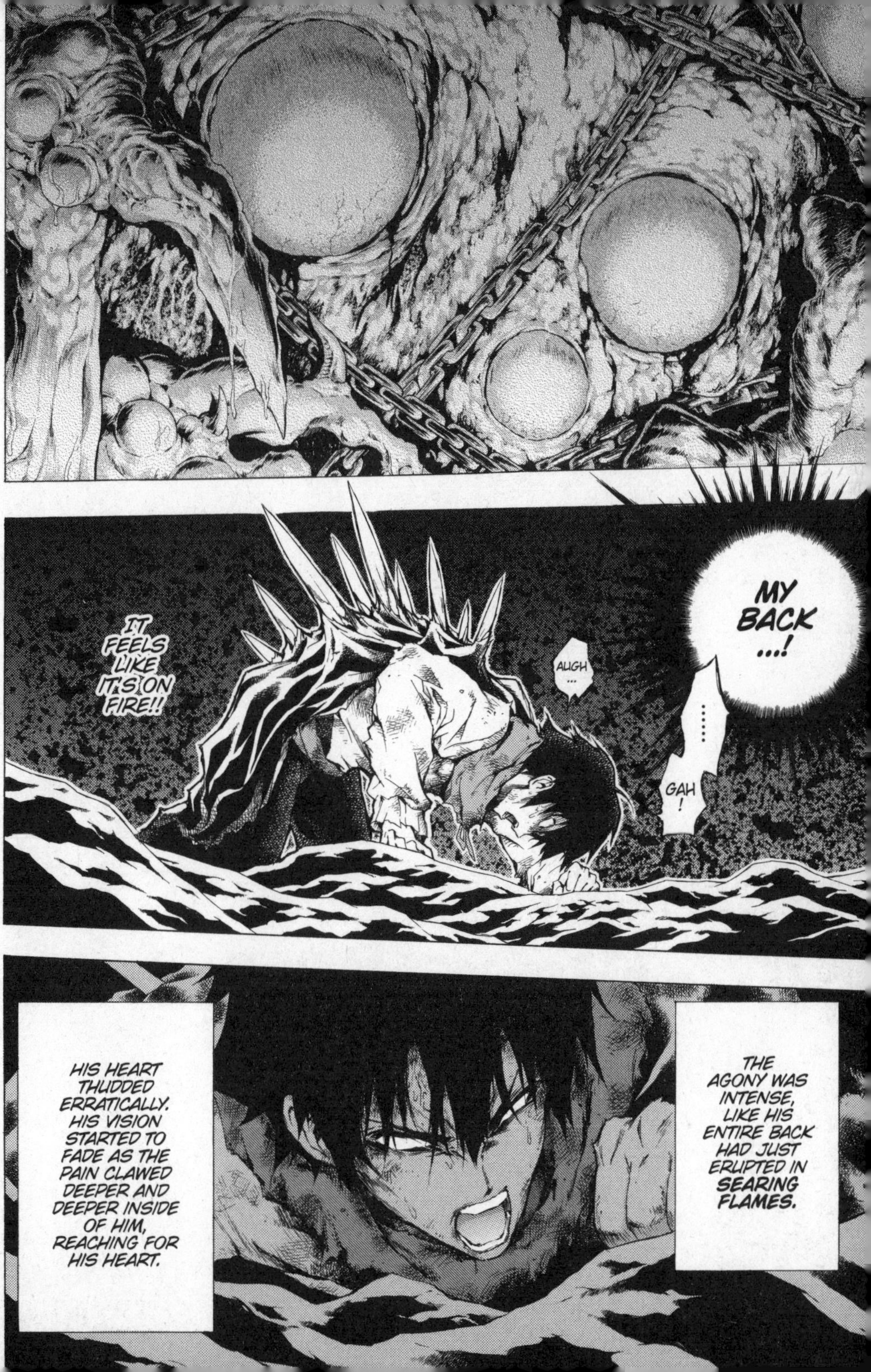
MY BACK ...!
...... GAH!
AUGH...
IT FEELS LIKE IT'S ON FIRE!!
THE AGONY WAS INTENSE, LIKE HIS ENTIRE BACK HAD JUST ERUPTED IN SEARING FLAMES.
HIS HEART THUDDED ERRATICALLY. HIS VISION STARTED TO FADE AS THE PAIN CLAWED DEEPER AND DEEPER INSIDE OF HIM, REACHING FOR HIS HEART.

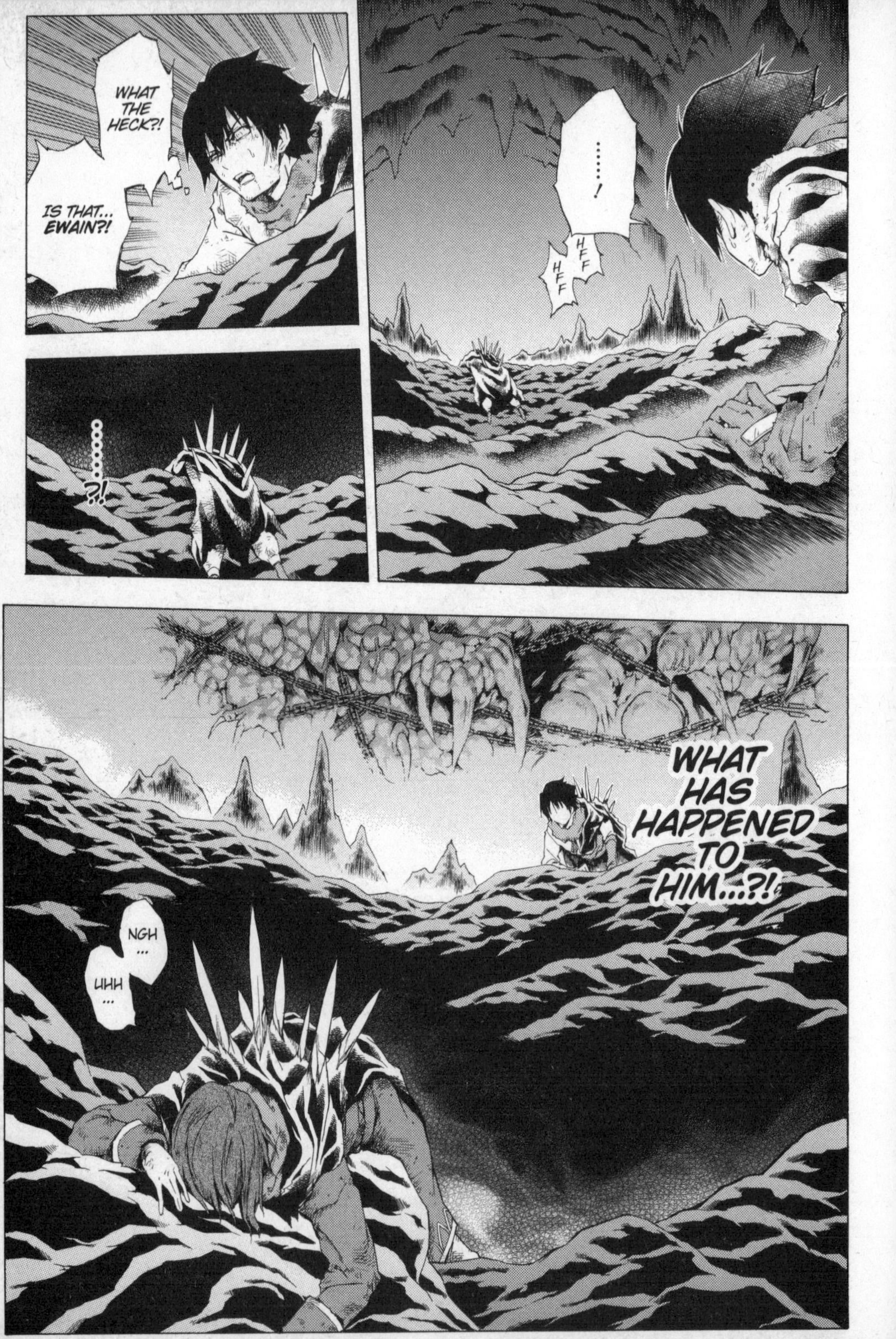
......!
HFF HFF
WHAT THE HECK?!
IS THAT... EWAIN?!
......?!
WHAT HAS HAPPENED TO HIM...?!
NGH...
UHH...

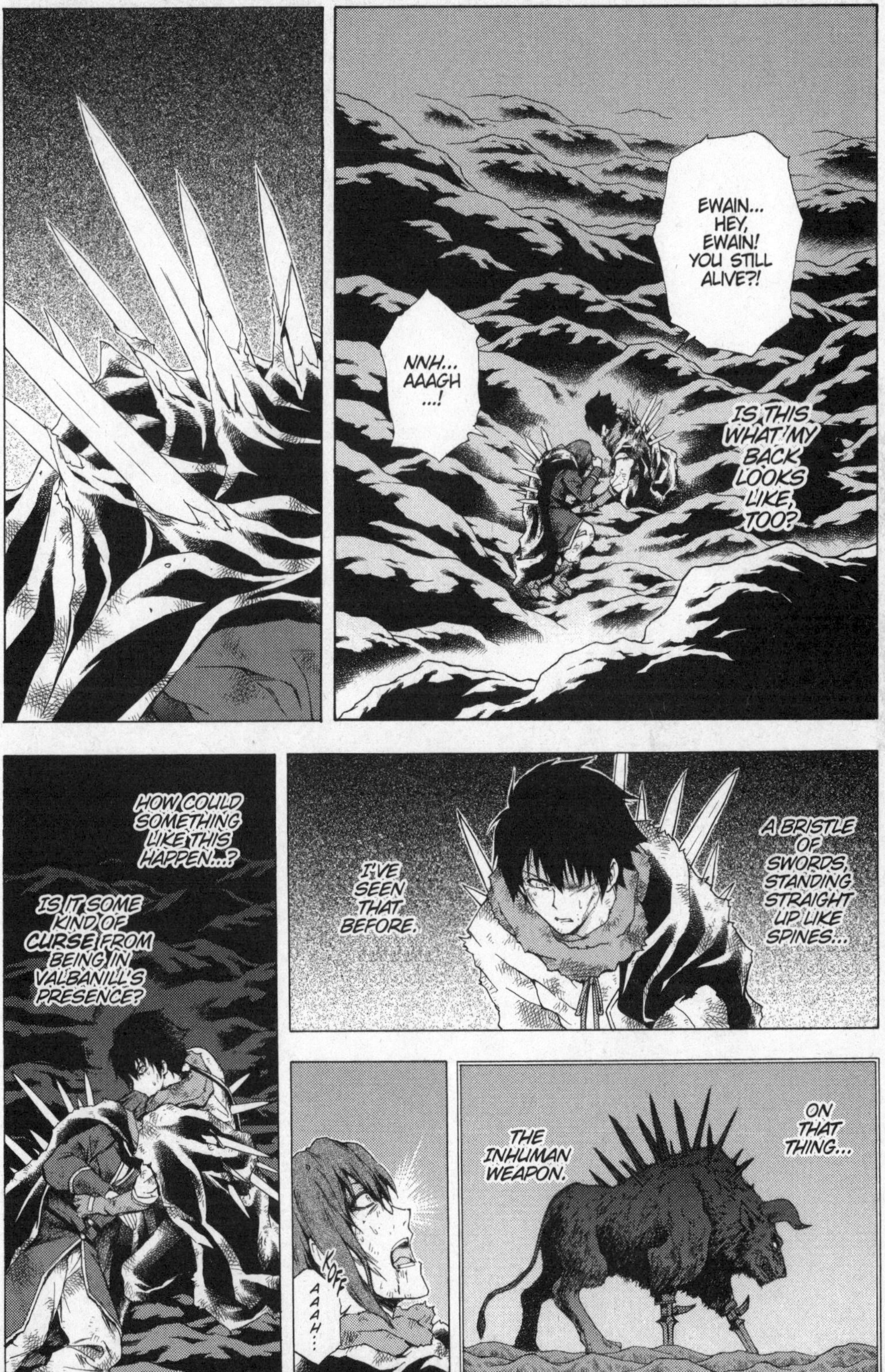
EWAIN... HEY, EWAIN! YOU STILL ALIVE?!
NNH... AAAGH ...!
IS THIS WHAT MY BACK LOOKS LIKE, TOO?
A BRISTLE OF SWORDS, STANDING STRAIGHT UP LIKE SPINES...
I'VE SEEN THAT BEFORE.
ON THAT THING...
THE INHUMAN WEAPON.
KOFF
AAAH...
HOW COULD SOMETHING LIKE THIS HAPPEN...?
IS IT SOME KIND OF CURSE FROM BEING IN VALBANILL'S PRESENCE?

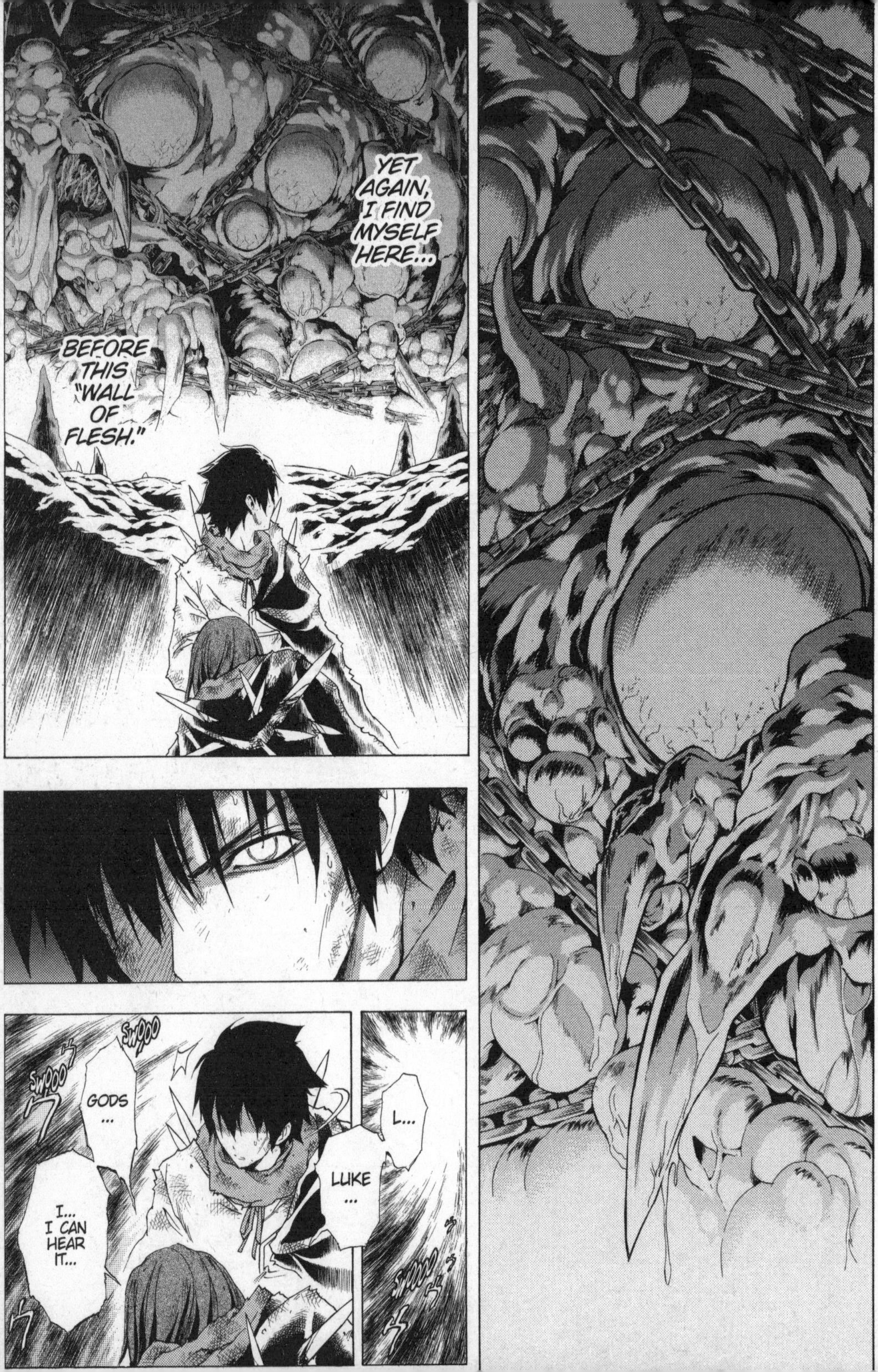
YET AGAIN, I FIND MYSELF HERE...
BEFORE THIS "WALL OF FLESH."
L...
LUKE ...
SWOOOO
SWOOO
SWOOO
GODS ...
I... I CAN HEAR IT...

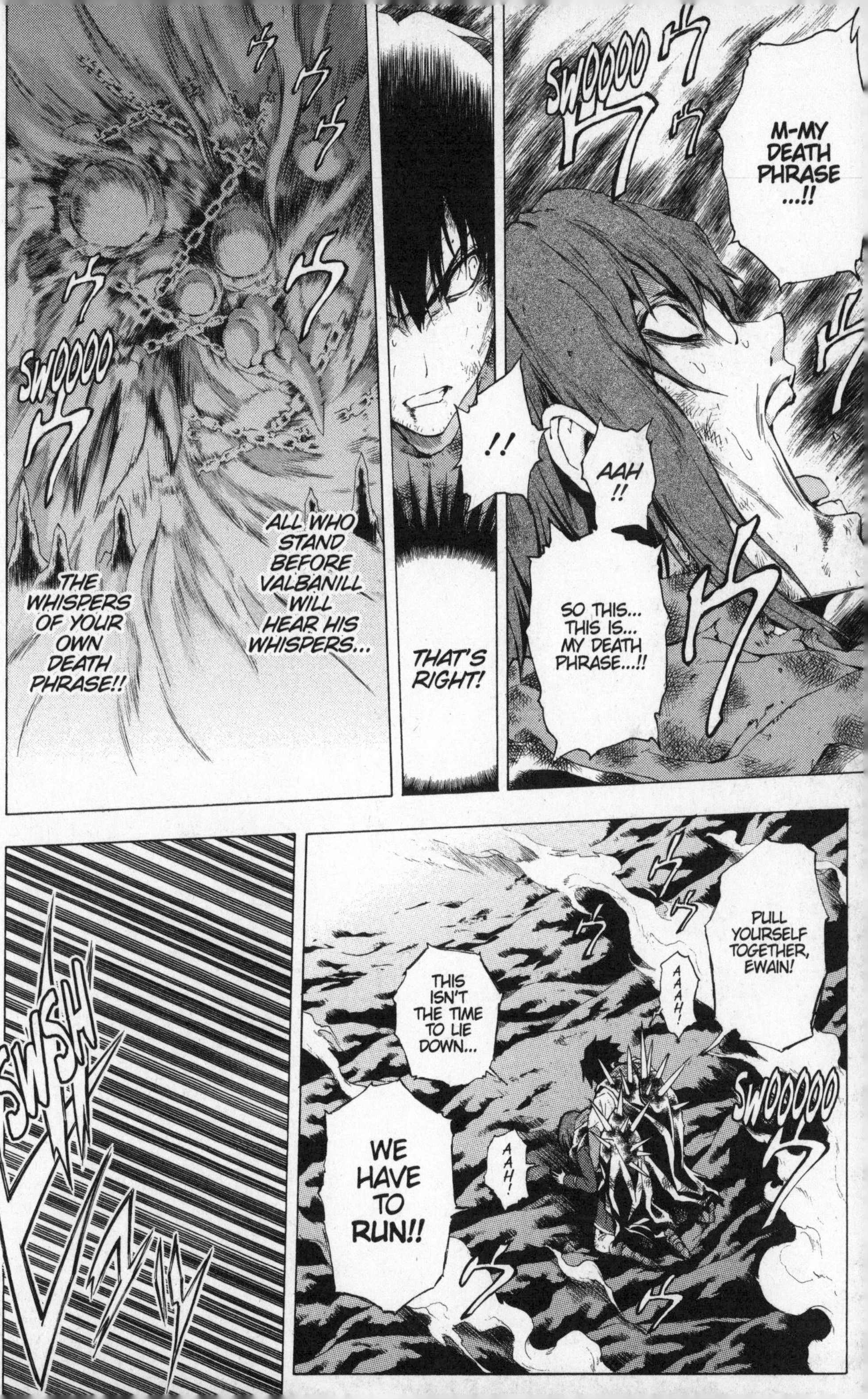
SWOOOO
M-MY DEATH PHRASE ...!!
AAH !!
SO THIS... THIS IS... MY DEATH PHRASE...!!
!!
THAT'S RIGHT!
ALL WHO STAND BEFORE VALBANILL WILL HEAR HIS WHISPERS...
THE WHISPERS OF YOUR OWN DEATH PHRASE!!
SWOOOO
PULL YOURSELF TOGETHER, EWAIN!
AAAH!
THIS ISN'T THE TIME TO LIE DOWN...
SWOOOOO
AAH!
WE HAVE TO RUN!!
SWSH

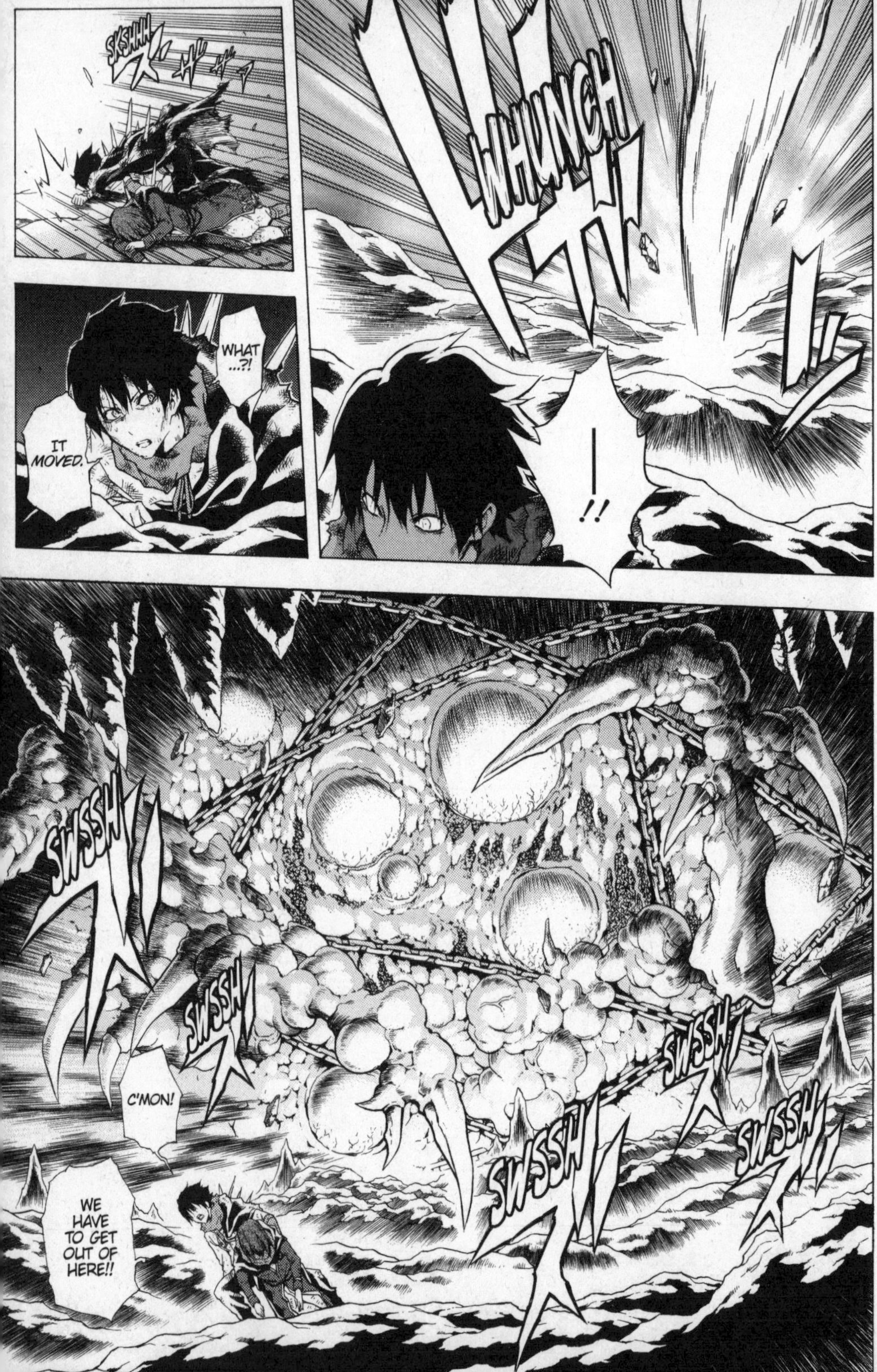
WHUNCH
!!
SKSHHH
WHAT ...?!
IT MOVED.
SWSSH
SWSSH
SWSSH
SWSSH
SWSSH
C'MON!
WE HAVE TO GET OUT OF HERE!!

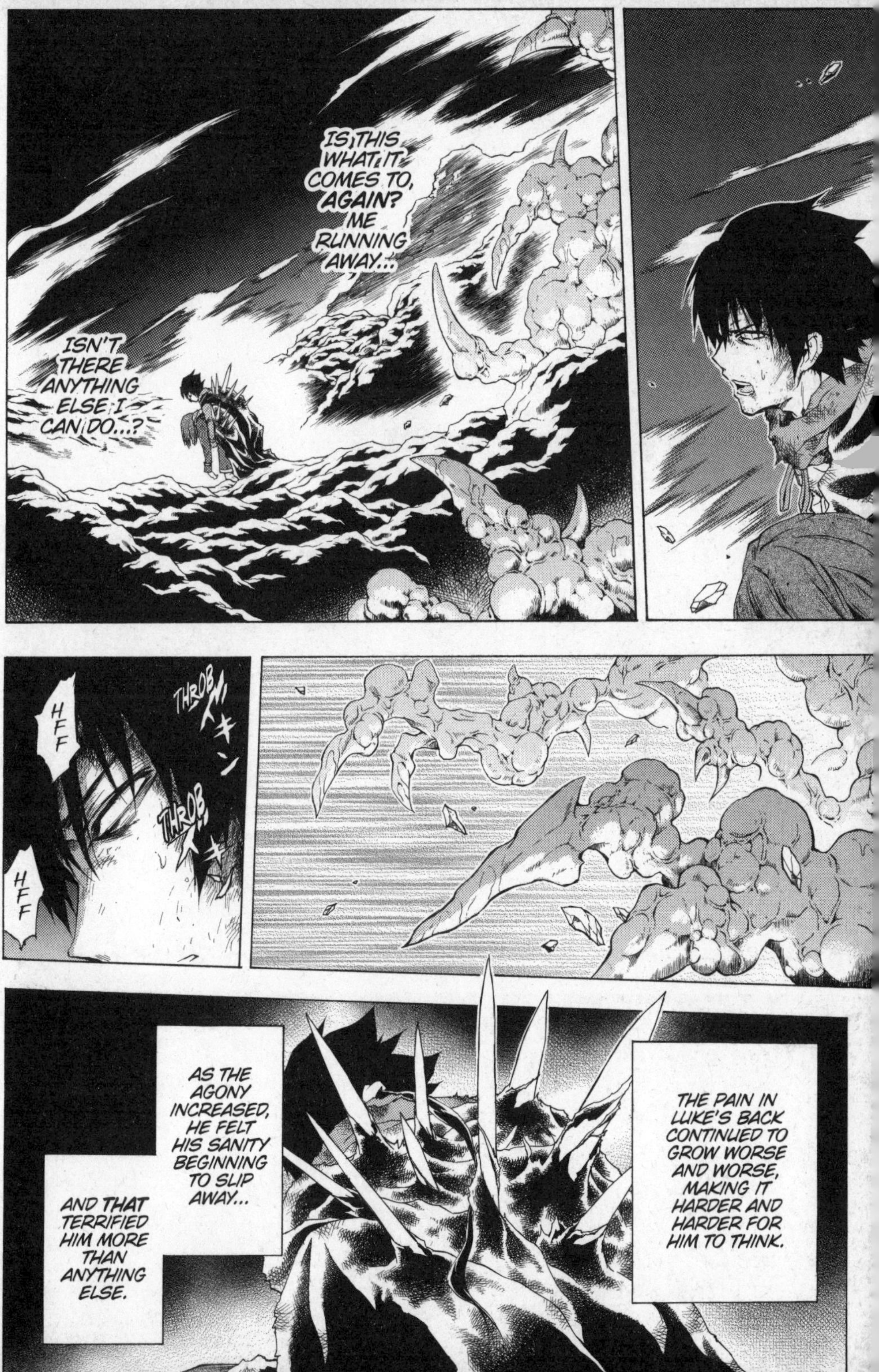
IS THIS WHAT IT COMES TO, AGAIN? ME RUNNING AWAY...
ISN'T THERE ANYTHING ELSE I CAN DO...?
THROB
HFF
THROB
HFF
THE PAIN IN LUKE'S BACK CONTINUED TO GROW WORSE AND WORSE, MAKING IT HARDER AND HARDER FOR HIM TO THINK.
AS THE AGONY INCREASED, HE FELT HIS SANITY BEGINNING TO SLIP AWAY...
AND THAT TERRIFIED HIM MORE THAN ANYTHING ELSE.

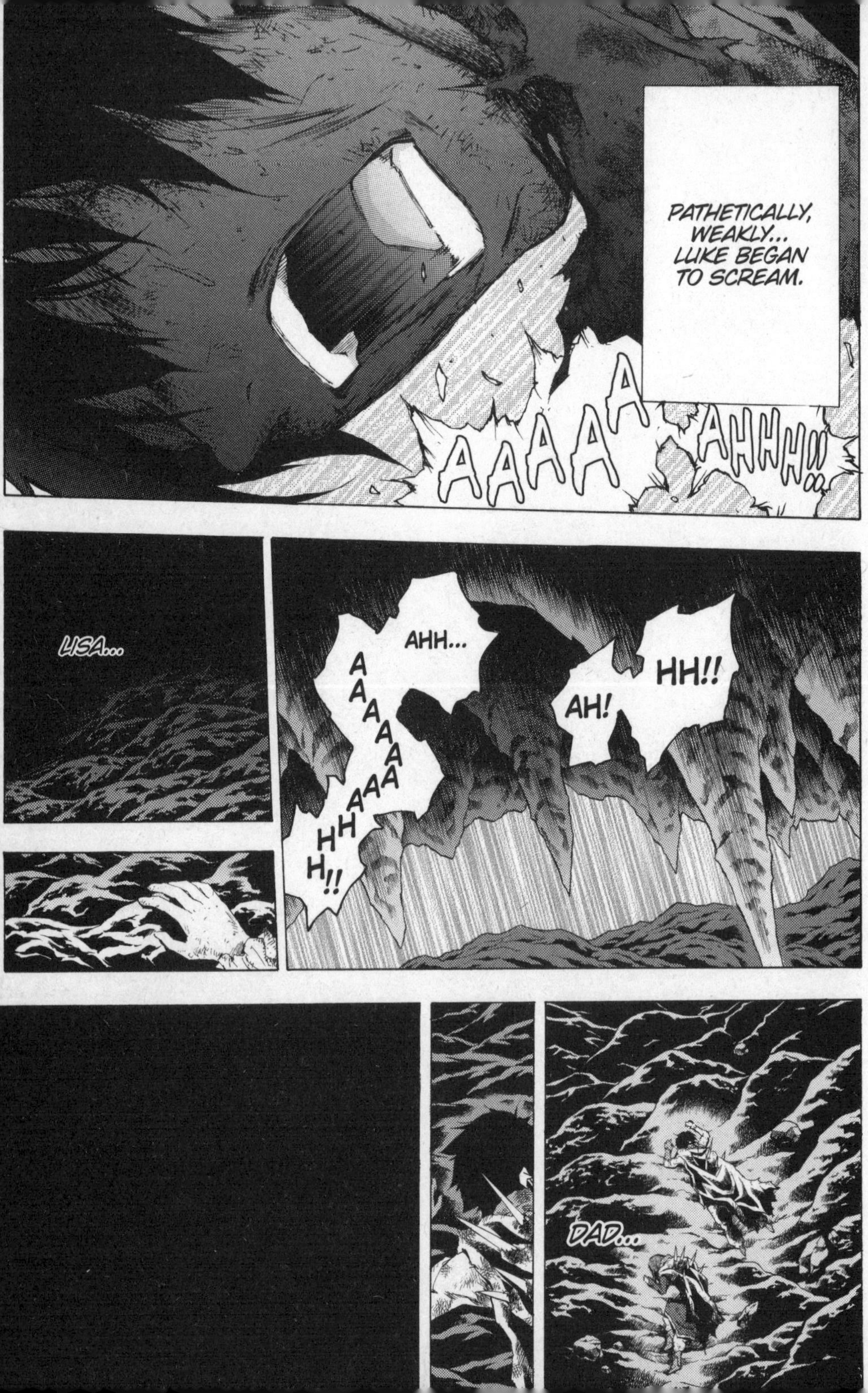
PATHETICALLY, WEAKLY... LUKE BEGAN TO SCREAM.
AAAAA AHHHH!!
AHH... AAAAAAAAAHHH!!
AH! HH!!
USA...
DAD...

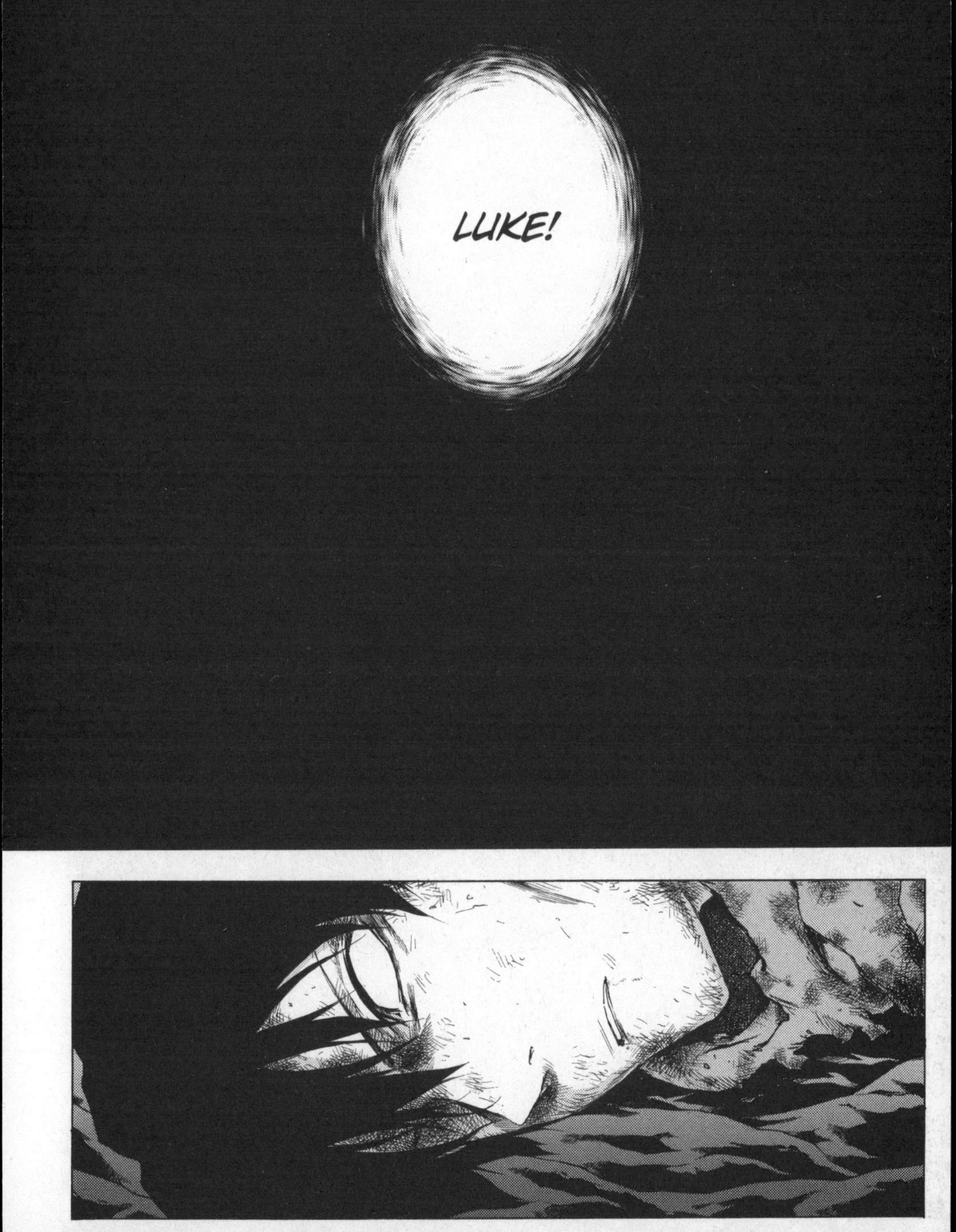
LUKE!

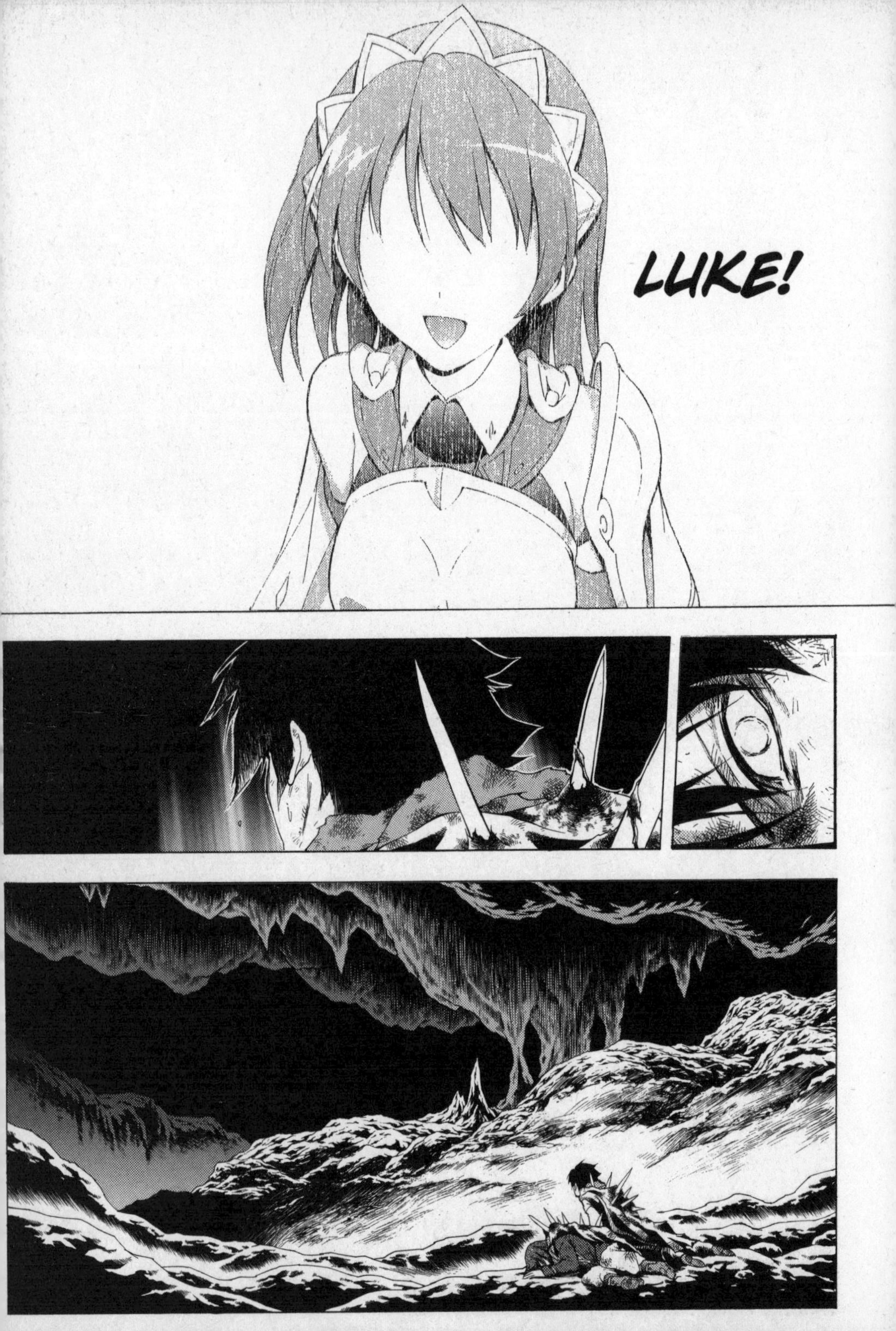
LUKE!

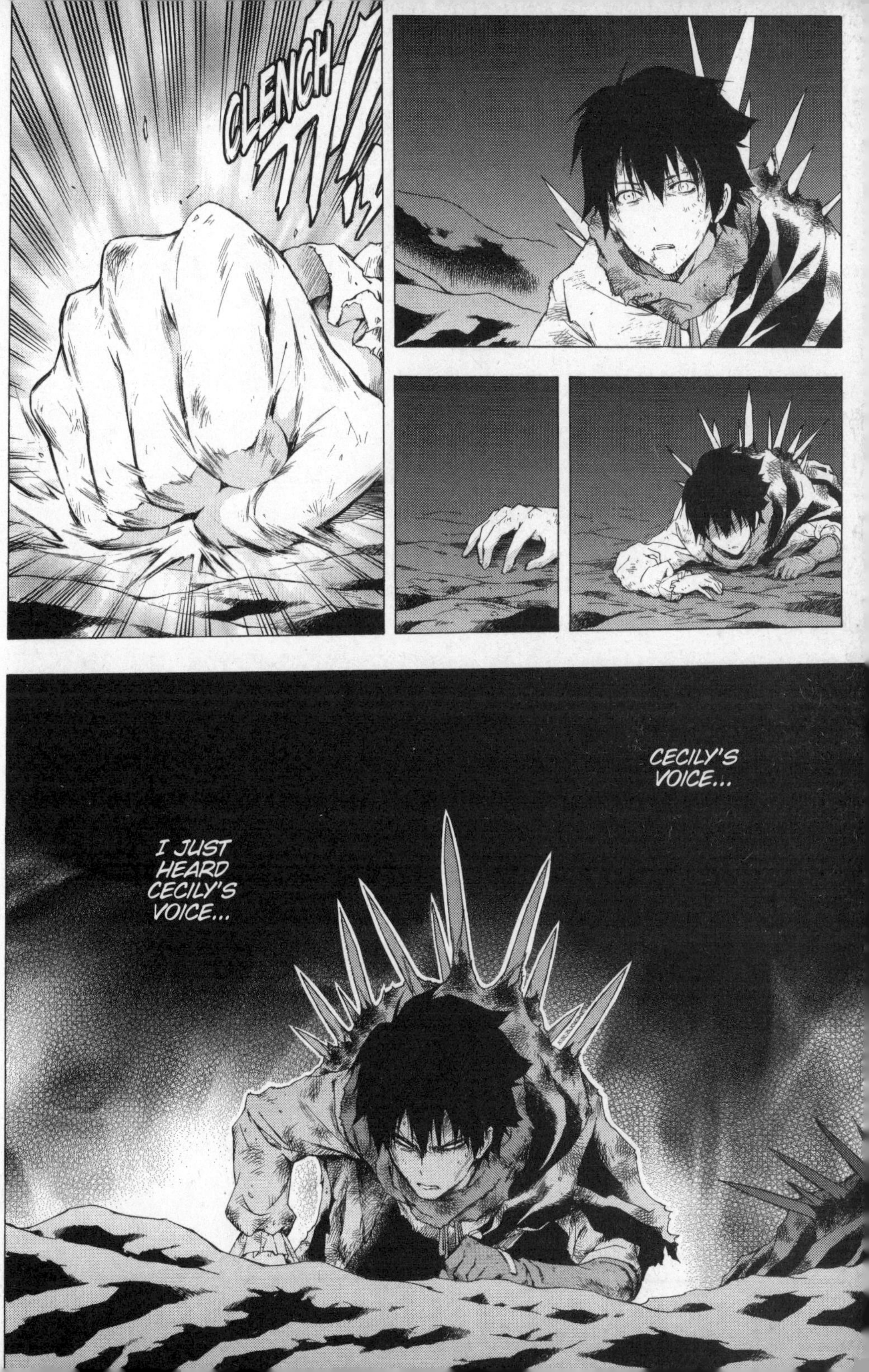
CLENCH
CECILY'S VOICE...
I JUST HEARD CECILY'S VOICE...

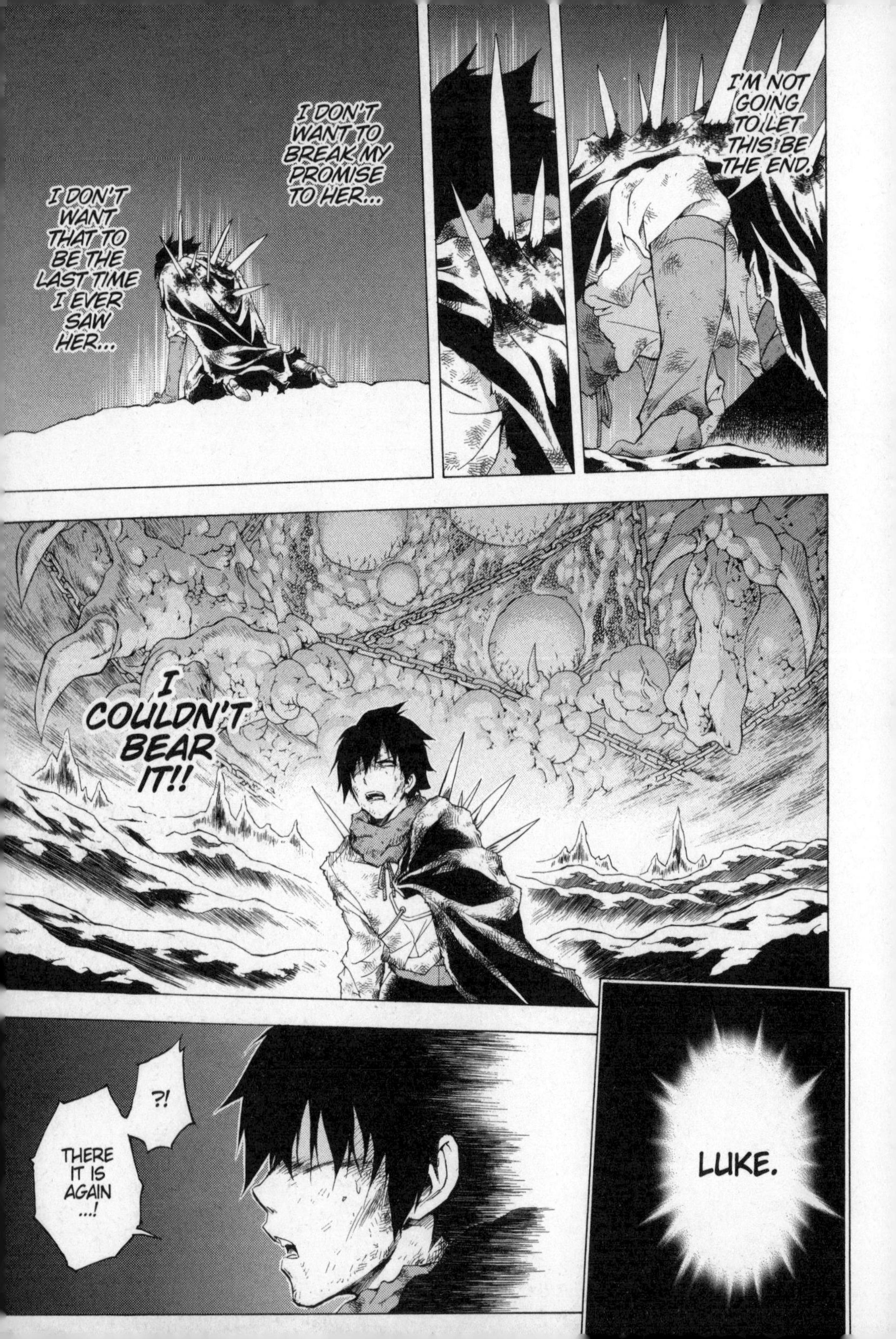
I'M NOT GOING TO LET THIS BE THE END.
I DON'T WANT TO BREAK MY PROMISE TO HER...
I DON'T WANT THAT TO BE THE LAST TIME I EVER SAW HER...
I COULDN'T BEAR IT!!
LUKE.
?!
THERE IT IS AGAIN...!

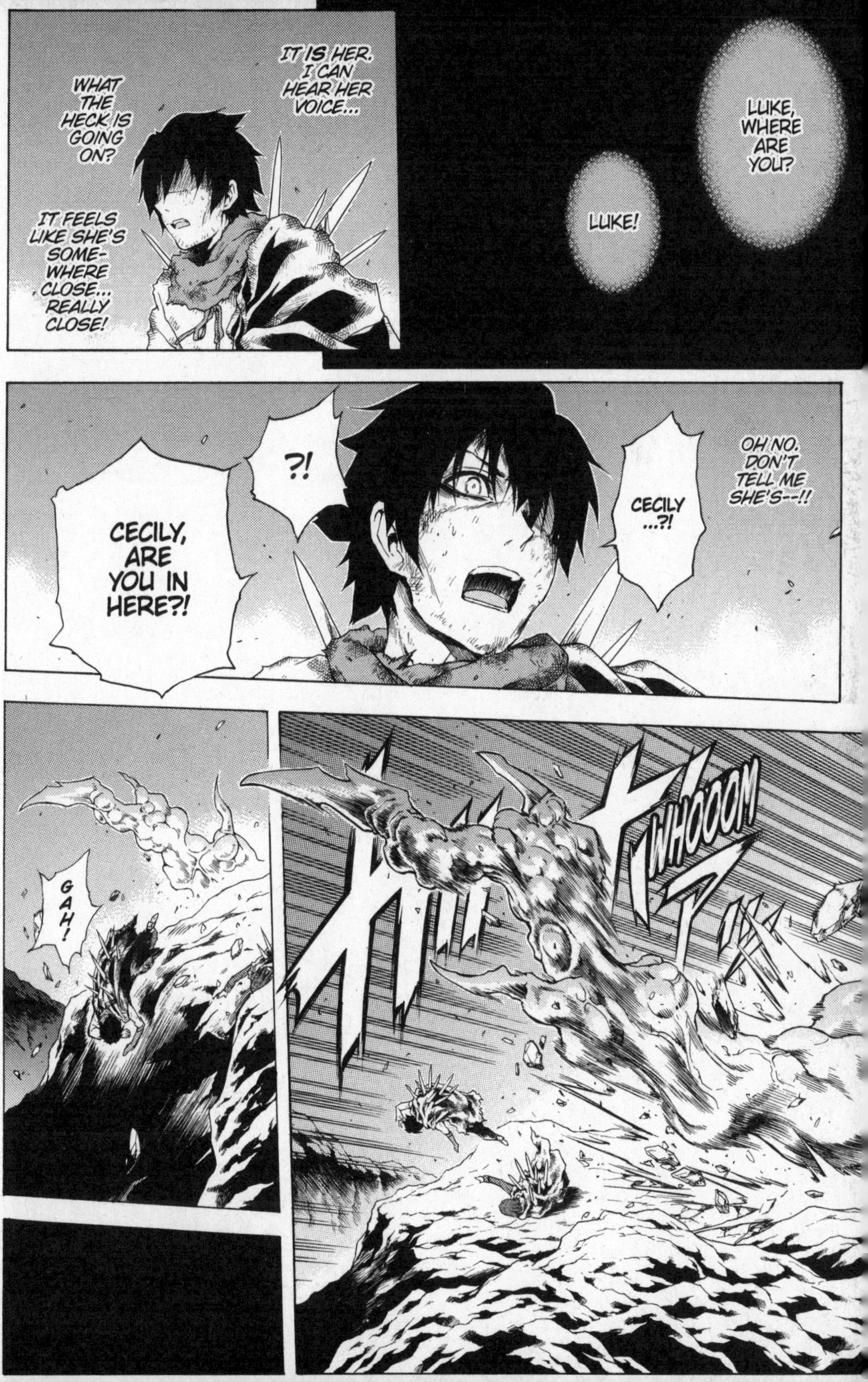
LUKE, WHERE ARE YOU?
LUKE!
IT IS HER. I CAN HEAR HER VOICE...
WHAT THE HECK IS GOING ON?
IT FEELS LIKE SHE'S SOME-WHERE CLOSE... REALLY CLOSE!
OH NO. DON'T TELL ME SHE'S--!!
CECILY ...?!
?!
CECILY, ARE YOU IN HERE?!
WHOOOM
GAH!

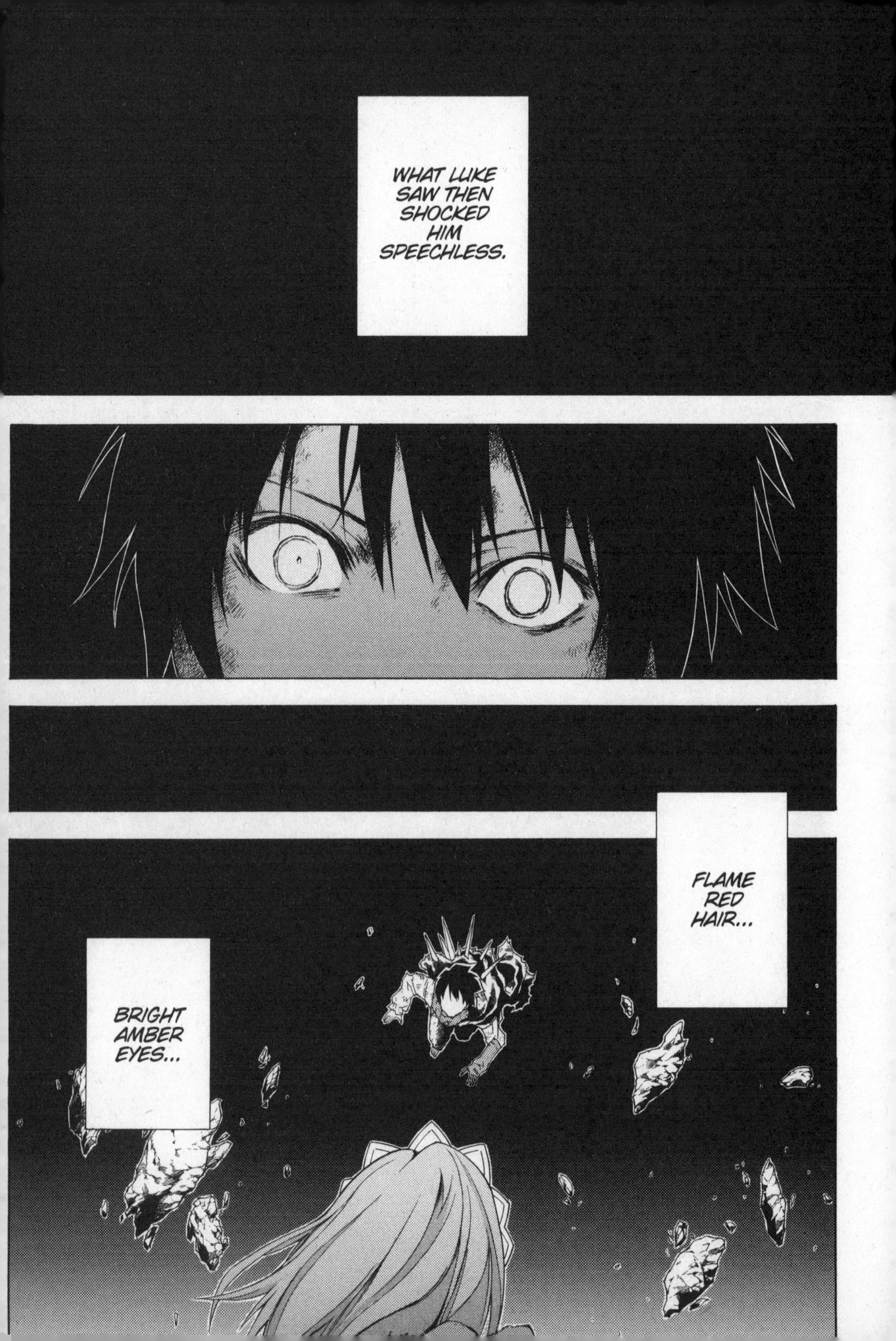
WHAT LUKE SAW THEN SHOCKED HIM SPEECHLESS.
FLAME RED HAIR...
BRIGHT AMBER EYES...

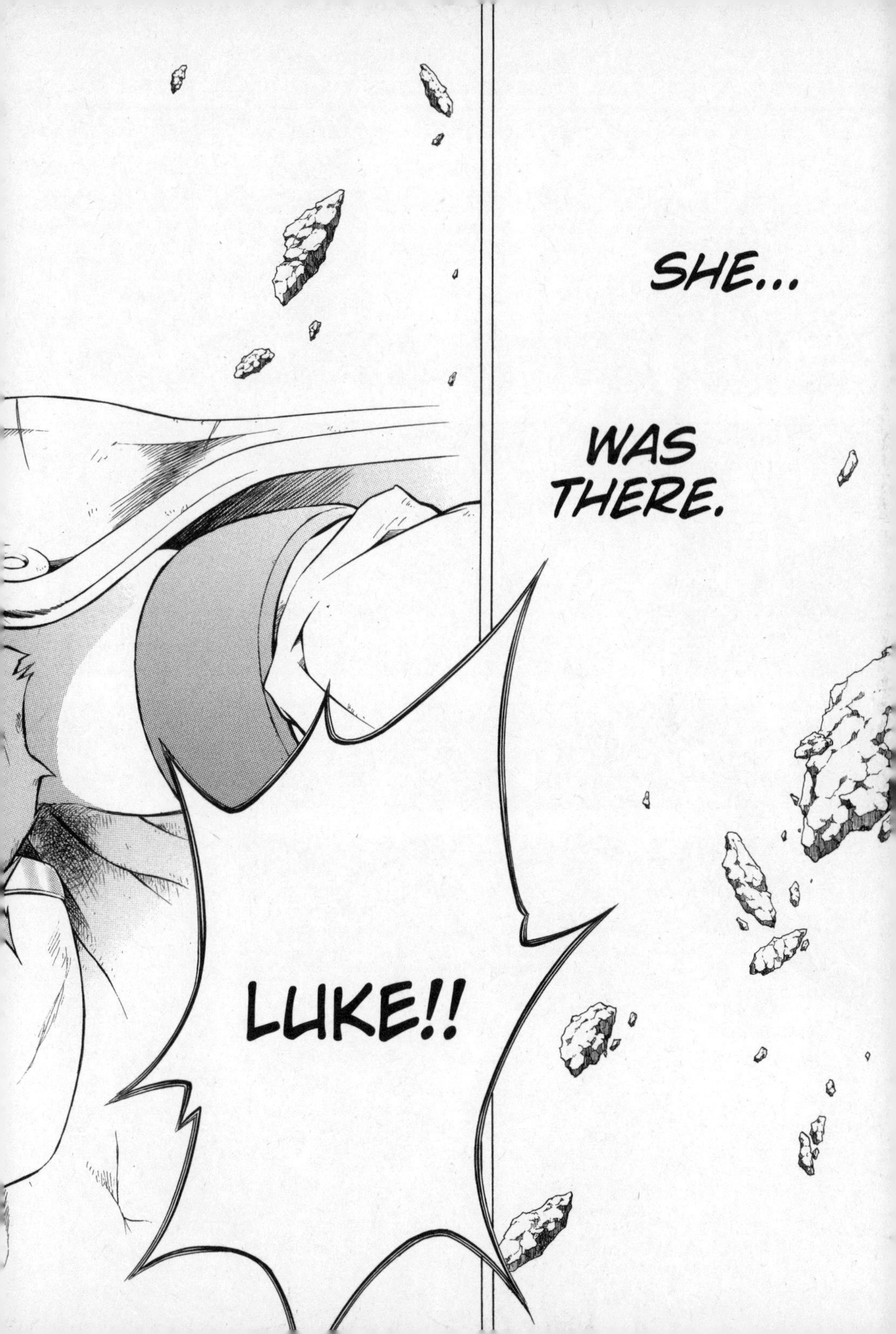
SHE...
WAS THERE.
LUKE!!

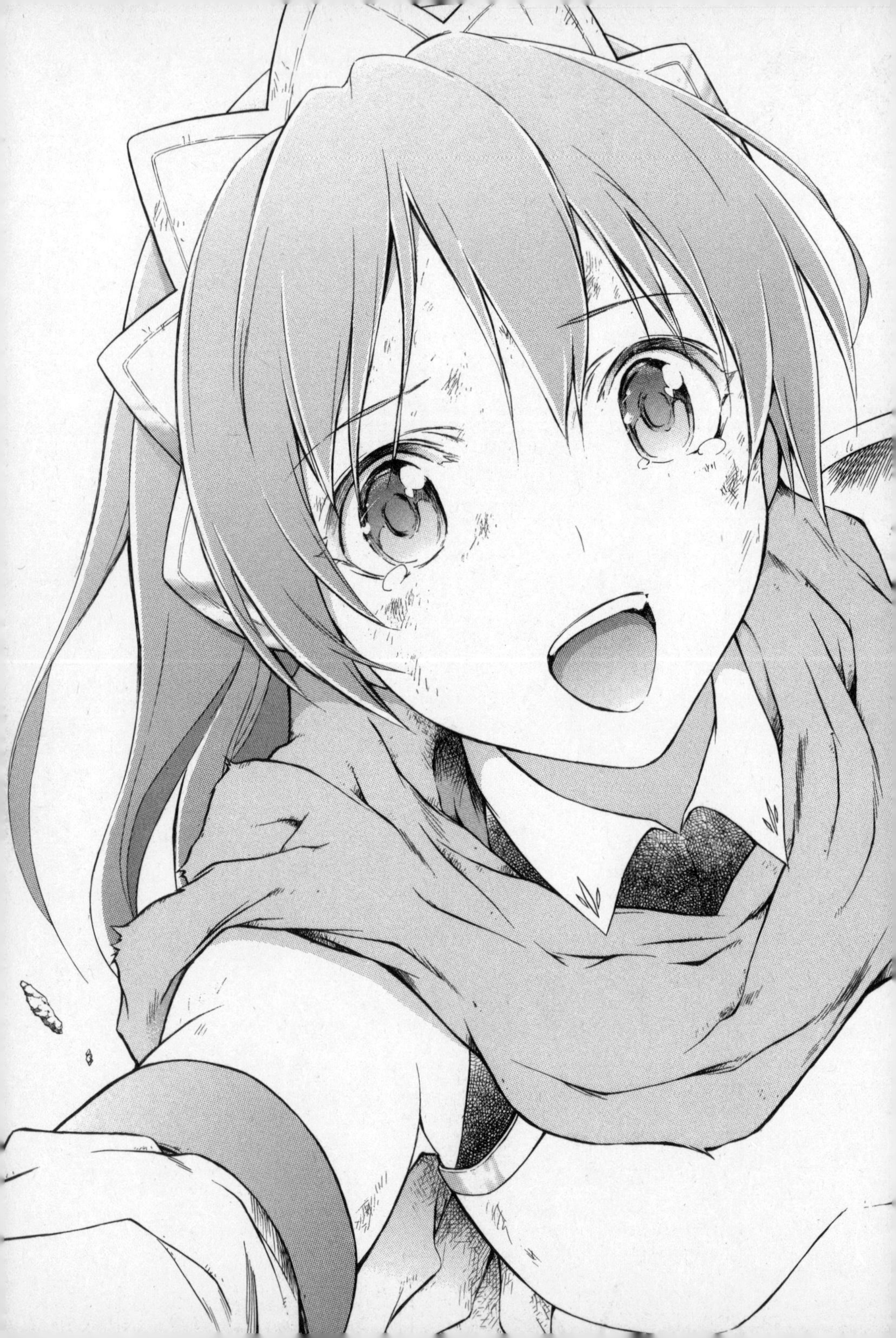

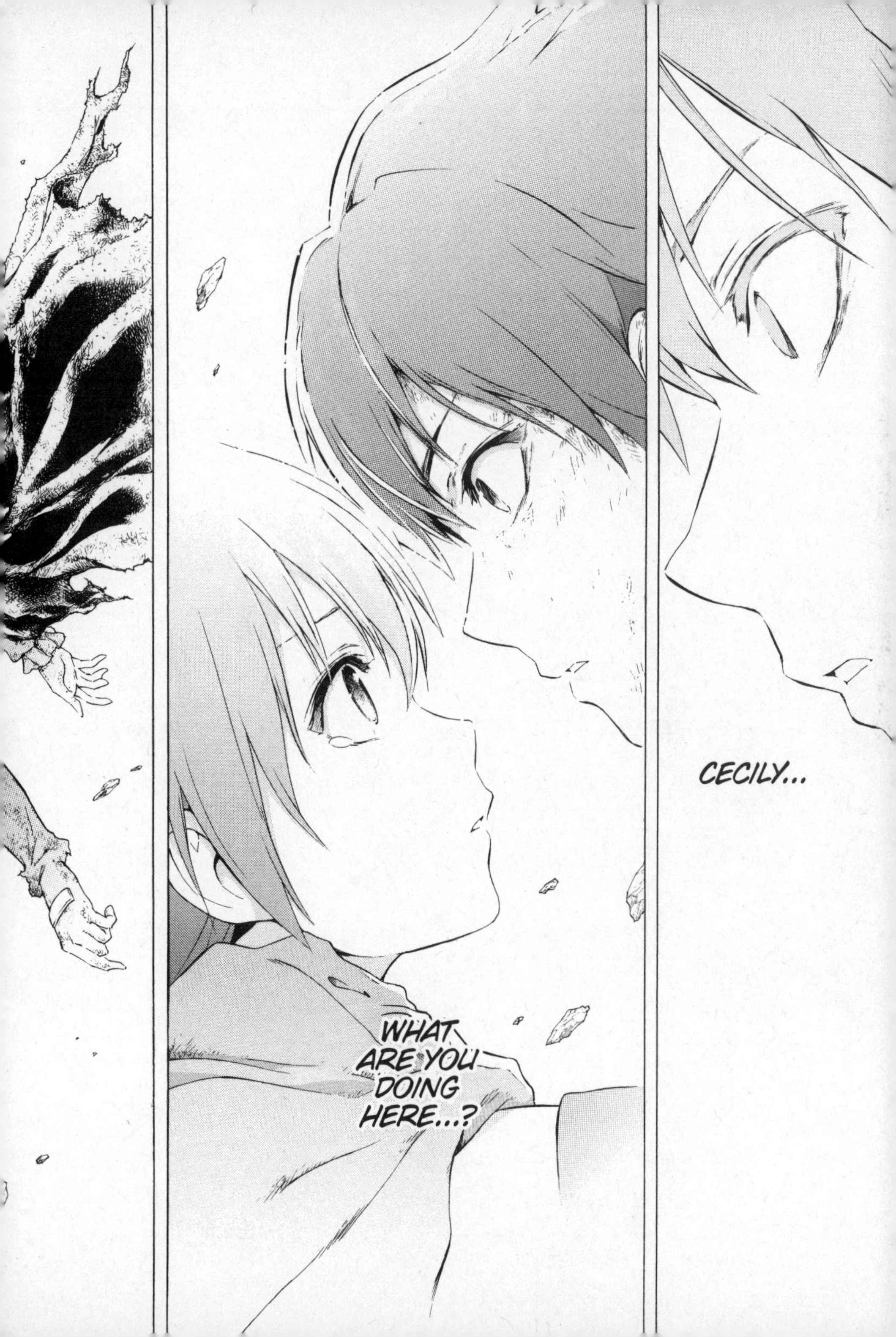
CECILY...
WHAT ARE YOU DOING HERE...?

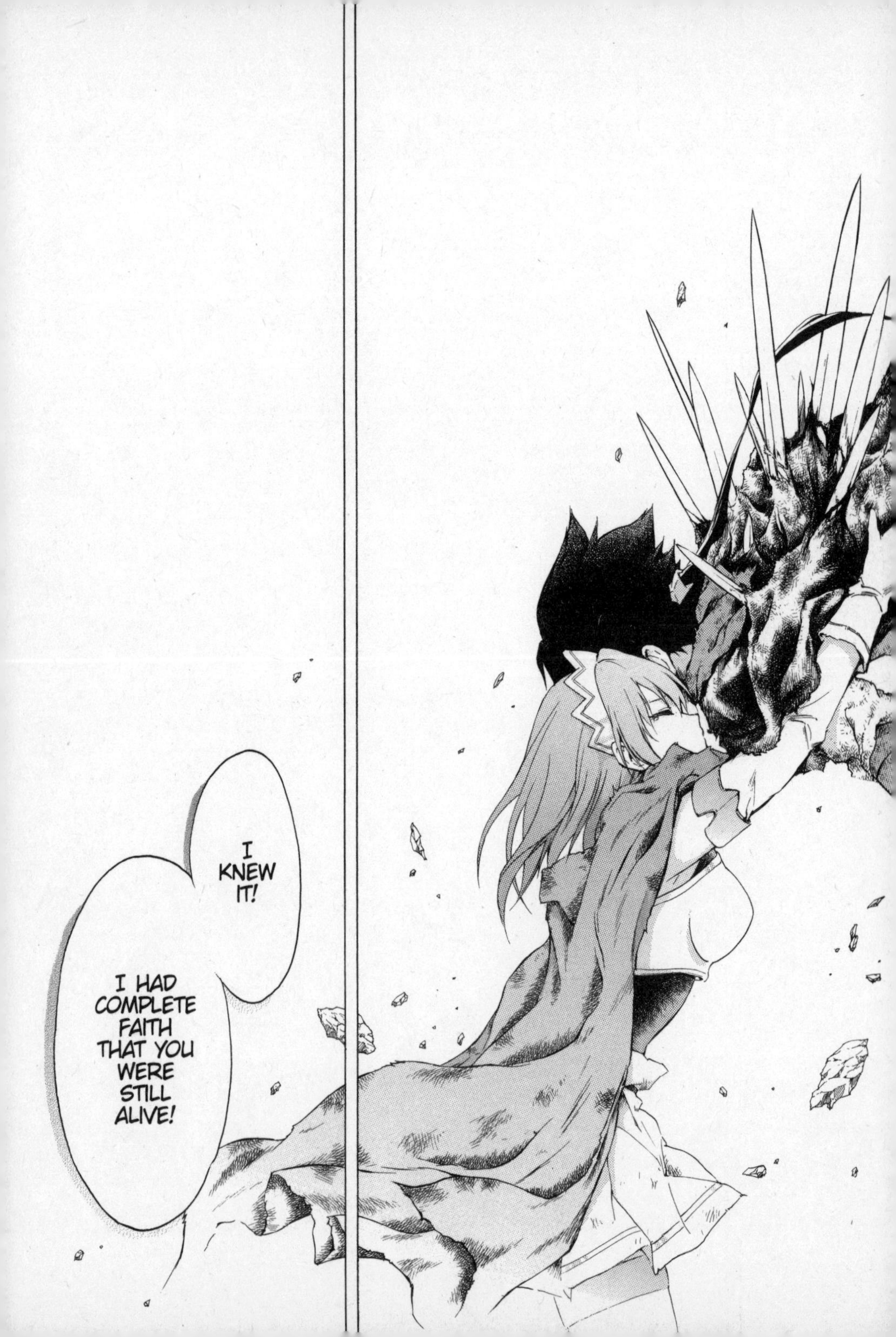
I KNEW IT!
I HAD COMPLETE FAITH THAT YOU WERE STILL ALIVE!

The Sacred Blacksmith

聖剣の刀鍛冶

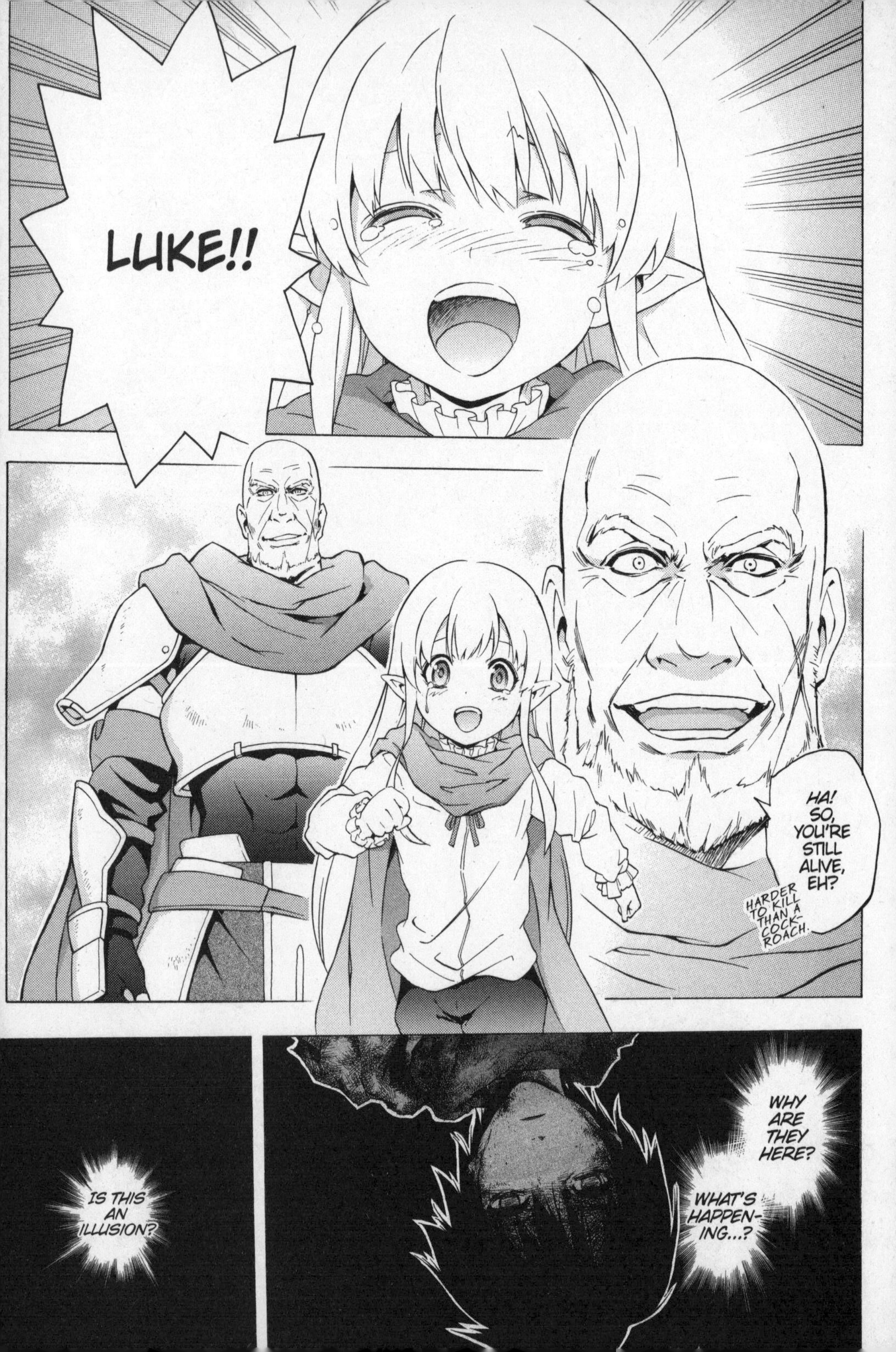
LUKE!!
HA! SO, YOU'RE STILL ALIVE, EH?
HARDER TO KILL THAN A COCK-ROACH.
WHY ARE THEY HERE?
WHAT'S HAPPEN-ING...?
IS THIS AN ILLUSION?

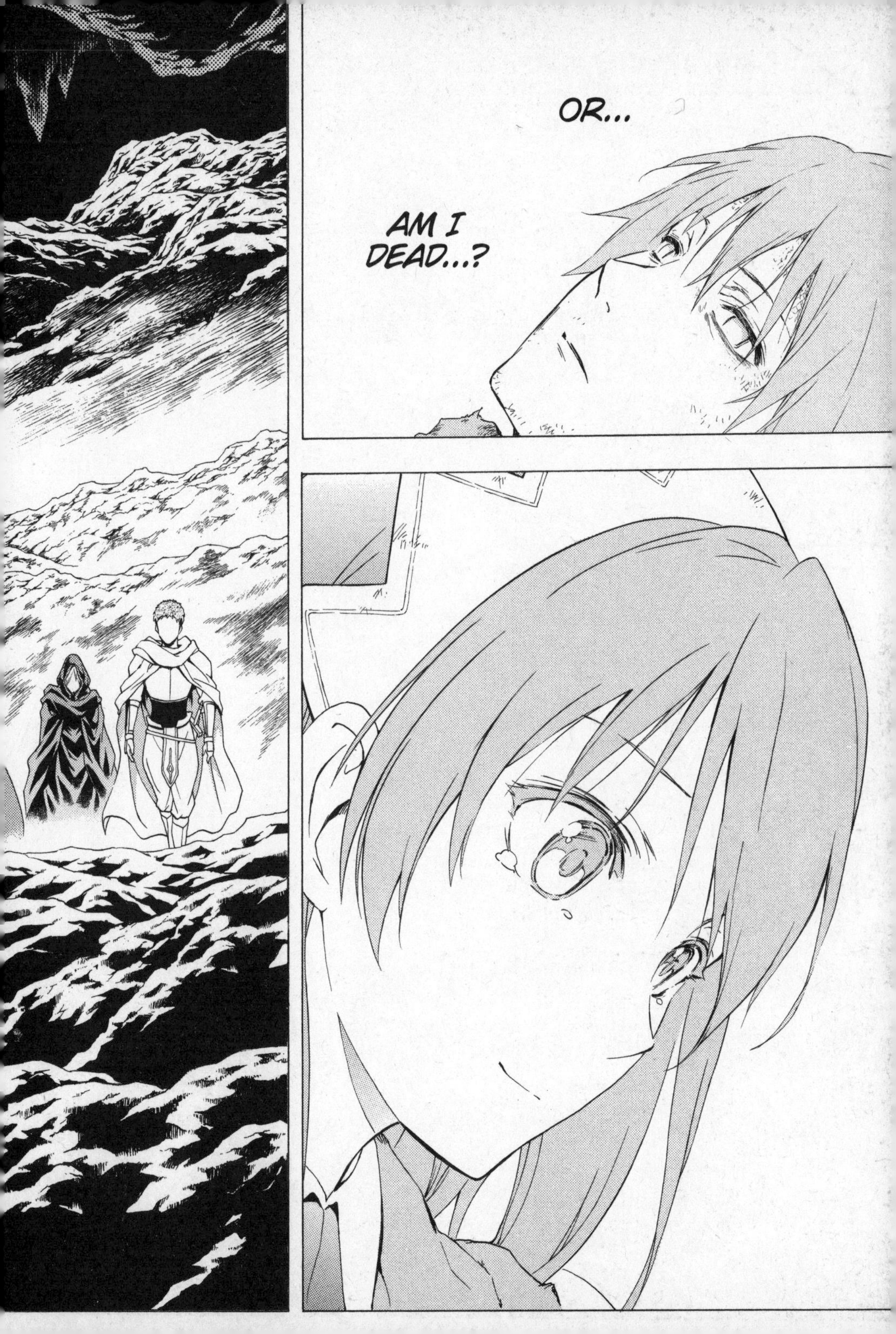
OR...
AM I DEAD...?

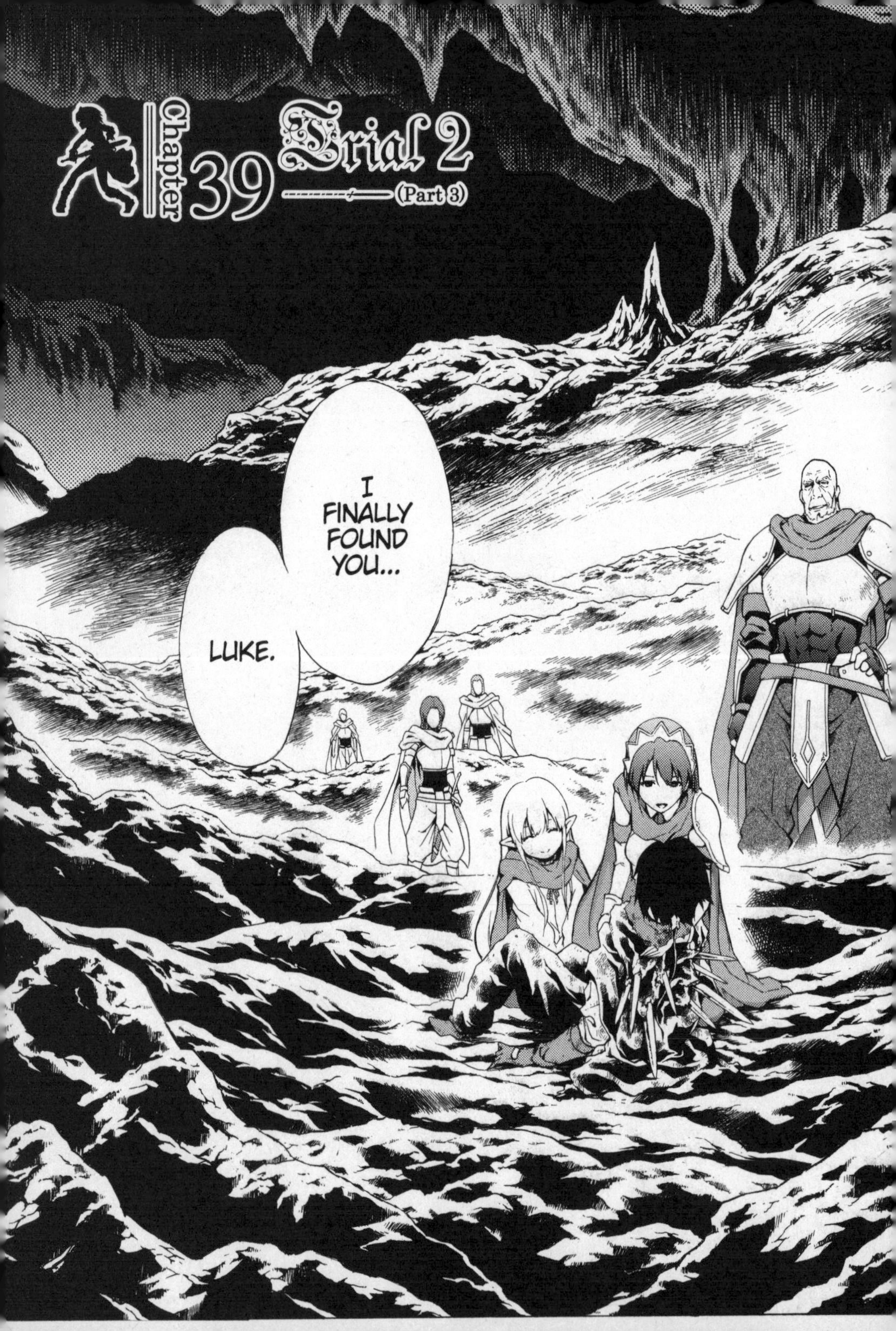
Chapter 39 Trial 2 (Part 3)
I FINALLY FOUND YOU...
LUKE.

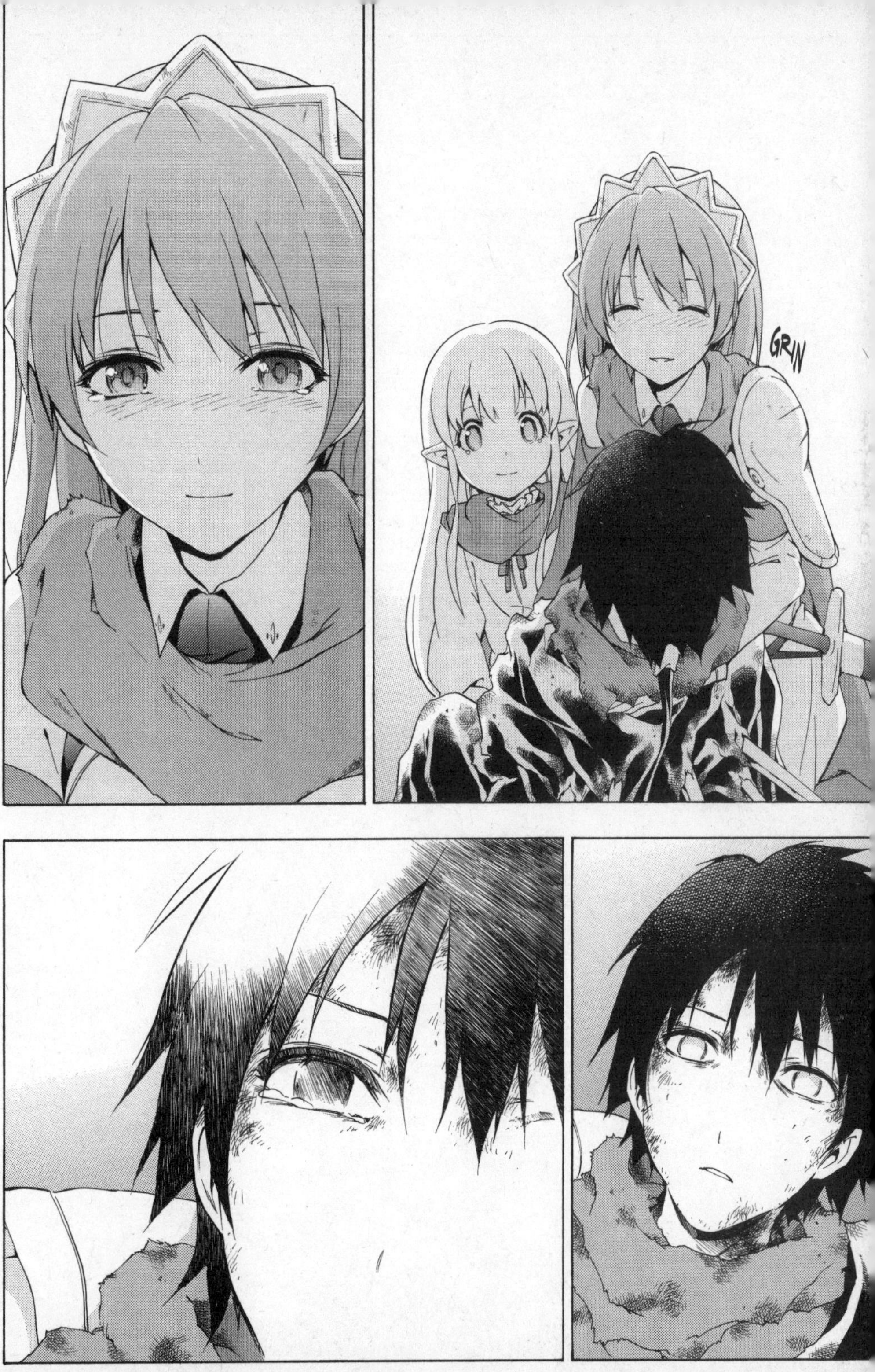
GRIN

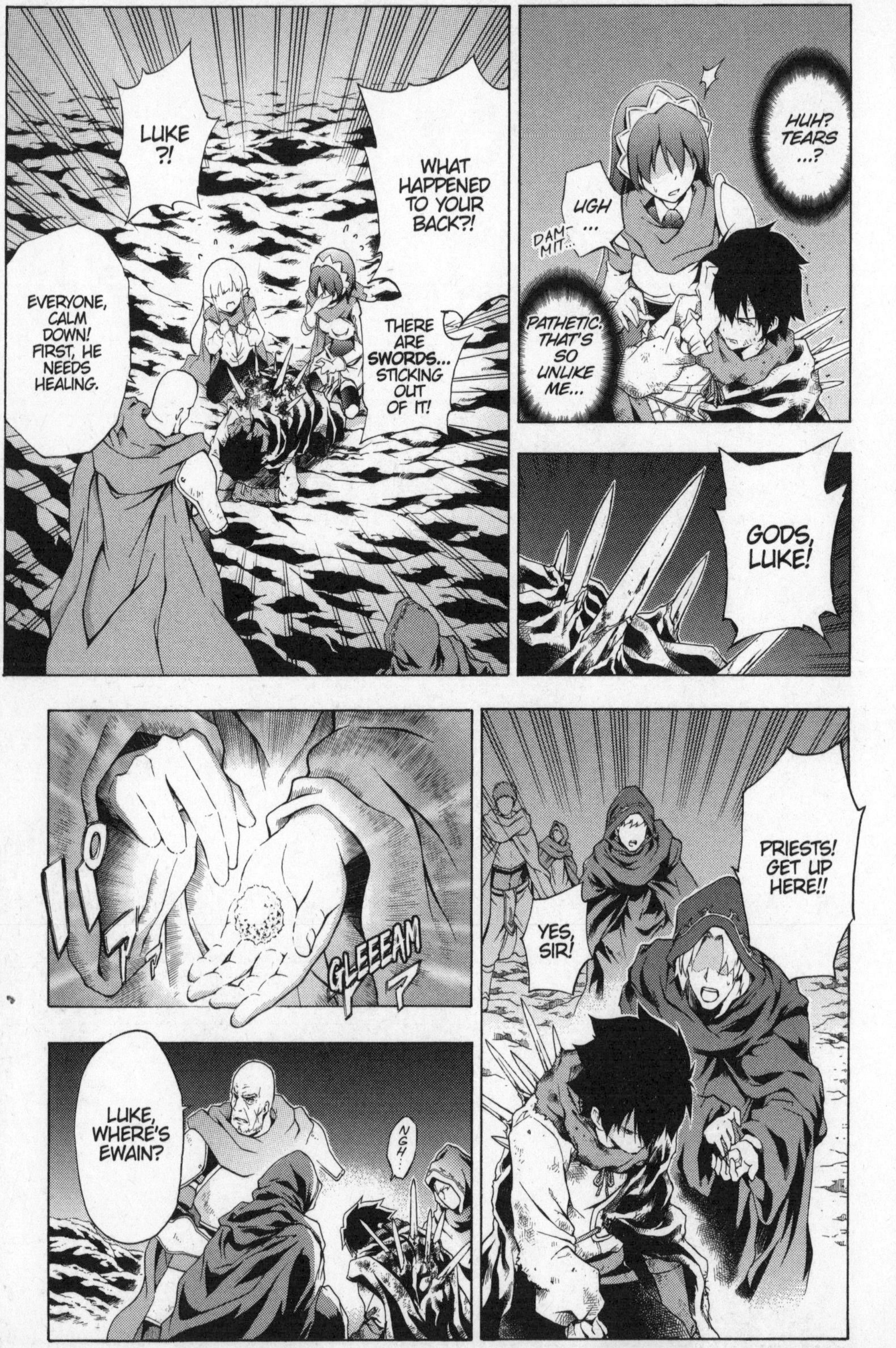
HUH? TEARS ...?
UGH ...
DAM-MIT...
PATHETIC. THAT'S SO UNLIKE ME...
GODS, LUKE!
LUKE ?!
WHAT HAPPENED TO YOUR BACK?!
THERE ARE SWORDS... STICKING OUT OF IT!
EVERYONE, CALM DOWN! FIRST, HE NEEDS HEALING.
PRIESTS! GET UP HERE!!
YES, SIR!
GLEEEAM
LUKE, WHERE'S EWAIN?
NGH...

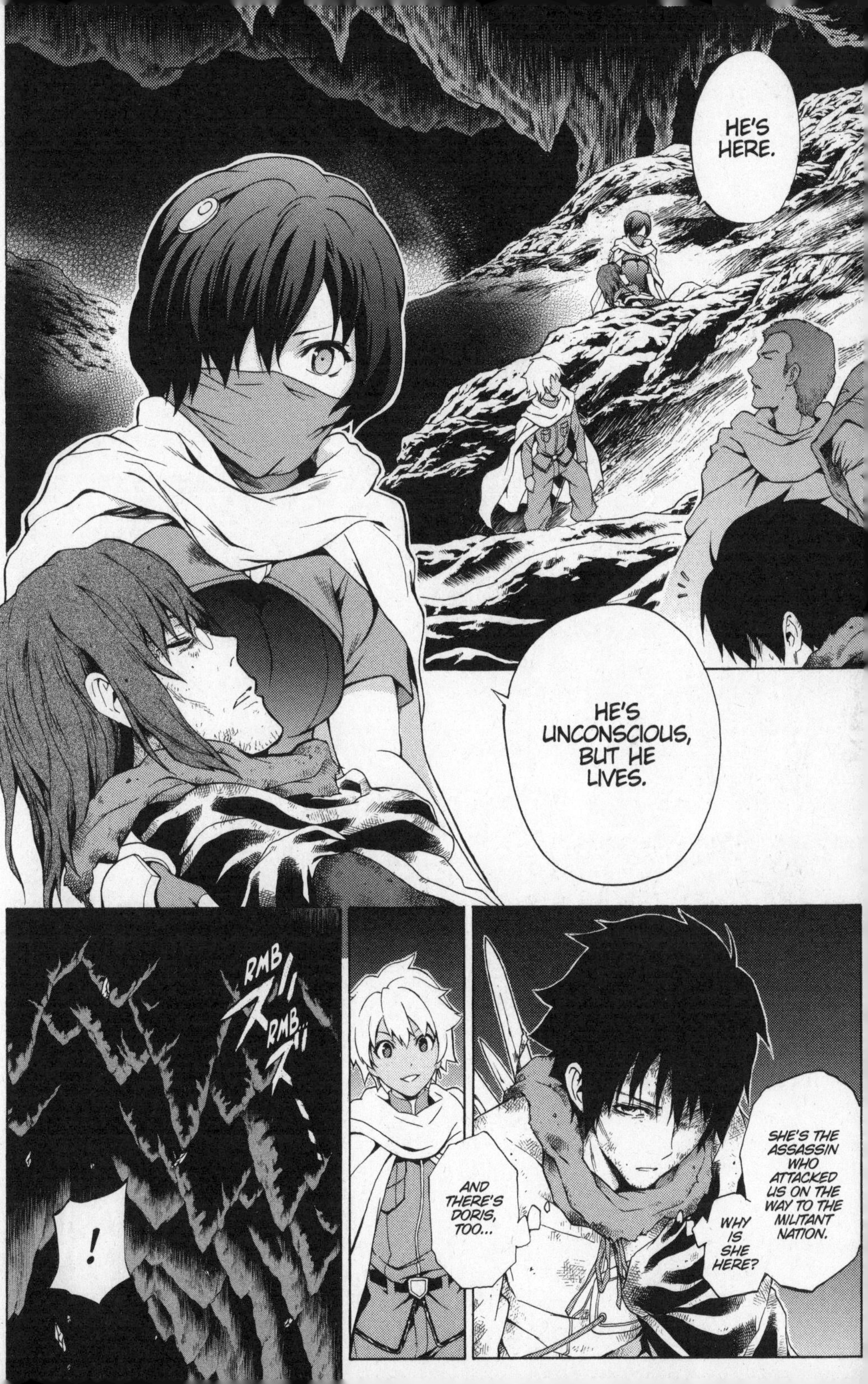
HE'S HERE.
HE'S UNCONSCIOUS, BUT HE LIVES.
SHE'S THE ASSASSIN WHO ATTACKED US ON THE WAY TO THE MILITANT NATION.
WHY IS SHE HERE?
AND THERE'S DORIS, TOO...
RMB RMB...
!

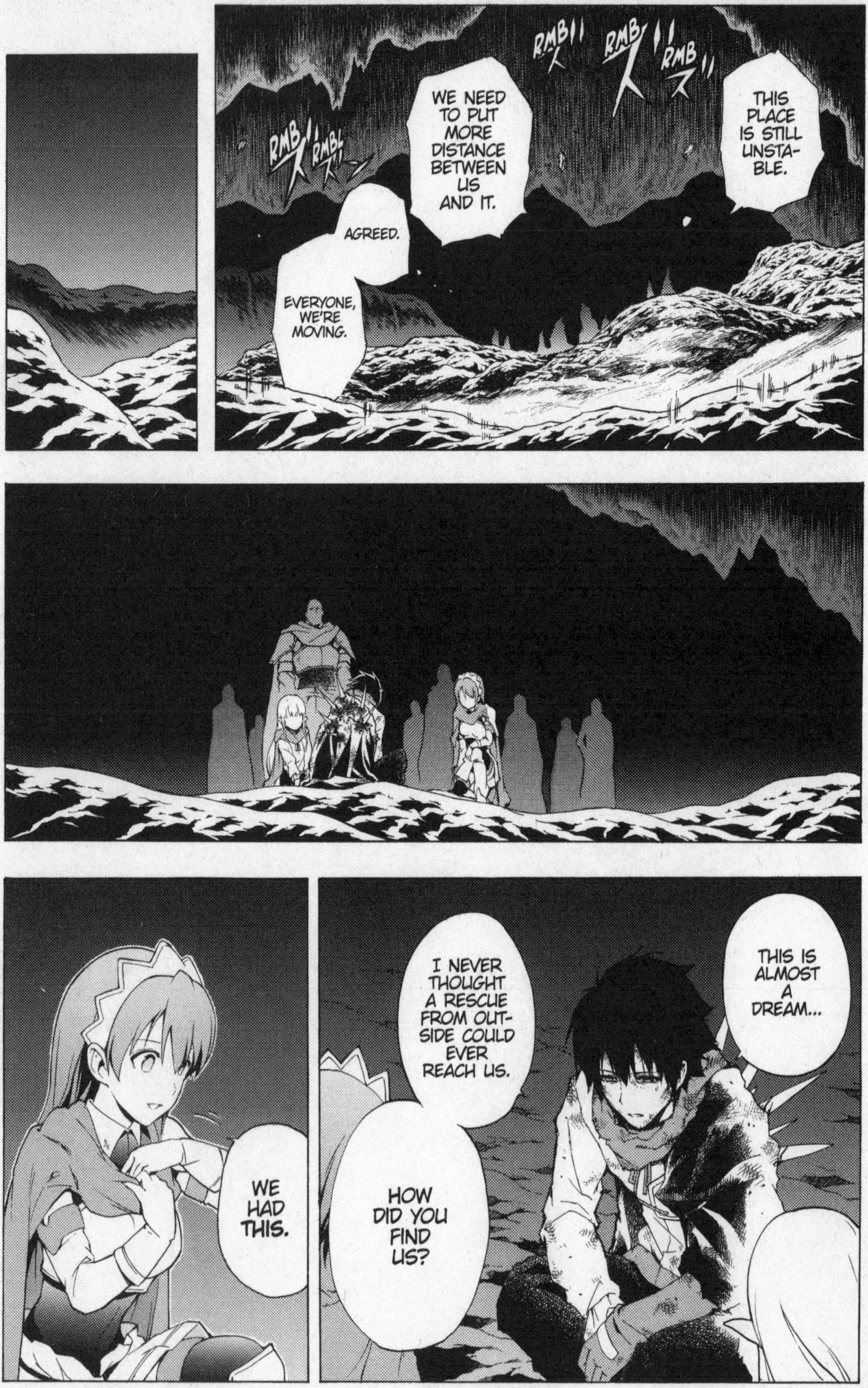
RMB
RMB
RMB
THIS PLACE IS STILL UNSTA-BLE.
WE NEED TO PUT MORE DISTANCE BETWEEN US AND IT.
AGREED.
EVERYONE, WE'RE MOVING.
RMB RMBL
THIS IS ALMOST A DREAM...
I NEVER THOUGHT A RESCUE FROM OUT-SIDE COULD EVER REACH US.
HOW DID YOU FIND US?
WE HAD THIS.

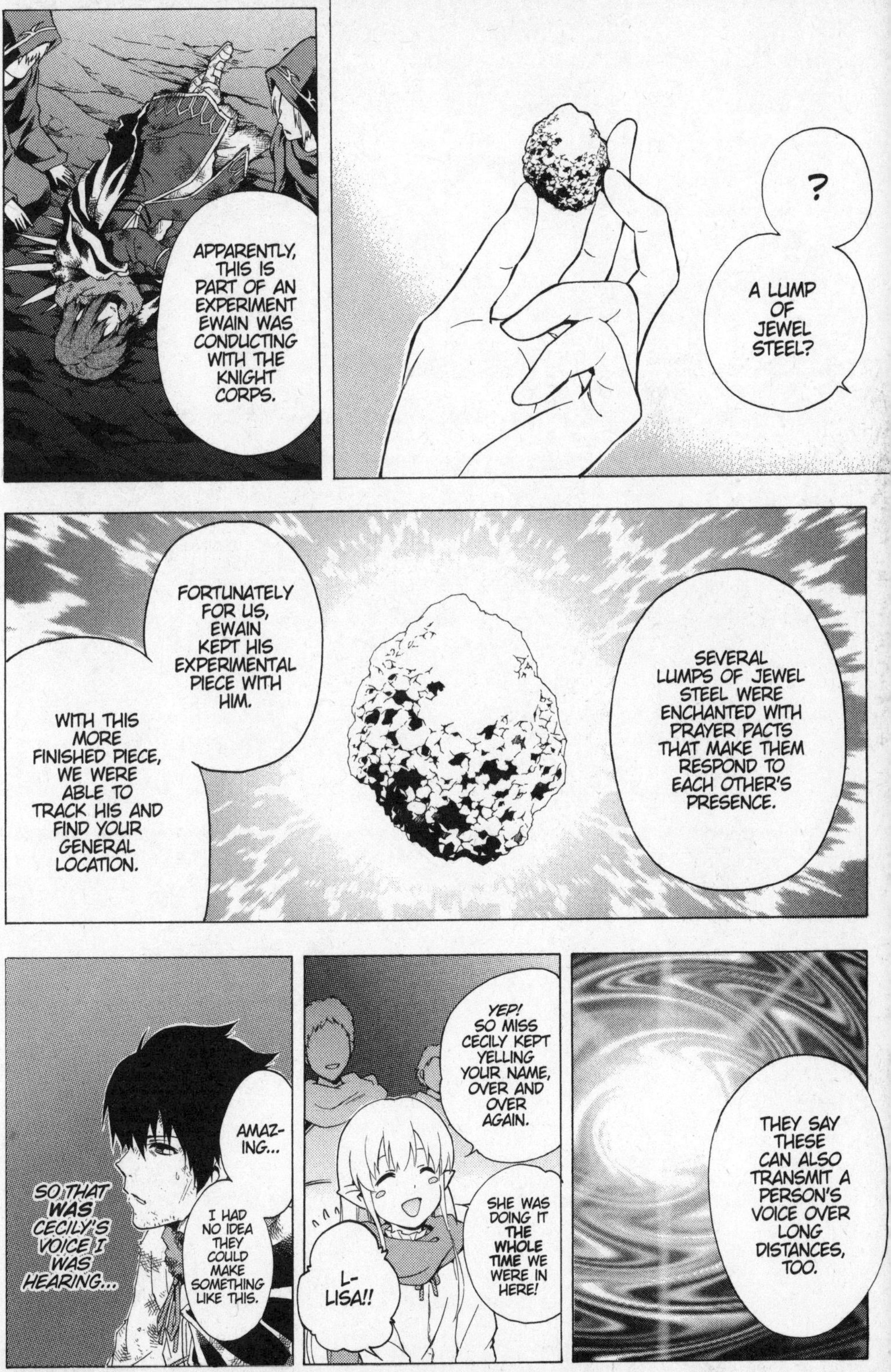
?
A LUMP OF JEWEL STEEL?
APPARENTLY, THIS IS PART OF AN EXPERIMENT EWAIN WAS CONDUCTING WITH THE KNIGHT CORPS.
SEVERAL LUMPS OF JEWEL STEEL WERE ENCHANTED WITH PRAYER PACTS THAT MAKE THEM RESPOND TO EACH OTHER'S PRESENCE.
FORTUNATELY FOR US, EWAIN KEPT HIS EXPERIMENTAL PIECE WITH HIM.
WITH THIS MORE FINISHED PIECE, WE WERE ABLE TO TRACK HIS AND FIND YOUR GENERAL LOCATION.
THEY SAY THESE CAN ALSO TRANSMIT A PERSON'S VOICE OVER LONG DISTANCES, TOO.
YEP! SO MISS CECILY KEPT YELLING YOUR NAME, OVER AND OVER AGAIN.
SHE WAS DOING IT THE WHOLE TIME WE WERE IN HERE!
L-LISA!!
AMAZ-ING...
I HAD NO IDEA THEY COULD MAKE SOMETHING LIKE THIS.
SO THAT WAS CECILY'S VOICE I WAS HEARING...

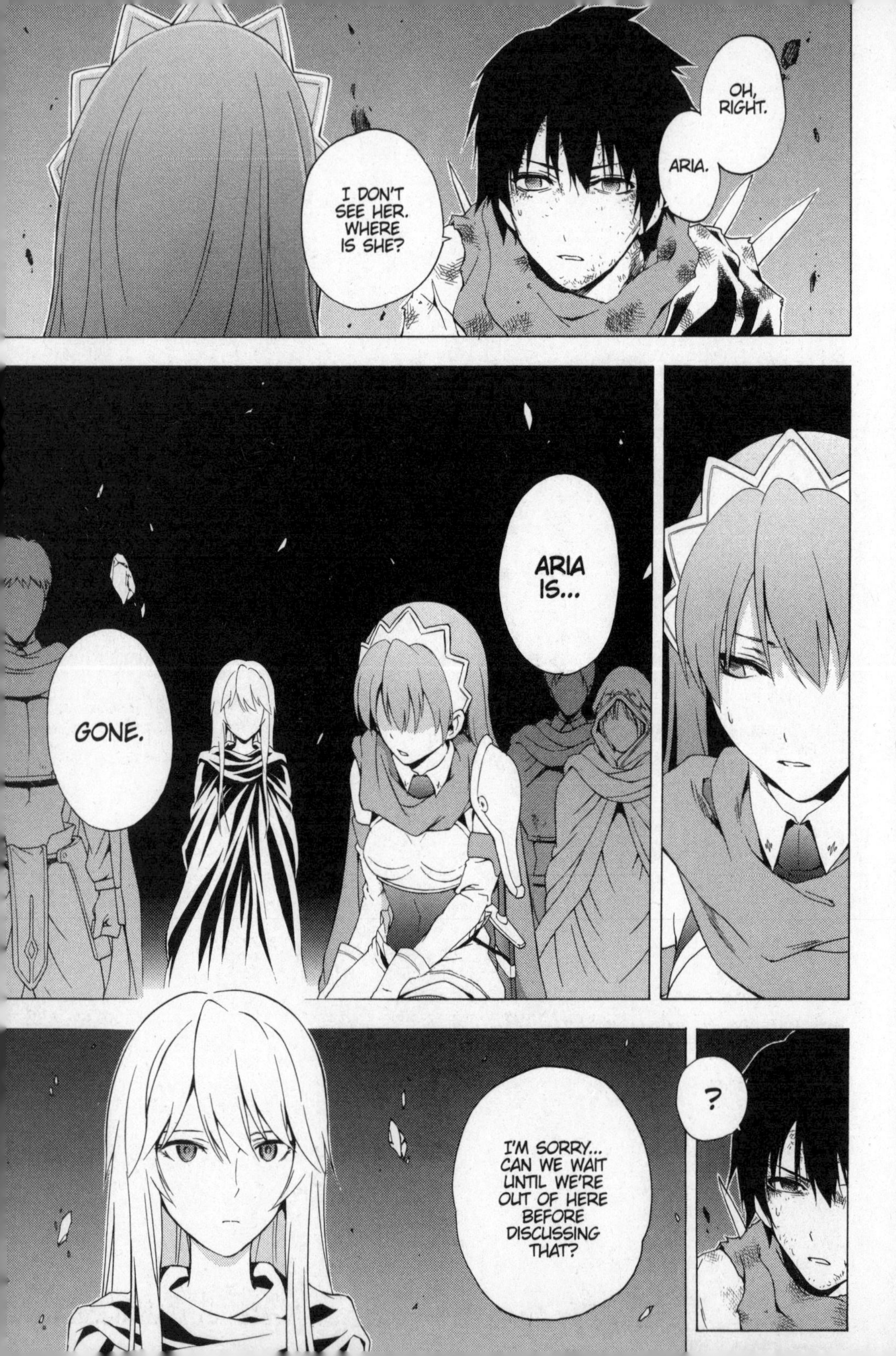
OH, RIGHT.
ARIA.
I DON'T SEE HER. WHERE IS SHE?
ARIA IS...
GONE.
?
I'M SORRY... CAN WE WAIT UNTIL WE'RE OUT OF HERE BEFORE DISCUSSING THAT?

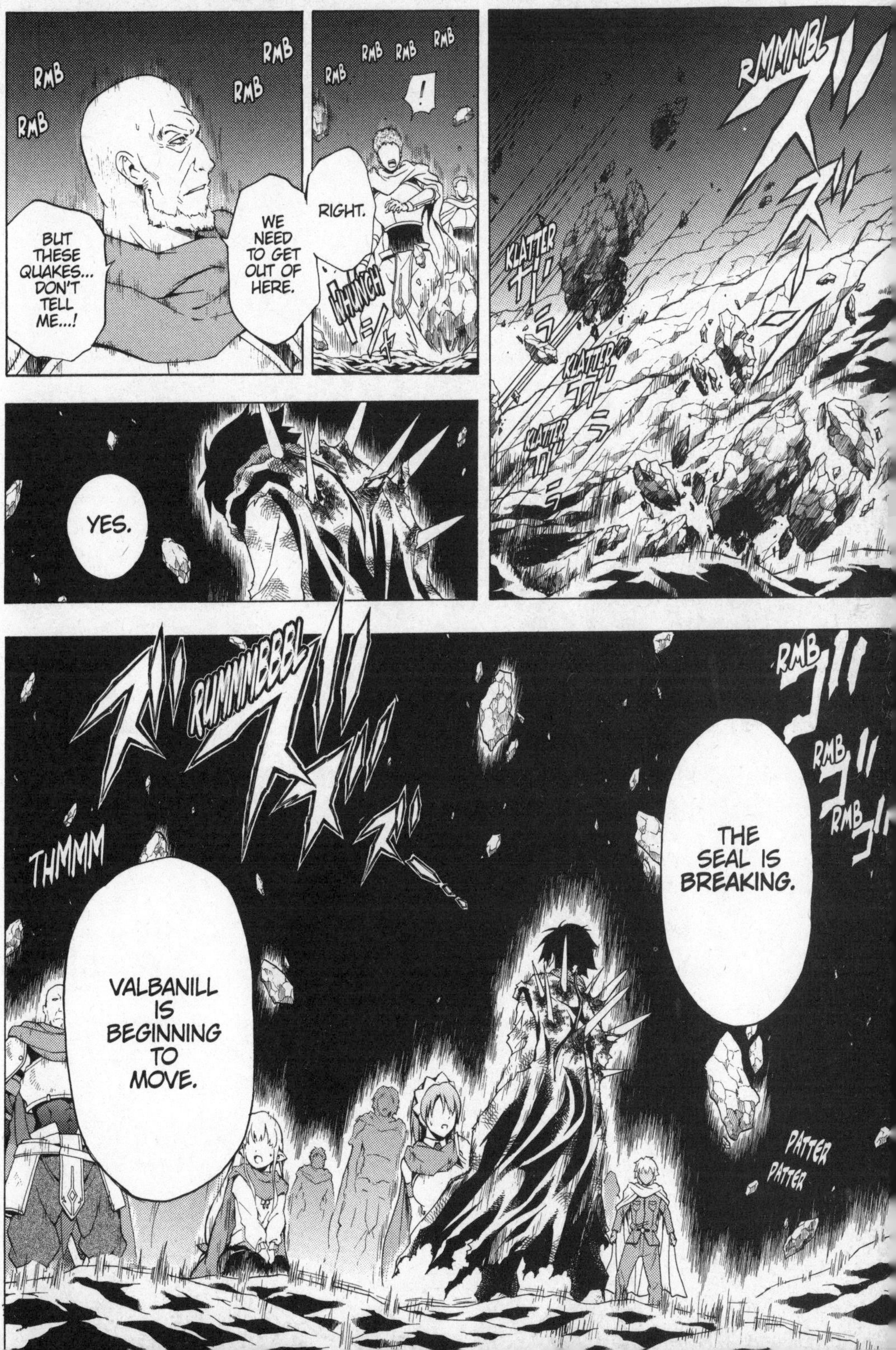

RMMMBL
KLATTER
KLATTER
KLATTER
RMB
RMB
RMB
RMB
!
RIGHT.
WE NEED TO GET OUT OF HERE.
WHUNCH
RMB
RMB
RMB
RMB
BUT THESE QUAKES... DON'T TELL ME...!
YES.
RMB
RMB
RMB
THE SEAL IS BREAKING.
RUMMMBBBL
THMMM
VALBANILL IS BEGINNING TO MOVE.
PATTER
PATTER

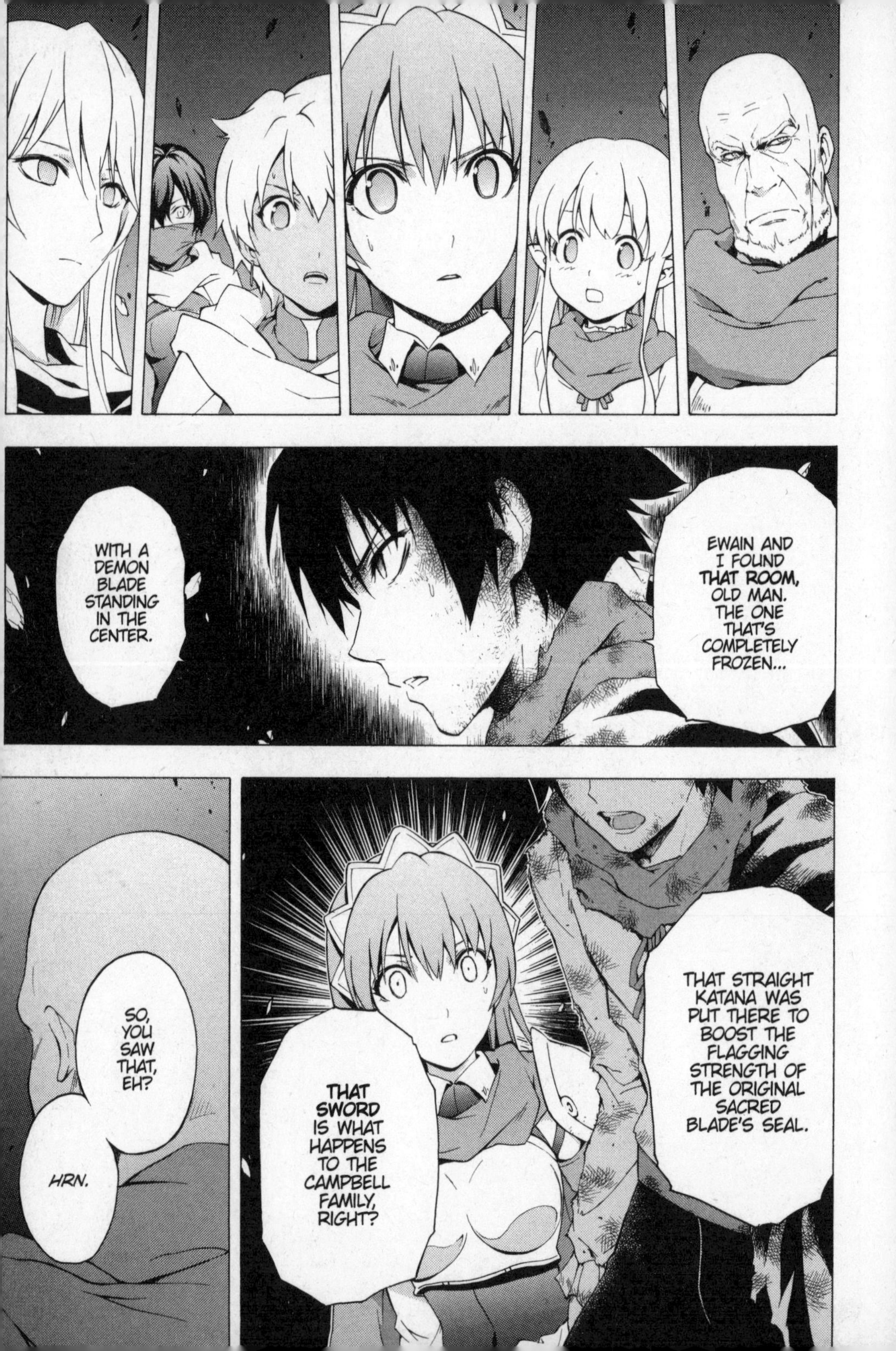
EWAIN AND I FOUND THAT ROOM, OLD MAN. THE ONE THAT'S COMPLETELY FROZEN...
WITH A DEMON BLADE STANDING IN THE CENTER.
THAT STRAIGHT KATANA WAS PUT THERE TO BOOST THE FLAGGING STRENGTH OF THE ORIGINAL SACRED BLADE'S SEAL.
THAT SWORD IS WHAT HAPPENS TO THE CAMPBELL FAMILY, RIGHT?
SO, YOU SAW THAT, EH?
HRN.

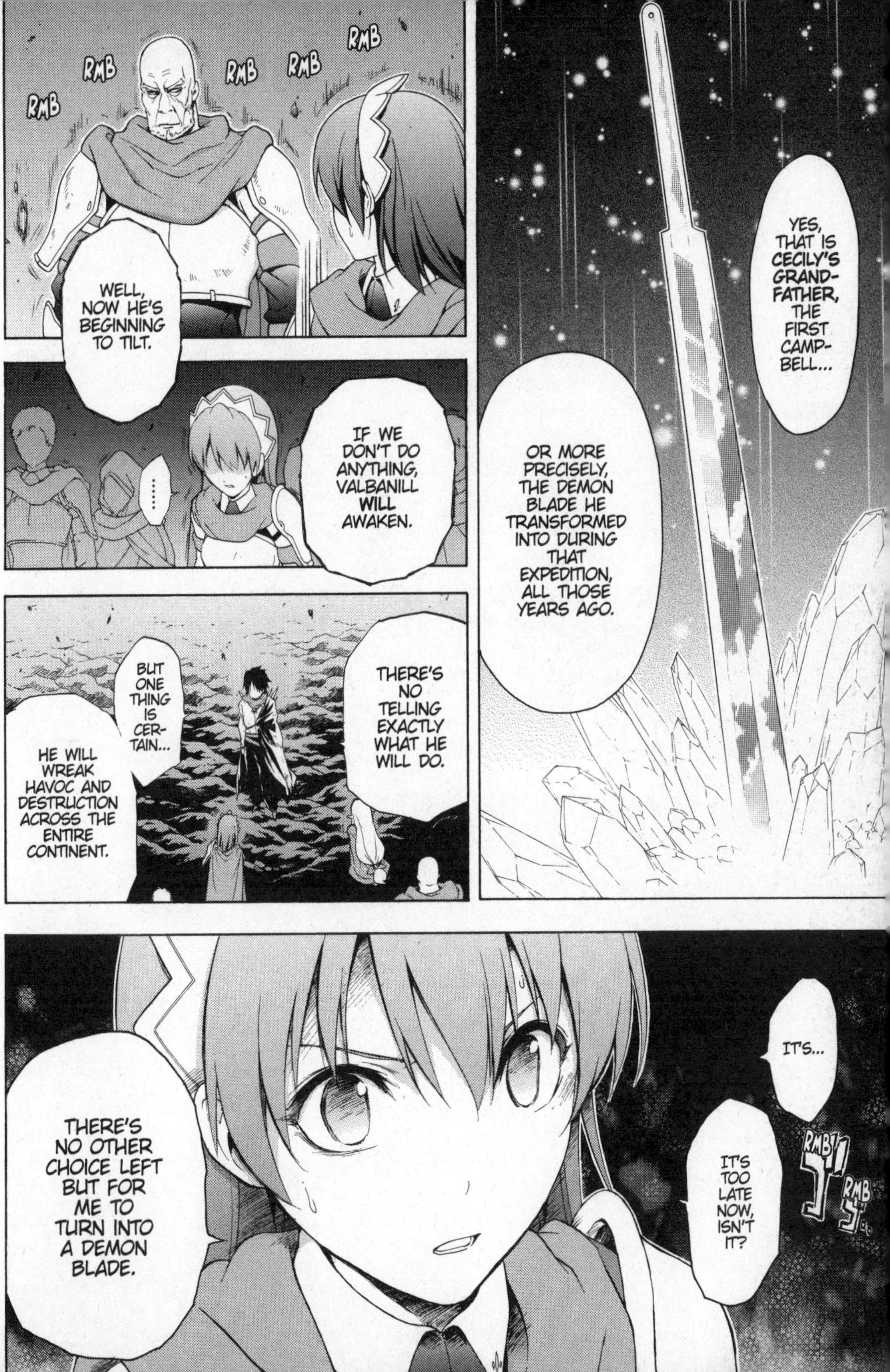
YES, THAT IS CECILY'S GRAND-FATHER, THE FIRST CAMP-BELL...
OR MORE PRECISELY, THE DEMON BLADE HE TRANSFORMED INTO DURING THAT EXPEDITION, ALL THOSE YEARS AGO.
RMB RMB RMB RMB RMB
WELL, NOW HE'S BEGINNING TO TILT.
IF WE DON'T DO ANYTHING, VALBANILL WILL AWAKEN.
......
THERE'S NO TELLING EXACTLY WHAT HE WILL DO.
BUT ONE THING IS CER-TAIN...
HE WILL WREAK HAVOC AND DESTRUCTION ACROSS THE ENTIRE CONTINENT.
IT'S...
IT'S TOO LATE NOW, ISN'T IT?
RMB RMB
THERE'S NO OTHER CHOICE LEFT BUT FOR ME TO TURN INTO A DEMON BLADE.

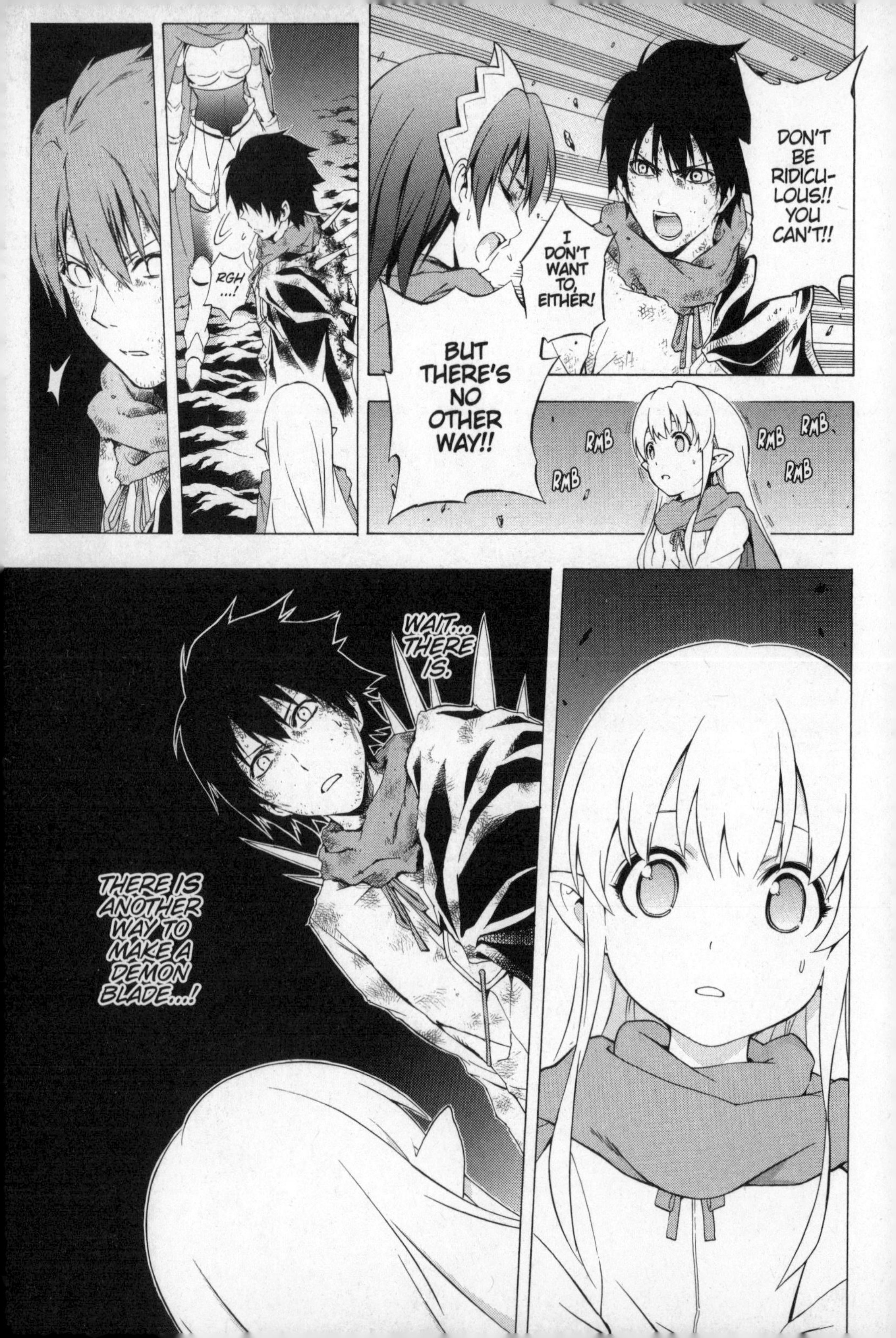

DON'T BE RIDICU-LOUS!! YOU CAN'T!!
I DON'T WANT TO, EITHER!
BUT THERE'S NO OTHER WAY!!
RMB
RMB
RMB
RMB
RMB
RGH ...!
WAIT... THERE IS.
THERE IS ANOTHER WAY TO MAKE A DEMON BLADE...!

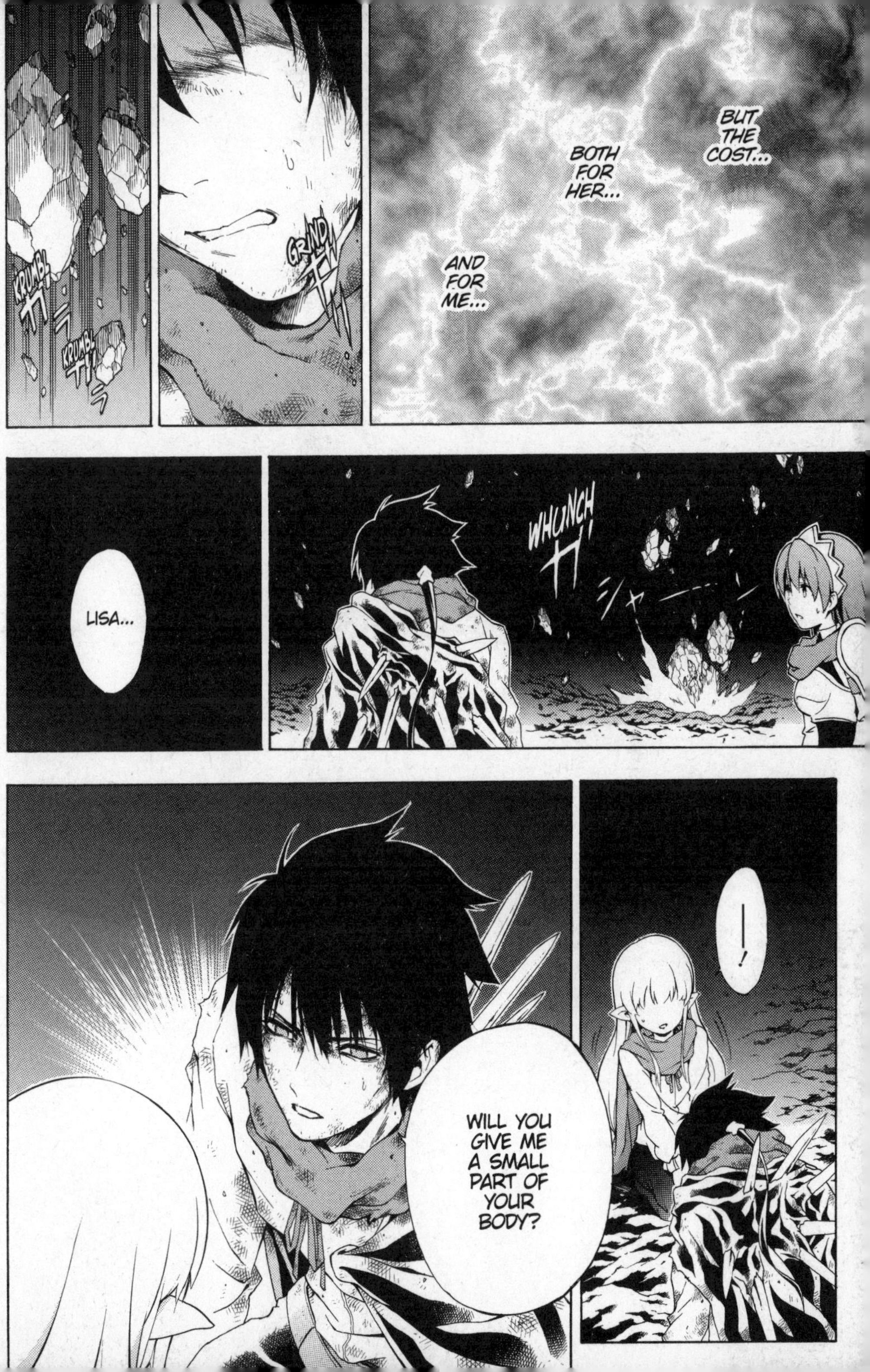
BUT THE COST...
BOTH FOR HER...
AND FOR ME...
GRIND
KRUMBL
KRUMBL
WHUNCH
LISA...
—!
WILL YOU GIVE ME A SMALL PART OF YOUR BODY?

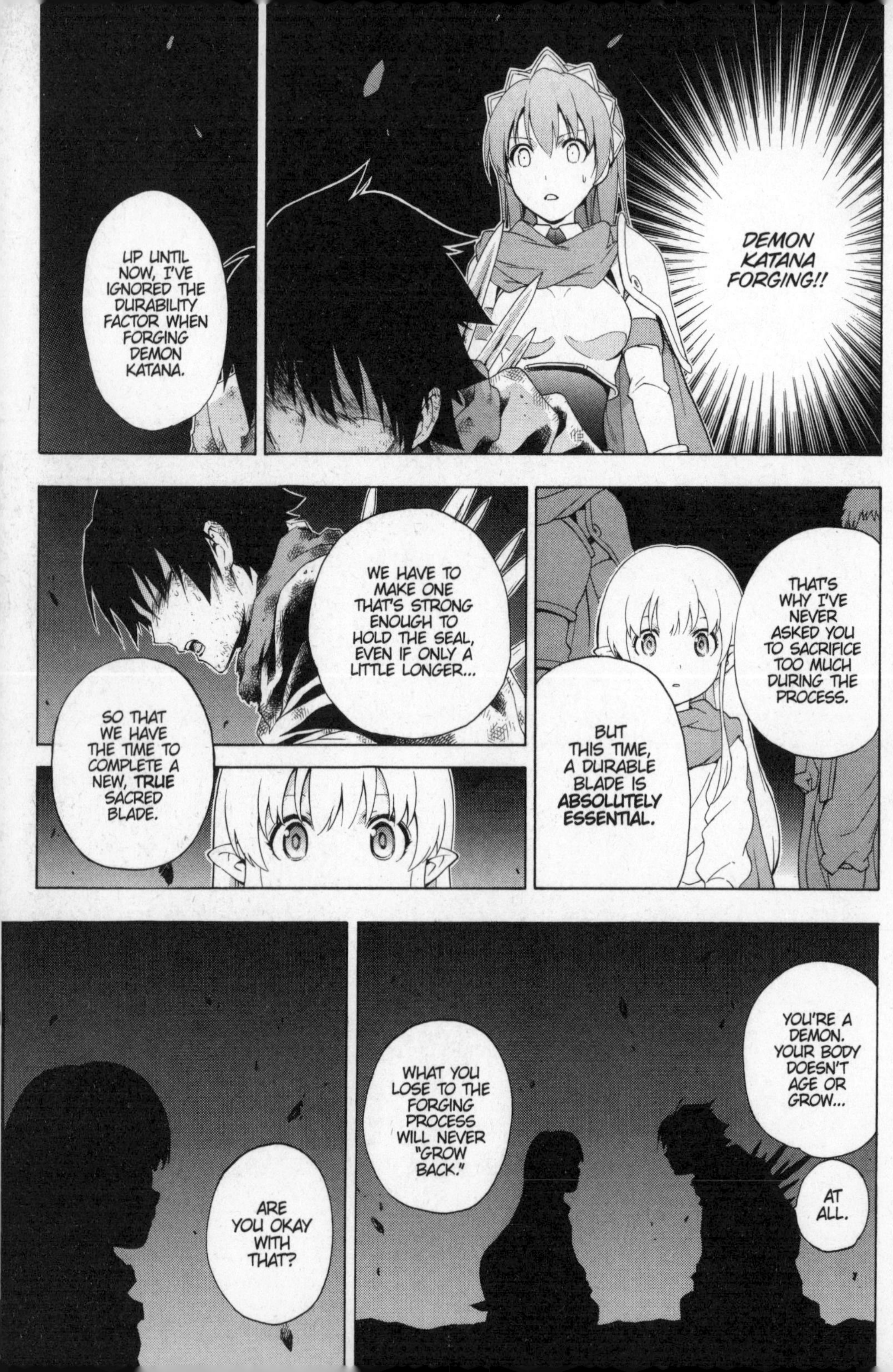
DEMON KATANA FORGING!!
UP UNTIL NOW, I'VE IGNORED THE DURABILITY FACTOR WHEN FORGING DEMON KATANA.
THAT'S WHY I'VE NEVER ASKED YOU TO SACRIFICE TOO MUCH DURING THE PROCESS.
BUT THIS TIME, A DURABLE BLADE IS **ABSOLUTELY ESSENTIAL.**
WE HAVE TO MAKE ONE THAT'S STRONG ENOUGH TO HOLD THE SEAL, EVEN IF ONLY A LITTLE LONGER...
SO THAT WE HAVE THE TIME TO COMPLETE A NEW, **TRUE** SACRED BLADE.
YOU'RE A DEMON. YOUR BODY DOESN'T AGE OR GROW...
AT ALL.
WHAT YOU LOSE TO THE FORGING PROCESS WILL NEVER "GROW BACK."
ARE YOU OKAY WITH THAT?

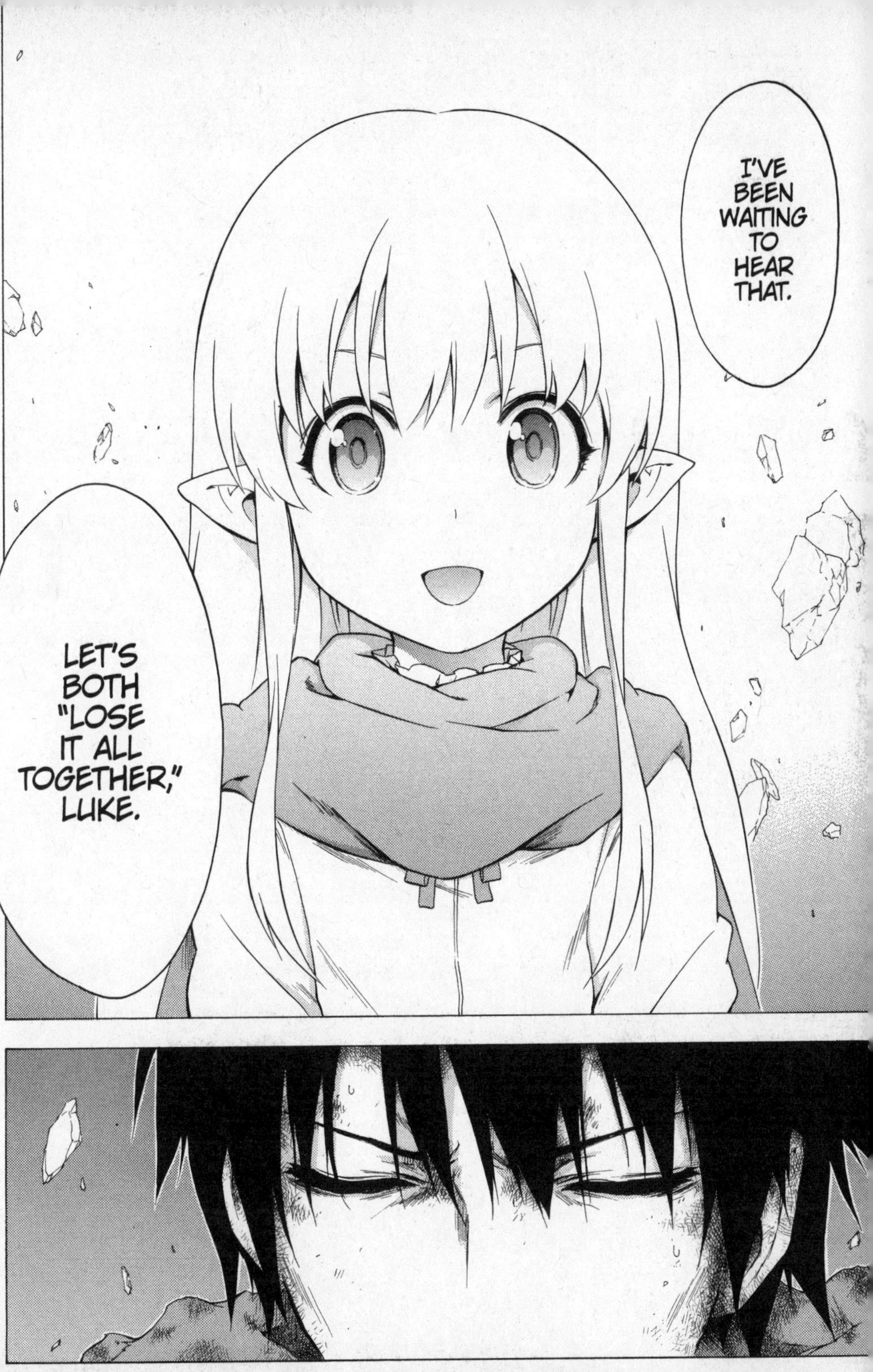
I'VE BEEN WAITING TO HEAR THAT.
LET'S BOTH "LOSE IT ALL TOGETHER," LUKE.

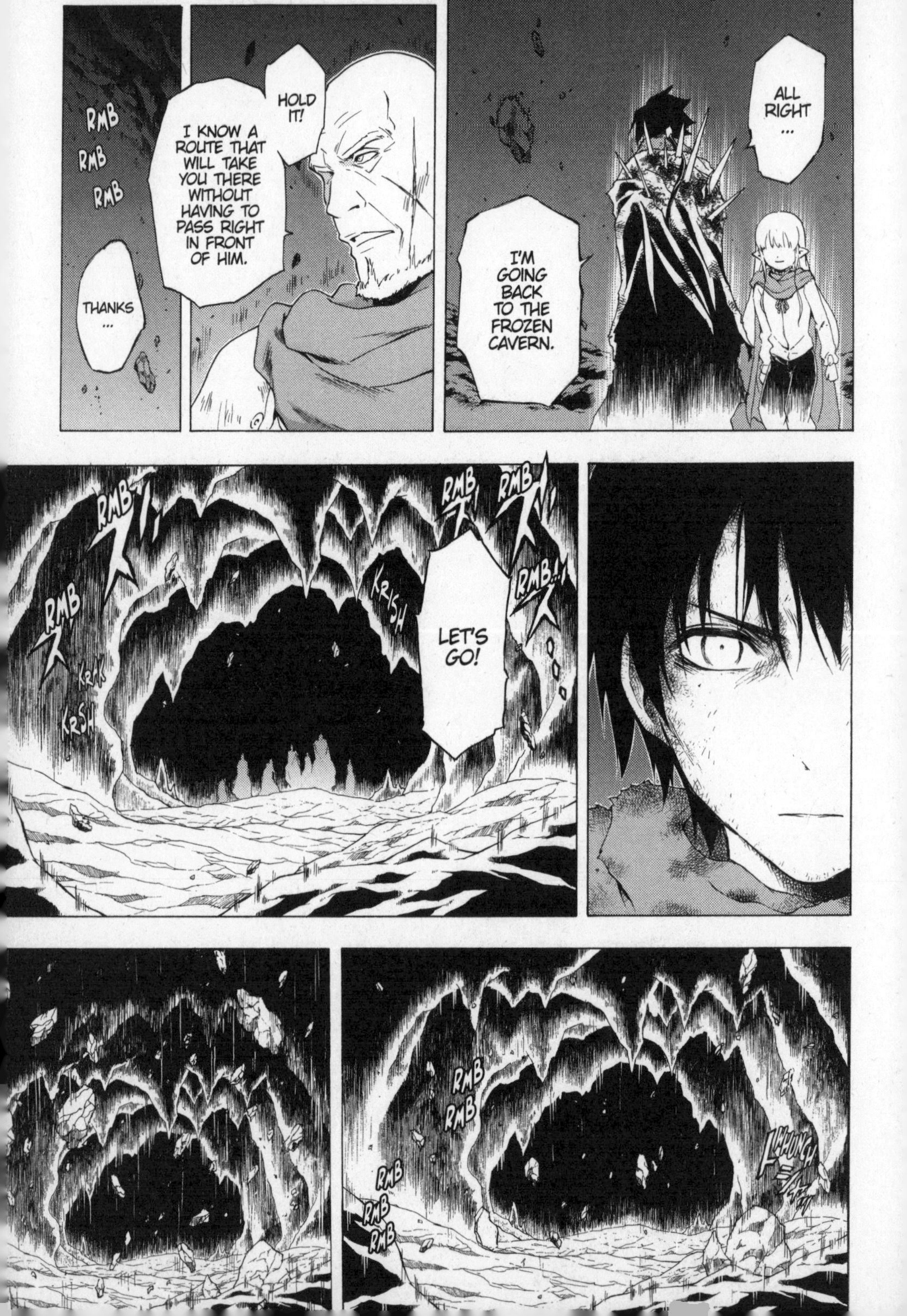
ALL RIGHT ...
I'M GOING BACK TO THE FROZEN CAVERN.
HOLD IT!
I KNOW A ROUTE THAT WILL TAKE YOU THERE WITHOUT HAVING TO PASS RIGHT IN FRONT OF HIM.
RMB RMB RMB
THANKS ...
RMB
RMB
RMB...
KRISH
LET'S GO!
RMB
RMB
KRAK
KRSH
RMB RMB
RMB RMB RMB
WHUNCH

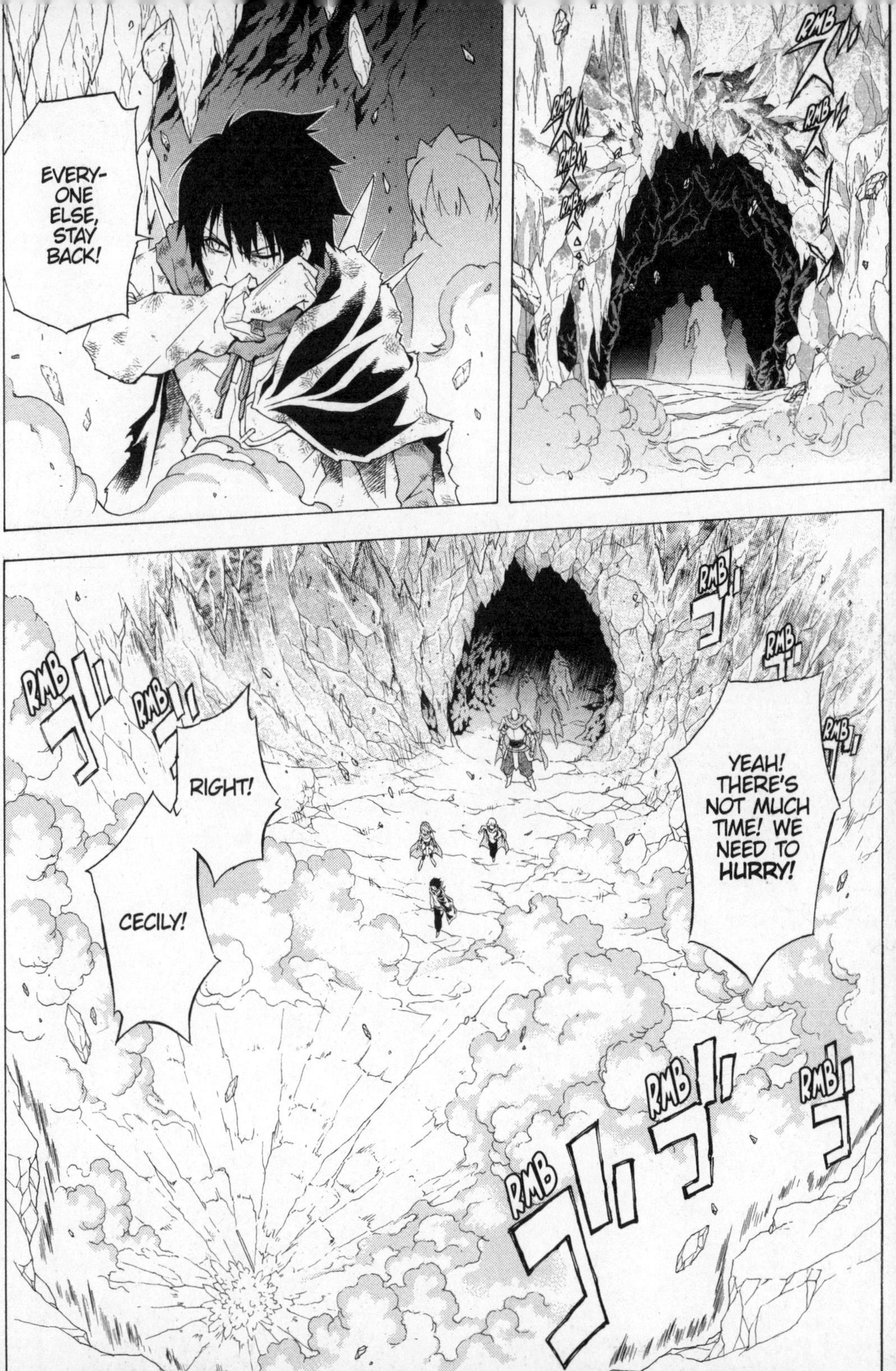
RMB
RMB
RMB
RMB
RMB
RMB
EVERY-ONE ELSE, STAY BACK!
RMB
RMB
RMB
YEAH! THERE'S NOT MUCH TIME! WE NEED TO HURRY!
RMB
RMB
RIGHT!
CECILY!
RMB
RMB
RMB

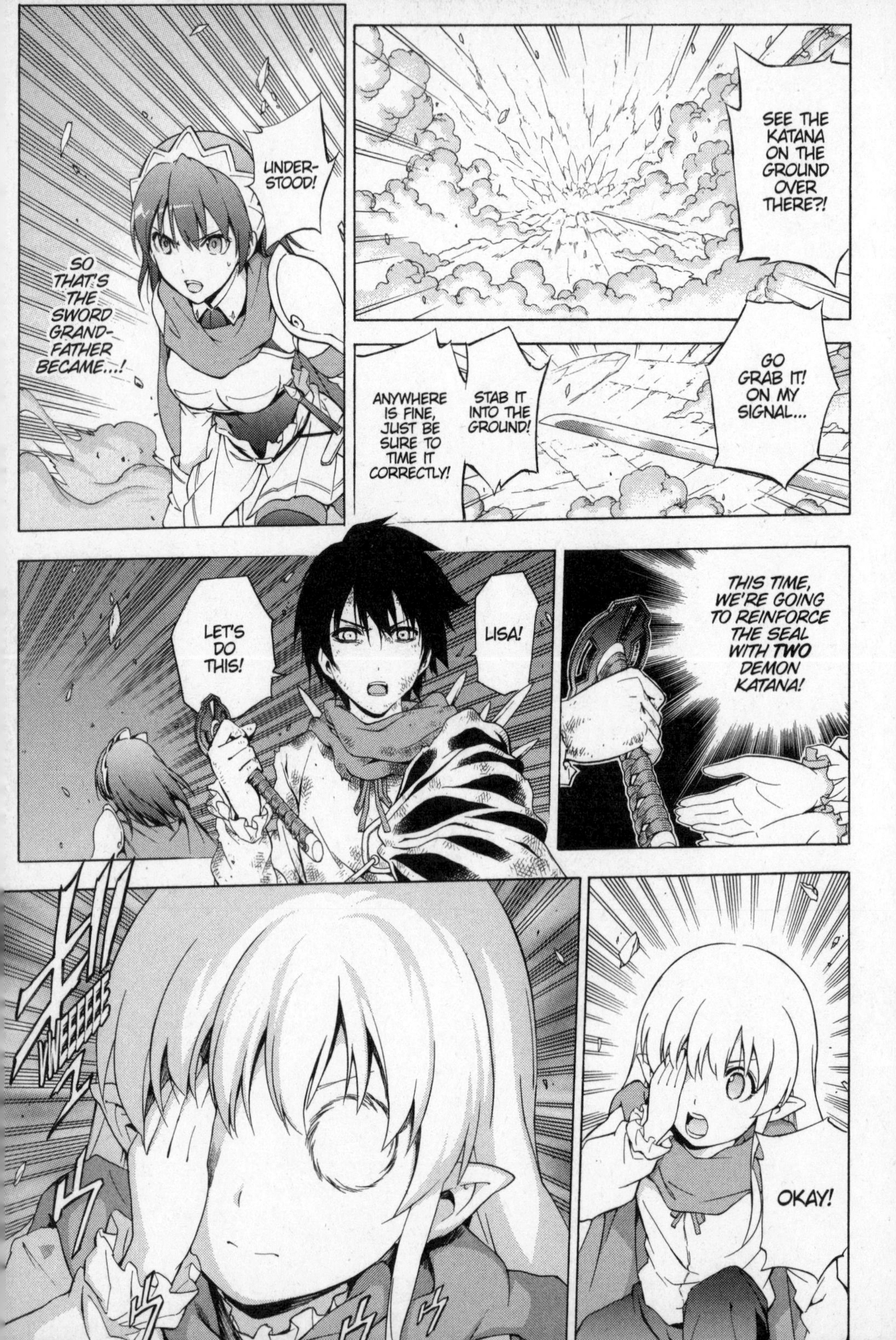
SEE THE KATANA ON THE GROUND OVER THERE?!
GO GRAB IT! ON MY SIGNAL...
STAB IT INTO THE GROUND!
ANYWHERE IS FINE, JUST BE SURE TO TIME IT CORRECTLY!
UNDER-STOOD!
SO THAT'S THE SWORD GRAND-FATHER BECAME...!
THIS TIME, WE'RE GOING TO REINFORCE THE SEAL WITH **TWO** DEMON KATANA!
LISA!
LET'S DO THIS!
OKAY!
VWEEEEEE

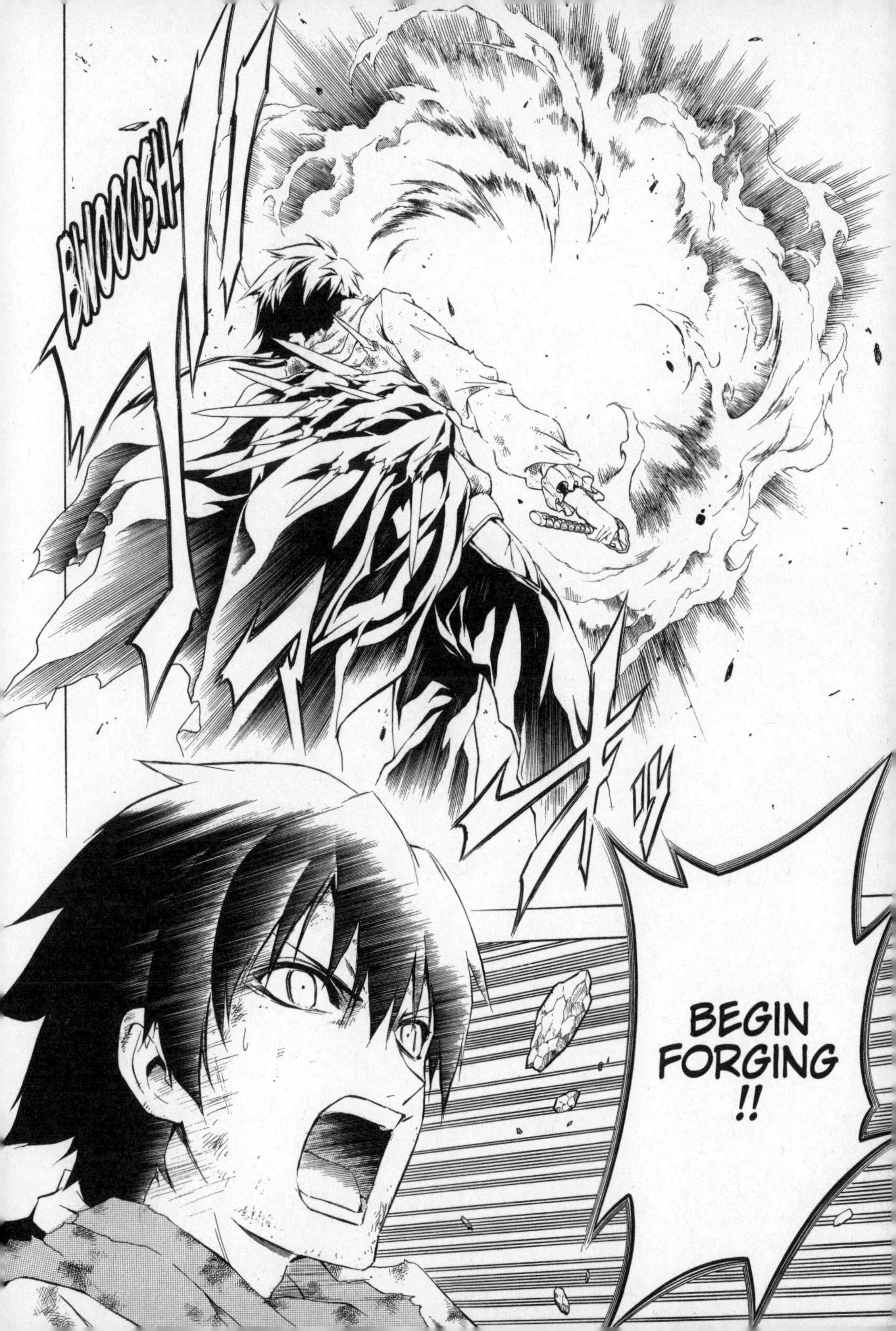
BWOOOSH
BEGIN FORGING !!

The Sacred Blacksmith

聖剣の刀鍛治

The Sacred Blacksmith

聖剣の刀鍛冶

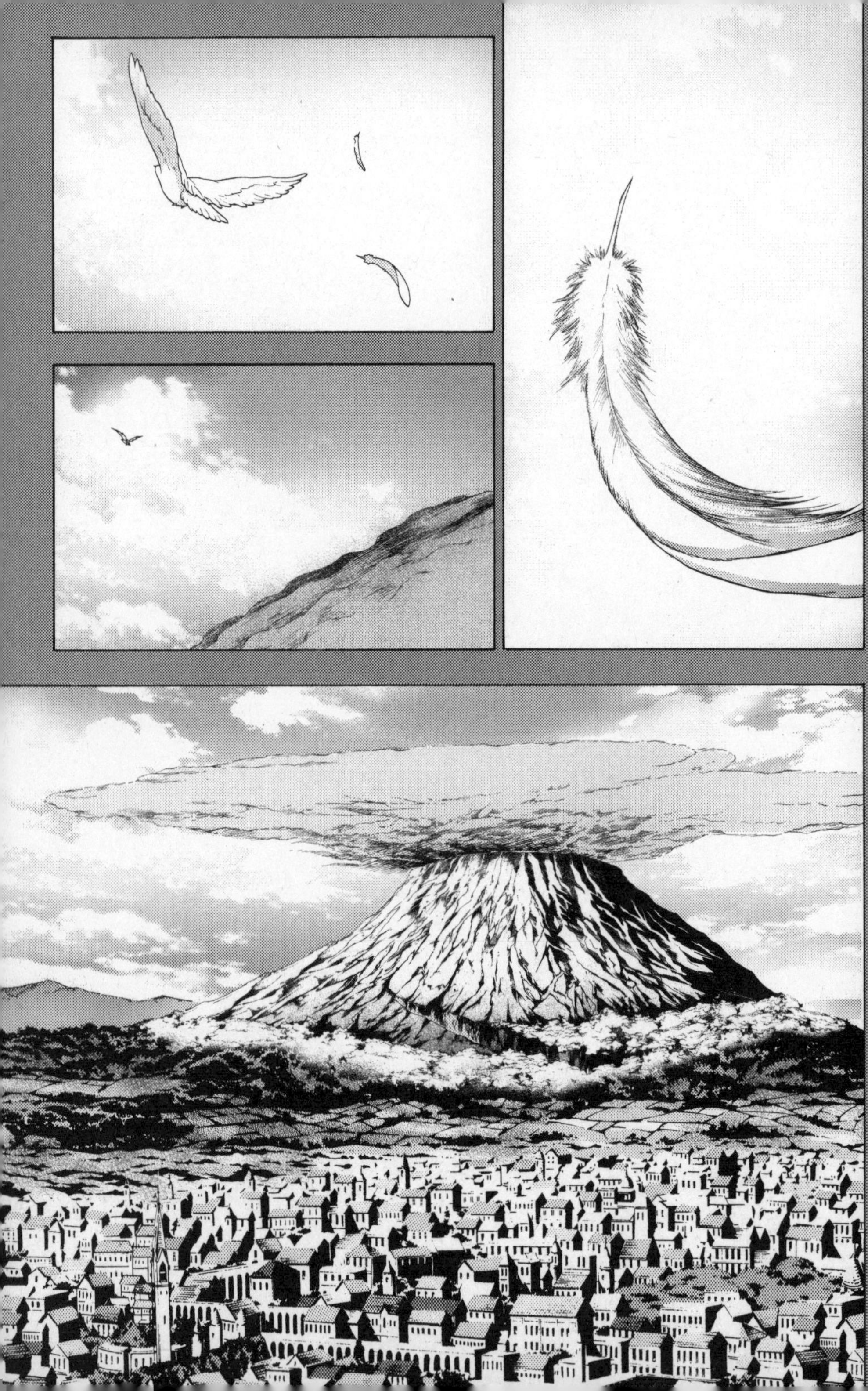

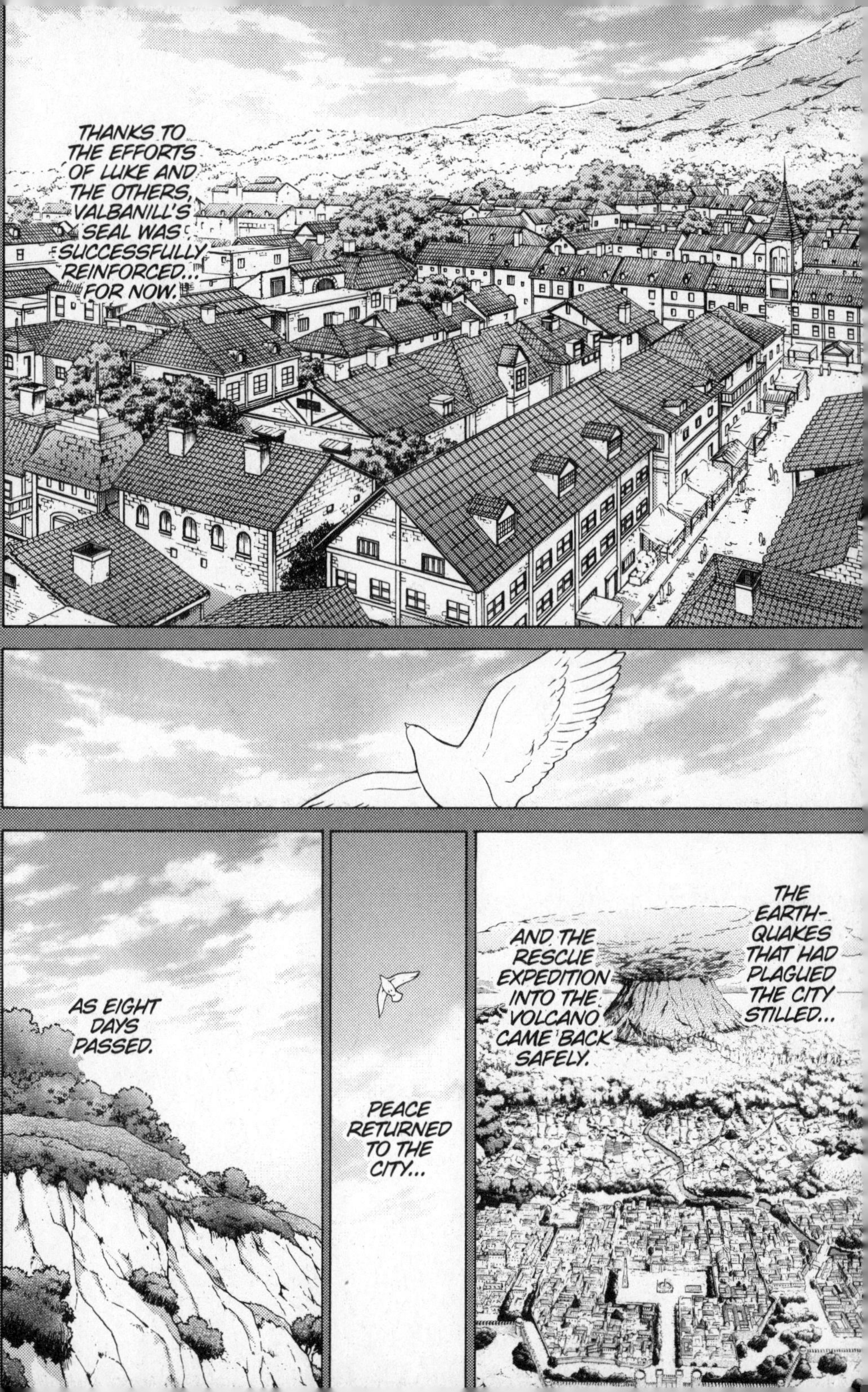
THANKS TO THE EFFORTS OF LUKE AND THE OTHERS, VALBANILL'S SEAL WAS SUCCESSFULLY REINFORCED... FOR NOW.
THE EARTH-QUAKES THAT HAD PLAGUED THE CITY STILLED...
AND THE RESCUE EXPEDITION INTO THE VOLCANO CAME BACK SAFELY.
PEACE RETURNED TO THE CITY...
AS EIGHT DAYS PASSED.

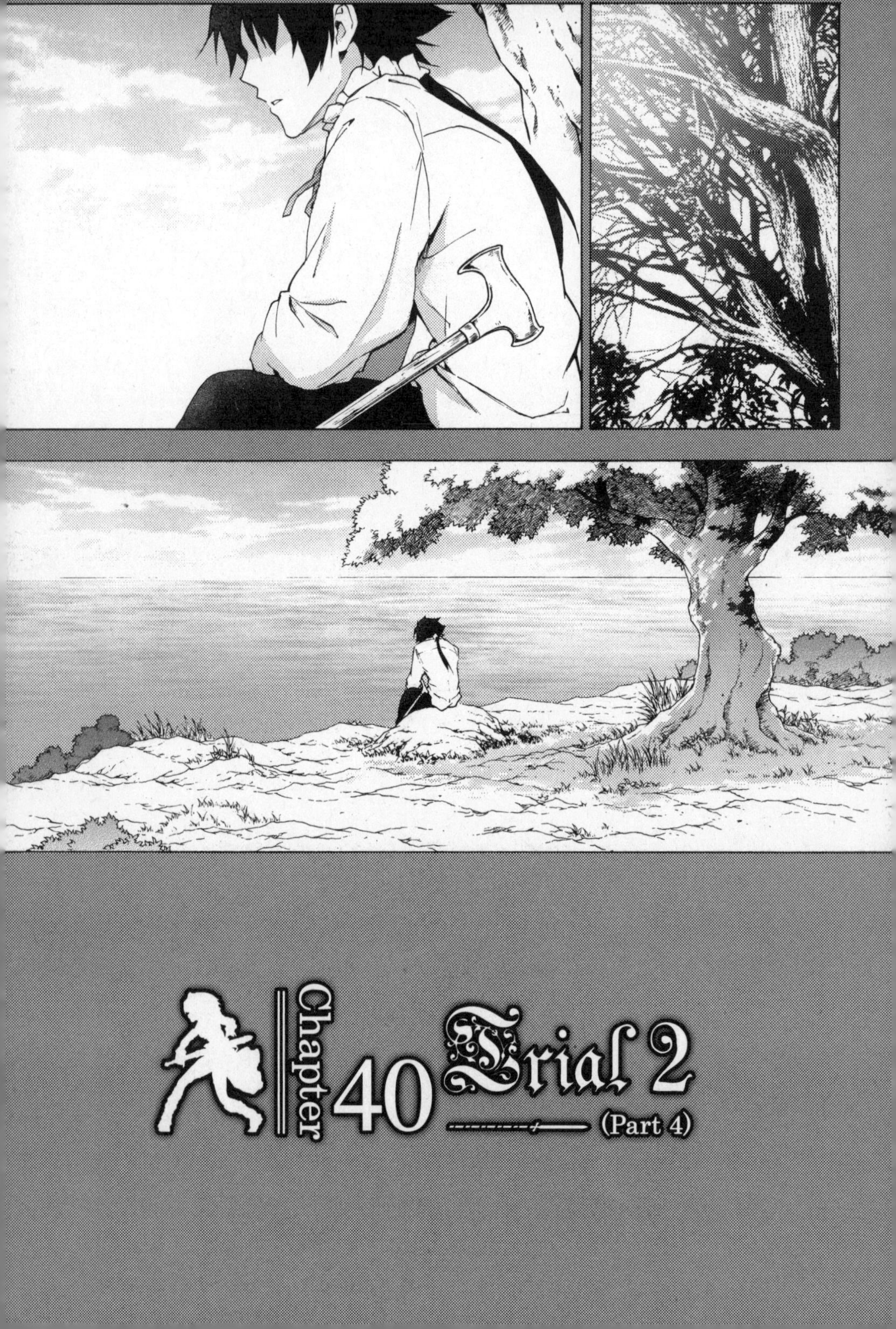

Chapter 40 Trial 2 (Part 4)

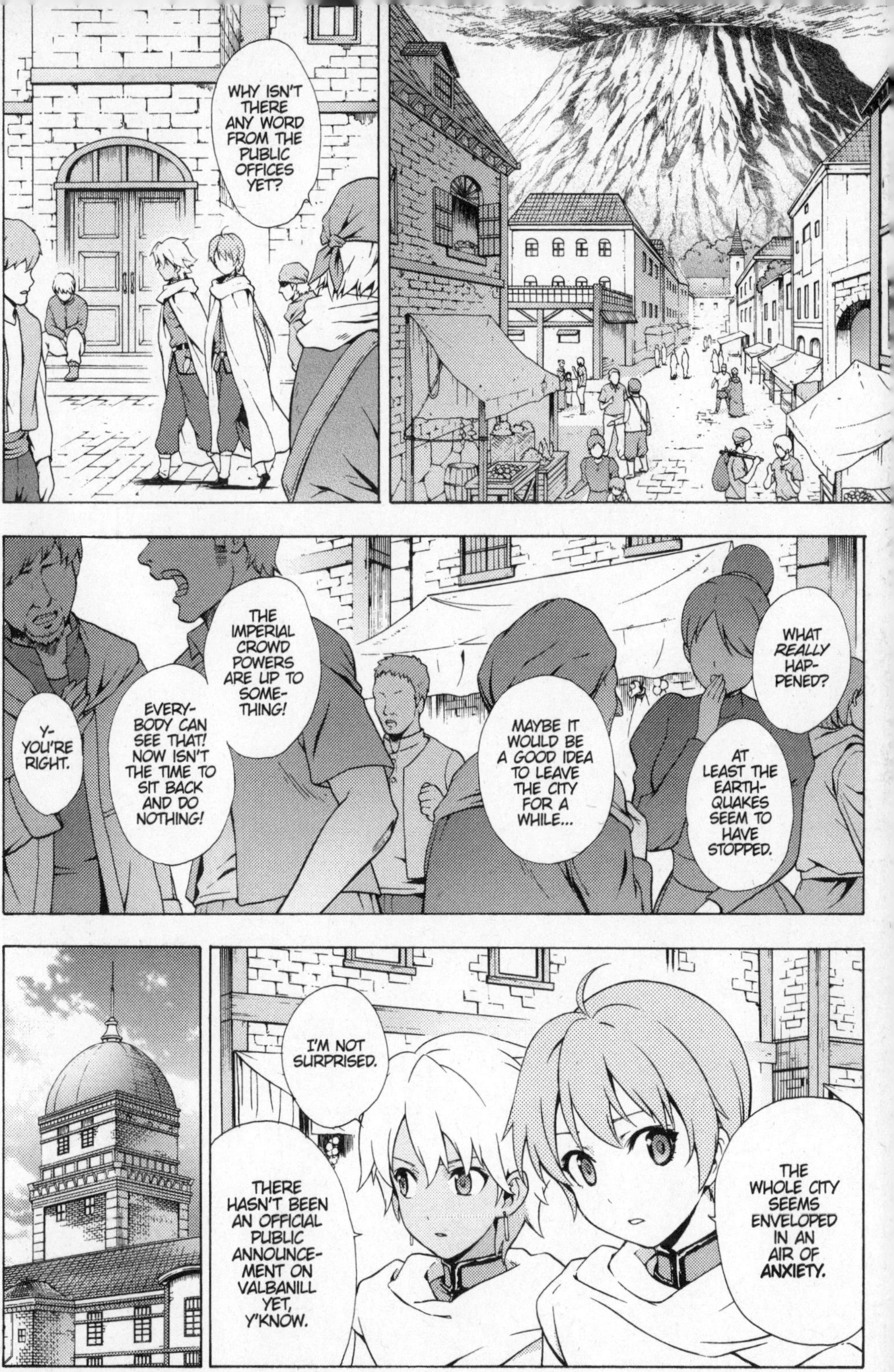
WHY ISN'T THERE ANY WORD FROM THE PUBLIC OFFICES YET?
WHAT *REALLY* HAPPENED?
AT LEAST THE EARTHQUAKES SEEM TO HAVE STOPPED.
MAYBE IT WOULD BE A GOOD IDEA TO LEAVE THE CITY FOR A WHILE...
THE IMPERIAL CROWD POWERS ARE UP TO SOMETHING!
EVERYBODY CAN SEE THAT! NOW ISN'T THE TIME TO SIT BACK AND DO NOTHING!
Y-YOU'RE RIGHT.
THE WHOLE CITY SEEMS ENVELOPED IN AN AIR OF **ANXIETY.**
I'M NOT SURPRISED.
THERE HASN'T BEEN AN OFFICIAL PUBLIC ANNOUNCEMENT ON VALBANILL YET, Y'KNOW.

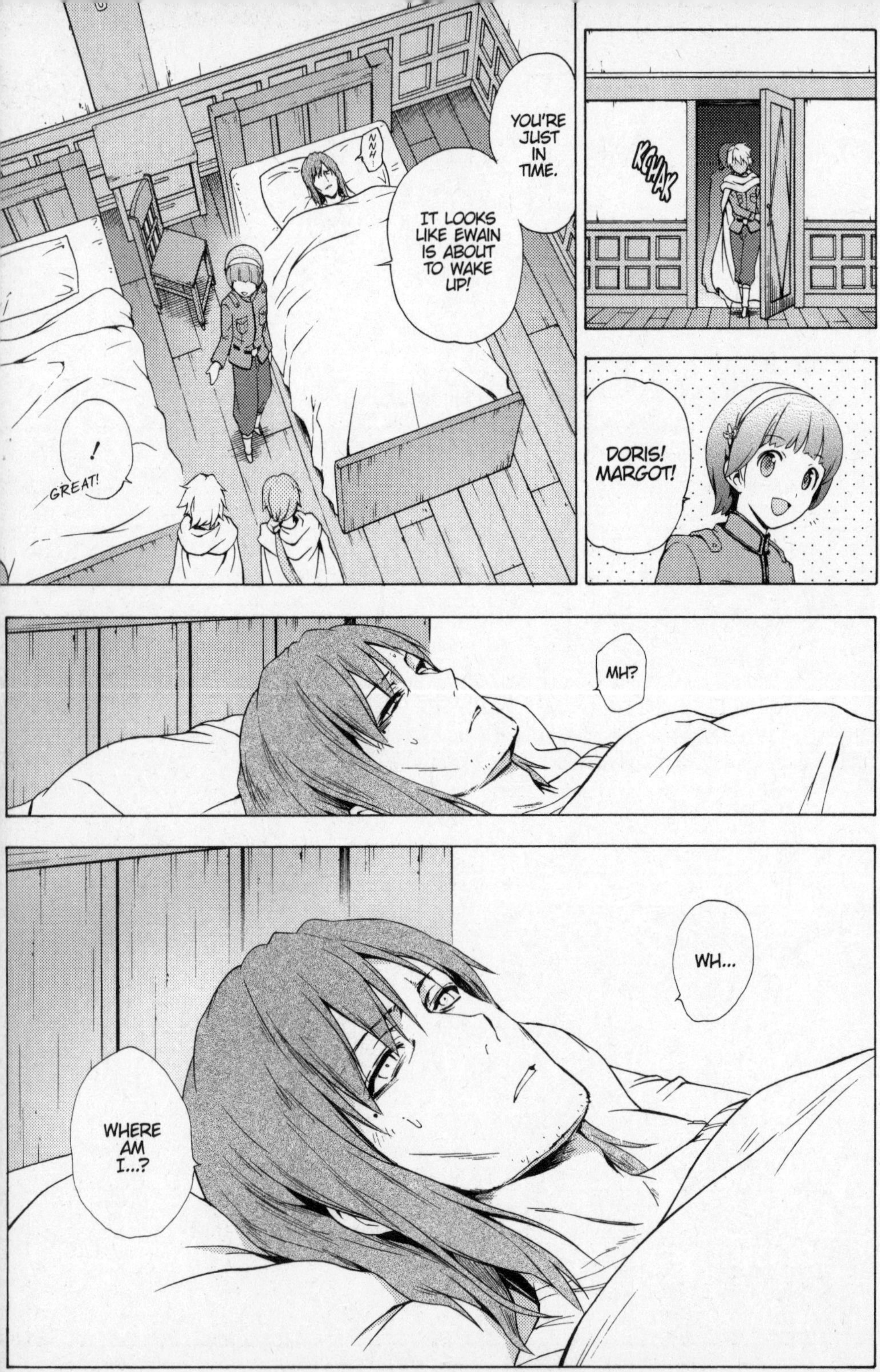
KCHAK
DORIS! MARGOT!
YOU'RE JUST IN TIME.
IT LOOKS LIKE EWAIN IS ABOUT TO WAKE UP!
NNH...
!
GREAT!
MH?
WH...
WHERE AM I...?

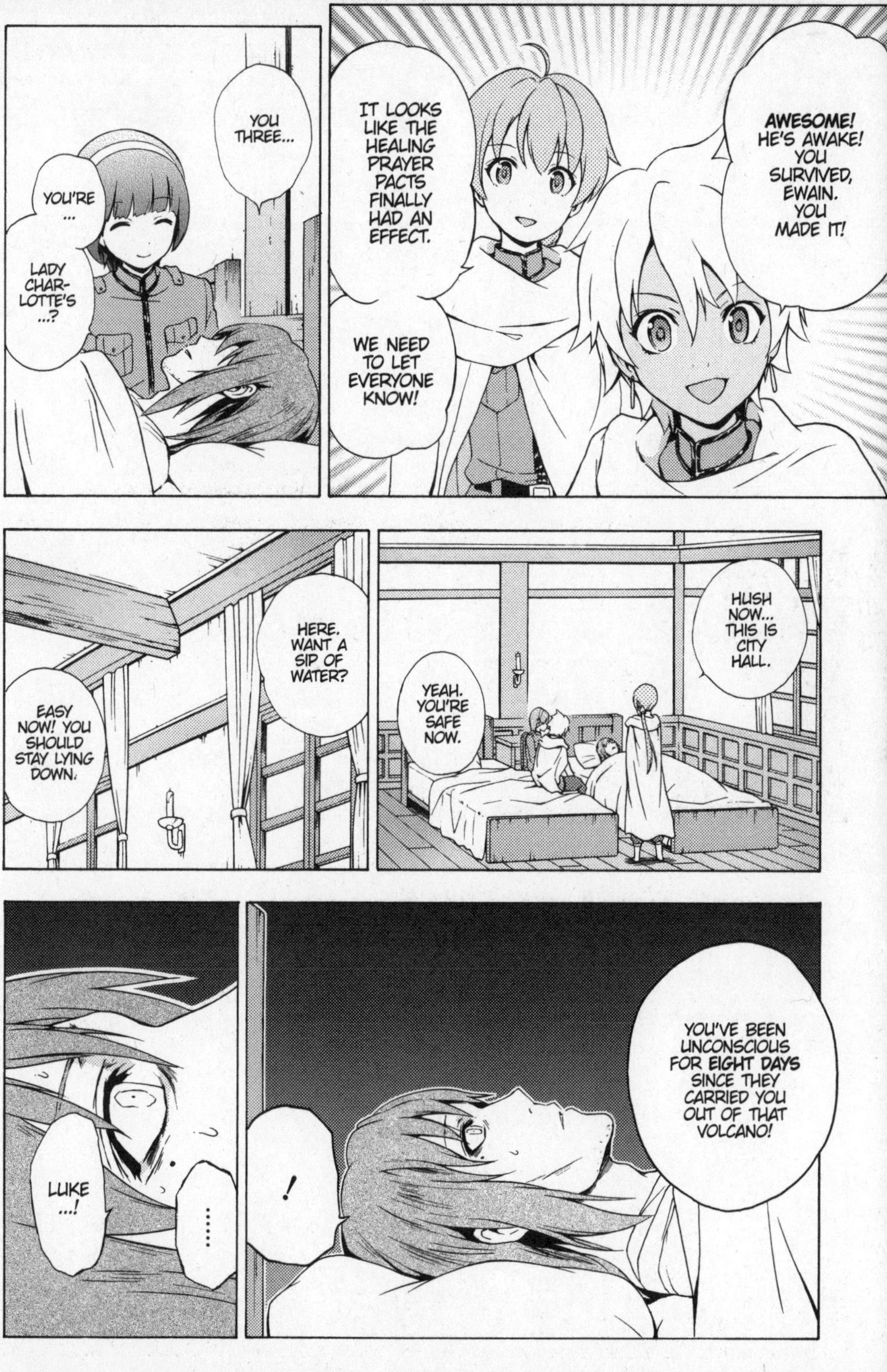
AWESOME! HE'S AWAKE! YOU SURVIVED, EWAIN. YOU MADE IT!
IT LOOKS LIKE THE HEALING PRAYER PACTS FINALLY HAD AN EFFECT.
WE NEED TO LET EVERYONE KNOW!
YOU THREE...
YOU'RE ...
LADY CHARLOTTE'S ...?
HUSH NOW... THIS IS CITY HALL.
YEAH. YOU'RE SAFE NOW.
HERE. WANT A SIP OF WATER?
EASY NOW! YOU SHOULD STAY LYING DOWN.
YOU'VE BEEN UNCONSCIOUS FOR EIGHT DAYS SINCE THEY CARRIED YOU OUT OF THAT VOLCANO!
!
......
LUKE ...!

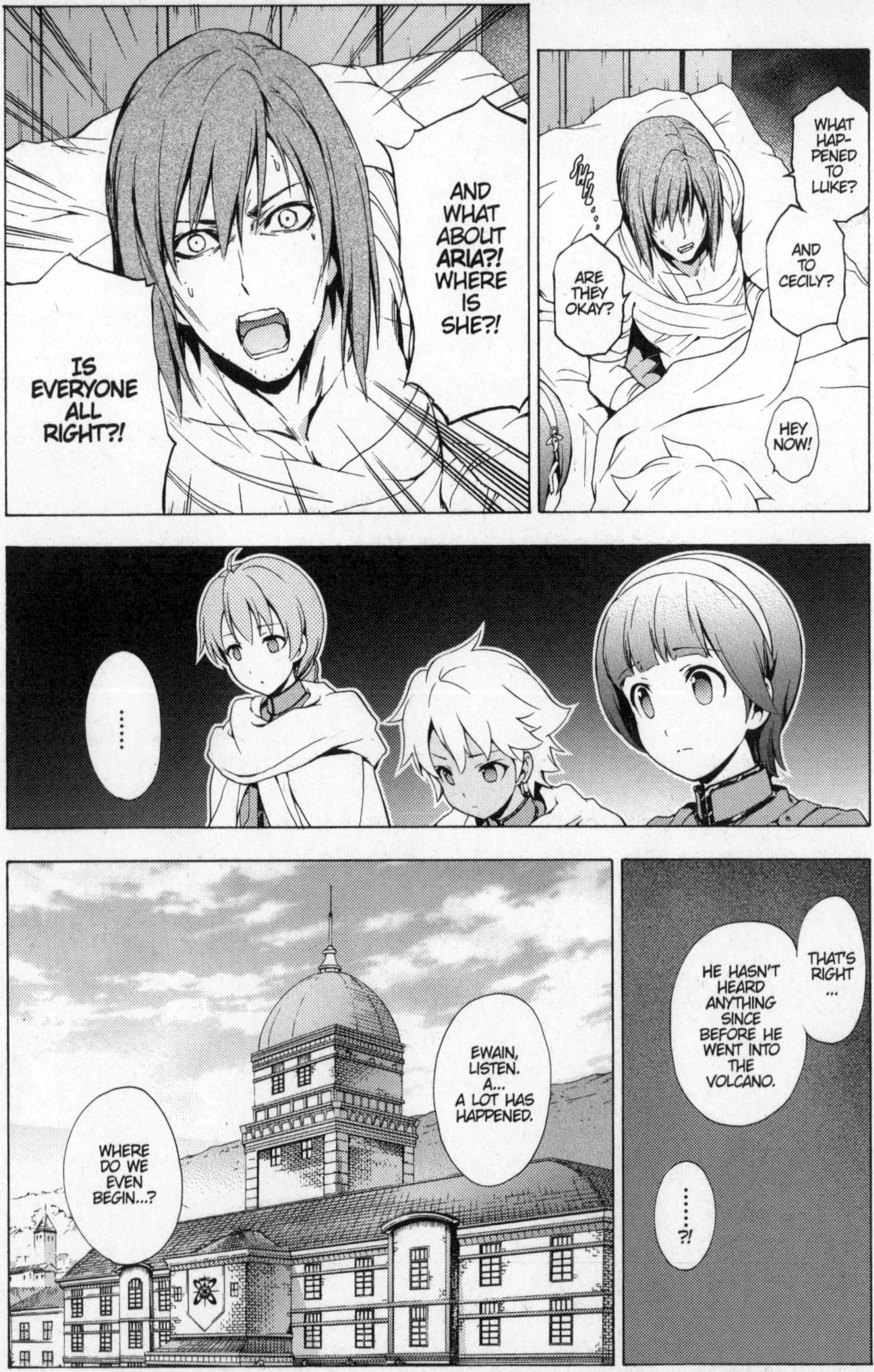
WHAT HAP-PENED TO LUKE?
AND TO CECILY?
ARE THEY OKAY?
HEY NOW!
AND WHAT ABOUT ARIA?! WHERE IS SHE?!
IS EVERYONE ALL RIGHT?!
……
THAT'S RIGHT ...
HE HASN'T HEARD ANYTHING SINCE BEFORE HE WENT INTO THE VOLCANO.
……?!
EWAIN, LISTEN. A... A LOT HAS HAPPENED.
WHERE DO WE EVEN BEGIN...?

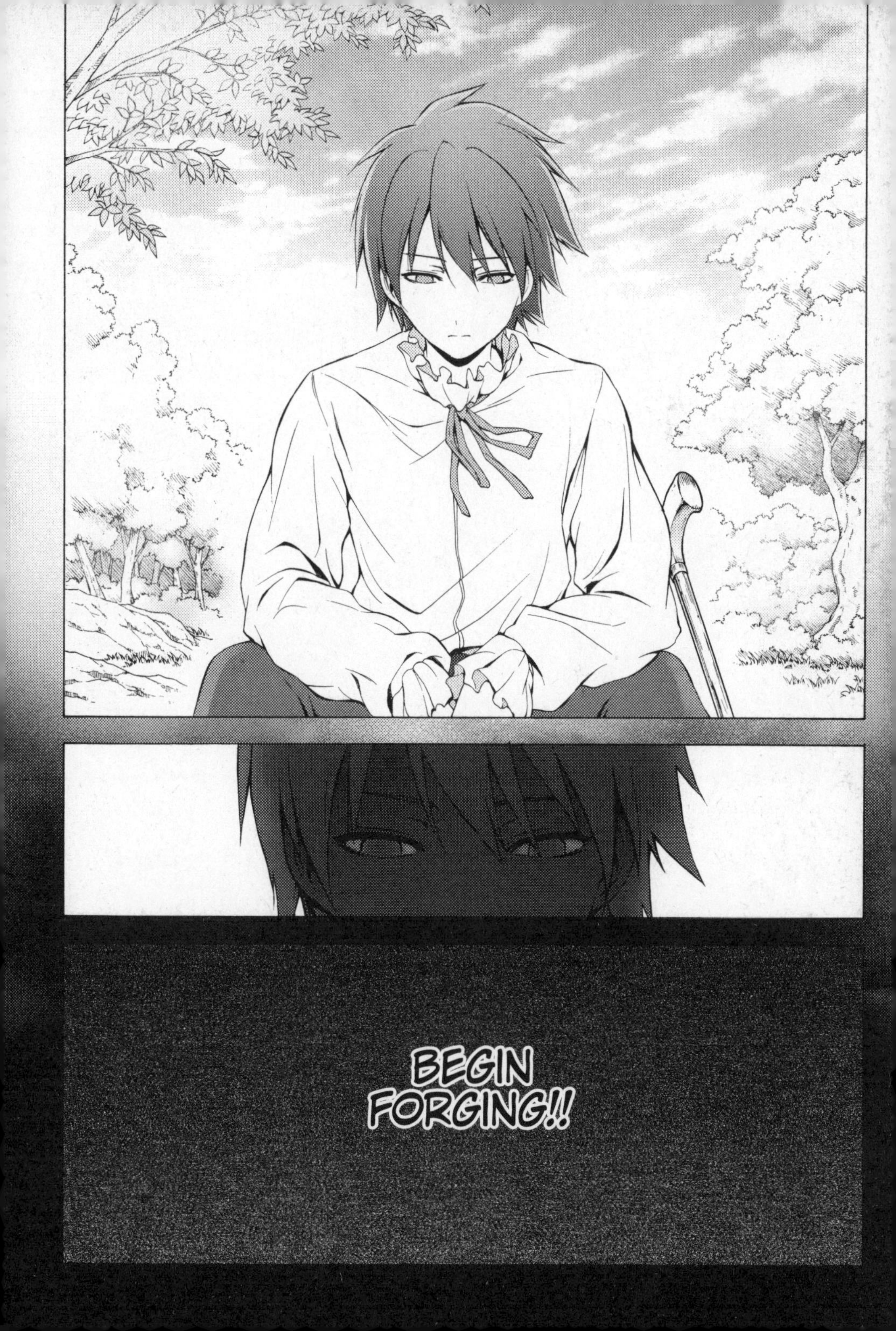
BEGIN FORGING!!

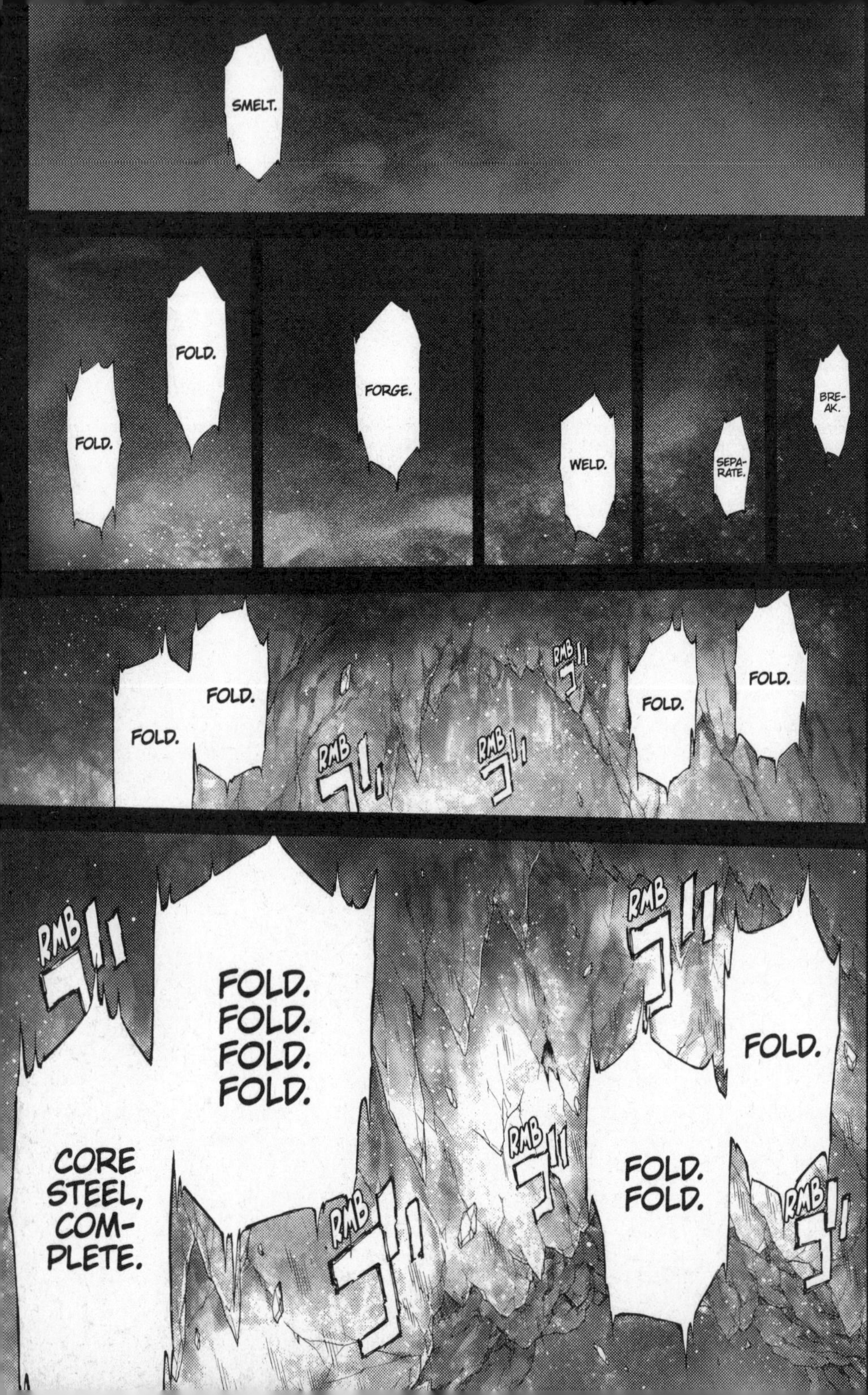
SMELT.
BRE-AK.
SEPA-RATE.
WELD.
FORGE.
FOLD.
FOLD.
FOLD.
FOLD.
RMB
RMB
RMB
FOLD.
FOLD.
RMB
FOLD.
RMB
FOLD.
FOLD.
RMB
RMB
FOLD.
FOLD.
FOLD.
FOLD.
RMB
CORE STEEL, COMP-LETE.

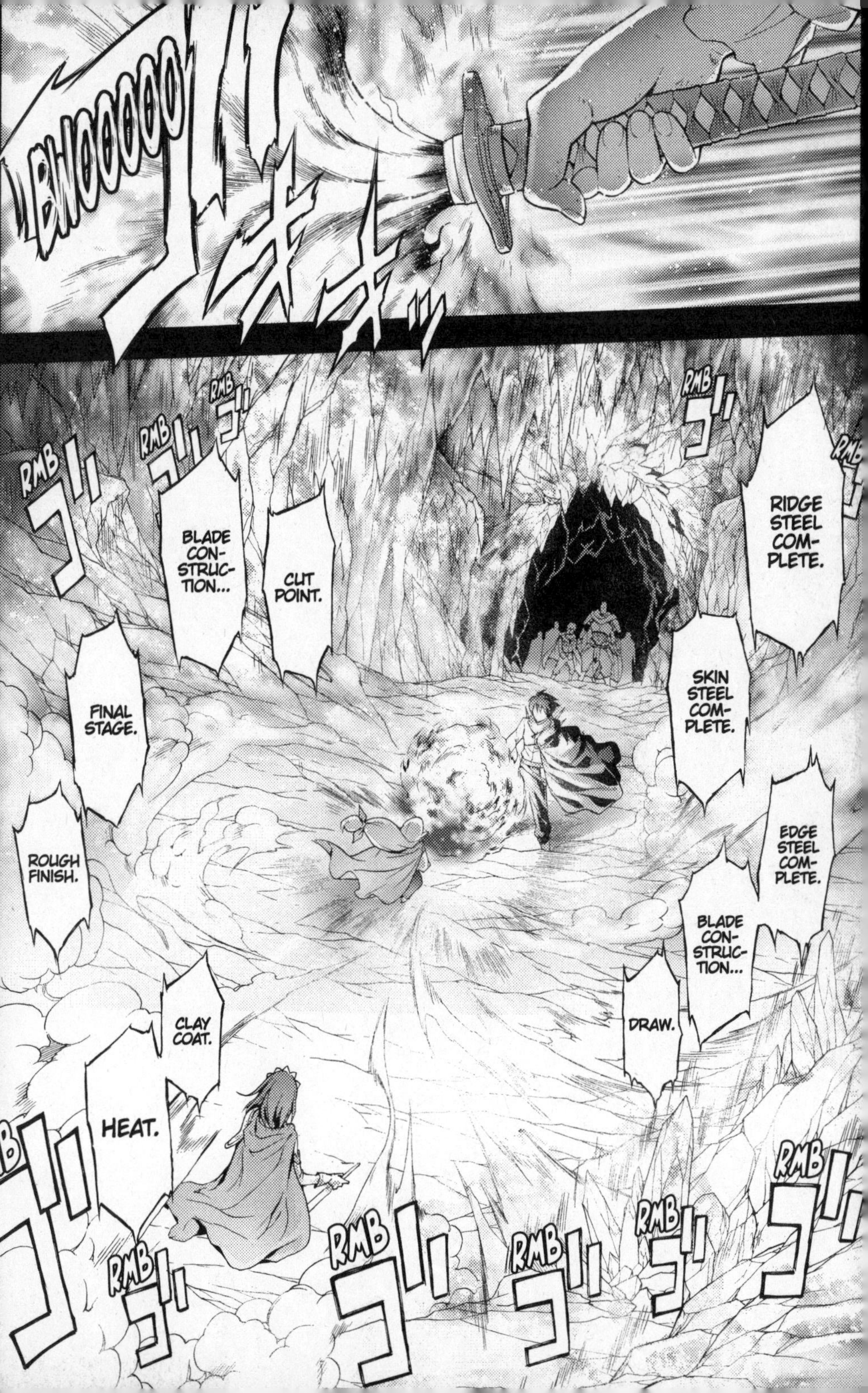
BWOOOO
RMB
RIDGE STEEL COMPLETE.
SKIN STEEL COMPLETE.
EDGE STEEL COMPLETE.
BLADE CONSTRUCTION...
DRAW.
RMB
RMB
RMB
CUT POINT.
BLADE CONSTRUCTION...
FINAL STAGE.
ROUGH FINISH.
CLAY COAT.
HEAT.
RMB
RMB
RMB
RMB
RMB
RMB
RMB

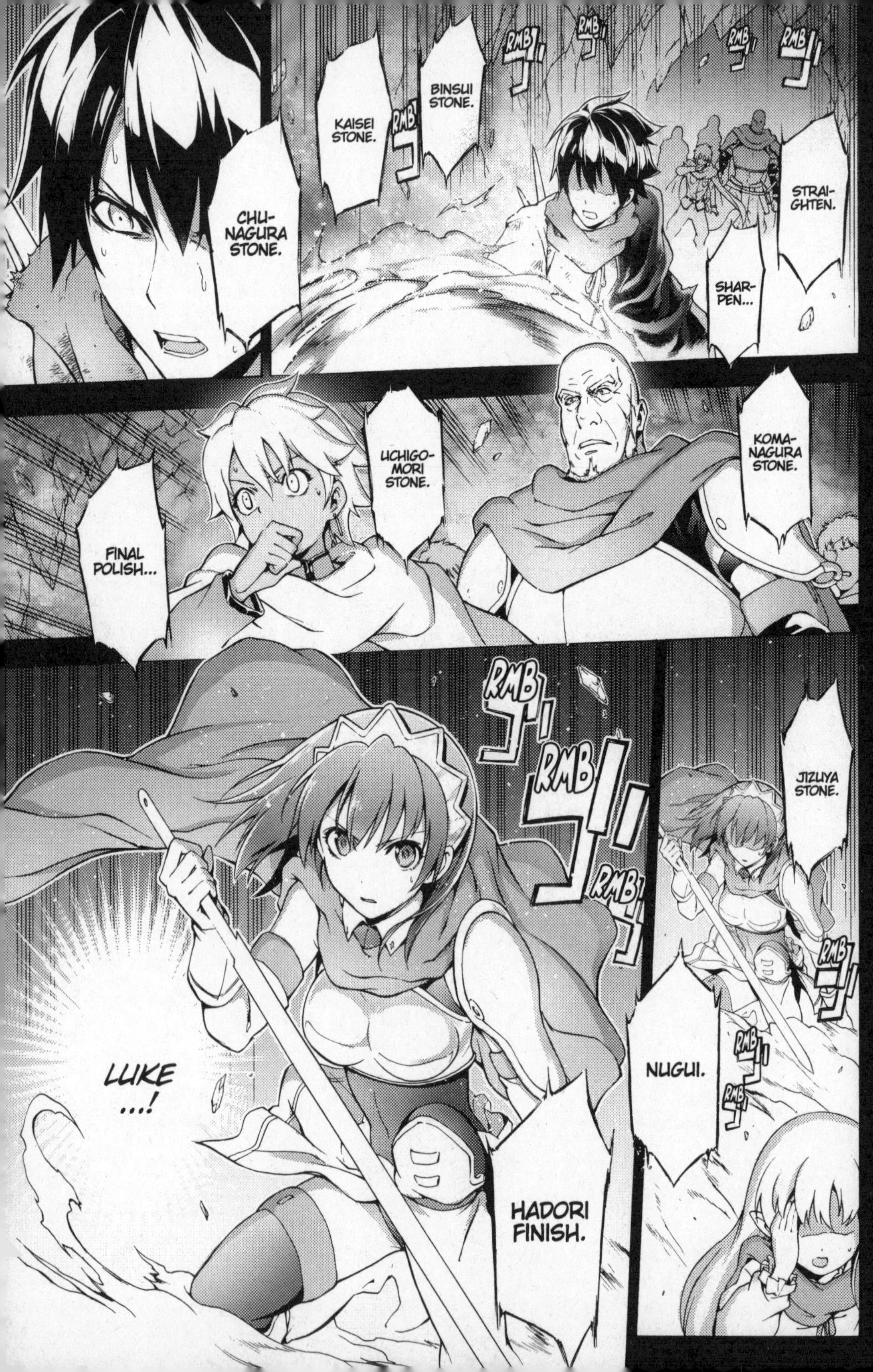
RMB
RMB
RMB
RMB
STRAIGHTEN.
SHARPEN...
BINSUI STONE.
RMB
KAISEI STONE.
CHUNAGURA STONE.
KOMANAGURA STONE.
UCHIGOMORI STONE.
FINAL POLISH...
JIZUYA STONE.
RMB
RMB
RMB
NUGUI.
RMB
RMB
RMB
RMB
HADORI FINISH.
LUKE ...!

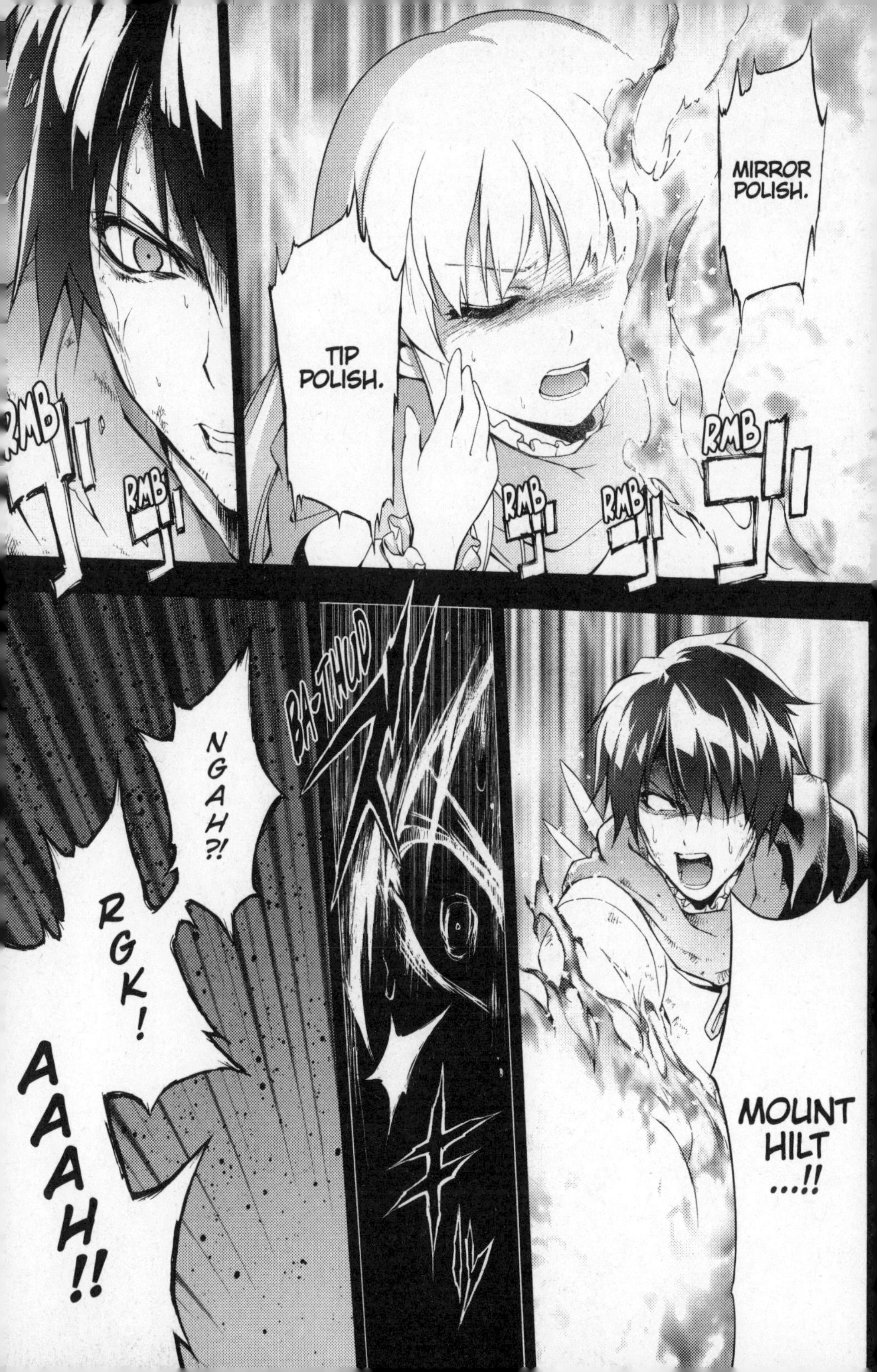
MIRROR POLISH.
TIP POLISH.
RMB
RMB
RMB
RMB
RMB
MOUNT HILT ...!!
BA-THUD
NGAH?!
RGK!
AAAH!!

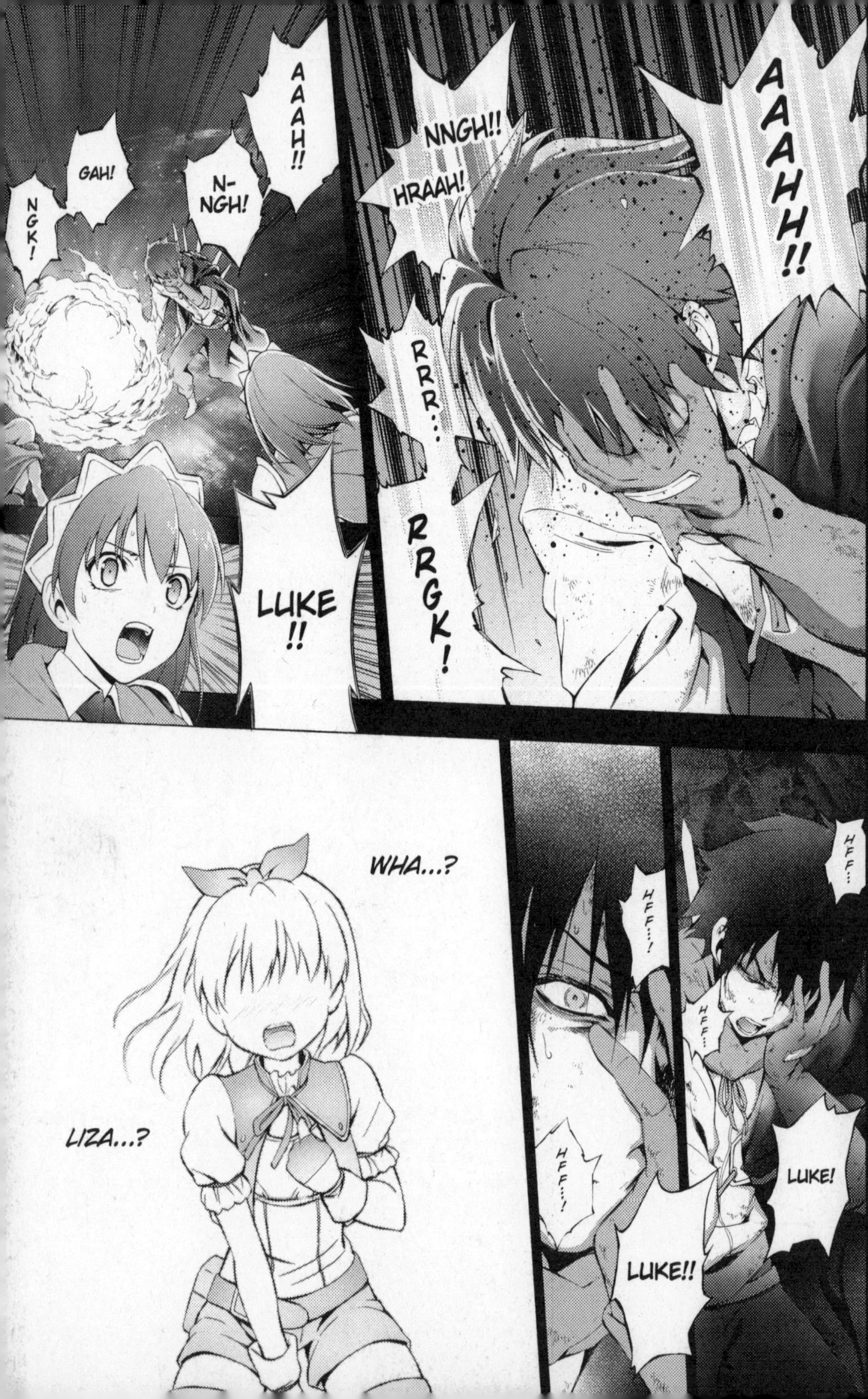
AAAAHH!!
NNGH!!
HRAAH!
RRR...
RRGK!
AAAAH!!
N-NGH!
GAH!
NGK!
LUKE!!
HFF...
HFF...
LUKE!
HFF...!
HFF...!
LUKE!!
WHA...?
LIZA...?

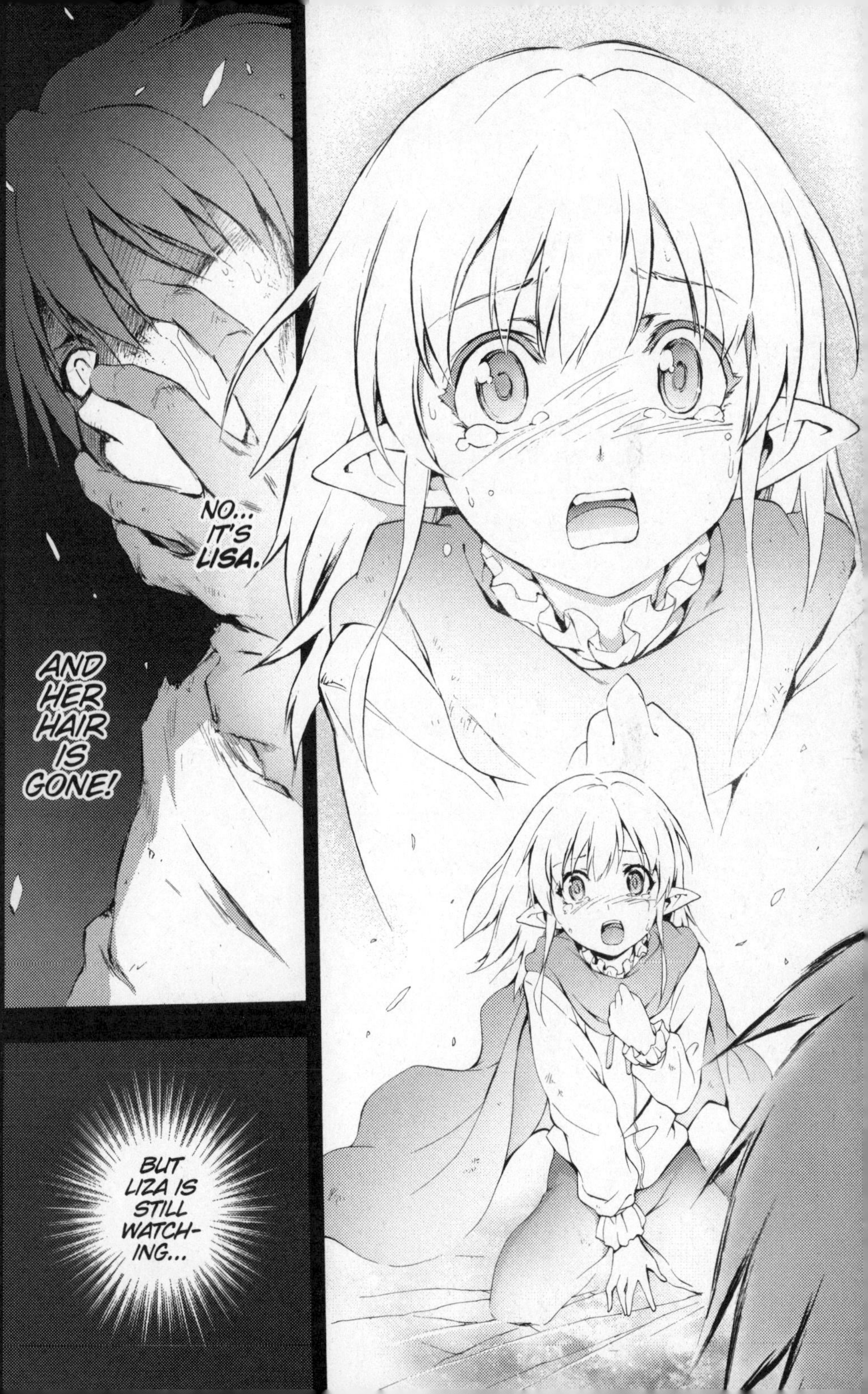
NO... IT'S LISA.
AND HER HAIR IS GONE!
BUT LIZA IS STILL WATCH-ING...

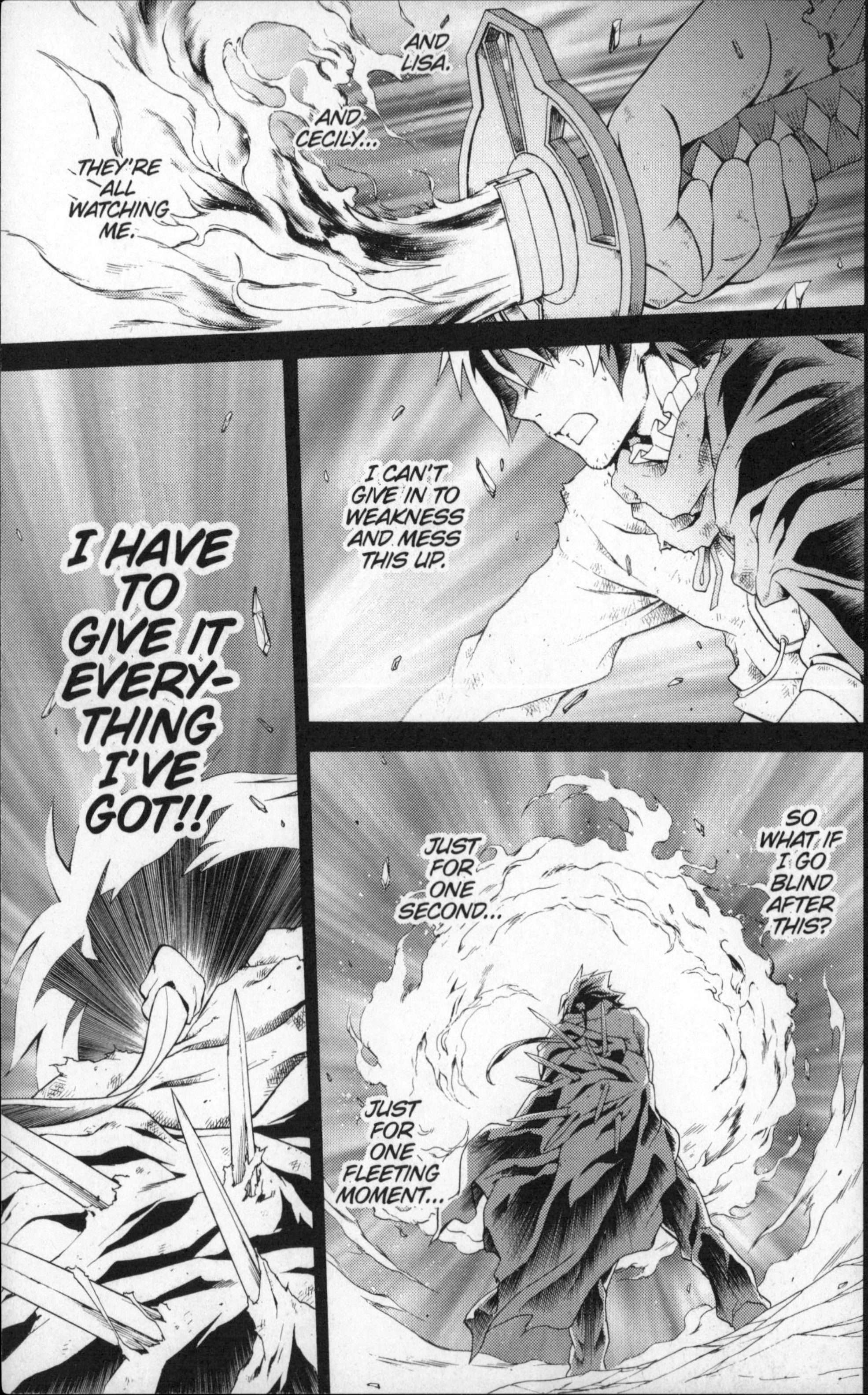
AND LISA.
AND CECILY...
THEY'RE ALL WATCHING ME.
I CAN'T GIVE IN TO WEAKNESS AND MESS THIS UP.
SO WHAT IF I GO BLIND AFTER THIS?
JUST FOR ONE SECOND...
JUST FOR ONE FLEETING MOMENT...
I HAVE TO GIVE IT EVERYTHING I'VE GOT!!

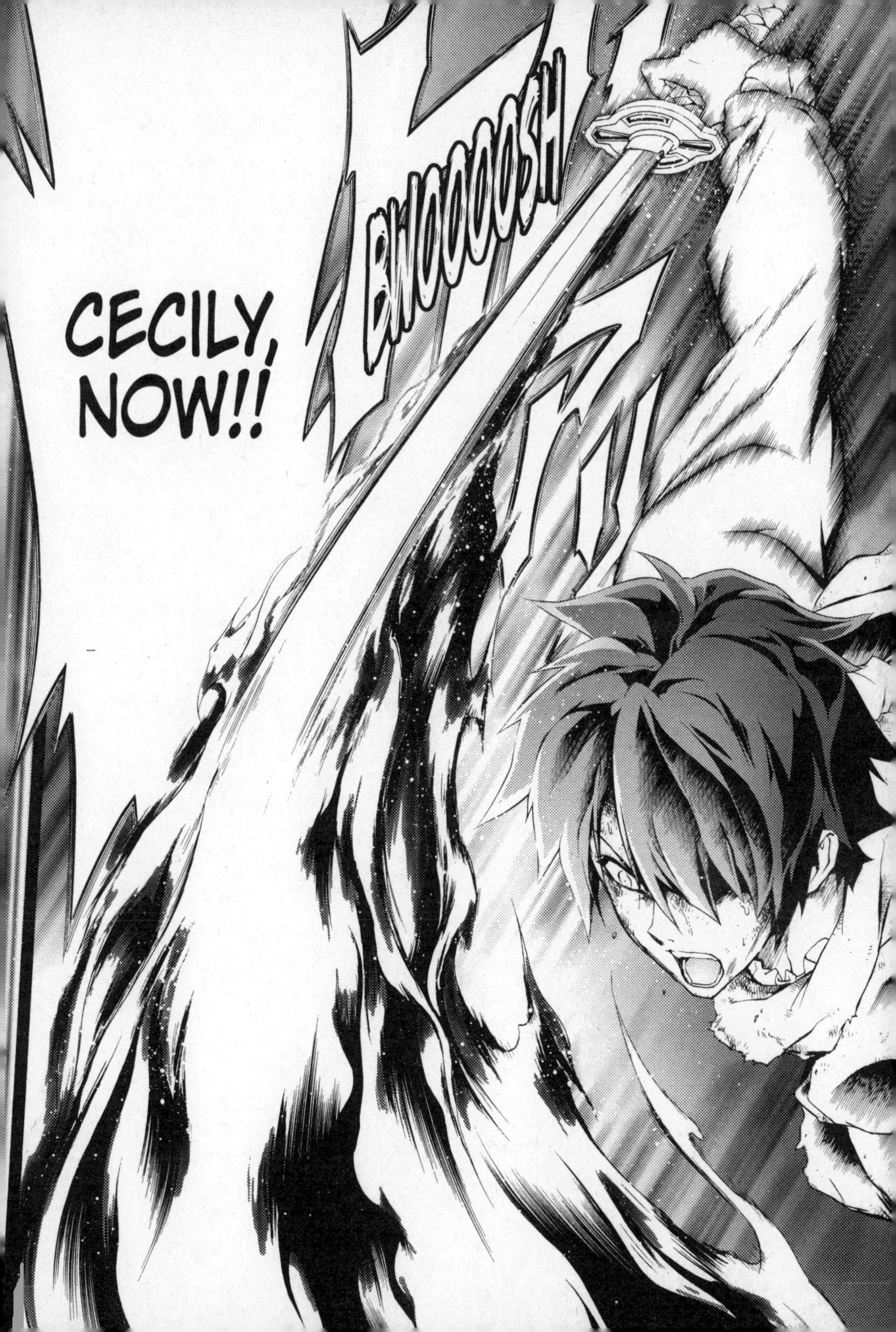
BWOOOOSH
CECILY, NOW!!

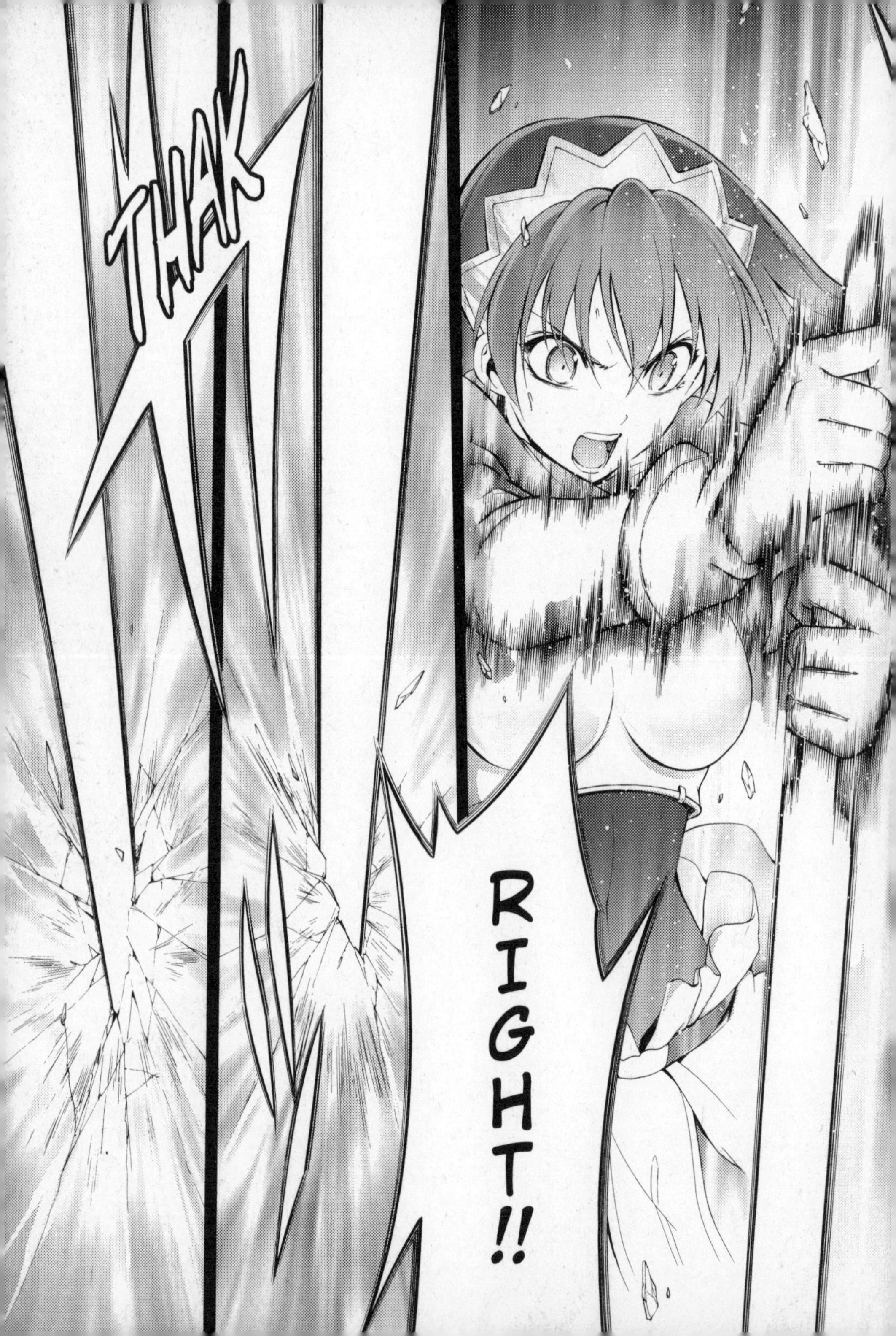
RIGHT!!
THAK

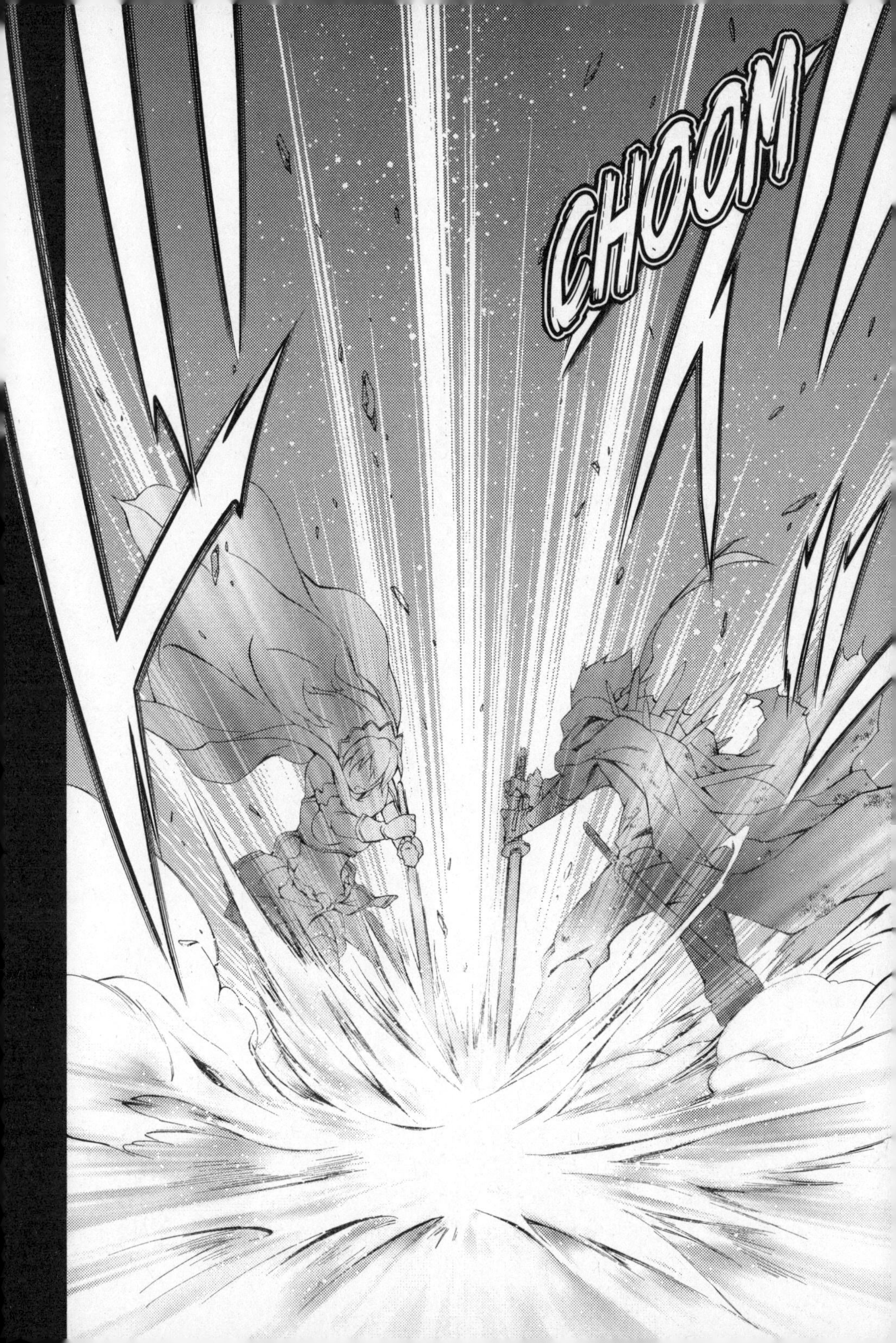
CHOOM

The Sacred Blacksmith

聖剣の刀鍛冶

The Sacred Blacksmith

聖剣の刀鍛治

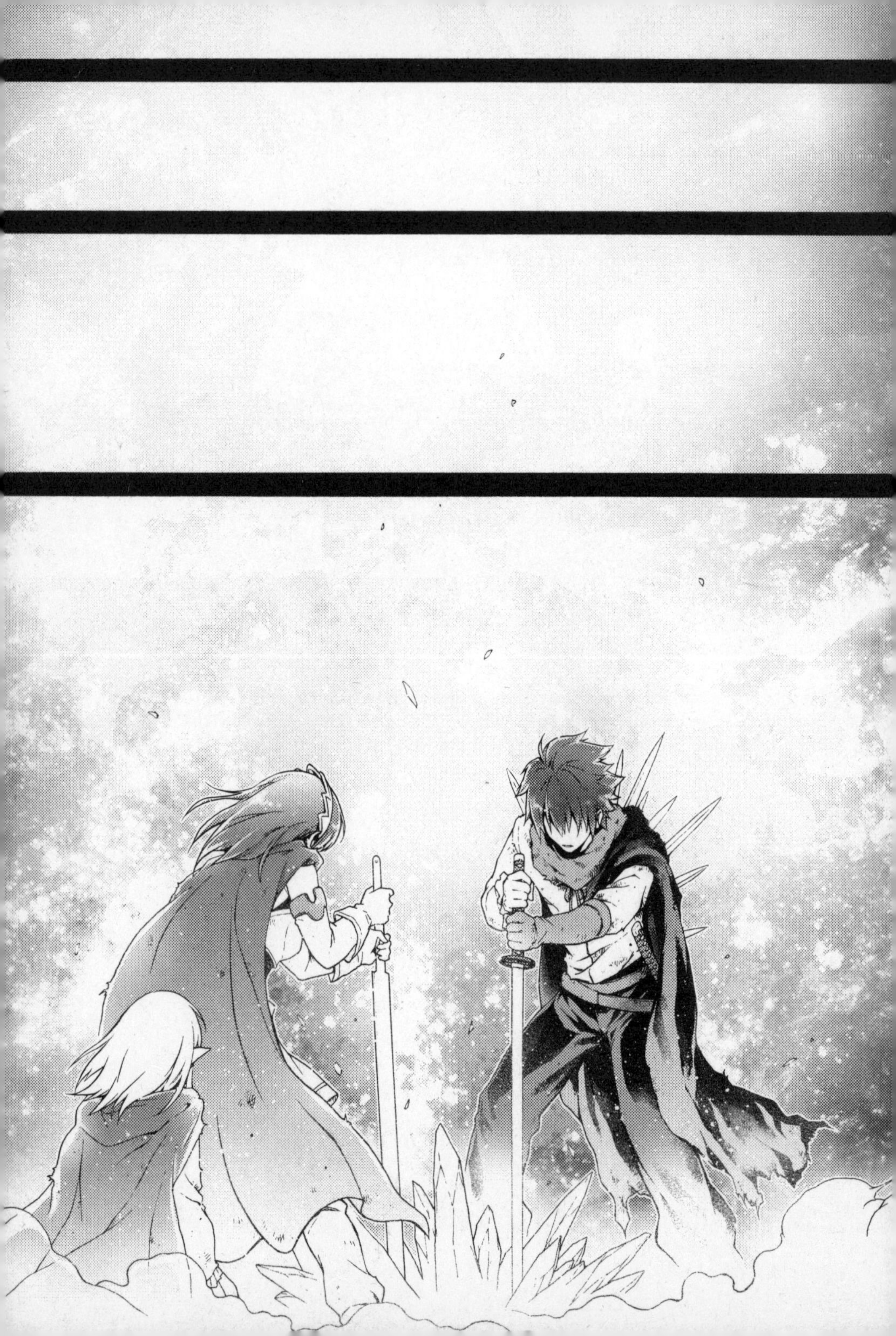

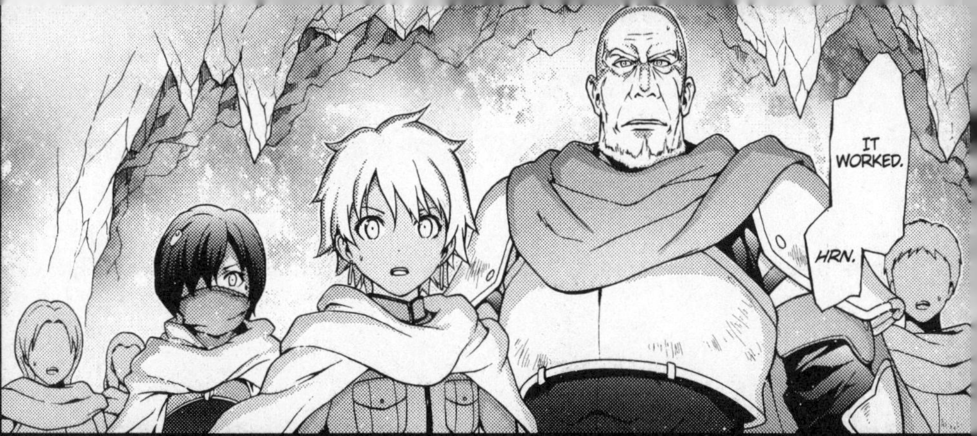
IT WORKED.
HRN.

Chapter 41 Trial 2 (Part 5)

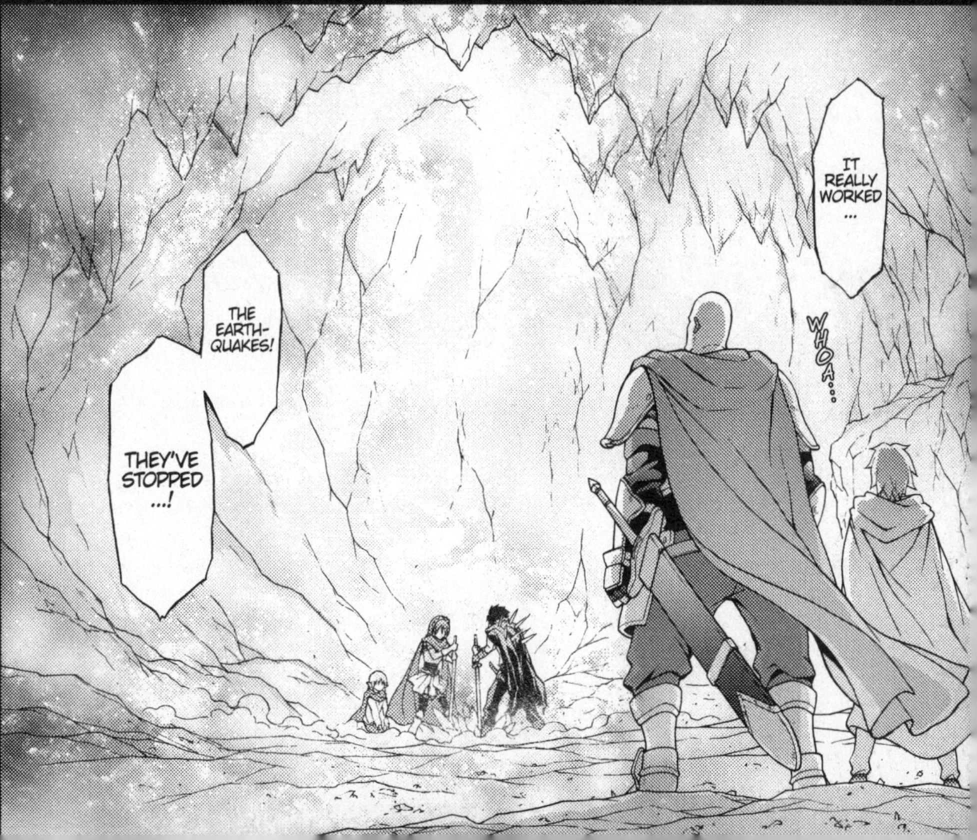
IT REALLY WORKED ...
WHOA...
THE EARTH-QUAKES!
THEY'VE STOPPED ...!

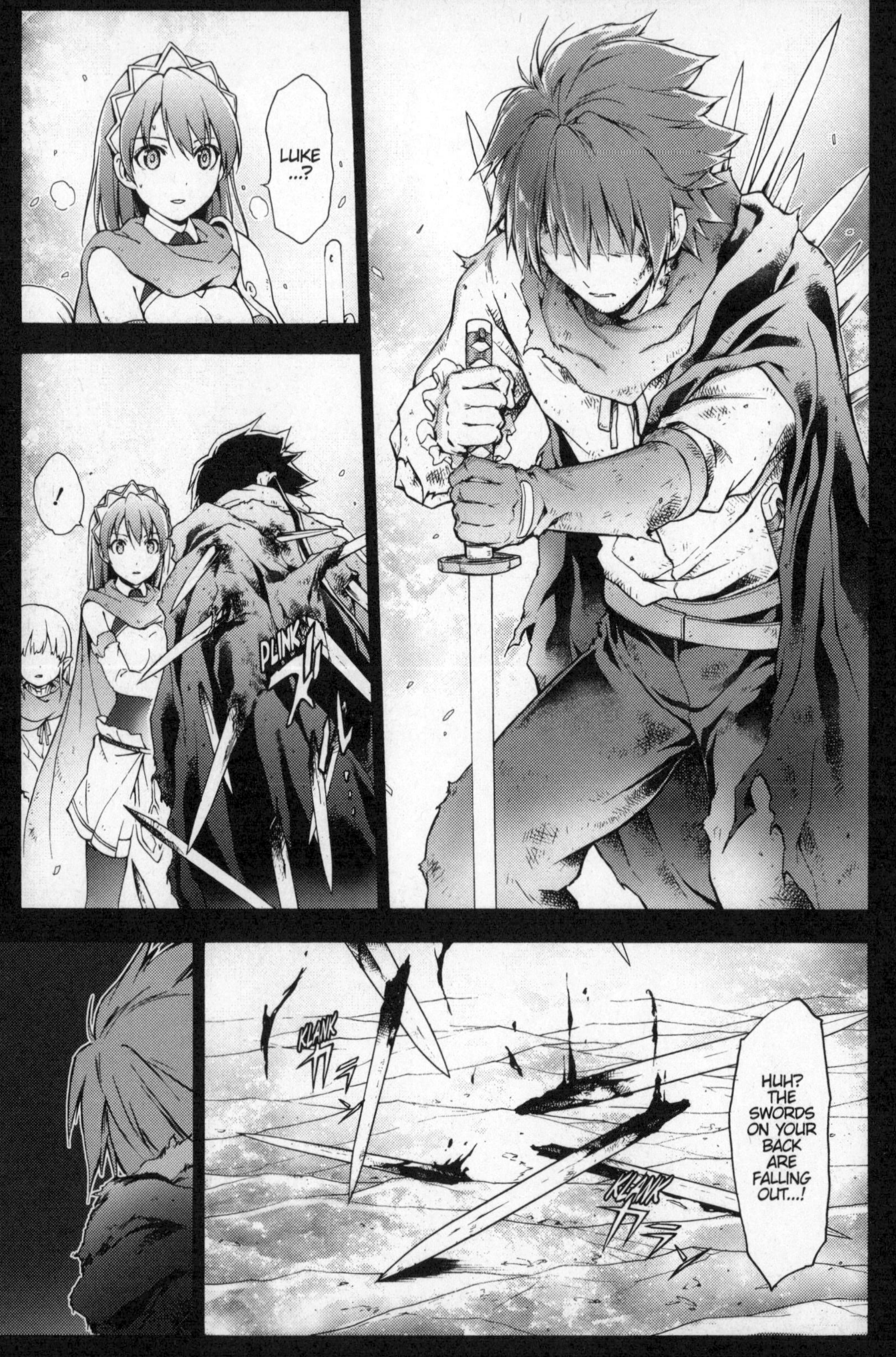
LUKE ...?
!
PLINK
HUH? THE SWORDS ON YOUR BACK ARE FALLING OUT...!
KLANK
KLANK

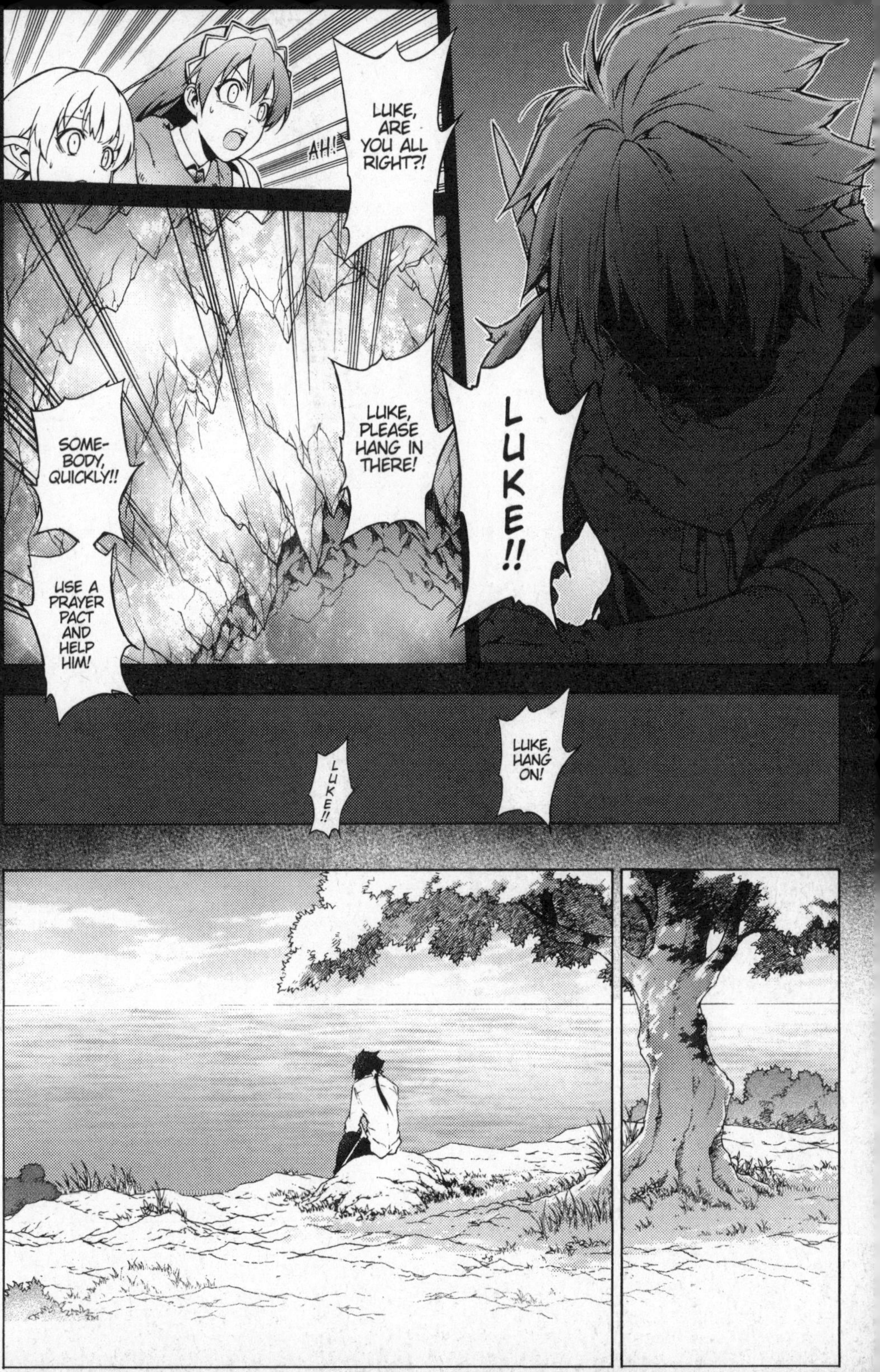
LUKE!!
AH!!
LUKE, ARE YOU ALL RIGHT?!
LUKE, PLEASE HANG IN THERE!
SOME-BODY, QUICKLY!!
USE A PRAYER PACT AND HELP HIM!
LUKE, HANG ON!
LUKE!!

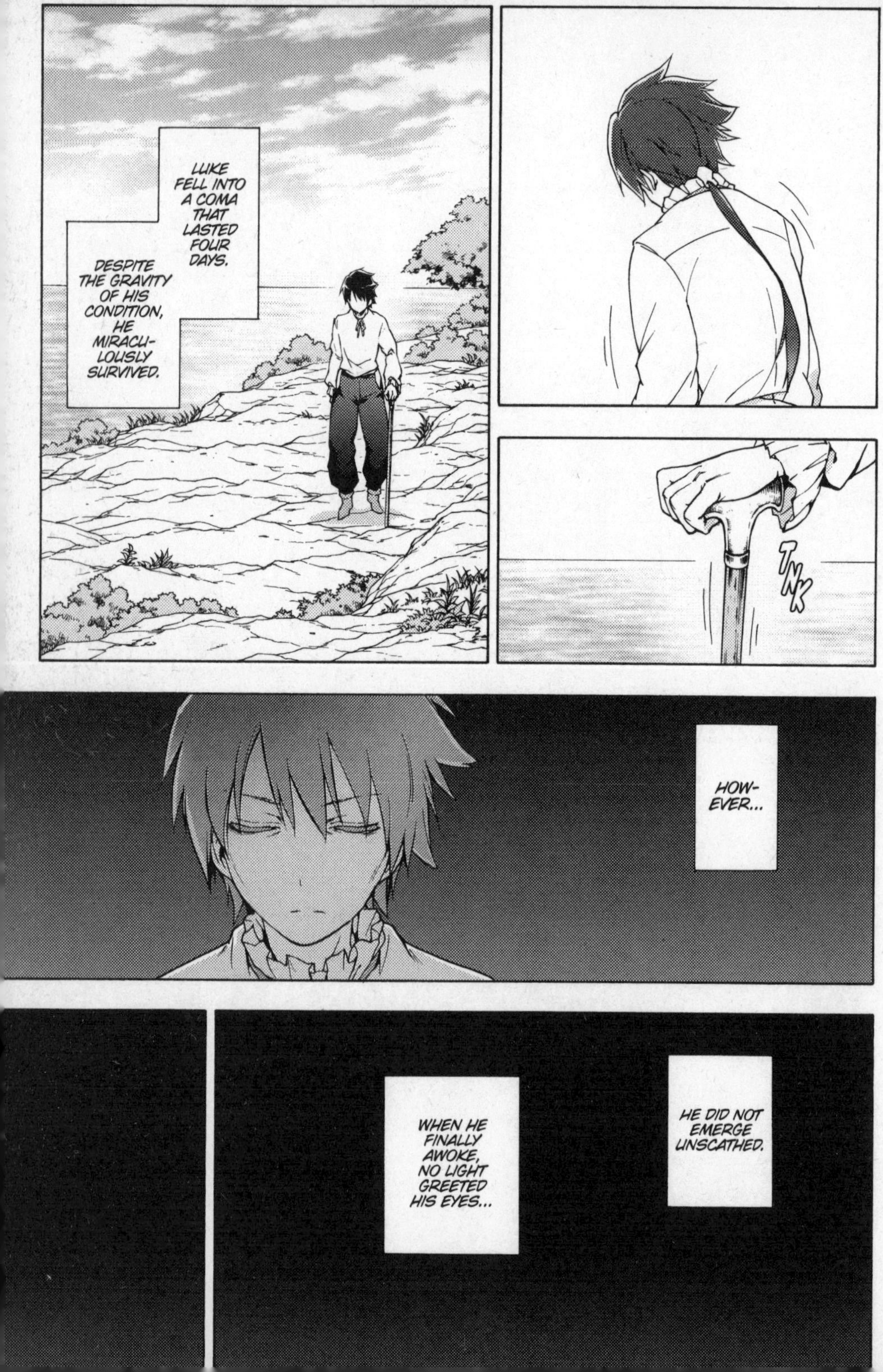
TNK
LUKE FELL INTO A COMA THAT LASTED FOUR DAYS.
DESPITE THE GRAVITY OF HIS CONDITION, HE MIRACULOUSLY SURVIVED.
HOW-EVER...
HE DID NOT EMERGE UNSCATHED.
WHEN HE FINALLY AWOKE, NO LIGHT GREETED HIS EYES...

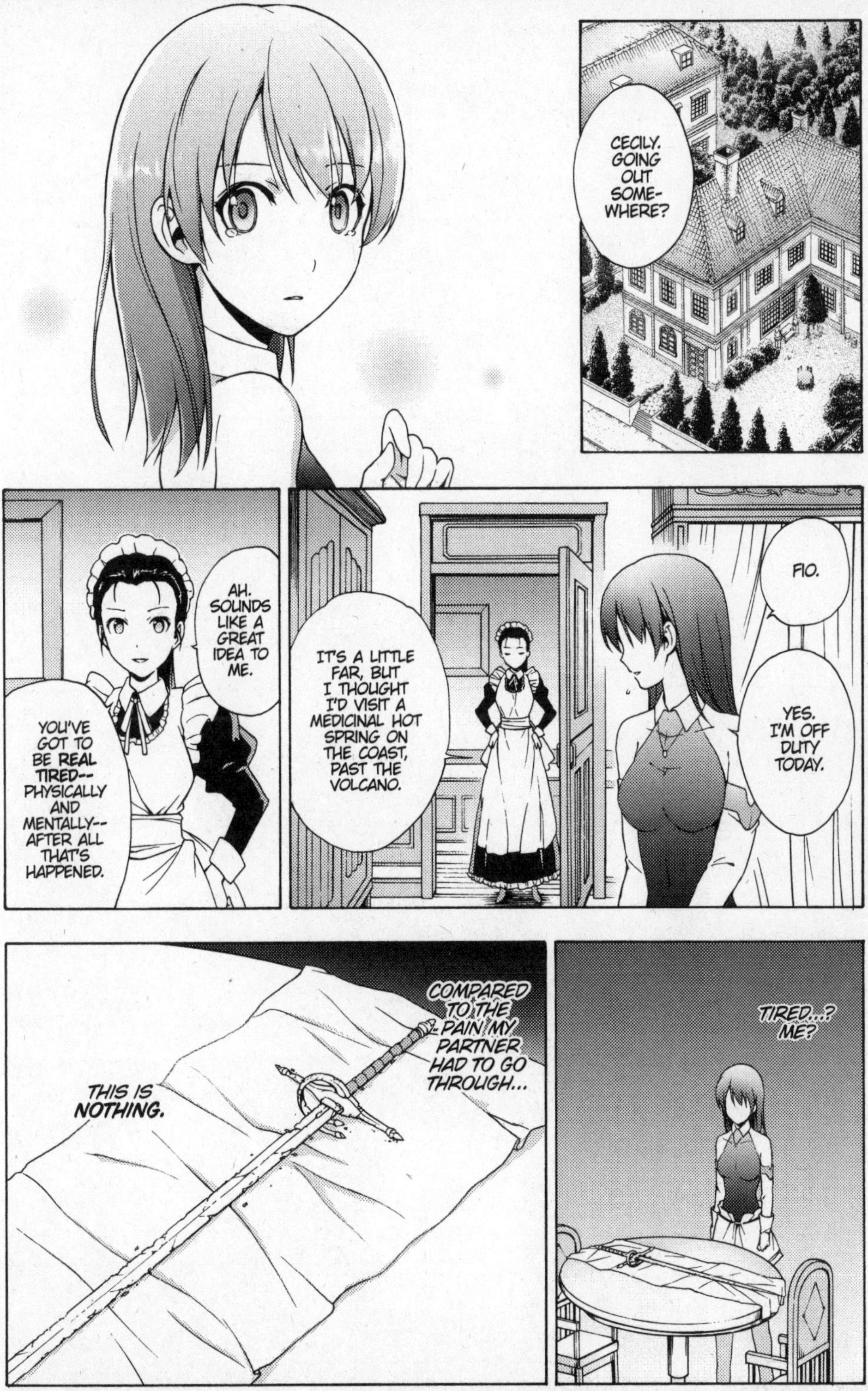
CECILY. GOING OUT SOME-WHERE?
FIO.
YES. I'M OFF DUTY TODAY.
IT'S A LITTLE FAR, BUT I THOUGHT I'D VISIT A MEDICINAL HOT SPRING ON THE COAST, PAST THE VOLCANO.
AH. SOUNDS LIKE A GREAT IDEA TO ME.
YOU'VE GOT TO BE REAL TIRED-- PHYSICALLY AND MENTALLY-- AFTER ALL THAT'S HAPPENED.
TIRED...? ME?
COMPARED TO THE PAIN MY PARTNER HAD TO GO THROUGH...
THIS IS NOTHING.

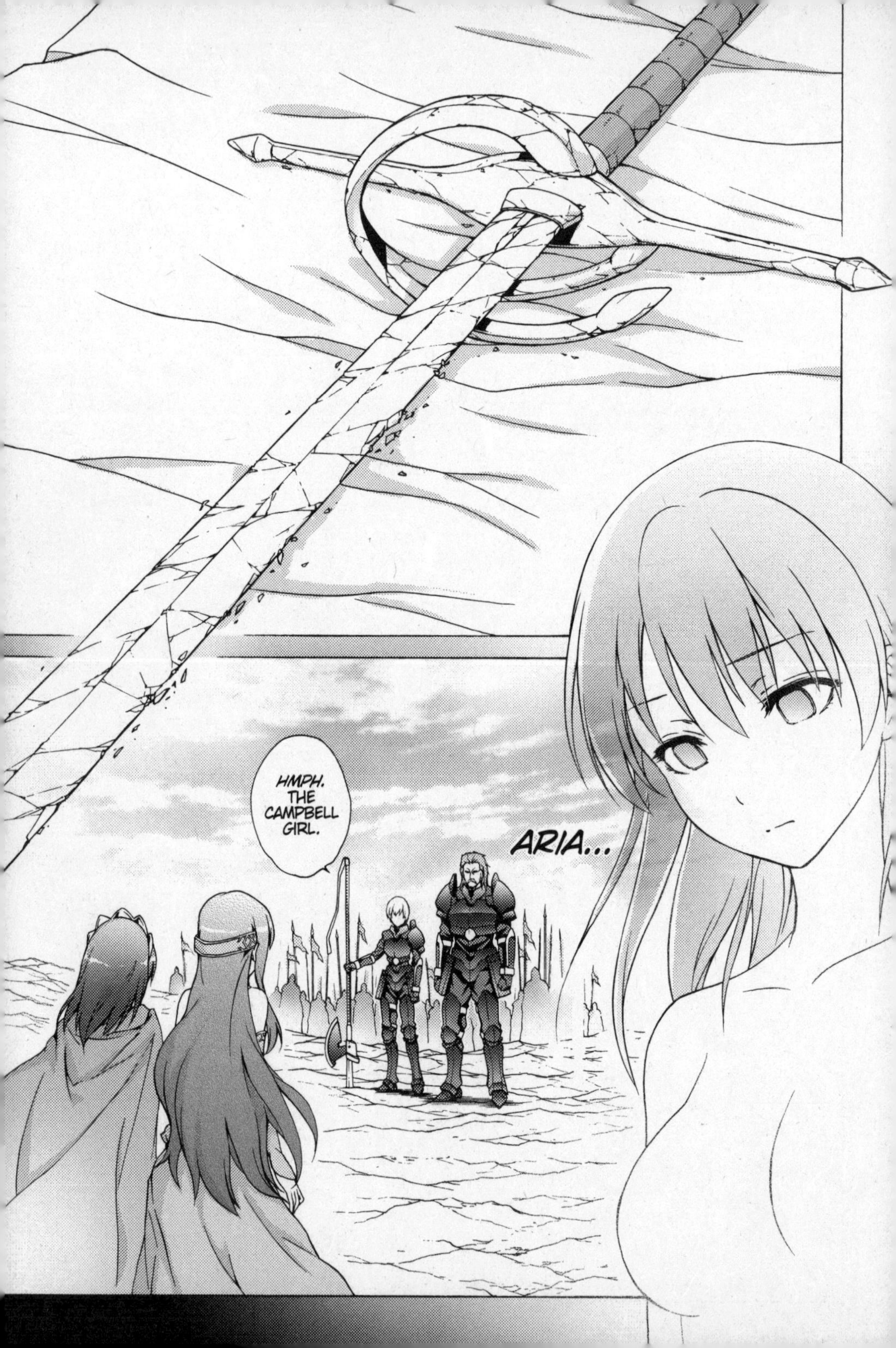
HMPH. THE CAMPBELL GIRL.
ARIA...

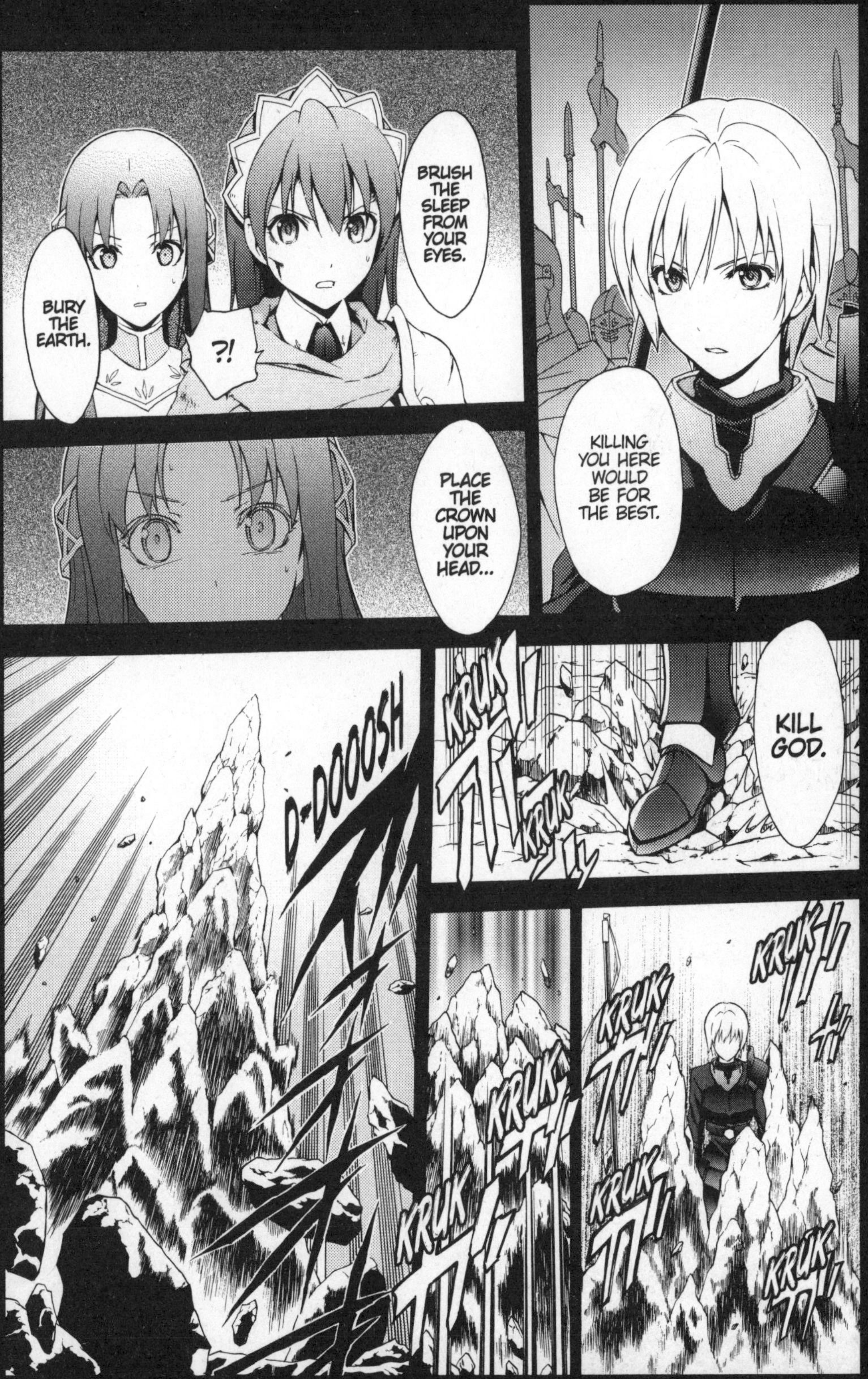
KILLING YOU HERE WOULD BE FOR THE BEST.
BRUSH THE SLEEP FROM YOUR EYES.
?!
BURY THE EARTH.
PLACE THE CROWN UPON YOUR HEAD...
KILL GOD.
KRUK
KRUK
KRUK
KRUK
KRUK
KRUK
KRUK
KRUK
D-DOOOSH

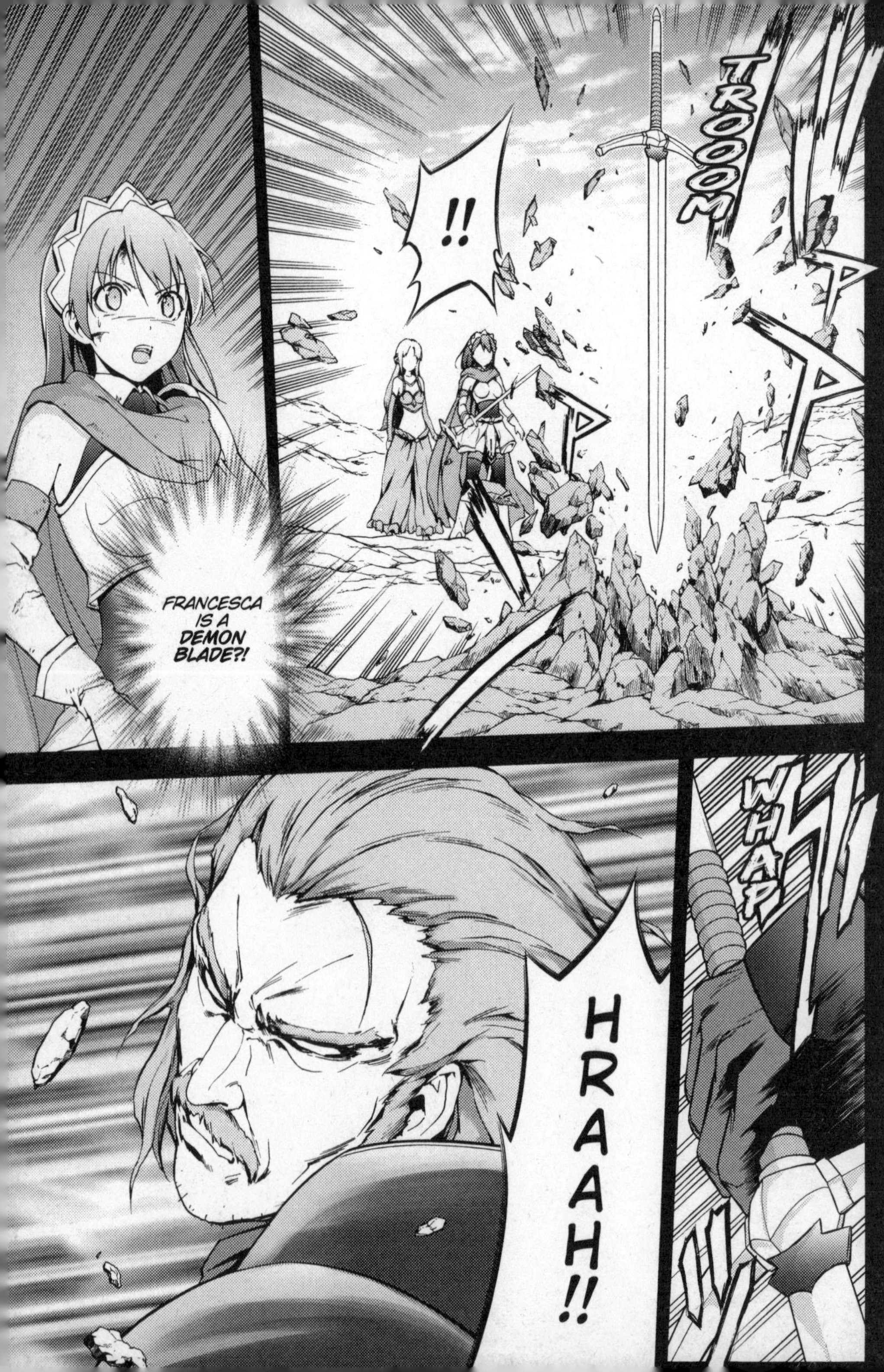
TROOOOM
!!
FRANCESCA IS A DEMON BLADE?!
WHAP
HRAAAH!!

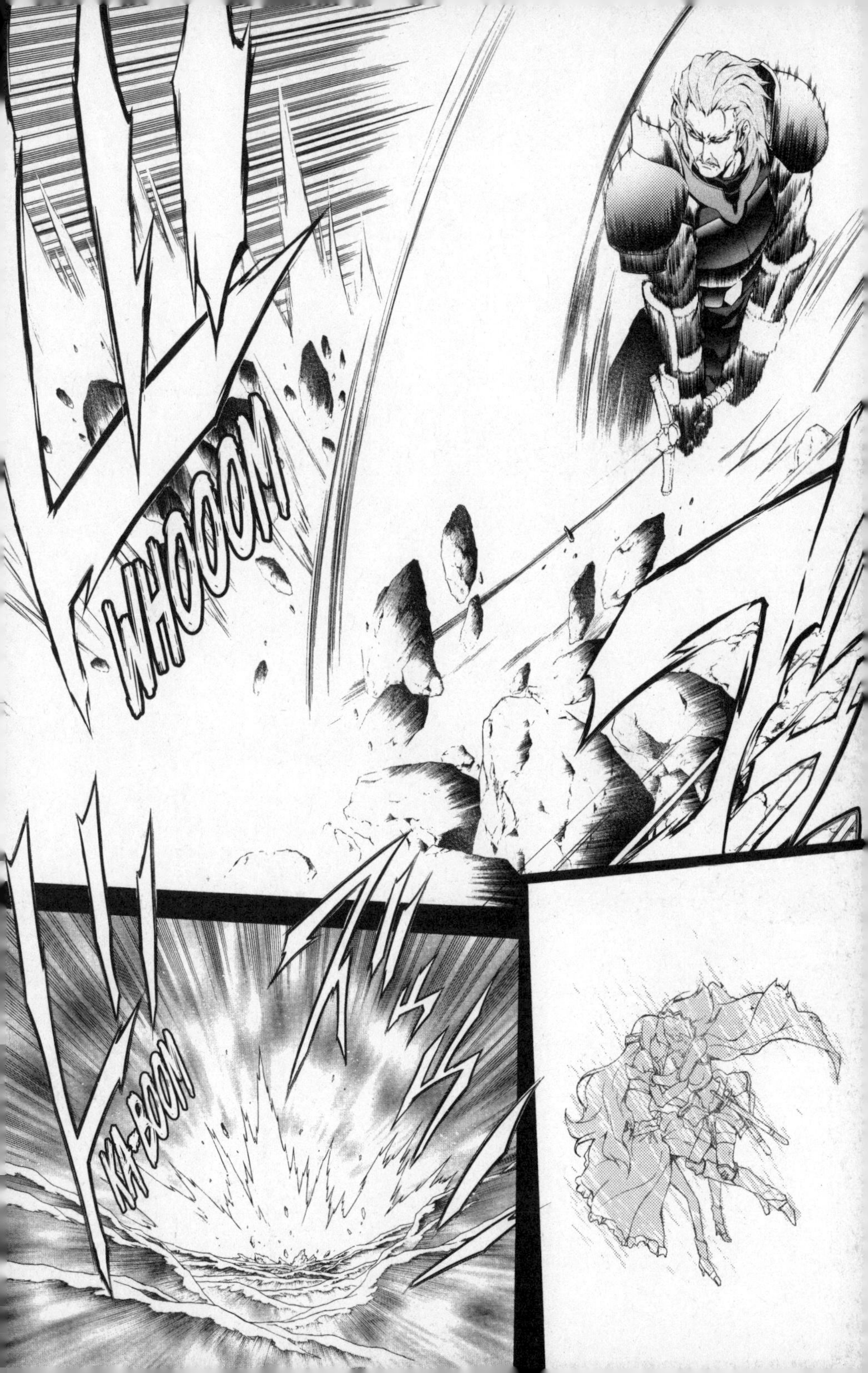
WHOOOM
KA-BOOM

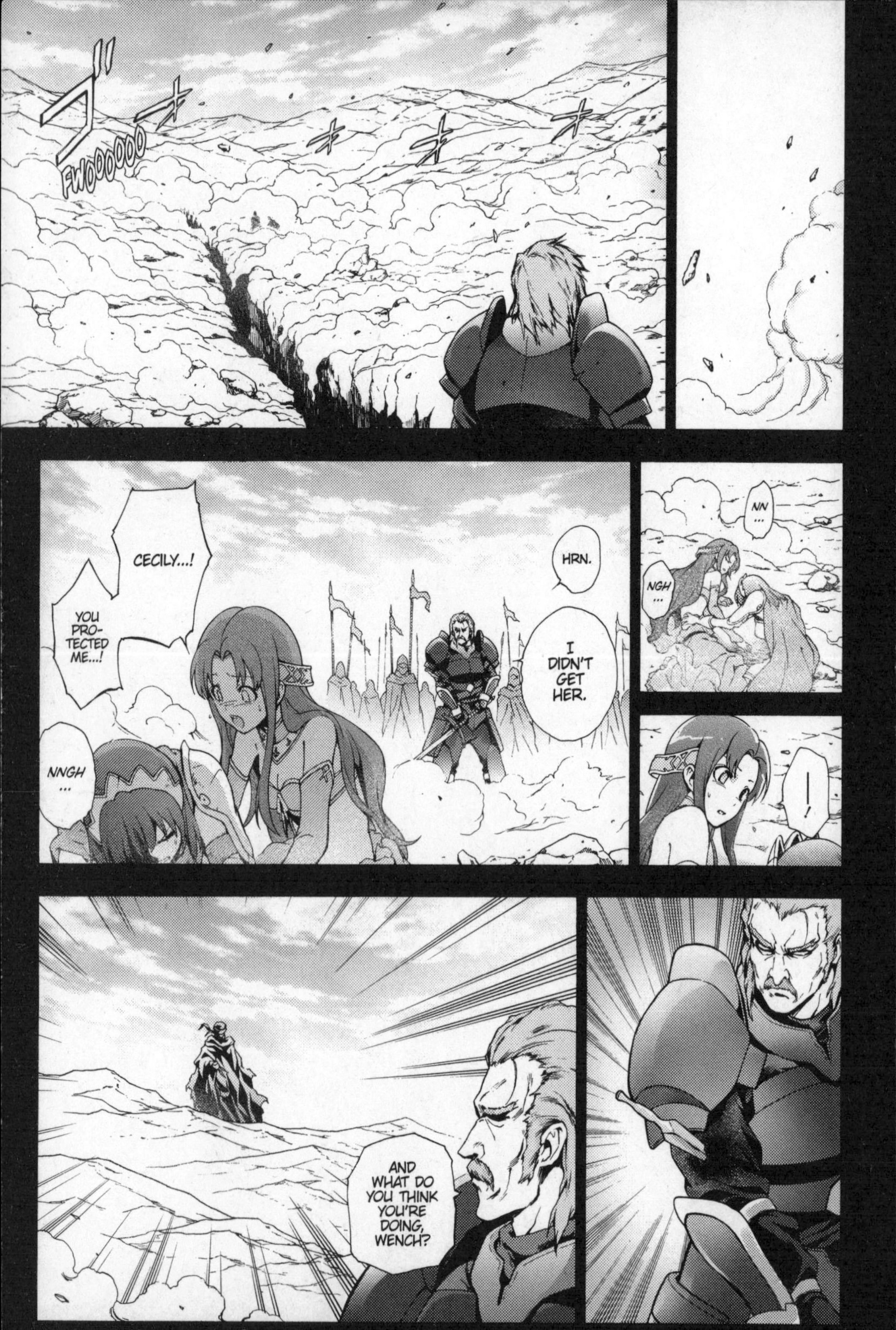
FWOOOOOO
NN ...
NGH ...
!
HRN.
I DIDN'T GET HER.
CECILY...!
YOU PROTECTED ME...!
NNGH ...
AND WHAT DO YOU THINK YOU'RE DOING, WENCH?

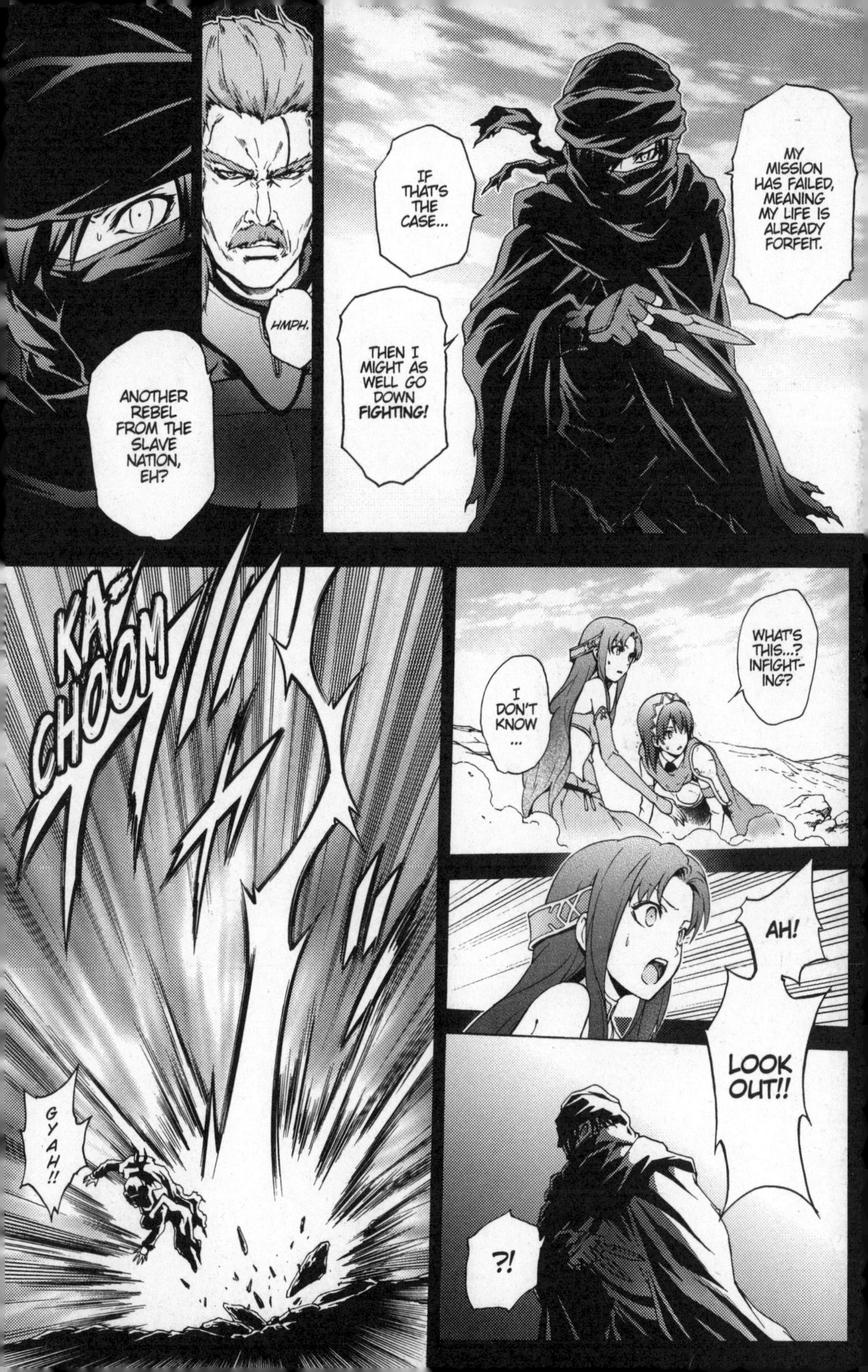
MY MISSION HAS FAILED, MEANING MY LIFE IS ALREADY FORFEIT.
IF THAT'S THE CASE...
THEN I MIGHT AS WELL GO DOWN FIGHTING!
HMPH.
ANOTHER REBEL FROM THE SLAVE NATION, EH?
WHAT'S THIS...? INFIGHTING?
I DON'T KNOW ...
AH!
LOOK OUT!!
?!
KA-CHOOM
GYAH!!

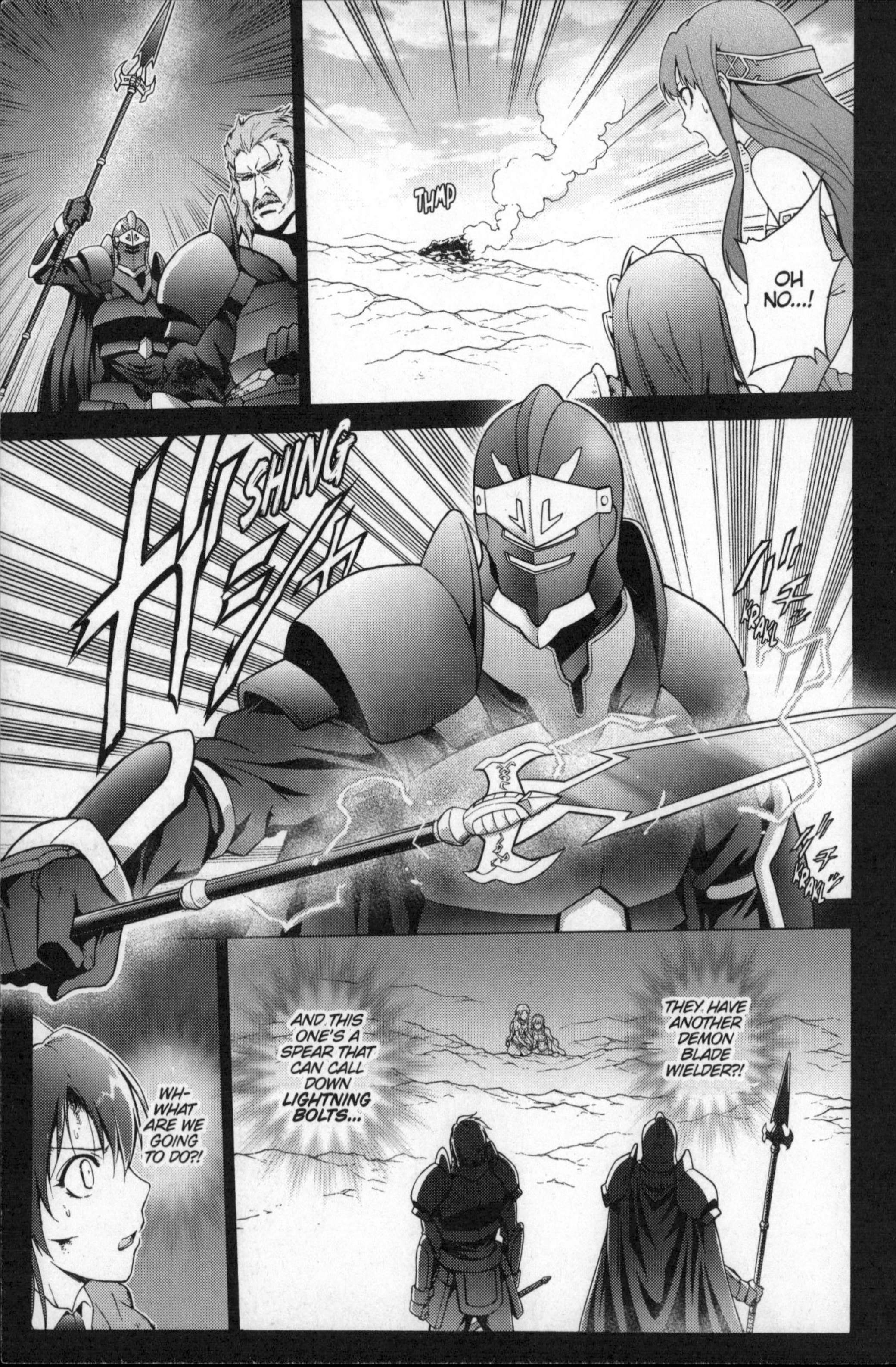
THMP
OH NO...!
SHING
KRAKL
KRAKL
THEY HAVE ANOTHER DEMON BLADE WIELDER?!
AND THIS ONE'S A SPEAR THAT CAN CALL DOWN LIGHTNING BOLTS...
WH- WHAT ARE WE GOING TO DO?!

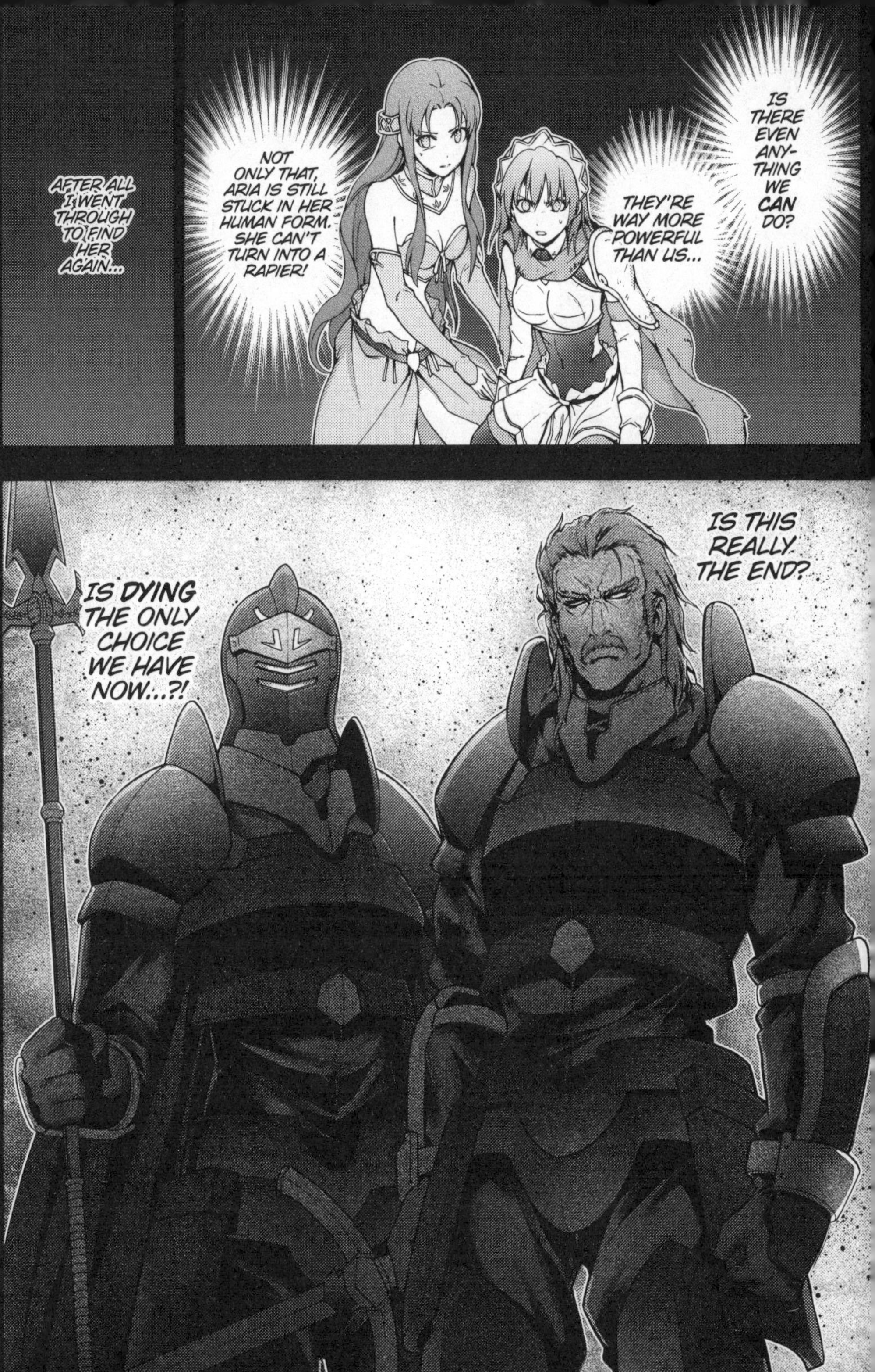
IS THERE EVEN ANYTHING WE CAN DO?
THEY'RE WAY MORE POWERFUL THAN US...
NOT ONLY THAT, ARIA IS STILL STUCK IN HER HUMAN FORM. SHE CAN'T TURN INTO A RAPIER!
AFTER ALL I WENT THROUGH TO FIND HER AGAIN...
IS THIS REALLY THE END?
IS DYING THE ONLY CHOICE WE HAVE NOW...?!

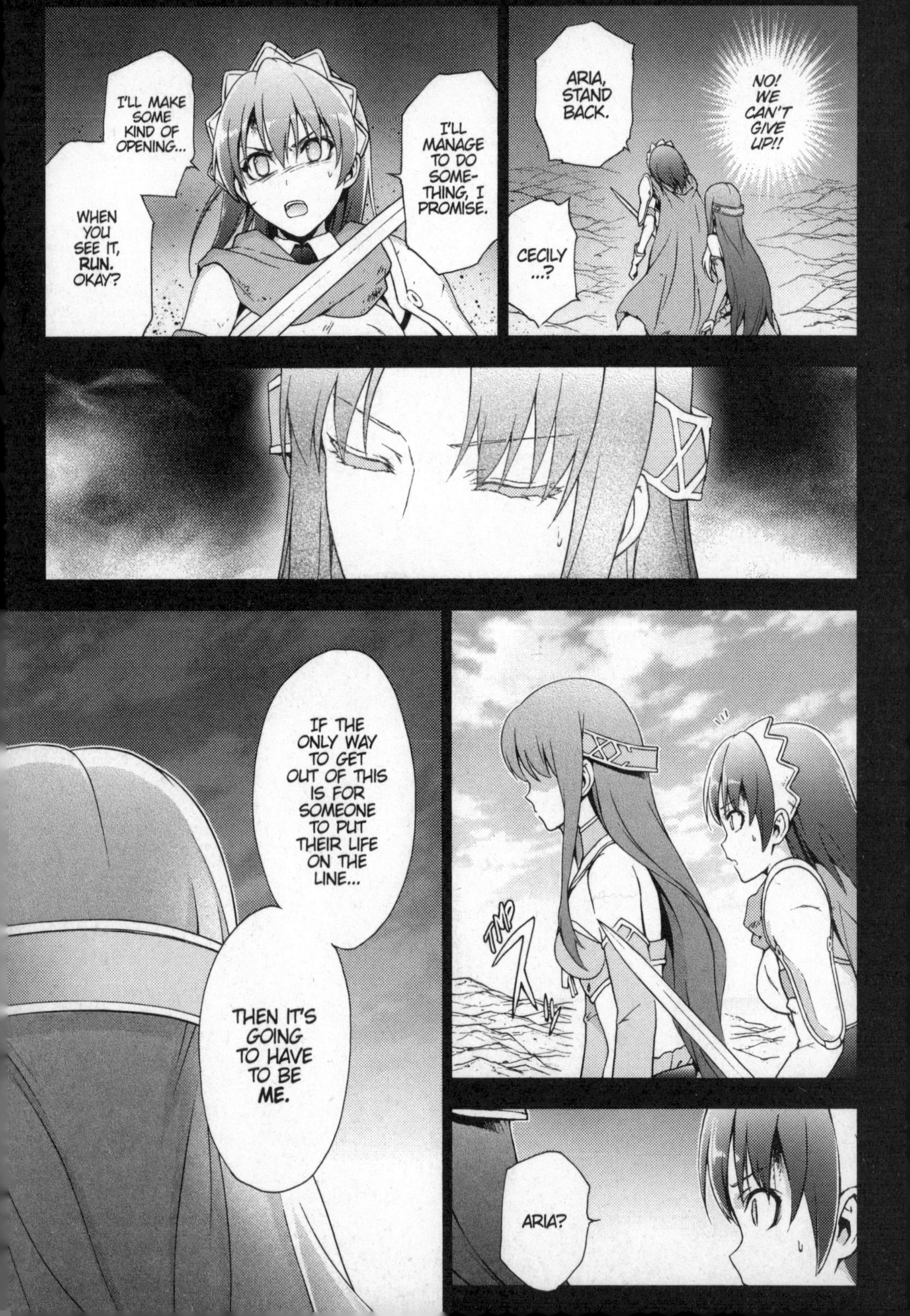
NO! WE CAN'T GIVE UP!!
ARIA, STAND BACK.
CECILY ...?
I'LL MANAGE TO DO SOME-THING, I PROMISE.
I'LL MAKE SOME KIND OF OPENING...
WHEN YOU SEE IT, RUN. OKAY?
TMP
ARIA?
IF THE ONLY WAY TO GET OUT OF THIS IS FOR SOMEONE TO PUT THEIR LIFE ON THE LINE...
THEN IT'S GOING TO HAVE TO BE ME.

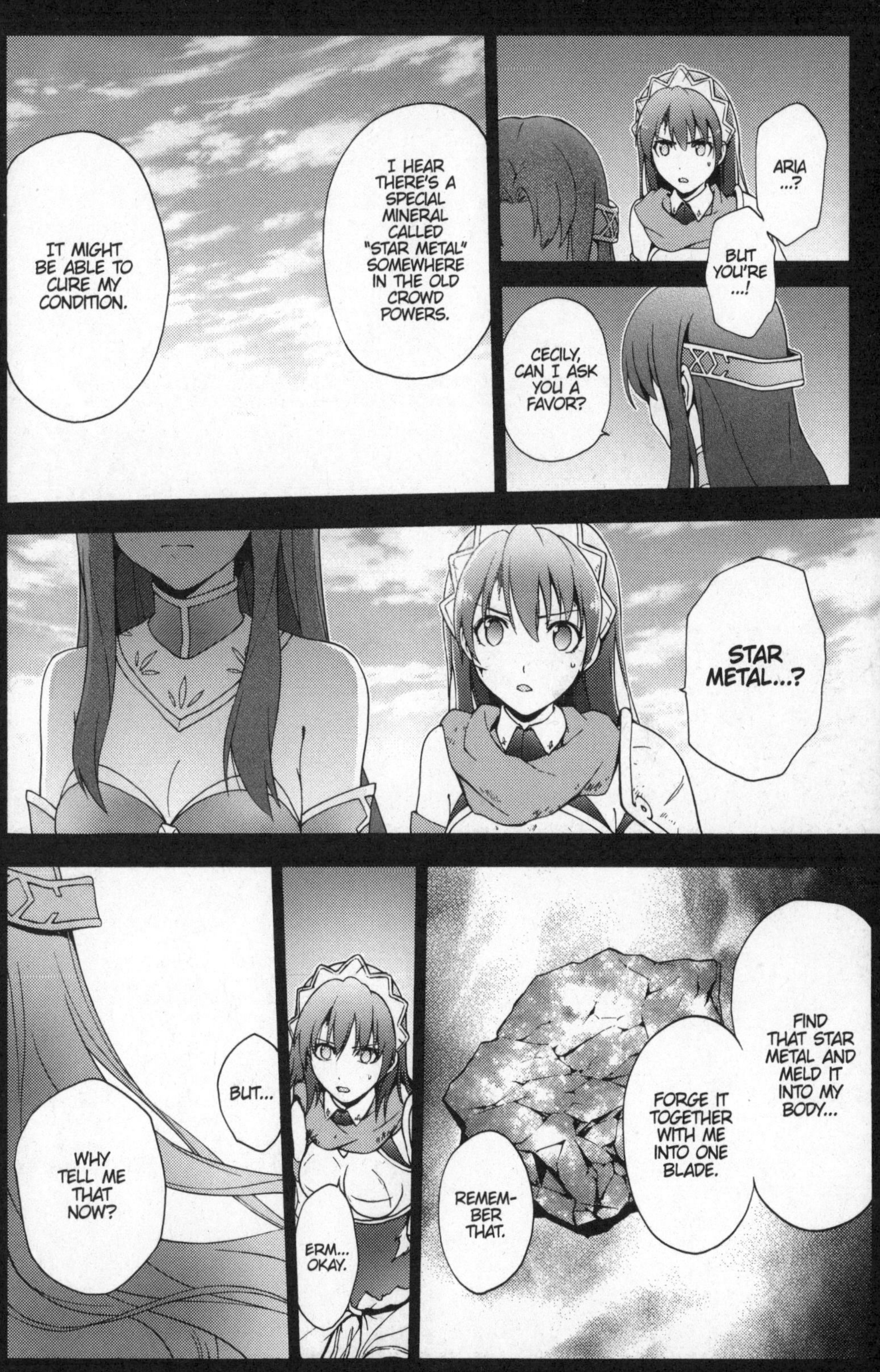
ARIA ...?
BUT YOU'RE ...!
CECILY, CAN I ASK YOU A FAVOR?
I HEAR THERE'S A SPECIAL MINERAL CALLED "STAR METAL" SOMEWHERE IN THE OLD CROWD POWERS.
IT MIGHT BE ABLE TO CURE MY CONDITION.
STAR METAL...?
FIND THAT STAR METAL AND MELD IT INTO MY BODY...
FORGE IT TOGETHER WITH ME INTO ONE BLADE.
REMEM-BER THAT.
BUT...
ERM... OKAY.
WHY TELL ME THAT NOW?

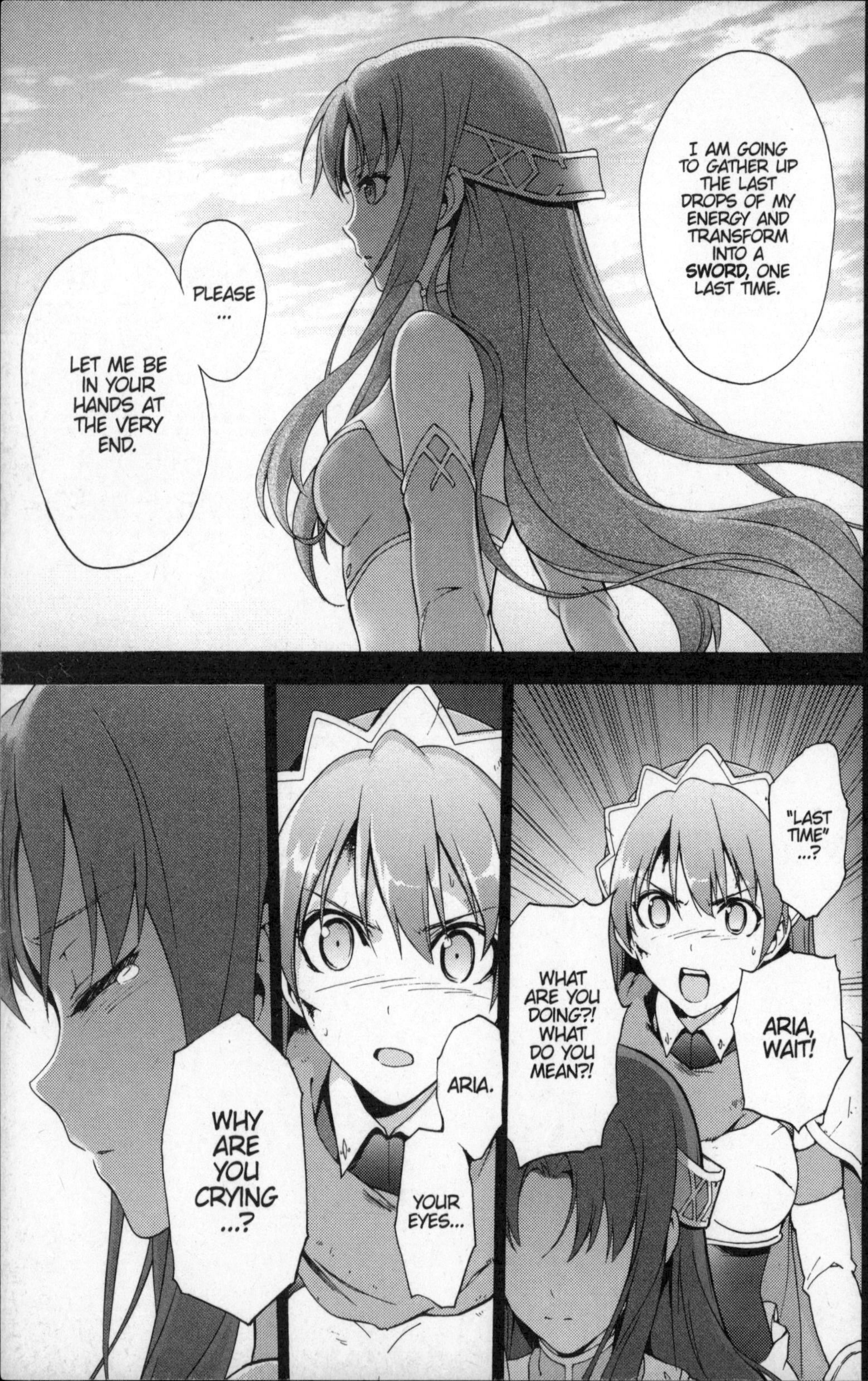
I AM GOING TO GATHER UP THE LAST DROPS OF MY ENERGY AND TRANSFORM INTO A **SWORD**, ONE LAST TIME.
PLEASE ...
LET ME BE IN YOUR HANDS AT THE VERY END.
"LAST TIME" ...?
ARIA, WAIT!
WHAT ARE YOU DOING?! WHAT DO YOU MEAN?!
ARIA.
YOUR EYES...
WHY ARE YOU CRYING ...?

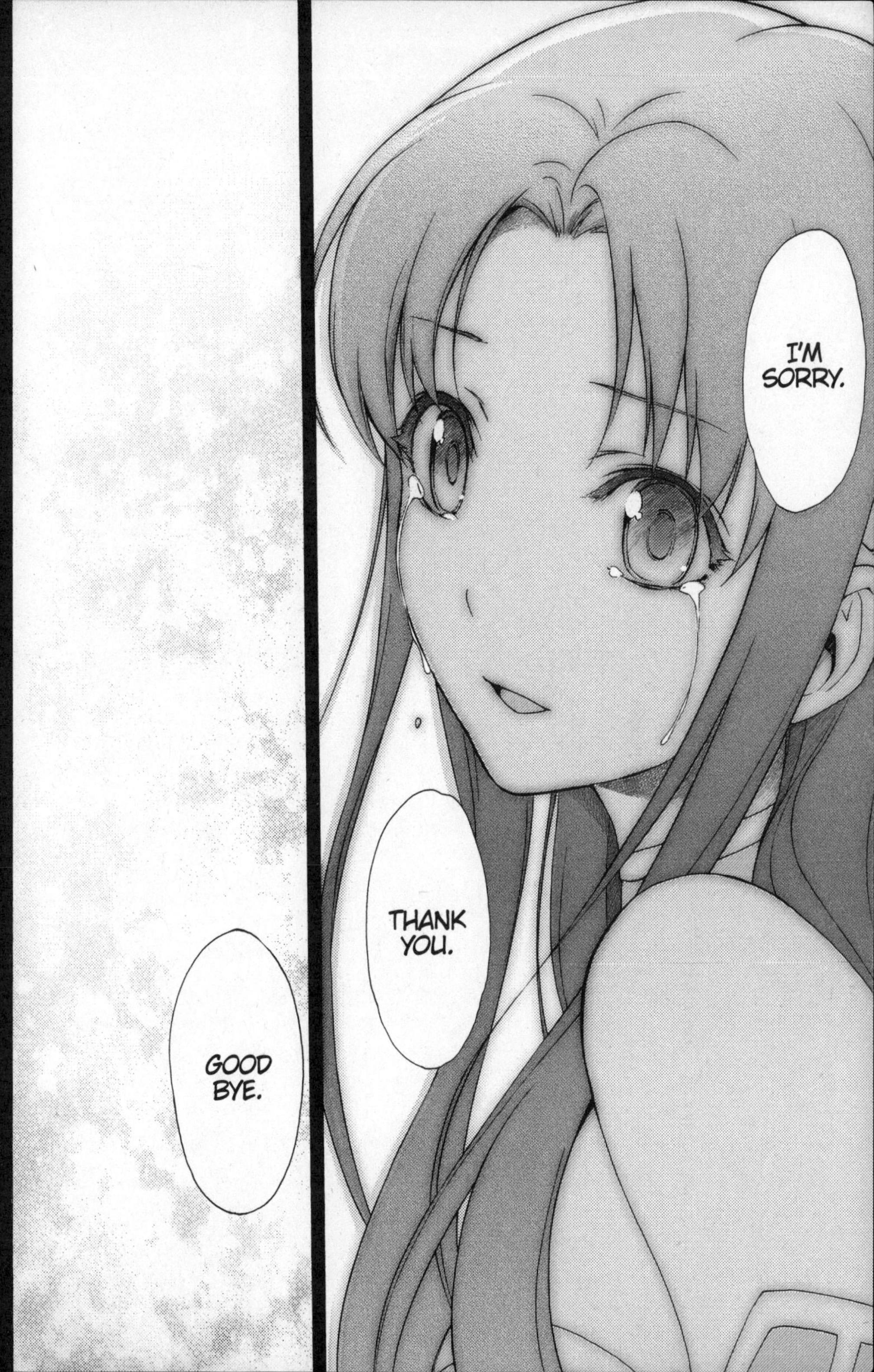
I'M SORRY.
THANK YOU.
GOOD BYE.

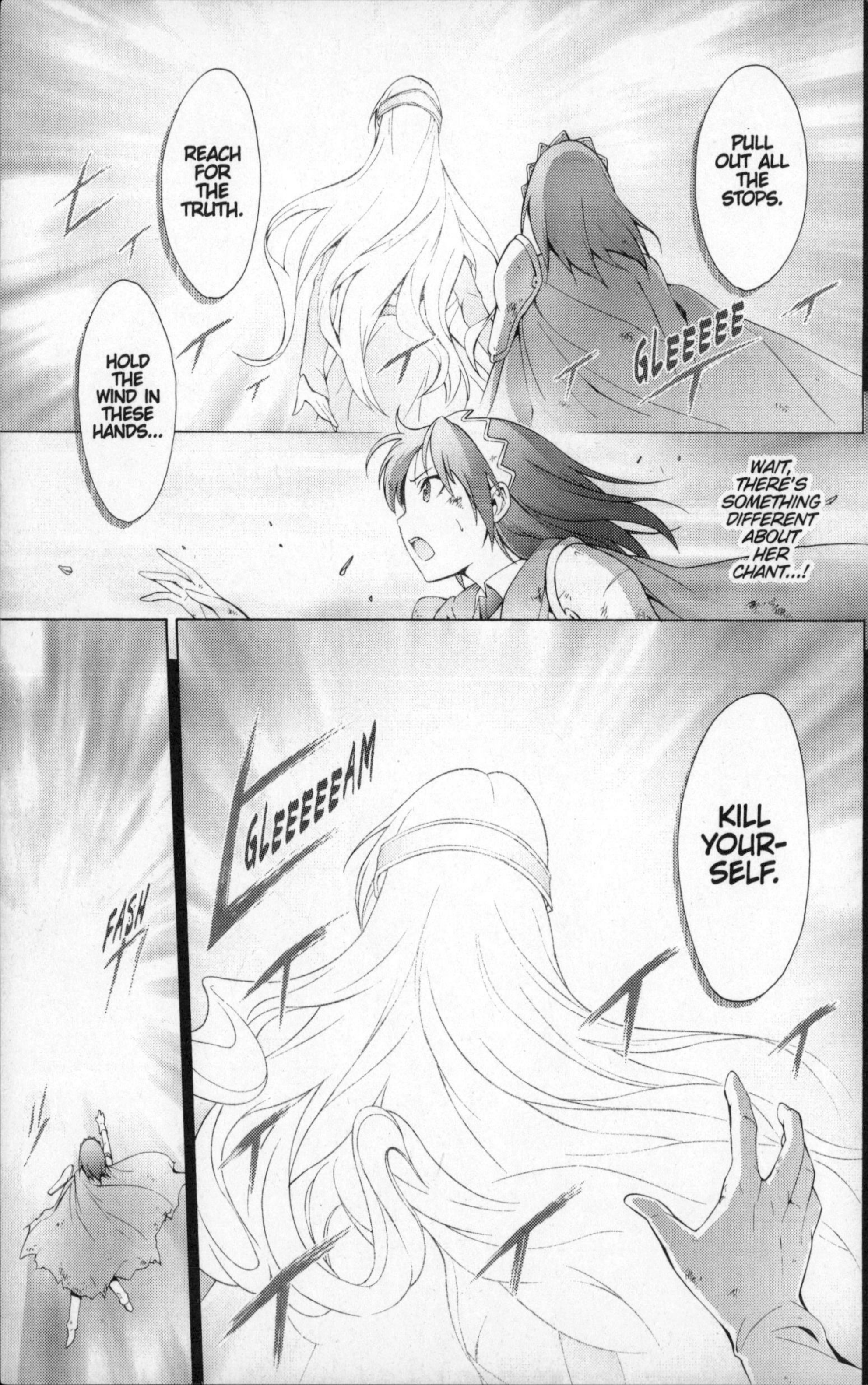
PULL OUT ALL THE STOPS.
REACH FOR THE TRUTH.
GLEEEEE
HOLD THE WIND IN THESE HANDS...
WAIT, THERE'S SOMETHING DIFFERENT ABOUT HER CHANT...!
KILL YOUR-SELF.
GLEEEEEAM
FASH

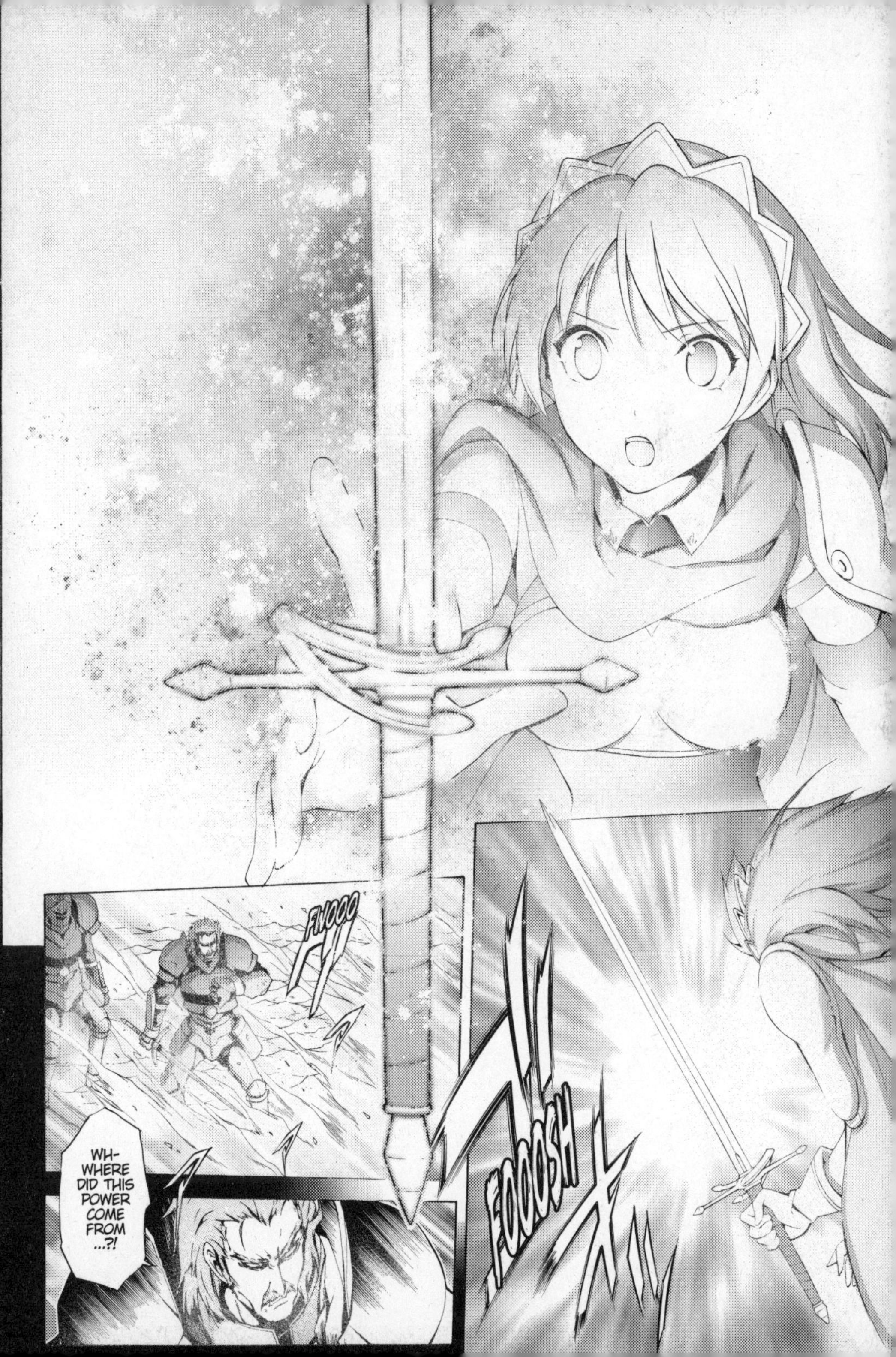
FOOOSH
FWOOO
WH-WHERE DID THIS POWER COME FROM ...?!

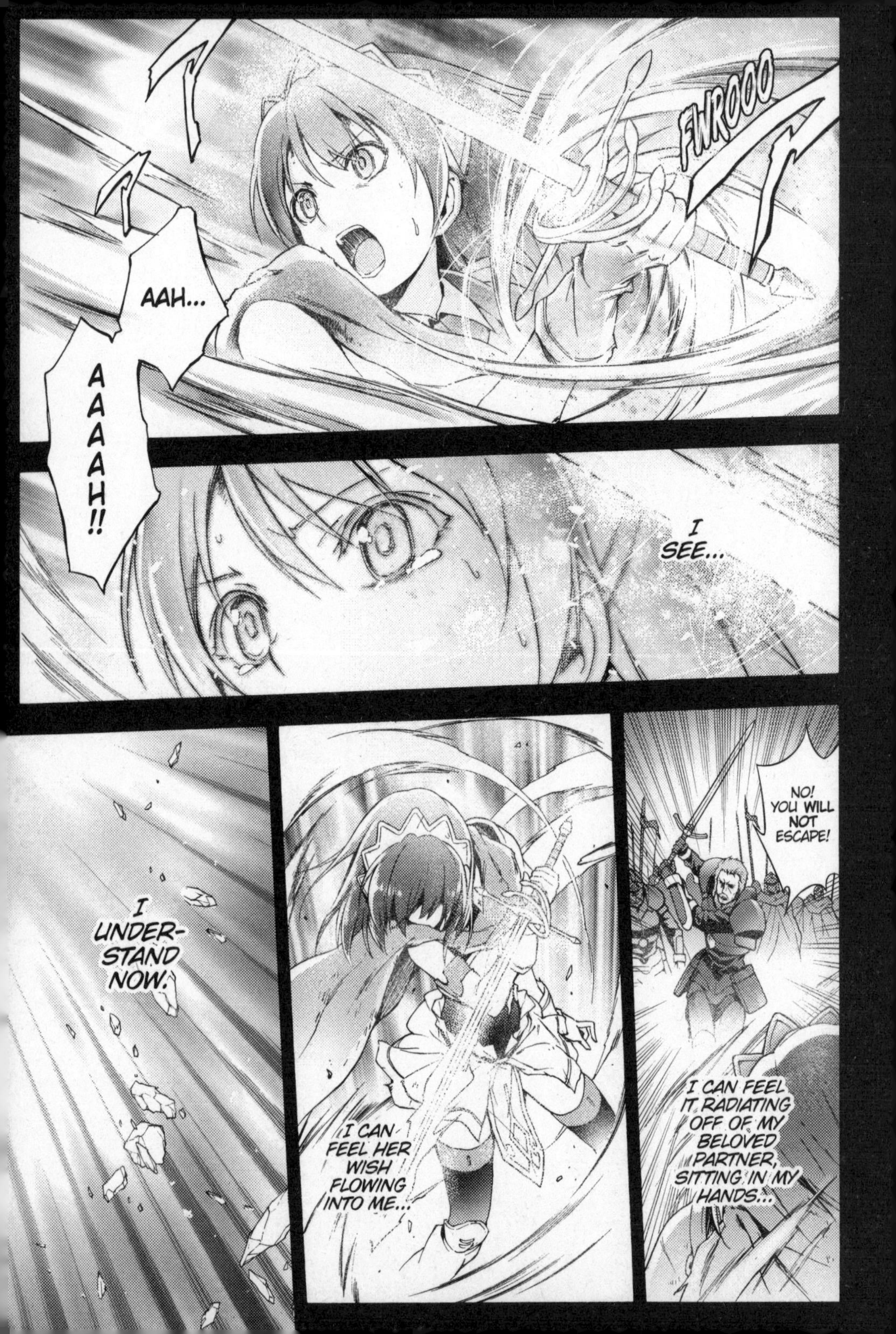
FWROOO
AAH...
AAAAAH!!
I SEE...
NO! YOU WILL NOT ESCAPE!
I CAN FEEL IT RADIATING OFF OF MY BELOVED PARTNER, SITTING IN MY HANDS...
I CAN FEEL HER WISH FLOWING INTO ME...
I UNDER-STAND NOW.

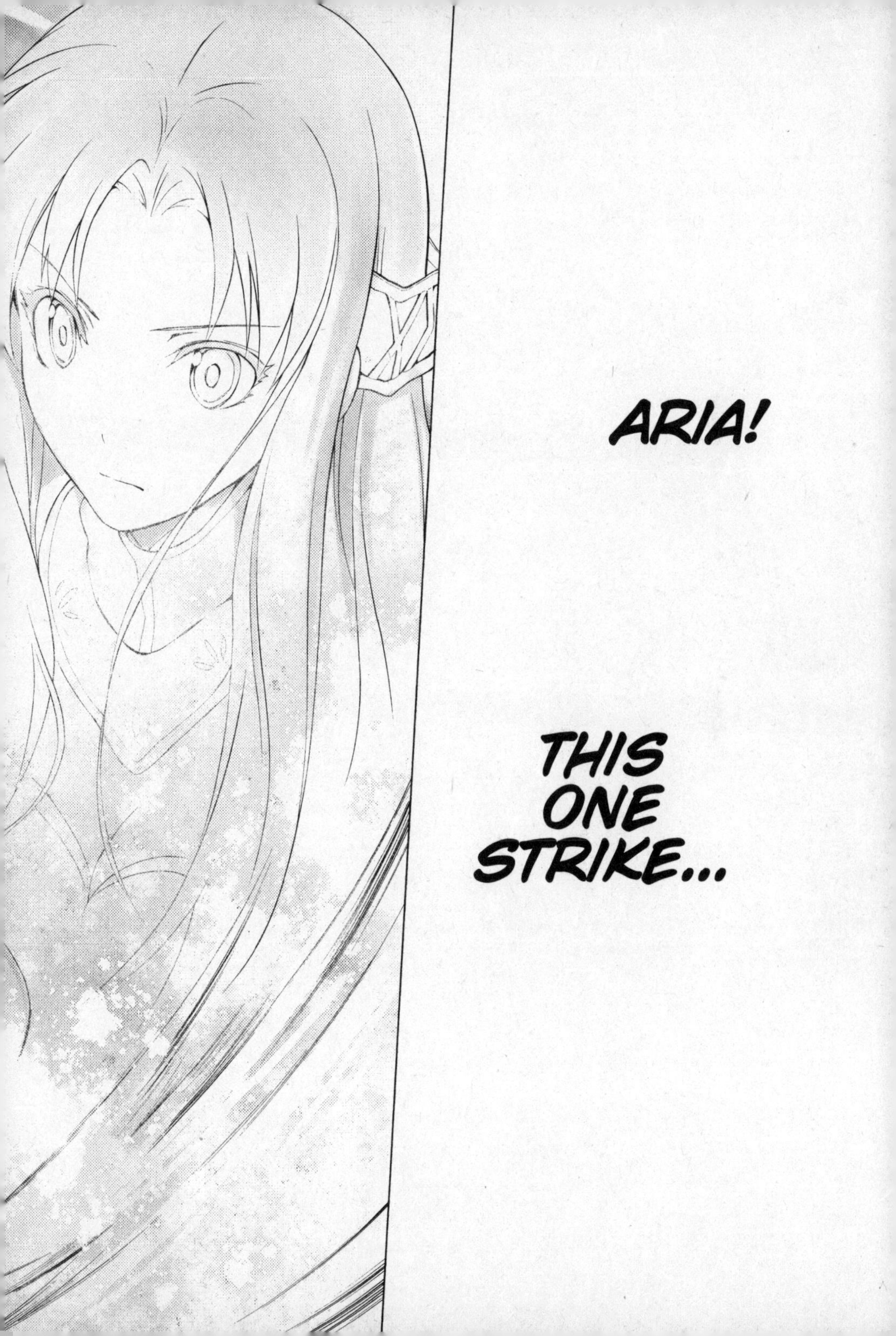
ARIA!
THIS ONE STRIKE...

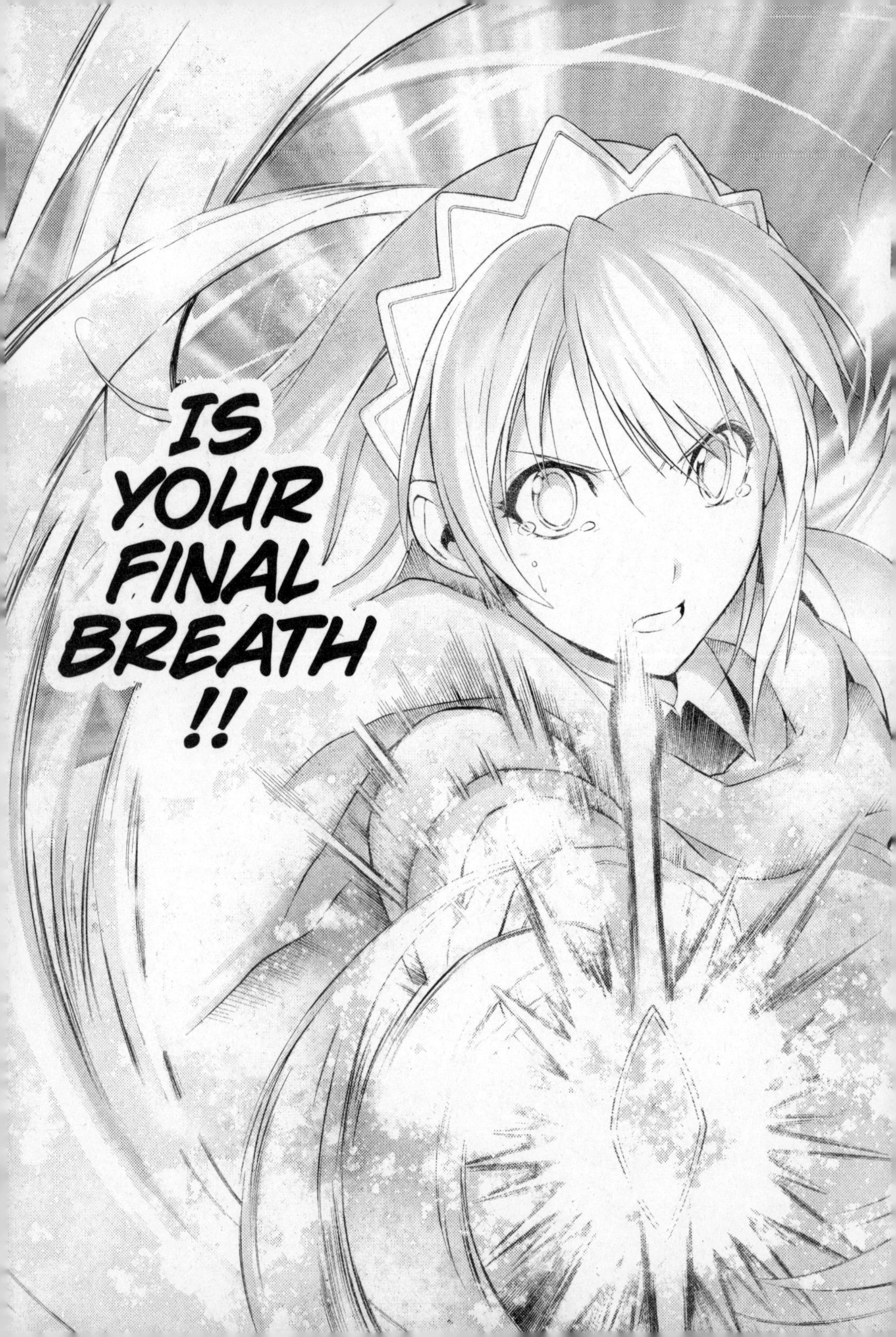
IS YOUR FINAL BREATH !!

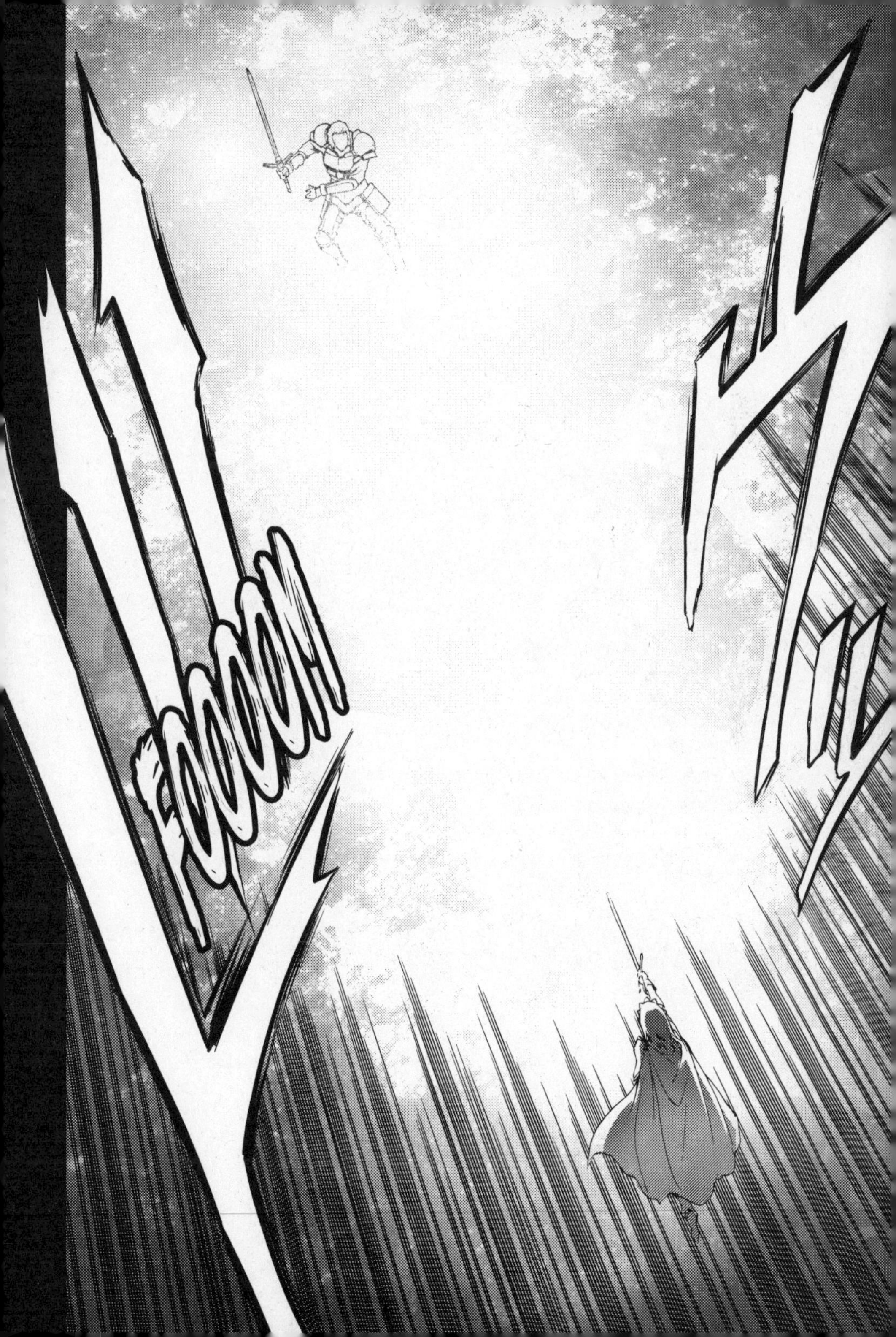
FOOOOM

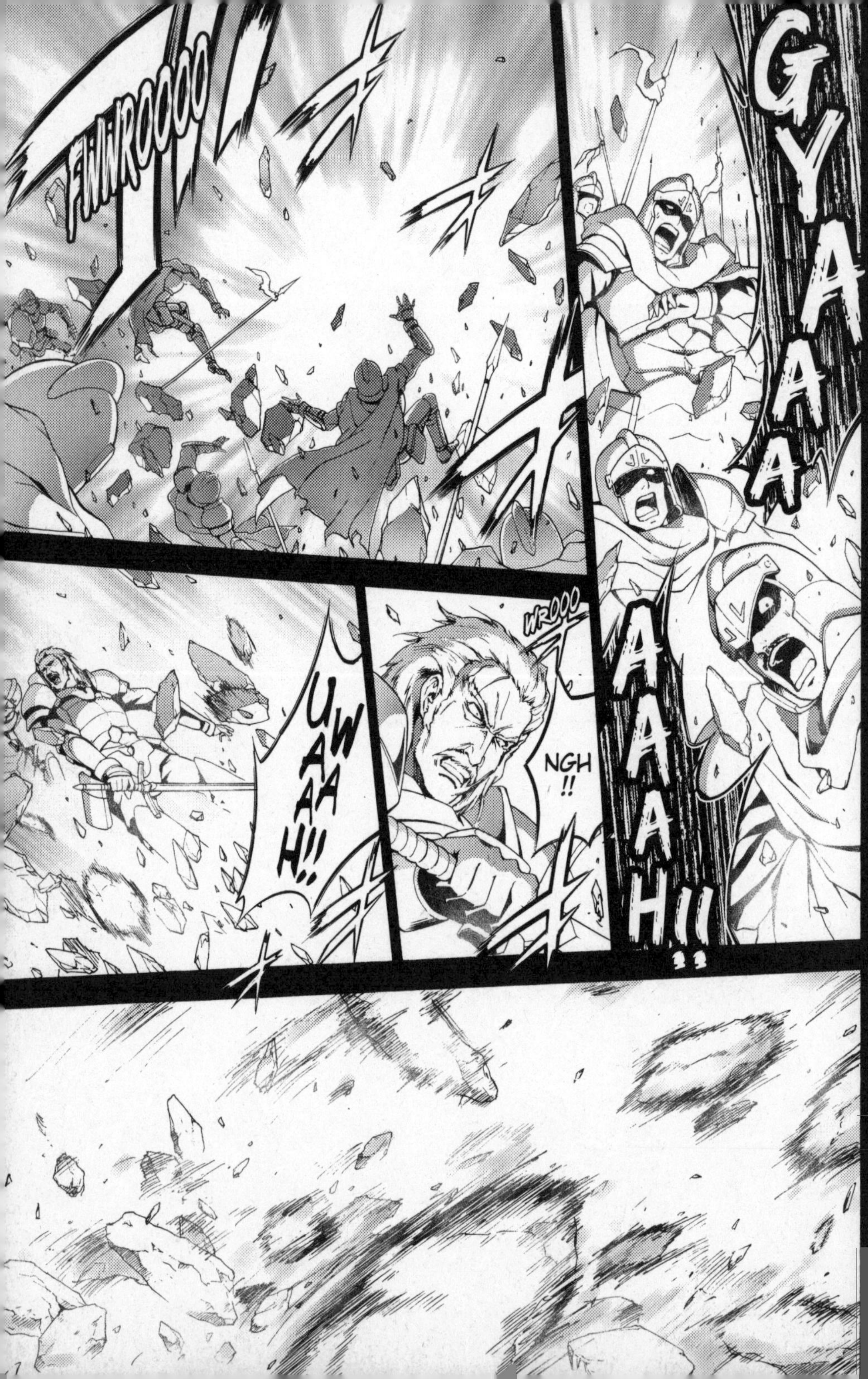
GYAAAAAAAH!!
FWROOOO
WROOO
NGH!!
UWAAAH!!

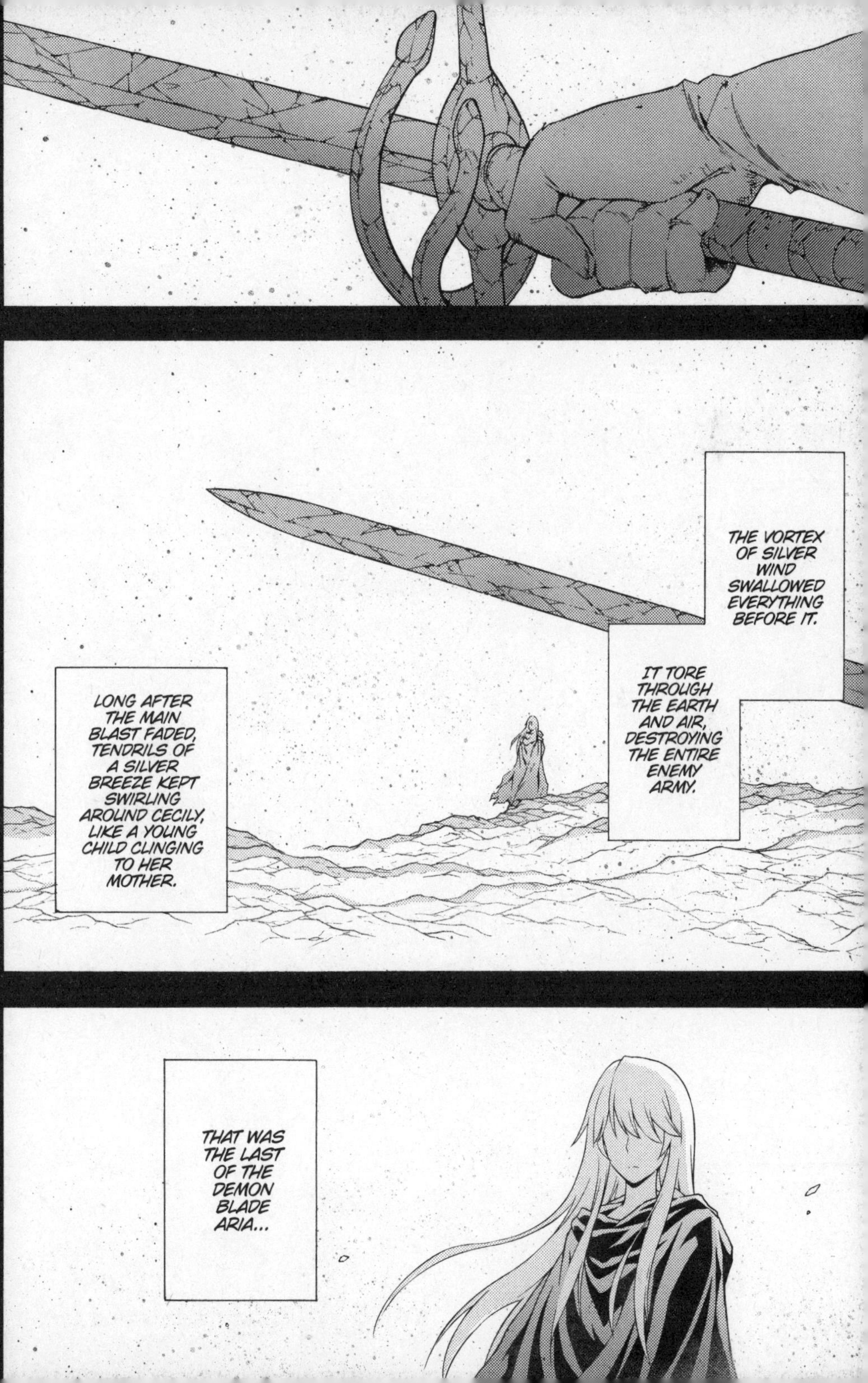
THE VORTEX OF SILVER WIND SWALLOWED EVERYTHING BEFORE IT.
IT TORE THROUGH THE EARTH AND AIR, DESTROYING THE ENTIRE ENEMY ARMY.
LONG AFTER THE MAIN BLAST FADED, TENDRILS OF A SILVER BREEZE KEPT SWIRLING AROUND CECILY, LIKE A YOUNG CHILD CLINGING TO HER MOTHER.
THAT WAS THE LAST OF THE DEMON BLADE ARIA...

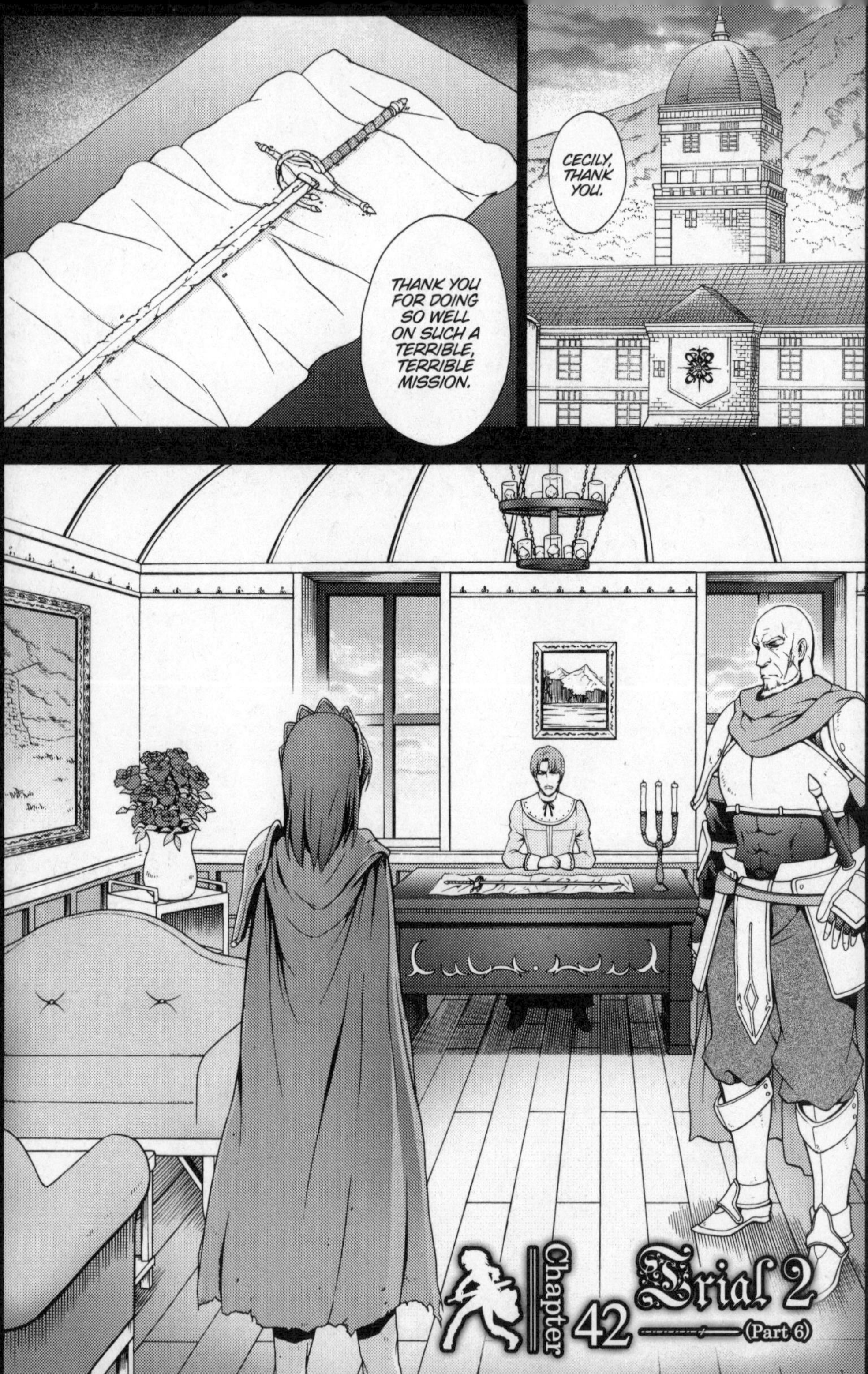
CECILY, THANK YOU.
THANK YOU FOR DOING SO WELL ON SUCH A TERRIBLE, TERRIBLE MISSION.
Chapter 42 Trial 2 (Part 6)

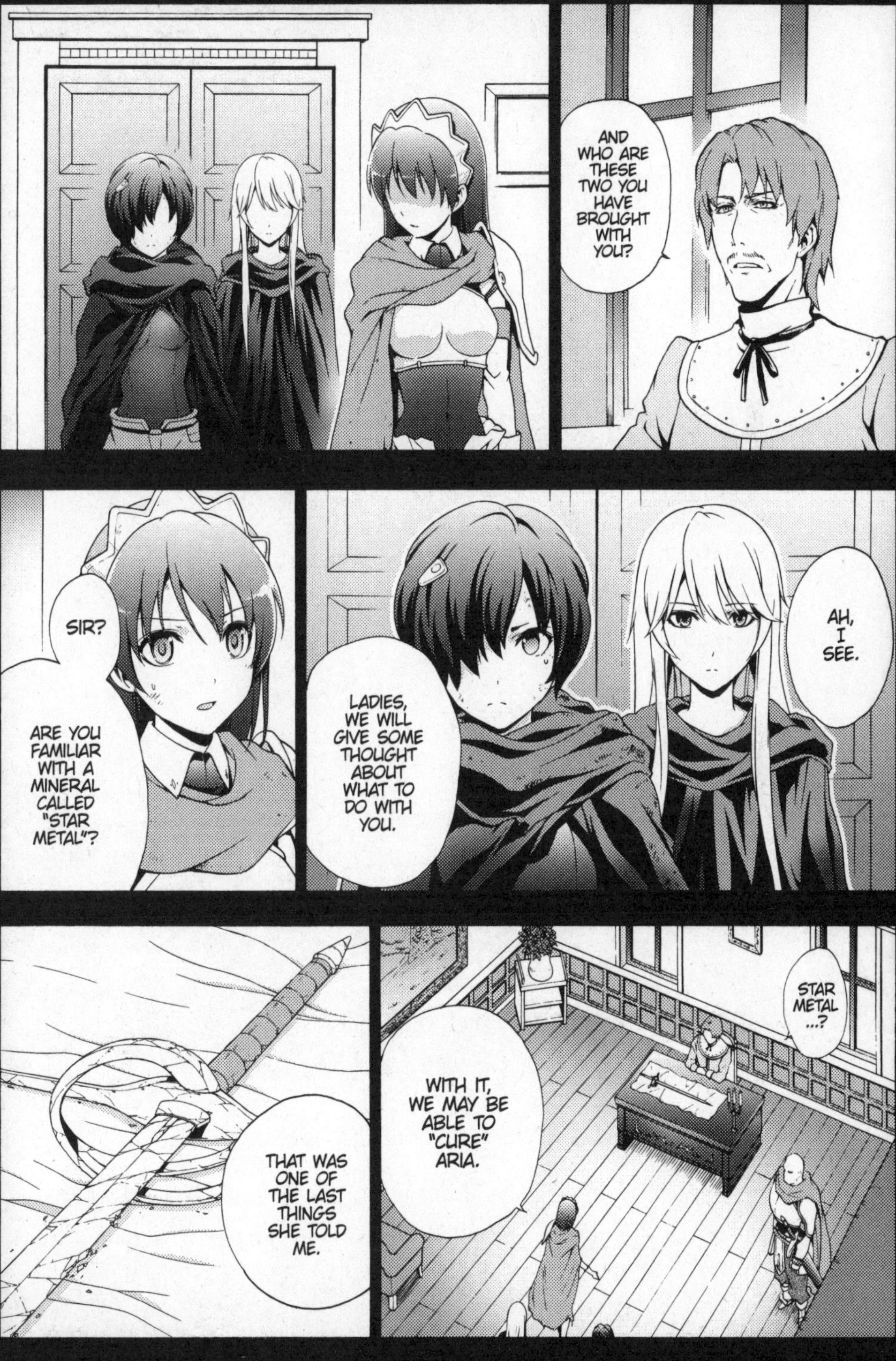
AND WHO ARE THESE TWO YOU HAVE BROUGHT WITH YOU?
AH, I SEE.
LADIES, WE WILL GIVE SOME THOUGHT ABOUT WHAT TO DO WITH YOU.
SIR?
ARE YOU FAMILIAR WITH A MINERAL CALLED "STAR METAL"?
STAR METAL ...?
WITH IT, WE MAY BE ABLE TO "CURE" ARIA.
THAT WAS ONE OF THE LAST THINGS SHE TOLD ME.

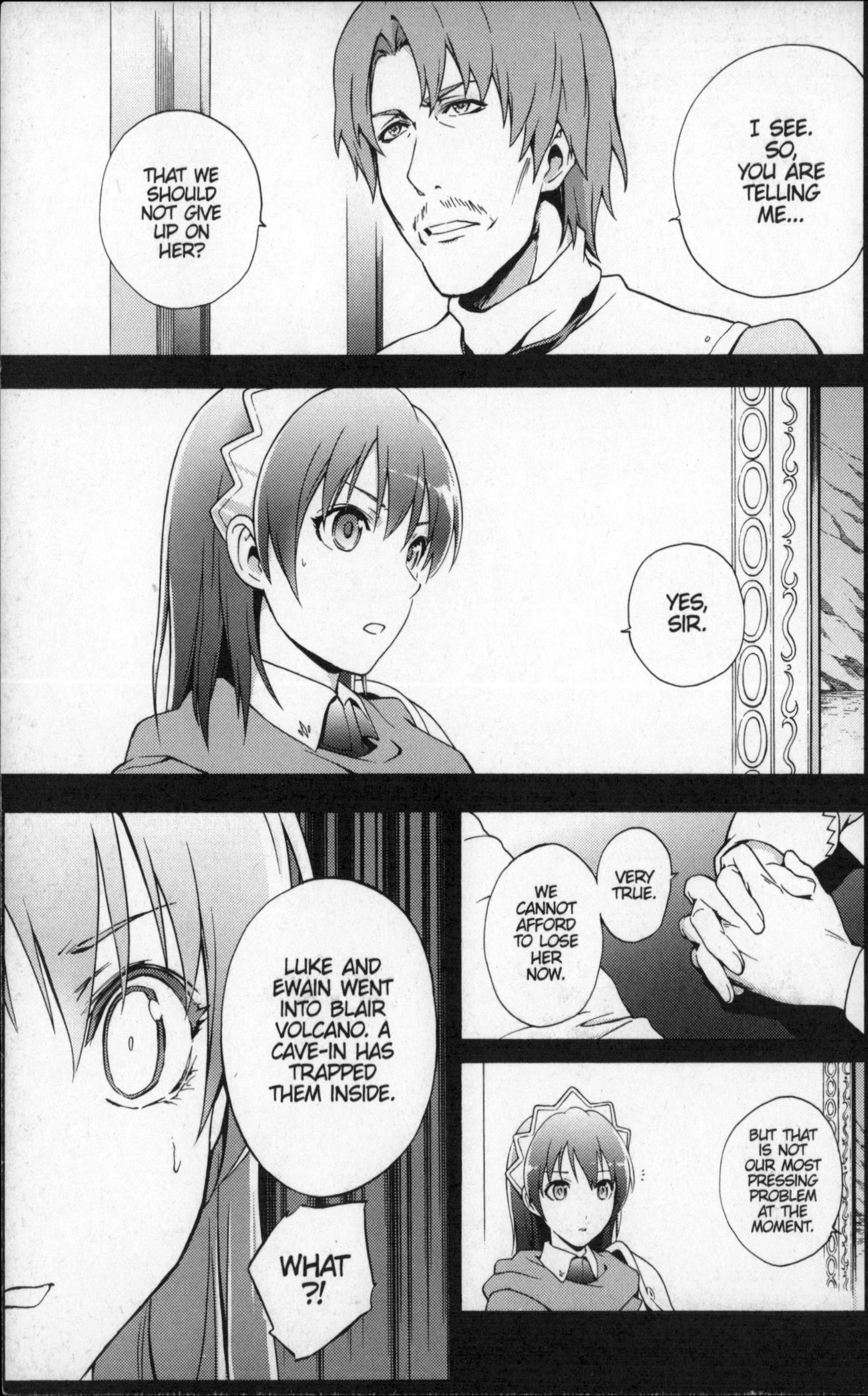
I SEE. SO, YOU ARE TELLING ME...
THAT WE SHOULD NOT GIVE UP ON HER?
YES, SIR.
VERY TRUE.
WE CANNOT AFFORD TO LOSE HER NOW.
BUT THAT IS NOT OUR MOST PRESSING PROBLEM AT THE MOMENT.
LUKE AND EWAIN WENT INTO BLAIR VOLCANO. A CAVE-IN HAS TRAPPED THEM INSIDE.
WHAT ?!

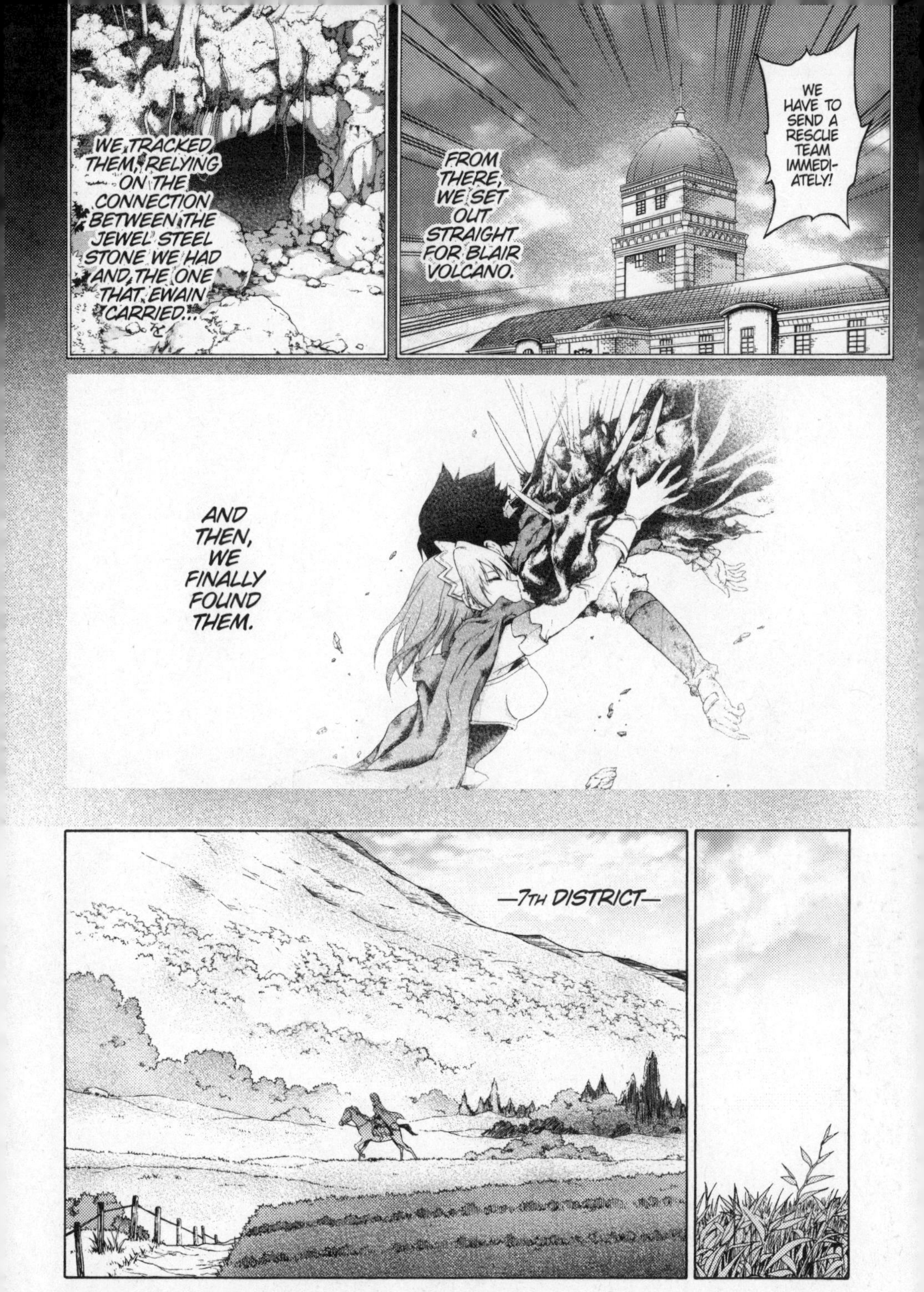
WE HAVE TO SEND A RESCUE TEAM IMMEDI-ATELY!
FROM THERE, WE SET OUT STRAIGHT FOR BLAIR VOLCANO.
WE TRACKED THEM, RELYING ON THE CONNECTION BETWEEN THE JEWEL STEEL STONE WE HAD AND THE ONE THAT EWAIN CARRIED...
AND THEN, WE FINALLY FOUND THEM.
—7TH DISTRICT—

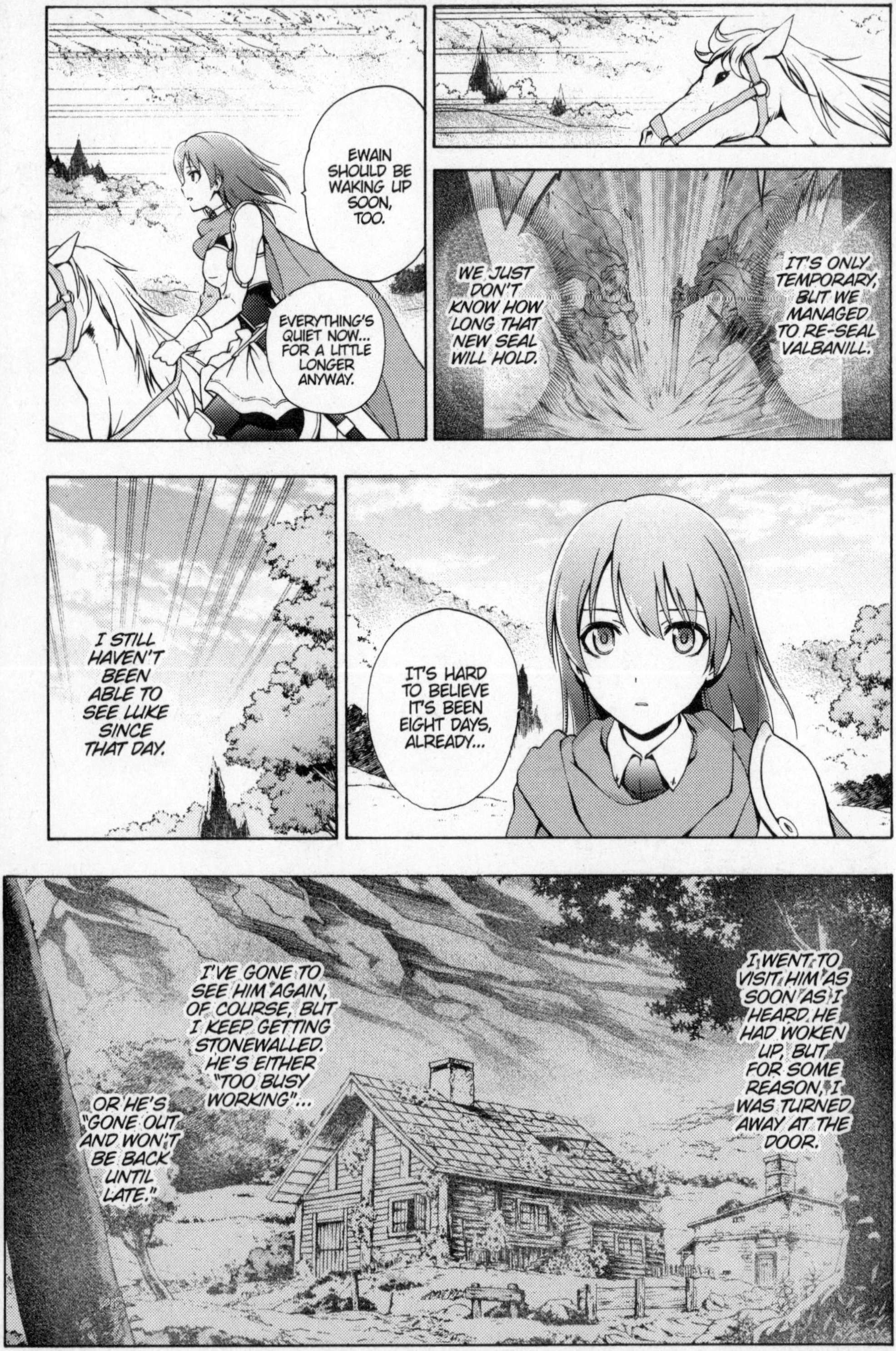
IT'S ONLY TEMPORARY, BUT WE MANAGED TO RE-SEAL VALBANILL.
WE JUST DON'T KNOW HOW LONG THAT NEW SEAL WILL HOLD.
EWAIN SHOULD BE WAKING UP SOON, TOO.
EVERYTHING'S QUIET NOW... FOR A LITTLE LONGER ANYWAY.
IT'S HARD TO BELIEVE IT'S BEEN EIGHT DAYS, ALREADY...
I STILL HAVEN'T BEEN ABLE TO SEE LUKE SINCE THAT DAY.
I WENT TO VISIT HIM AS SOON AS I HEARD HE HAD WOKEN UP, BUT FOR SOME REASON, I WAS TURNED AWAY AT THE DOOR.
I'VE GONE TO SEE HIM AGAIN, OF COURSE, BUT I KEEP GETTING STONEWALLED. HE'S EITHER "TOO BUSY WORKING"...
OR HE'S "GONE OUT AND WON'T BE BACK UNTIL LATE."

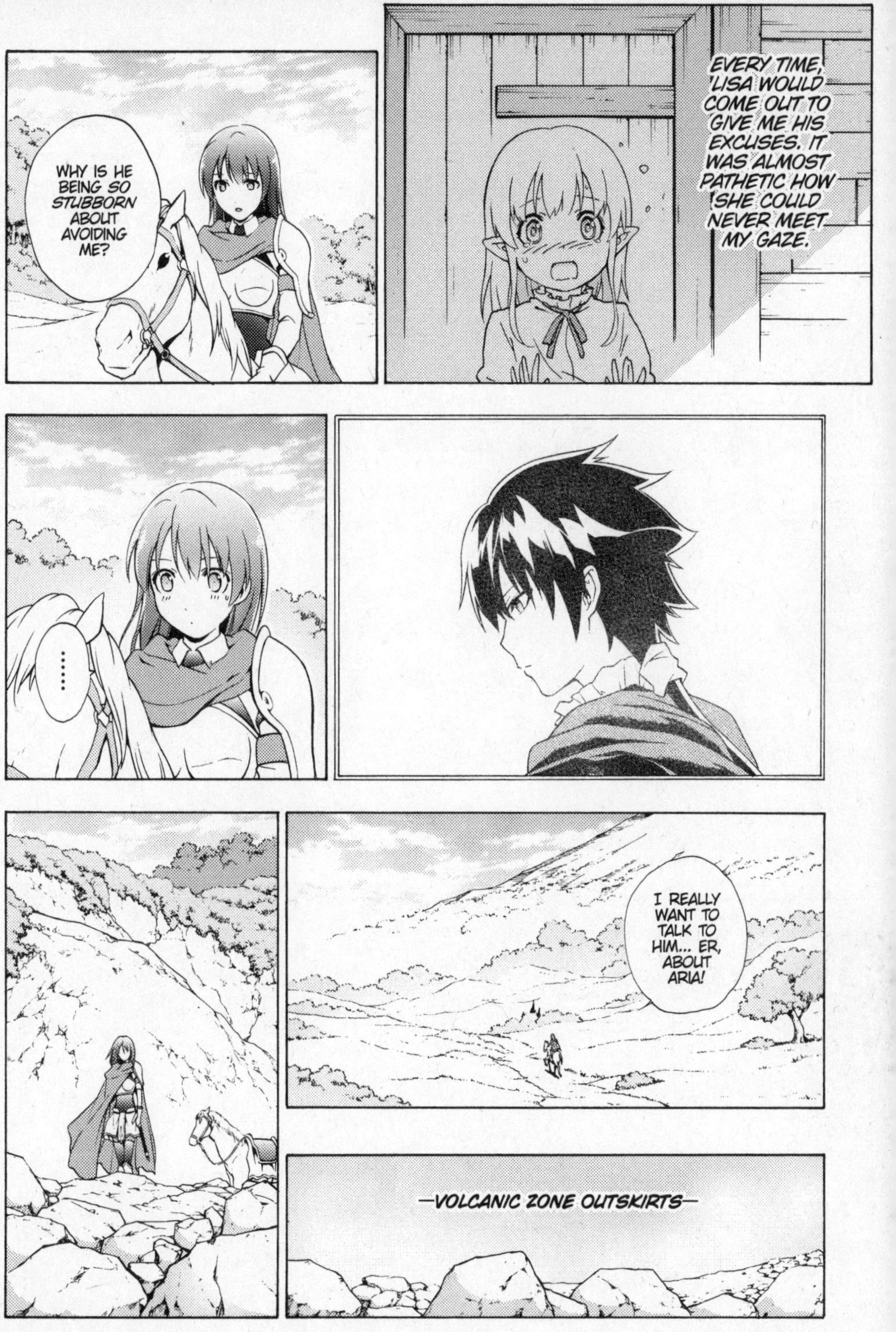
EVERY TIME, LISA WOULD COME OUT TO GIVE ME HIS EXCUSES. IT WAS ALMOST PATHETIC HOW SHE COULD NEVER MEET MY GAZE.
WHY IS HE BEING SO STUBBORN ABOUT AVOIDING ME?
......
I REALLY WANT TO TALK TO HIM... ER, ABOUT ARIA!
—VOLCANIC ZONE OUTSKIRTS—

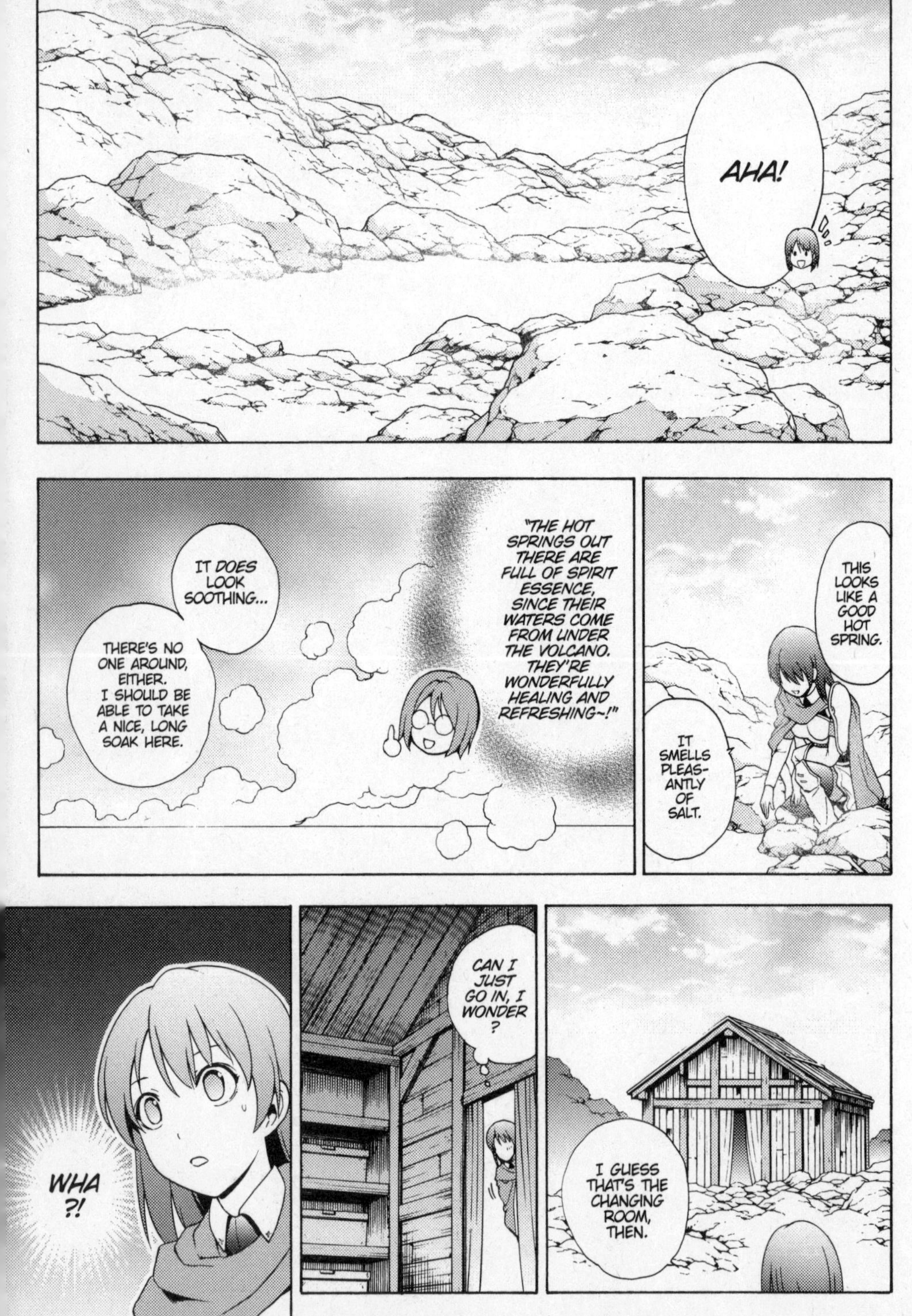
AHA!
THIS LOOKS LIKE A GOOD HOT SPRING.
IT SMELLS PLEASANTLY OF SALT.
"THE HOT SPRINGS OUT THERE ARE FULL OF SPIRIT ESSENCE, SINCE THEIR WATERS COME FROM UNDER THE VOLCANO. THEY'RE WONDERFULLY HEALING AND REFRESHING~!"
IT DOES LOOK SOOTHING...
THERE'S NO ONE AROUND, EITHER. I SHOULD BE ABLE TO TAKE A NICE, LONG SOAK HERE.
I GUESS THAT'S THE CHANGING ROOM, THEN.
CAN I JUST GO IN, I WONDER?
WHA?!

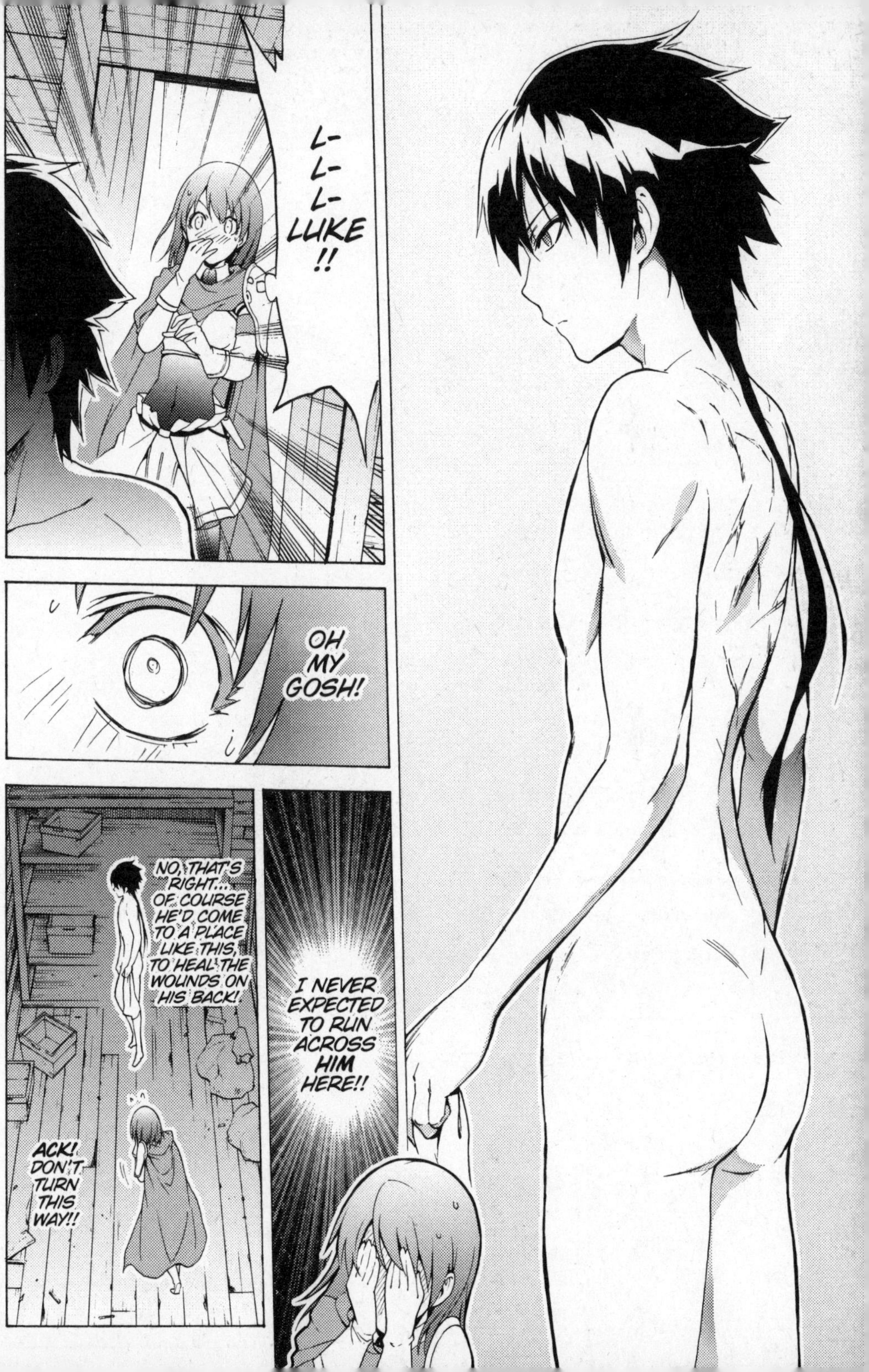
L-L-L-LUKE!!
OH MY GOSH!
I NEVER EXPECTED TO RUN ACROSS HIM HERE!!
NO, THAT'S RIGHT... OF COURSE HE'D COME TO A PLACE LIKE THIS, TO HEAL THE WOUNDS ON HIS BACK!
ACK! DON'T TURN THIS WAY!!

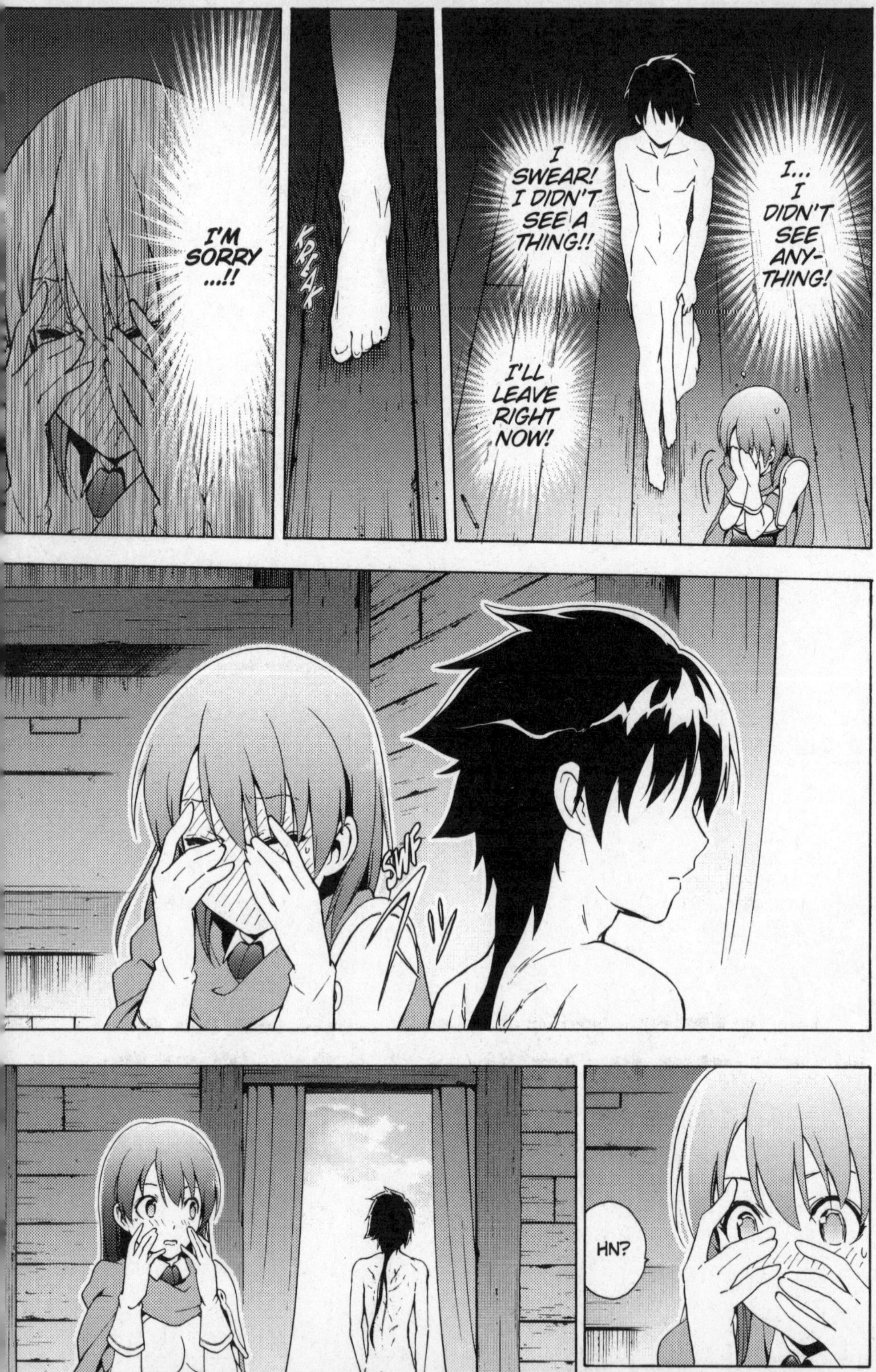
I... I DIDN'T SEE ANY-THING!
I SWEAR! I DIDN'T SEE A THING!!
I'LL LEAVE RIGHT NOW!
KREAK
I'M SORRY ...!!
SWF
HN?

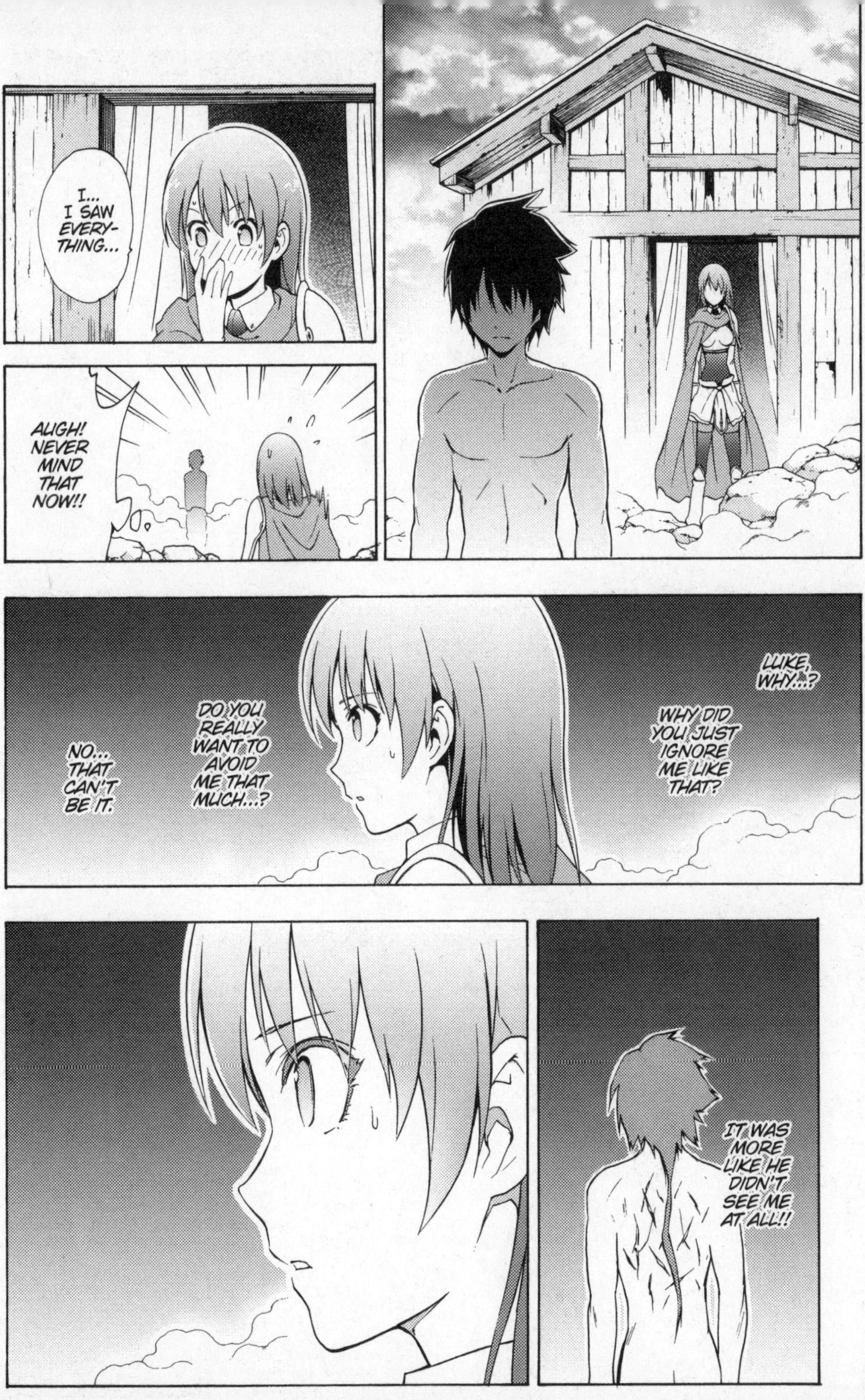
I... I SAW EVERY-THING...
AUGH! NEVER MIND THAT NOW!!
LUKE, WHY...?
WHY DID YOU JUST IGNORE ME LIKE THAT?
DO YOU REALLY WANT TO AVOID ME THAT MUCH...?
NO... THAT CAN'T BE IT.
IT WAS MORE LIKE HE DIDN'T SEE ME AT ALL!!

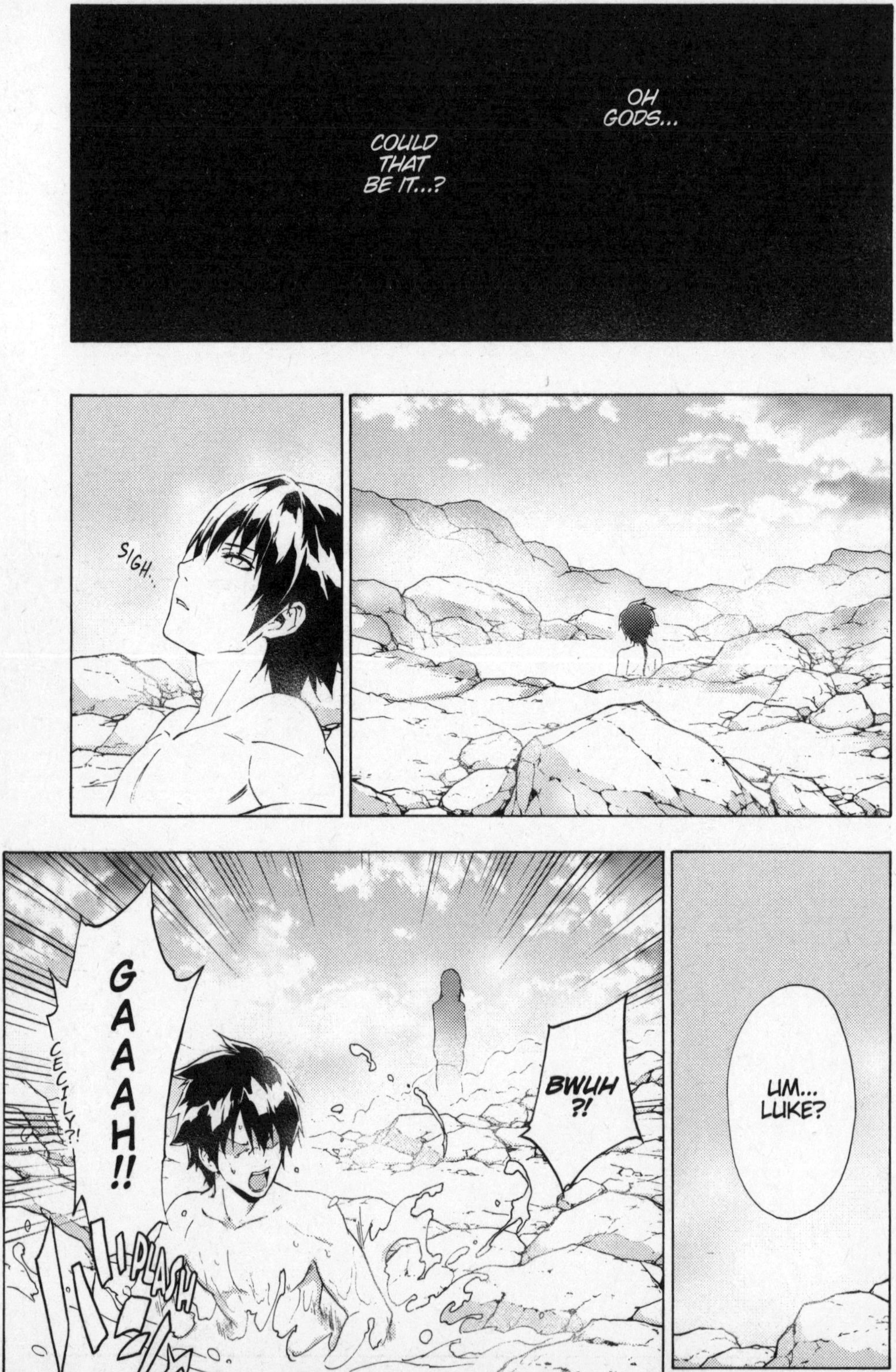
OH GODS...
COULD THAT BE IT...?
SIGH...
UM... LUKE?
BWUH ?!
GAAAAH!!
CECILY?!
PLASH

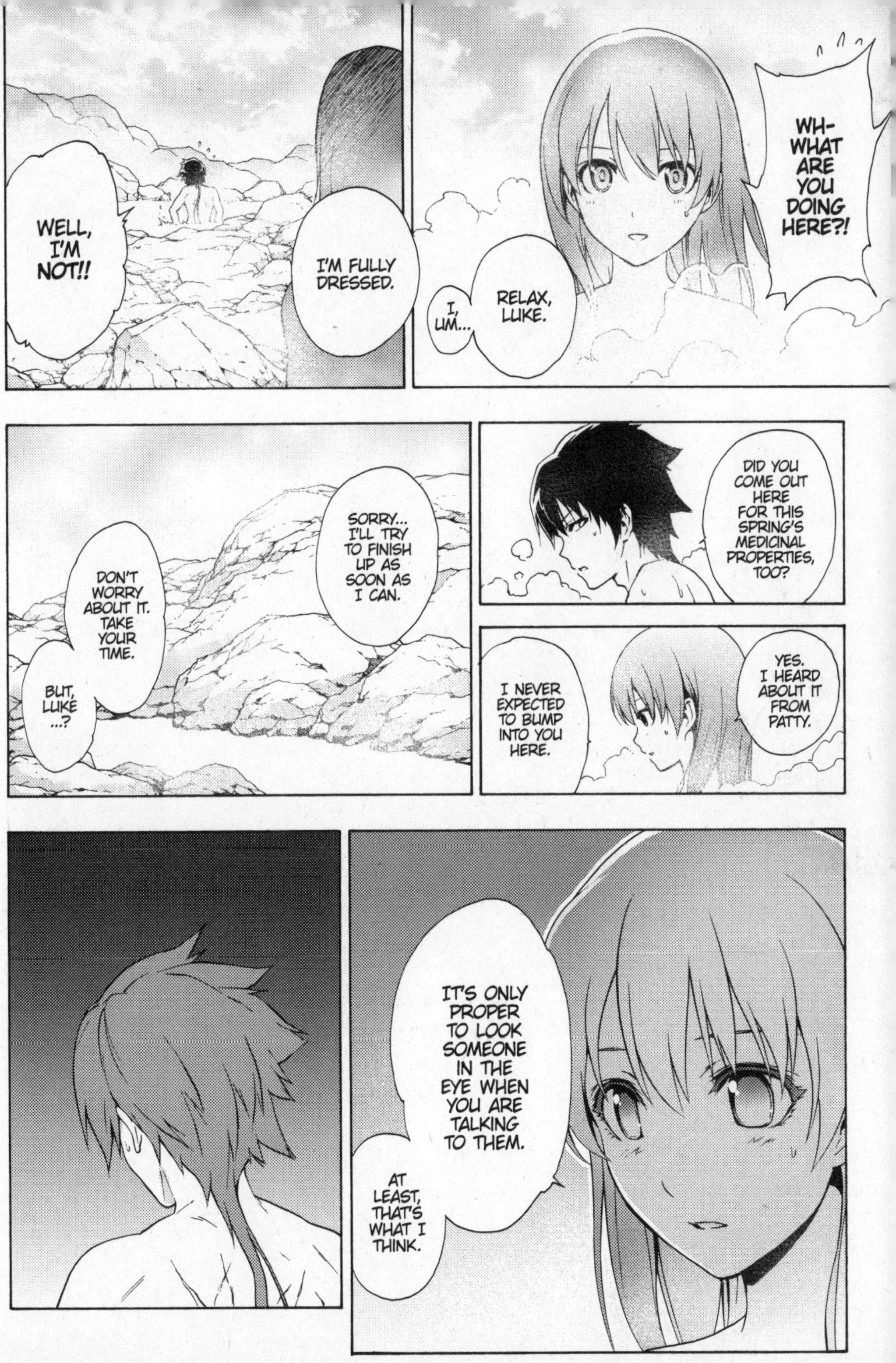
WH-WHAT ARE YOU DOING HERE?!
RELAX, LUKE.
I, UM...
I'M FULLY DRESSED.
WELL, I'M NOT!!
DID YOU COME OUT HERE FOR THIS SPRING'S MEDICINAL PROPERTIES, TOO?
YES. I HEARD ABOUT IT FROM PATTY.
I NEVER EXPECTED TO BUMP INTO YOU HERE.
SORRY... I'LL TRY TO FINISH UP AS SOON AS I CAN.
DON'T WORRY ABOUT IT. TAKE YOUR TIME.
BUT, LUKE ...?
IT'S ONLY PROPER TO LOOK SOMEONE IN THE EYE WHEN YOU ARE TALKING TO THEM.
AT LEAST, THAT'S WHAT I THINK.

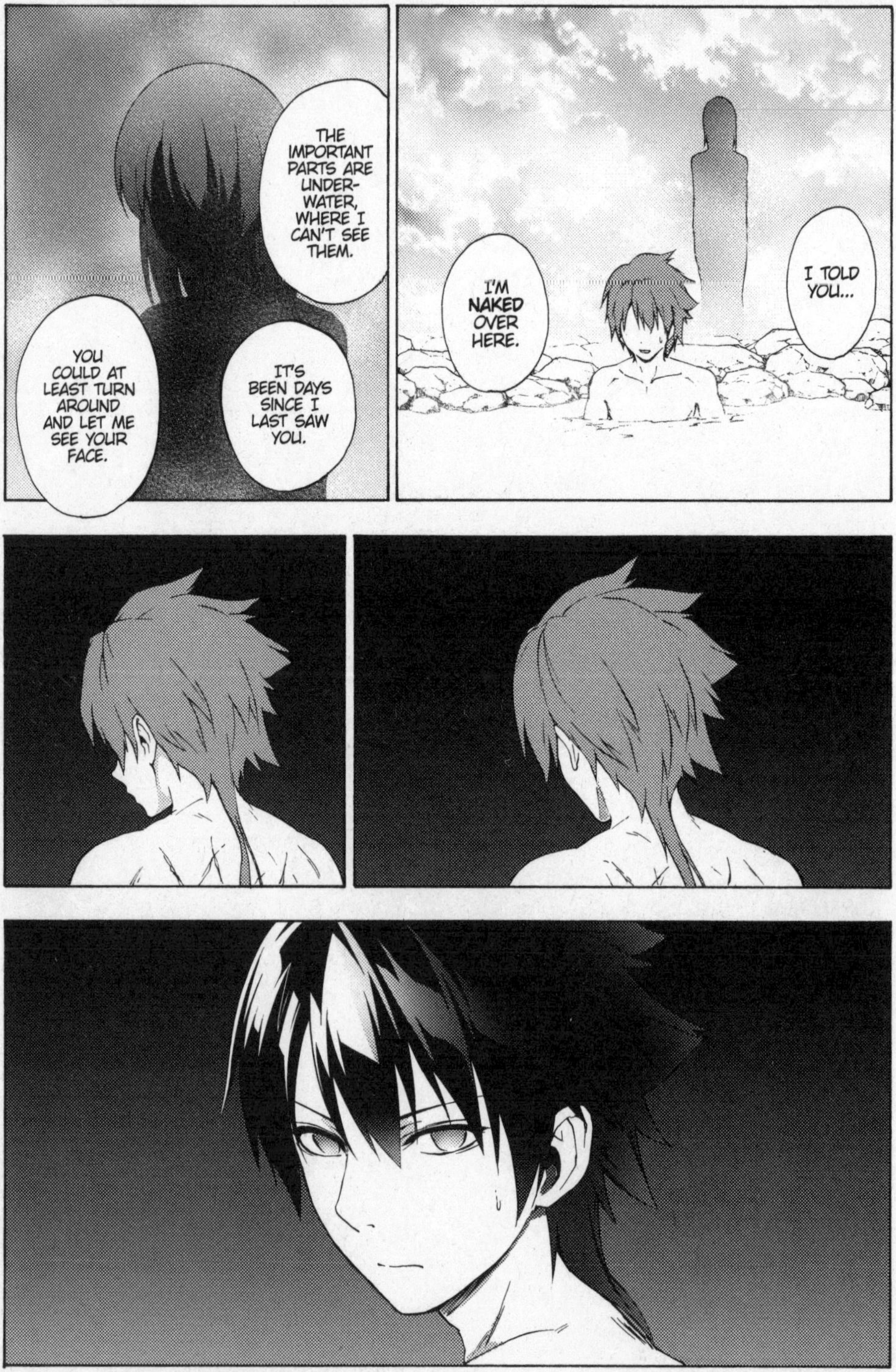
I TOLD YOU...
I'M NAKED OVER HERE.
THE IMPORTANT PARTS ARE UNDER-WATER, WHERE I CAN'T SEE THEM.
IT'S BEEN DAYS SINCE I LAST SAW YOU.
YOU COULD AT LEAST TURN AROUND AND LET ME SEE YOUR FACE.

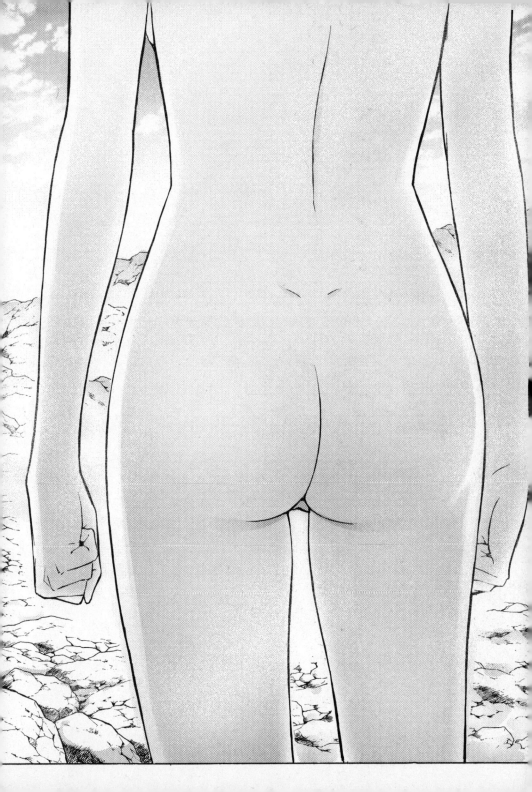

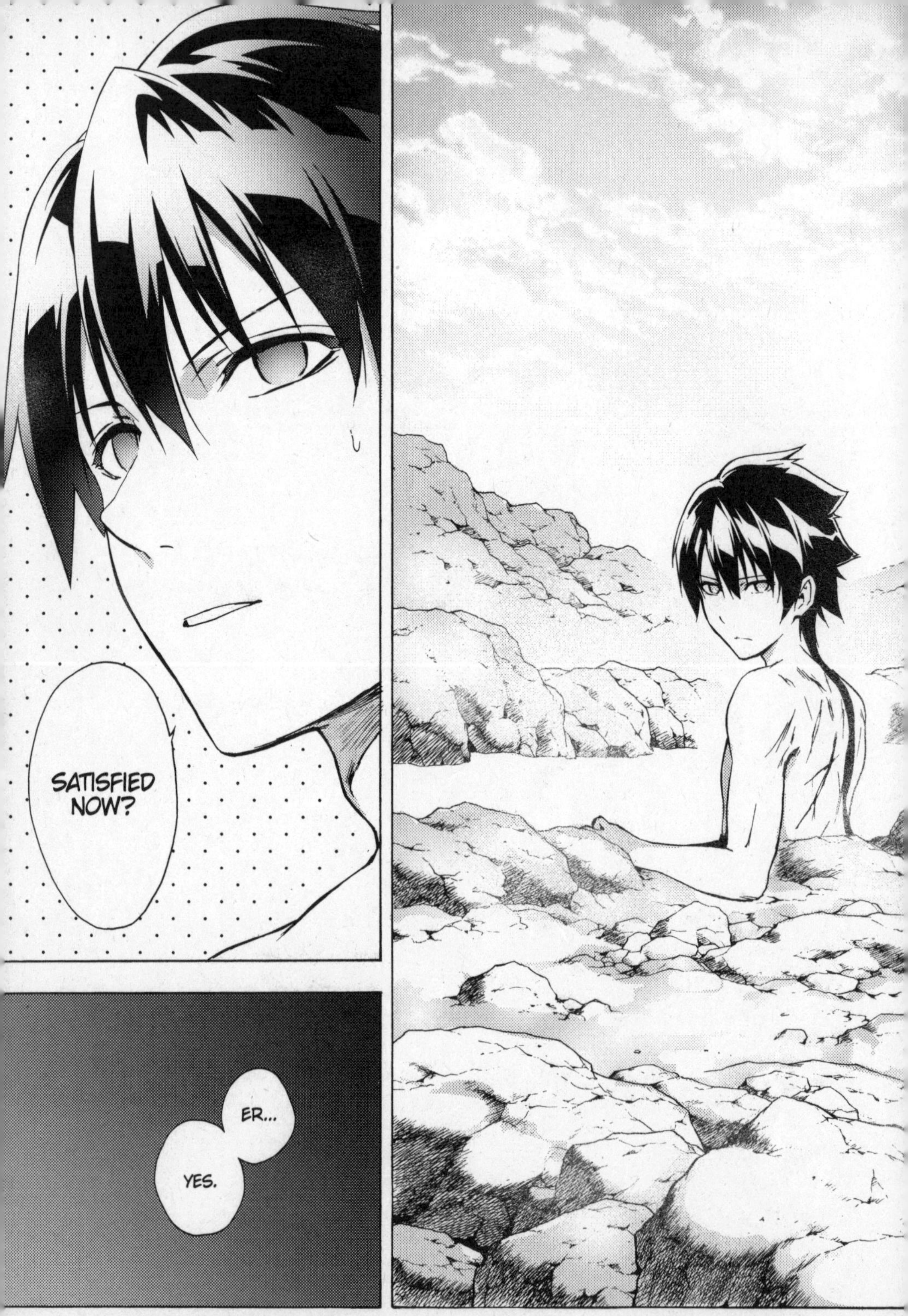
SATISFIED NOW?
ER...
YES.

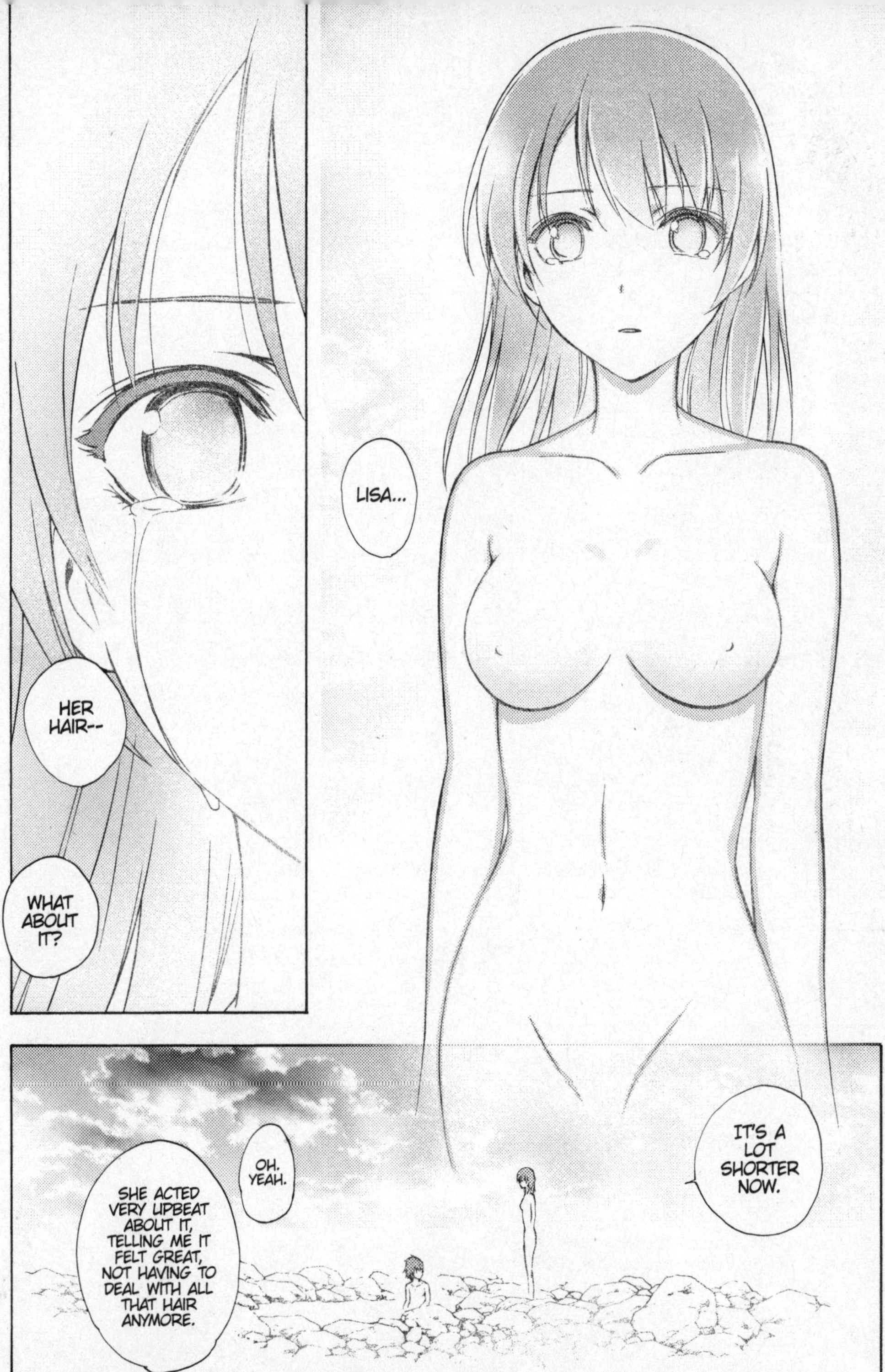
LISA...
HER HAIR--
WHAT ABOUT IT?
IT'S A LOT SHORTER NOW.
OH. YEAH.
SHE ACTED VERY UPBEAT ABOUT IT, TELLING ME IT FELT GREAT, NOT HAVING TO DEAL WITH ALL THAT HAIR ANYMORE.

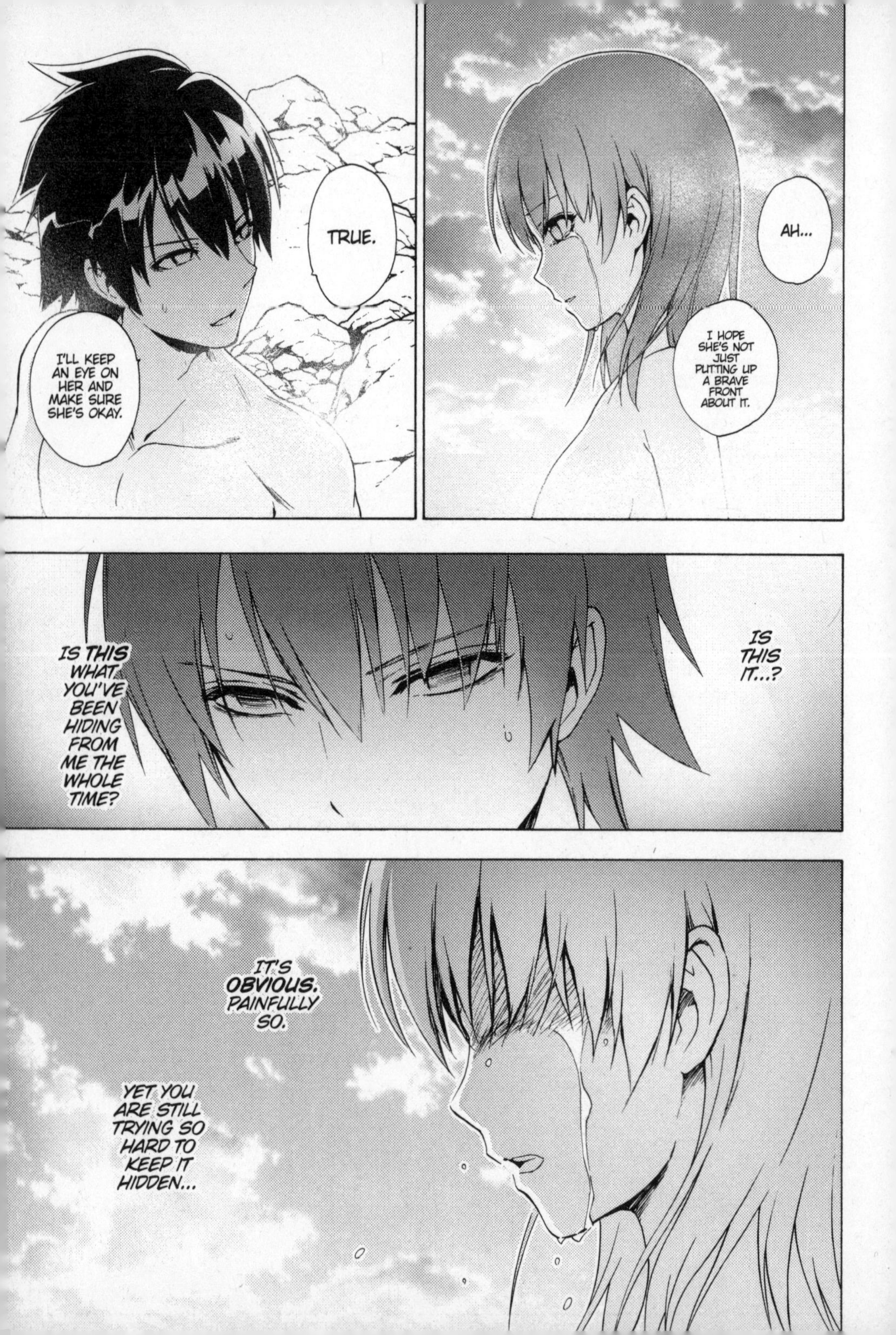
AH...
I HOPE SHE'S NOT JUST PUTTING UP A BRAVE FRONT ABOUT IT.
TRUE.
I'LL KEEP AN EYE ON HER AND MAKE SURE SHE'S OKAY.
IS THIS IT...?
IS THIS WHAT YOU'VE BEEN HIDING FROM ME THE WHOLE TIME?
IT'S OBVIOUS. PAINFULLY SO.
YET YOU ARE STILL TRYING SO HARD TO KEEP IT HIDDEN...

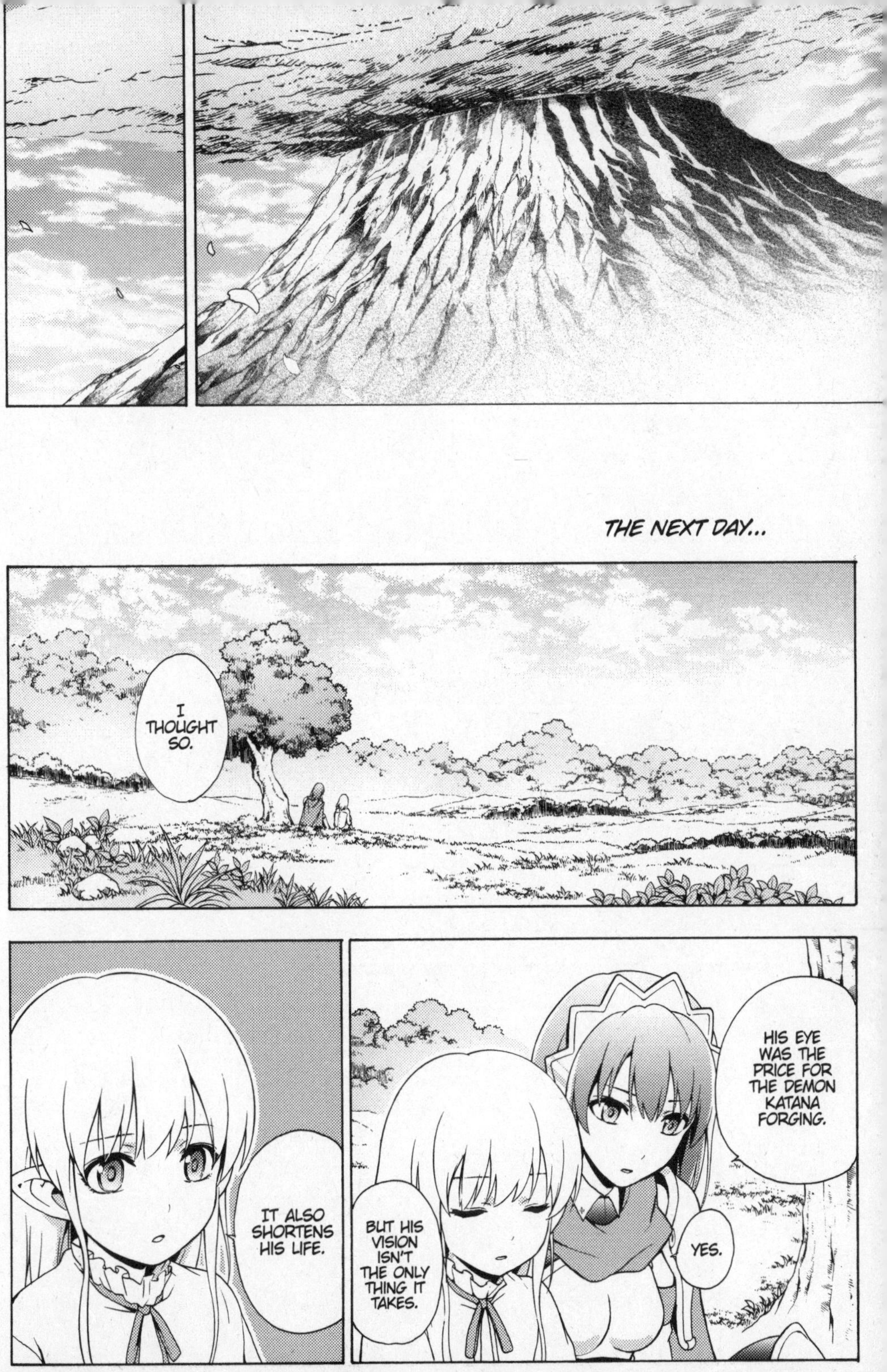
THE NEXT DAY...
I THOUGHT SO.
HIS EYE WAS THE PRICE FOR THE DEMON KATANA FORGING.
YES.
BUT HIS VISION ISN'T THE ONLY THING IT TAKES.
IT ALSO SHORTENS HIS LIFE.

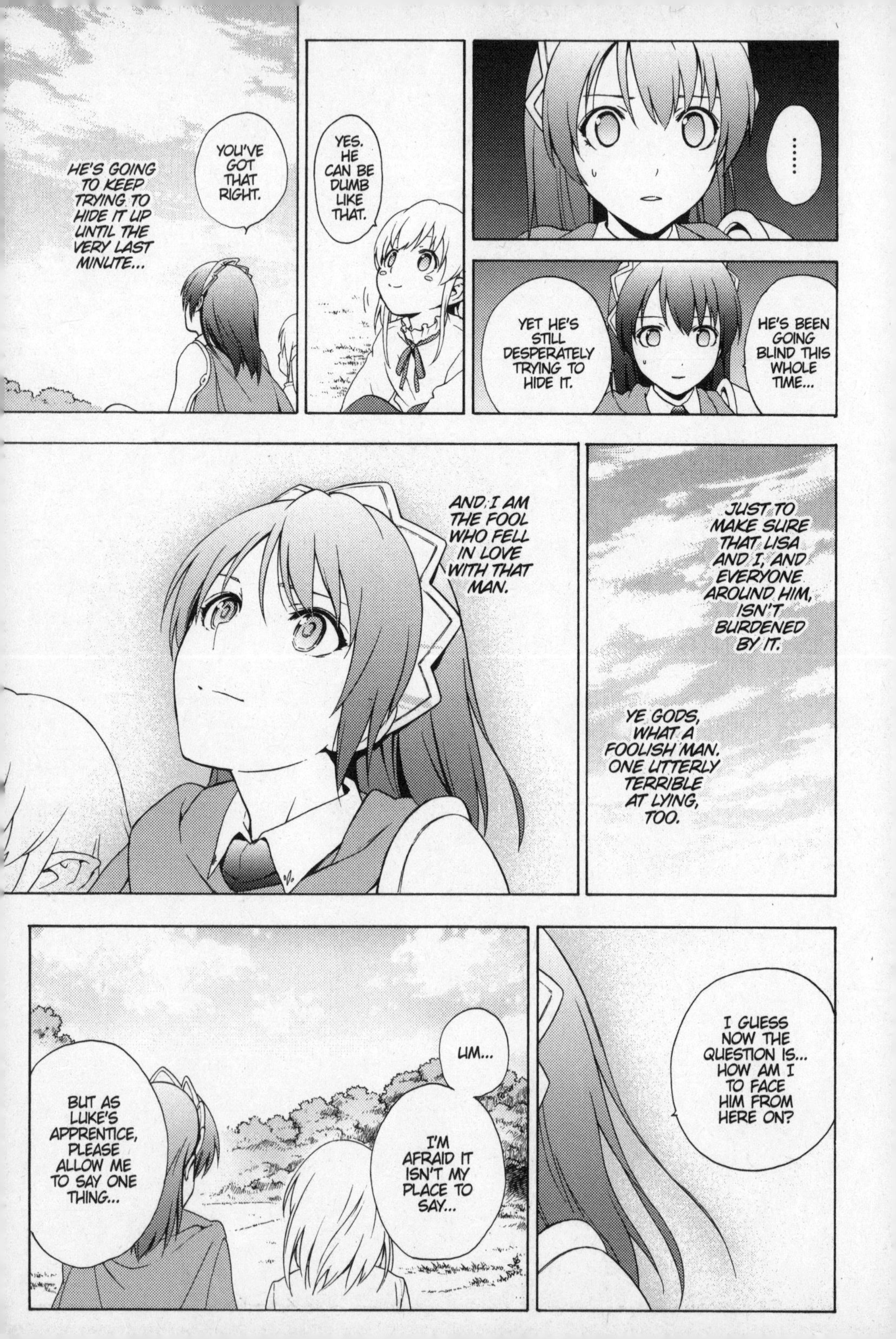
……
HE'S BEEN GOING BLIND THIS WHOLE TIME...
YET HE'S STILL DESPERATELY TRYING TO HIDE IT.
YES. HE CAN BE DUMB LIKE THAT.
YOU'VE GOT THAT RIGHT.
HE'S GOING TO KEEP TRYING TO HIDE IT UP UNTIL THE VERY LAST MINUTE...
JUST TO MAKE SURE THAT LISA AND I, AND EVERYONE AROUND HIM, ISN'T BURDENED BY IT.
YE GODS, WHAT A FOOLISH MAN. ONE UTTERLY TERRIBLE AT LYING, TOO.
AND I AM THE FOOL WHO FELL IN LOVE WITH THAT MAN.
I GUESS NOW THE QUESTION IS... HOW AM I TO FACE HIM FROM HERE ON?
UM...
I'M AFRAID IT ISN'T MY PLACE TO SAY...
BUT AS LUKE'S APPRENTICE, PLEASE ALLOW ME TO SAY ONE THING...

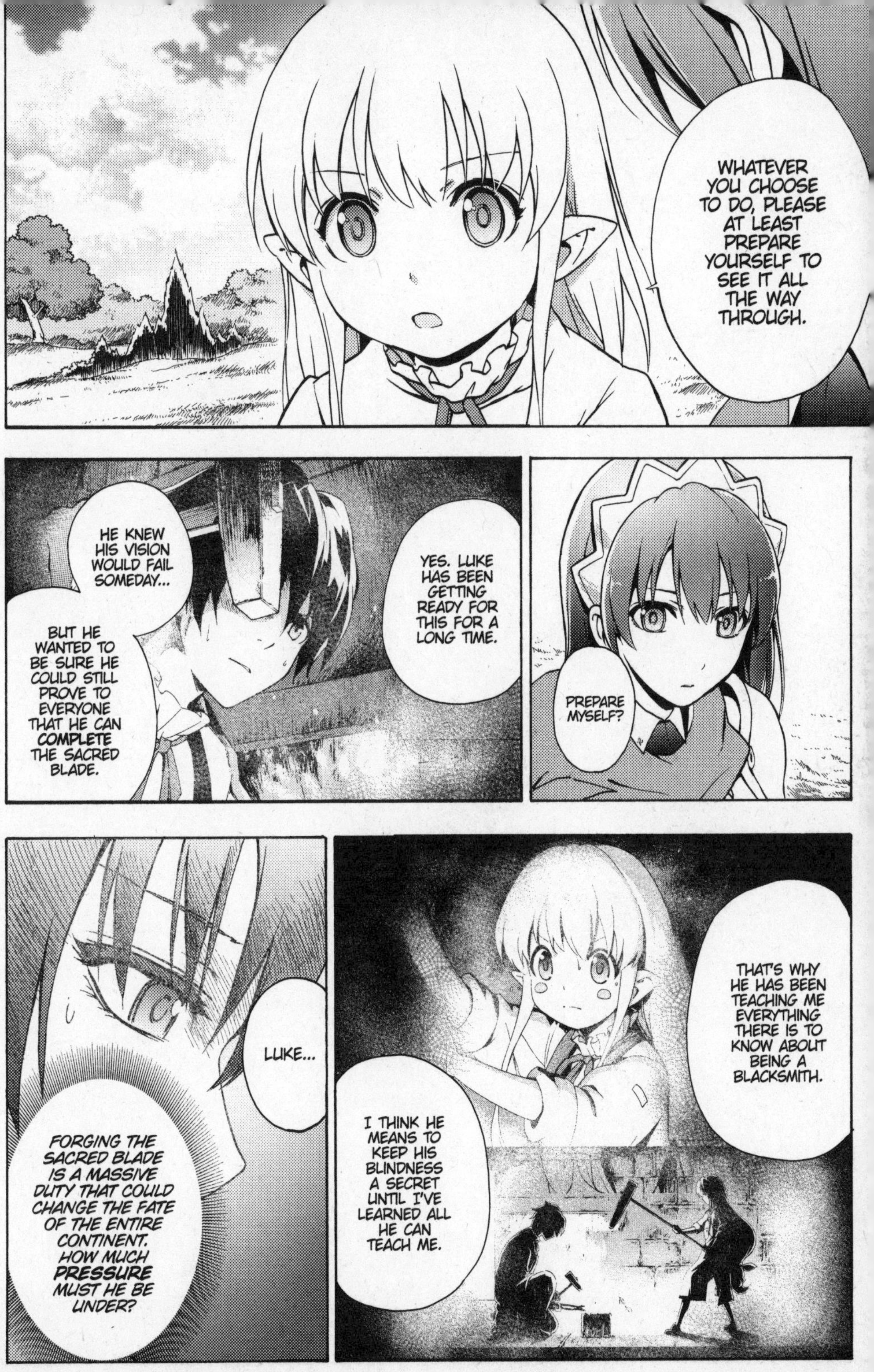
WHATEVER YOU CHOOSE TO DO, PLEASE AT LEAST PREPARE YOURSELF TO SEE IT ALL THE WAY THROUGH.
PREPARE MYSELF?
YES. LUKE HAS BEEN GETTING READY FOR THIS FOR A LONG TIME.
HE KNEW HIS VISION WOULD FAIL SOMEDAY...
BUT HE WANTED TO BE SURE HE COULD STILL PROVE TO EVERYONE THAT HE CAN **COMPLETE** THE SACRED BLADE.
THAT'S WHY HE HAS BEEN TEACHING ME EVERYTHING THERE IS TO KNOW ABOUT BEING A BLACKSMITH.
I THINK HE MEANS TO KEEP HIS BLINDNESS A SECRET UNTIL I'VE LEARNED ALL HE CAN TEACH ME.
LUKE...
FORGING THE SACRED BLADE IS A MASSIVE DUTY THAT COULD CHANGE THE FATE OF THE ENTIRE CONTINENT. HOW MUCH ***PRESSURE*** *MUST HE BE UNDER?*

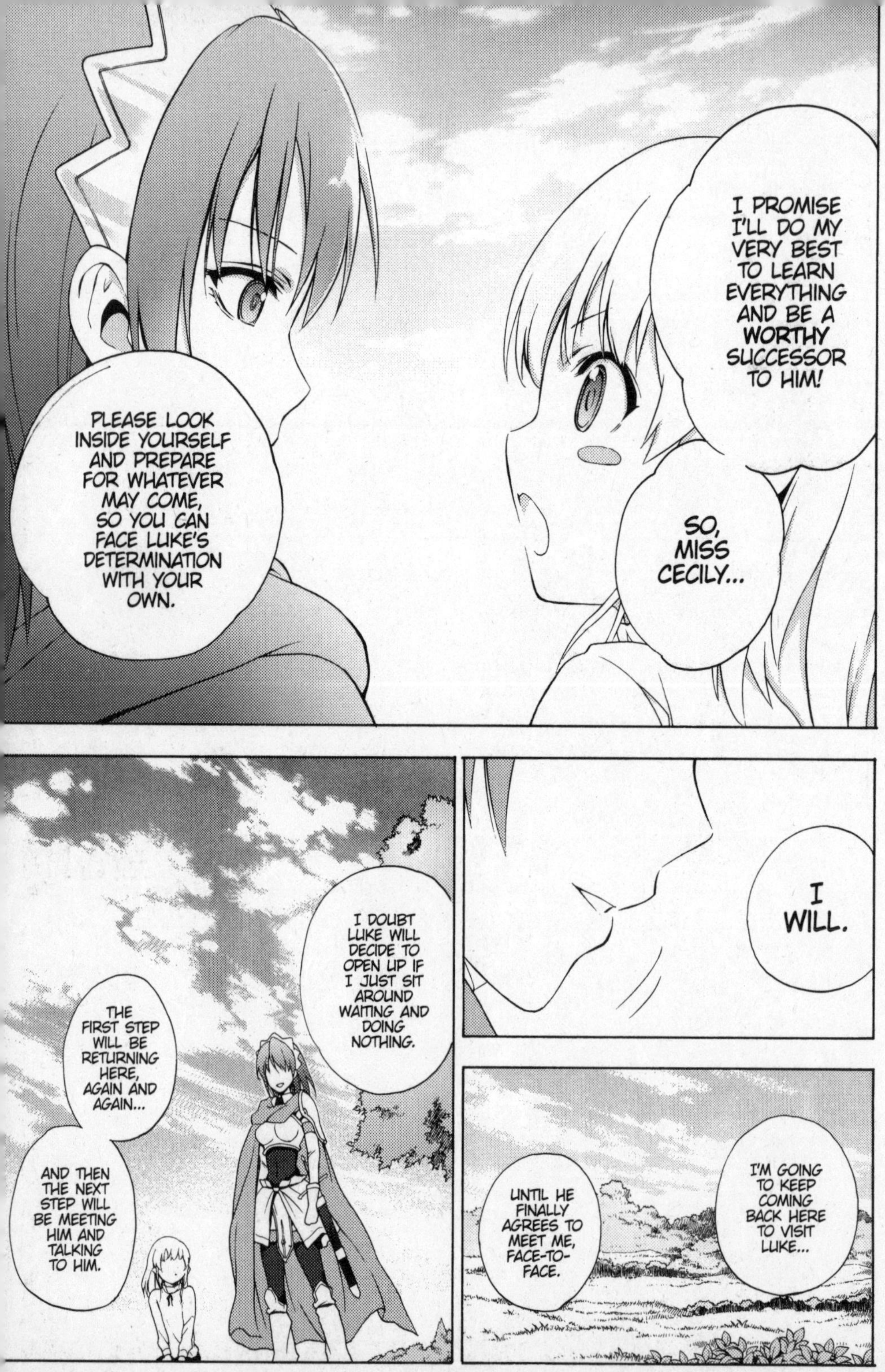
I PROMISE I'LL DO MY VERY BEST TO LEARN EVERYTHING AND BE A WORTHY SUCCESSOR TO HIM!
SO, MISS CECILY...
PLEASE LOOK INSIDE YOURSELF AND PREPARE FOR WHATEVER MAY COME, SO YOU CAN FACE LUKE'S DETERMINATION WITH YOUR OWN.
I WILL.
I'M GOING TO KEEP COMING BACK HERE TO VISIT LUKE...
UNTIL HE FINALLY AGREES TO MEET ME, FACE-TO-FACE.
I DOUBT LUKE WILL DECIDE TO OPEN UP IF I JUST SIT AROUND WAITING AND DOING NOTHING.
THE FIRST STEP WILL BE RETURNING HERE, AGAIN AND AGAIN...
AND THEN THE NEXT STEP WILL BE MEETING HIM AND TALKING TO HIM.

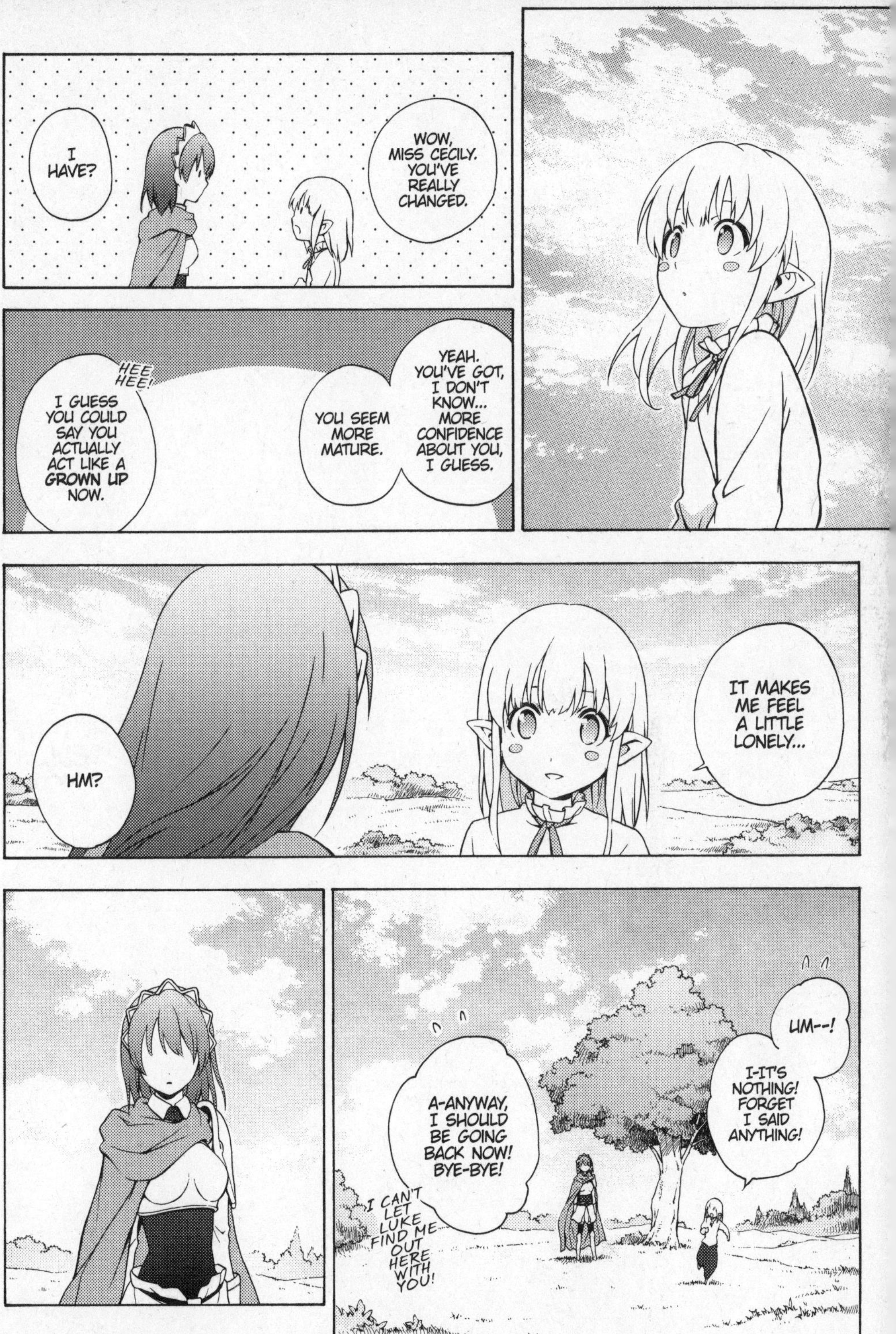
WOW, MISS CECILY. YOU'VE REALLY CHANGED.
I HAVE?
YEAH. YOU'VE GOT, I DON'T KNOW... MORE CONFIDENCE ABOUT YOU, I GUESS.
YOU SEEM MORE MATURE.
HEE HEE!
I GUESS YOU COULD SAY YOU ACTUALLY ACT LIKE A GROWN UP NOW.
IT MAKES ME FEEL A LITTLE LONELY...
HM?
UM--!
I-IT'S NOTHING! FORGET I SAID ANYTHING!
A-ANYWAY, I SHOULD BE GOING BACK NOW! BYE-BYE!
I CAN'T LET LUKE FIND ME OUT HERE WITH YOU!

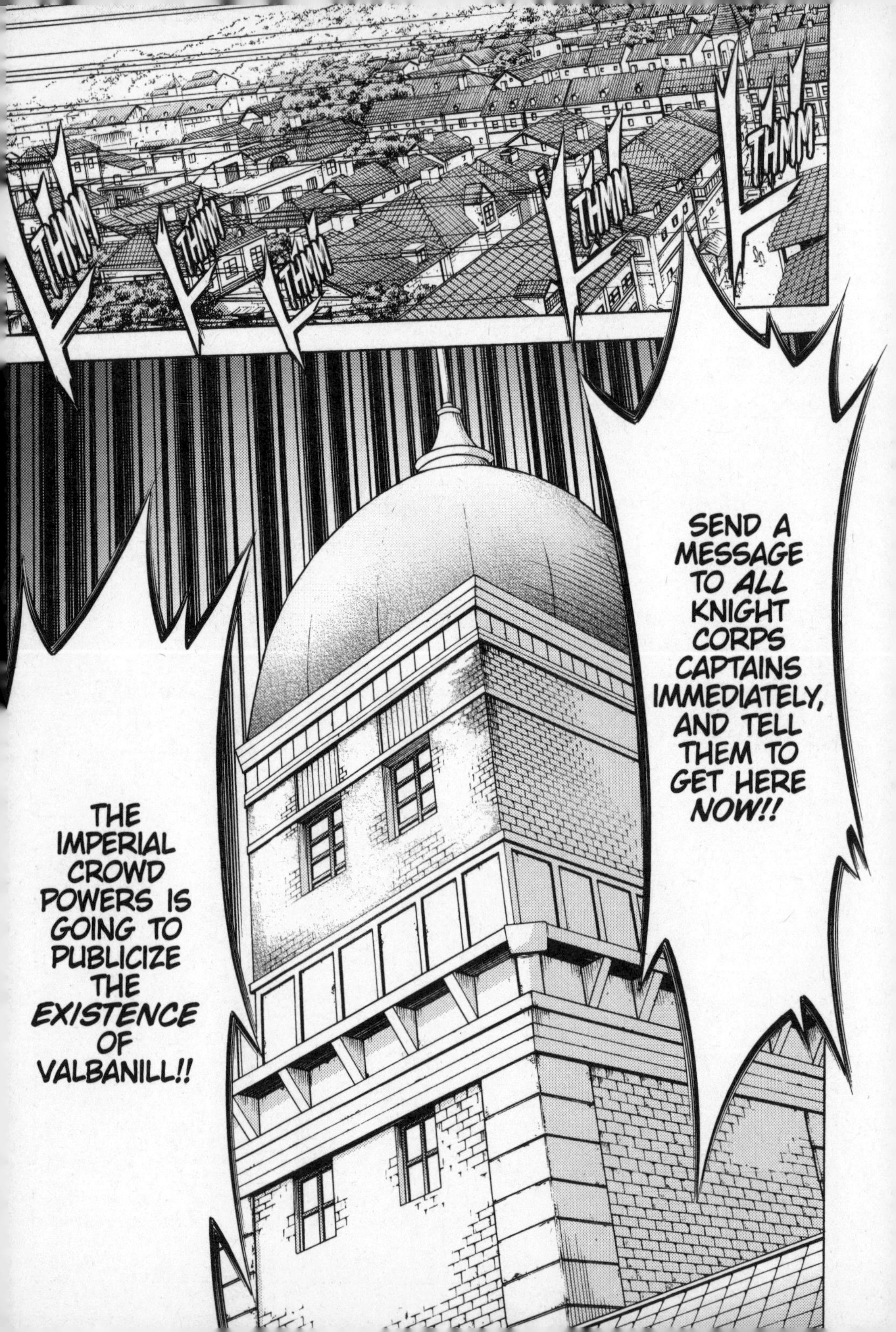
THMM
THMM
THMM
THMM
THMM
SEND A MESSAGE TO ALL KNIGHT CORPS CAPTAINS IMMEDIATELY, AND TELL THEM TO GET HERE NOW!!
THE IMPERIAL CROWD POWERS IS GOING TO PUBLICIZE THE EXISTENCE OF VALBANILL!!

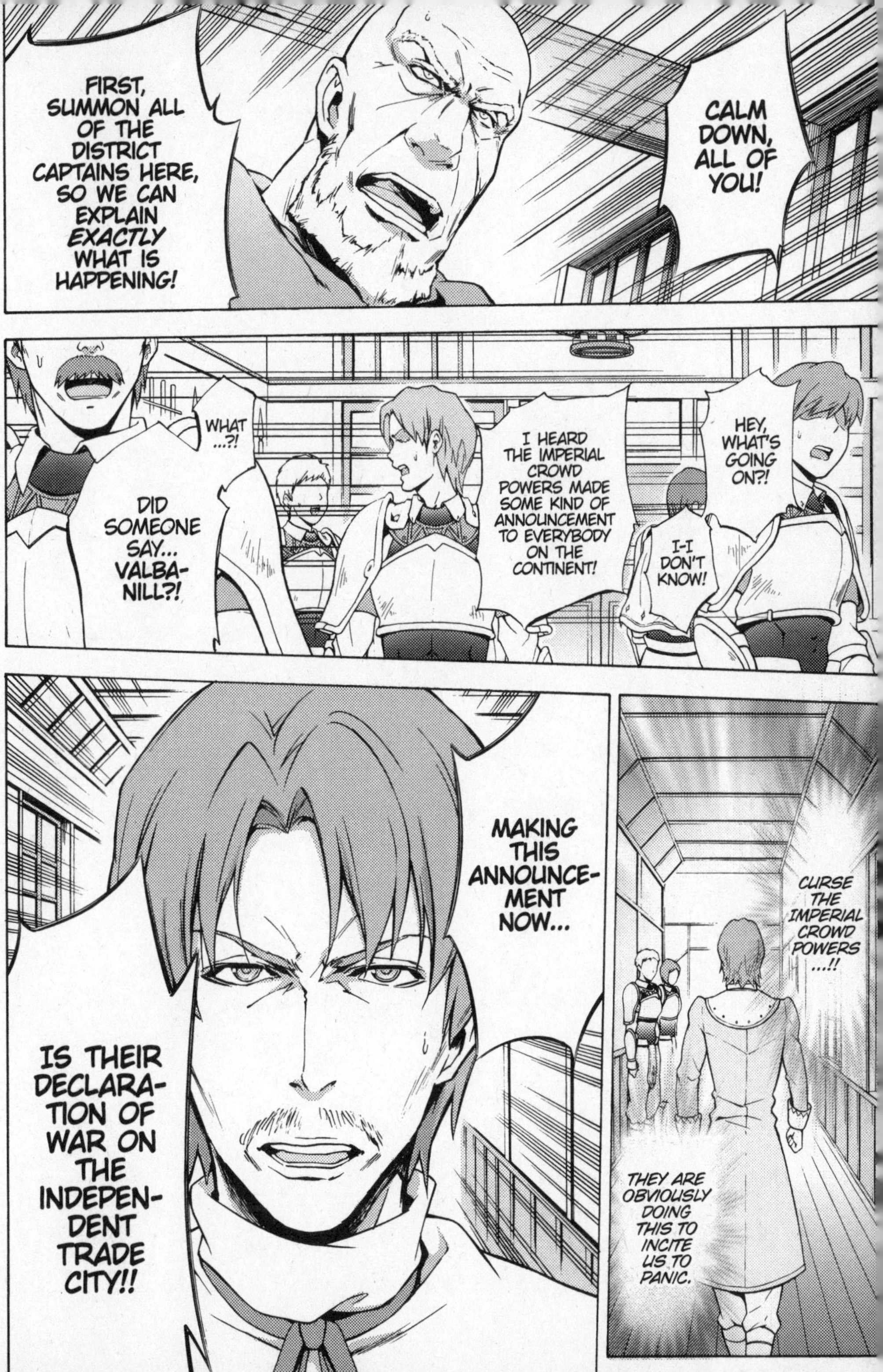
CALM DOWN, ALL OF YOU!
FIRST, SUMMON ALL OF THE DISTRICT CAPTAINS HERE, SO WE CAN EXPLAIN *EXACTLY* WHAT IS HAPPENING!
HEY, WHAT'S GOING ON?!
I-I DON'T KNOW!
I HEARD THE IMPERIAL CROWD POWERS MADE SOME KIND OF ANNOUNCEMENT TO EVERYBODY ON THE CONTINENT!
WHAT ...?!
DID SOMEONE SAY... VALBANILL?!
CURSE THE IMPERIAL CROWD POWERS ...!!
THEY ARE OBVIOUSLY DOING THIS TO INCITE US TO PANIC.
MAKING THIS ANNOUNCEMENT NOW...
IS THEIR DECLARATION OF WAR ON THE INDEPENDENT TRADE CITY!!

The Sacred Blacksmith

聖剣の刀鍛治

The Sacred Blacksmith

聖剣の刀鍛治

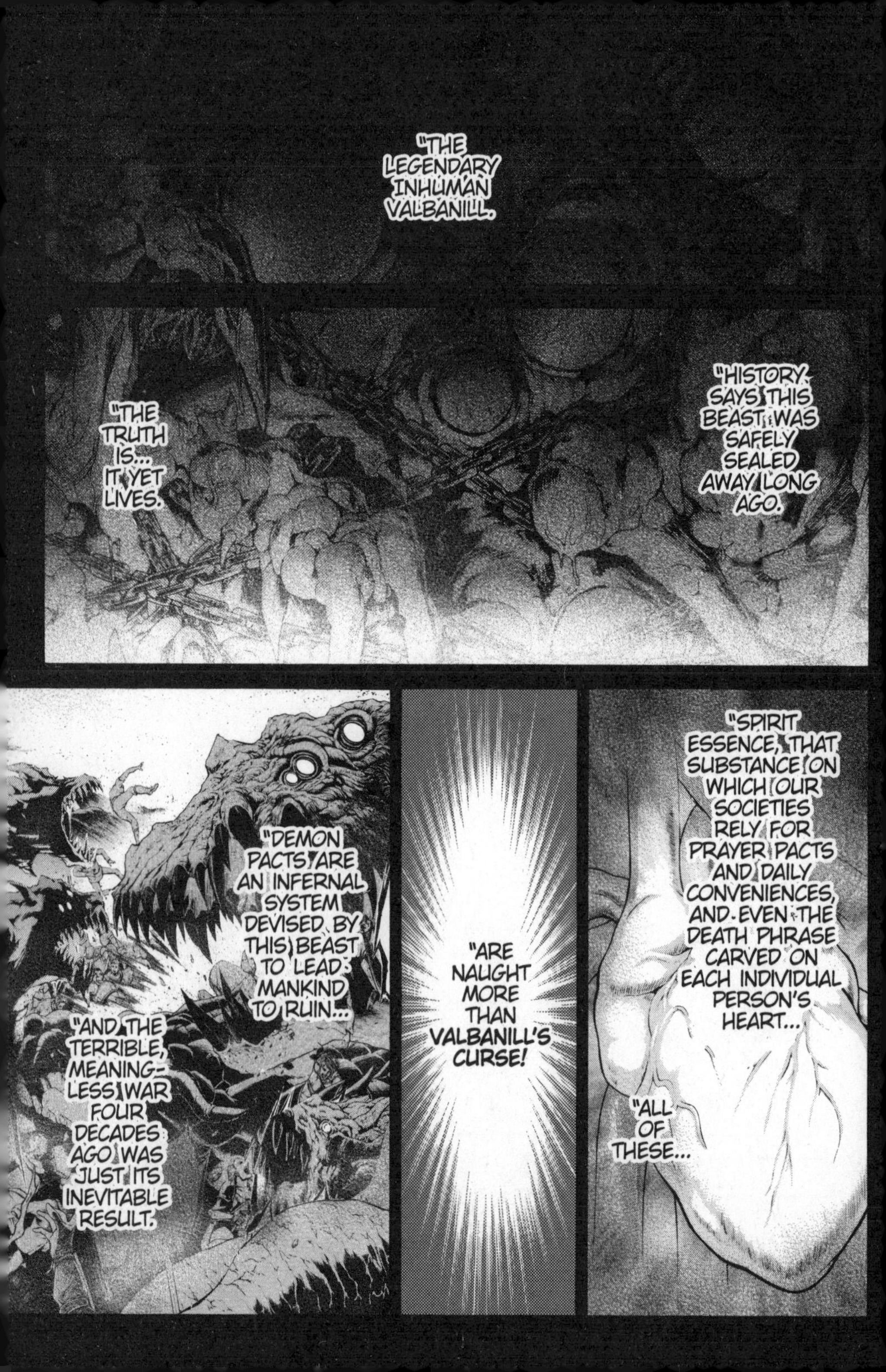
"THE LEGENDARY INHUMAN VALBANILL.
"HISTORY SAYS THIS BEAST WAS SAFELY SEALED AWAY LONG AGO.
"THE TRUTH IS... IT YET LIVES.
"SPIRIT ESSENCE, THAT SUBSTANCE ON WHICH OUR SOCIETIES RELY FOR PRAYER PACTS AND DAILY CONVENIENCES, AND EVEN THE DEATH PHRASE CARVED ON EACH INDIVIDUAL PERSON'S HEART...
"ALL OF THESE...
"ARE NAUGHT MORE THAN VALBANILL'S CURSE!
"DEMON PACTS ARE AN INFERNAL SYSTEM DEVISED BY THIS BEAST TO LEAD MANKIND TO RUIN...
"AND THE TERRIBLE, MEANING-LESS WAR FOUR DECADES AGO WAS JUST ITS INEVITABLE RESULT.

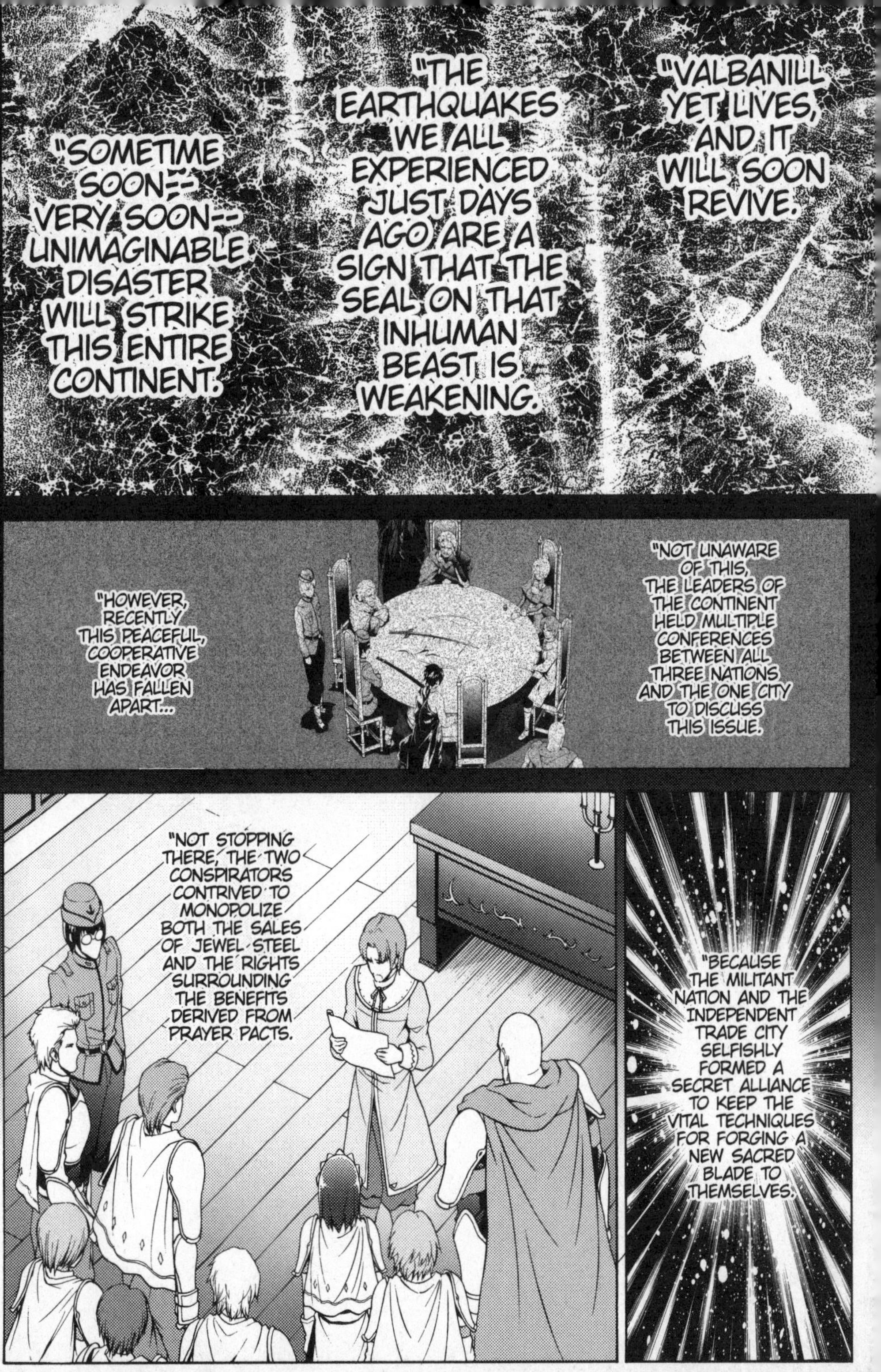
"VALBANILL YET LIVES, AND IT WILL SOON REVIVE.
"THE EARTHQUAKES WE ALL EXPERIENCED JUST DAYS AGO ARE A SIGN THAT THE SEAL ON THAT INHUMAN BEAST IS WEAKENING.
"SOMETIME SOON-- VERY SOON-- UNIMAGINABLE DISASTER WILL STRIKE THIS ENTIRE CONTINENT.
"NOT UNAWARE OF THIS, THE LEADERS OF THE CONTINENT HELD MULTIPLE CONFERENCES BETWEEN ALL THREE NATIONS AND THE ONE CITY TO DISCUSS THIS ISSUE.
"HOWEVER, RECENTLY THIS PEACEFUL, COOPERATIVE ENDEAVOR HAS FALLEN APART...
"BECAUSE THE MILITANT NATION AND THE INDEPENDENT TRADE CITY SELFISHLY FORMED A SECRET ALLIANCE TO KEEP THE VITAL TECHNIQUES FOR FORGING A NEW SACRED BLADE TO THEMSELVES.
"NOT STOPPING THERE, THE TWO CONSPIRATORS CONTRIVED TO MONOPOLIZE BOTH THE SALES OF JEWEL STEEL AND THE RIGHTS SURROUNDING THE BENEFITS DERIVED FROM PRAYER PACTS.

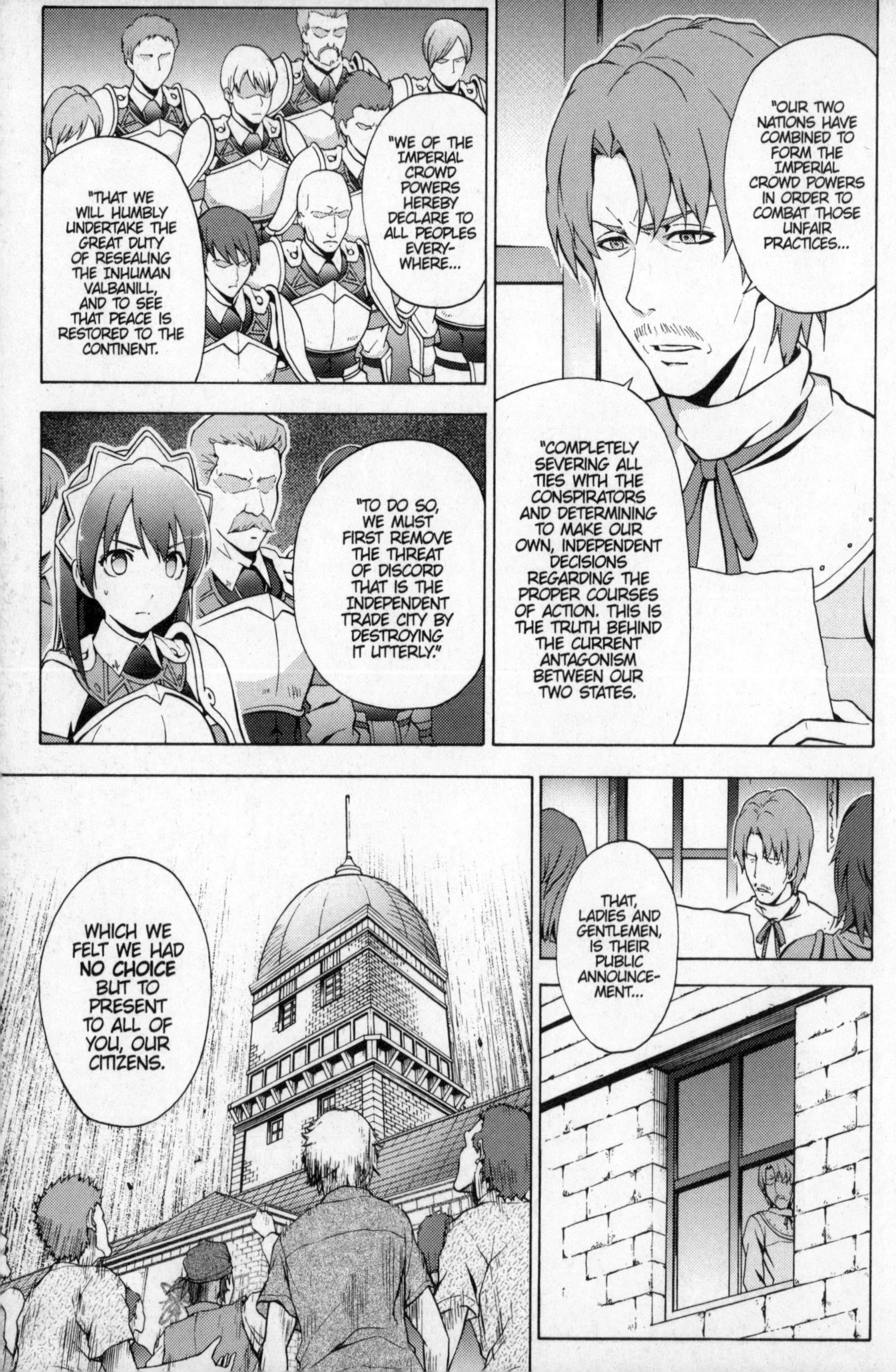
"OUR TWO NATIONS HAVE COMBINED TO FORM THE IMPERIAL CROWD POWERS IN ORDER TO COMBAT THOSE UNFAIR PRACTICES...
"COMPLETELY SEVERING ALL TIES WITH THE CONSPIRATORS AND DETERMINING TO MAKE OUR OWN, INDEPENDENT DECISIONS REGARDING THE PROPER COURSES OF ACTION. THIS IS THE TRUTH BEHIND THE CURRENT ANTAGONISM BETWEEN OUR TWO STATES.
"WE OF THE IMPERIAL CROWD POWERS HEREBY DECLARE TO ALL PEOPLES EVERY-WHERE...
"THAT WE WILL HUMBLY UNDERTAKE THE GREAT DUTY OF RESEALING THE INHUMAN VALBANILL, AND TO SEE THAT PEACE IS RESTORED TO THE CONTINENT.
"TO DO SO, WE MUST FIRST REMOVE THE THREAT OF DISCORD THAT IS THE INDEPENDENT TRADE CITY BY DESTROYING IT UTTERLY."
THAT, LADIES AND GENTLEMEN, IS THEIR PUBLIC ANNOUNCE-MENT...
WHICH WE FELT WE HAD NO CHOICE BUT TO PRESENT TO ALL OF YOU, OUR CITIZENS.

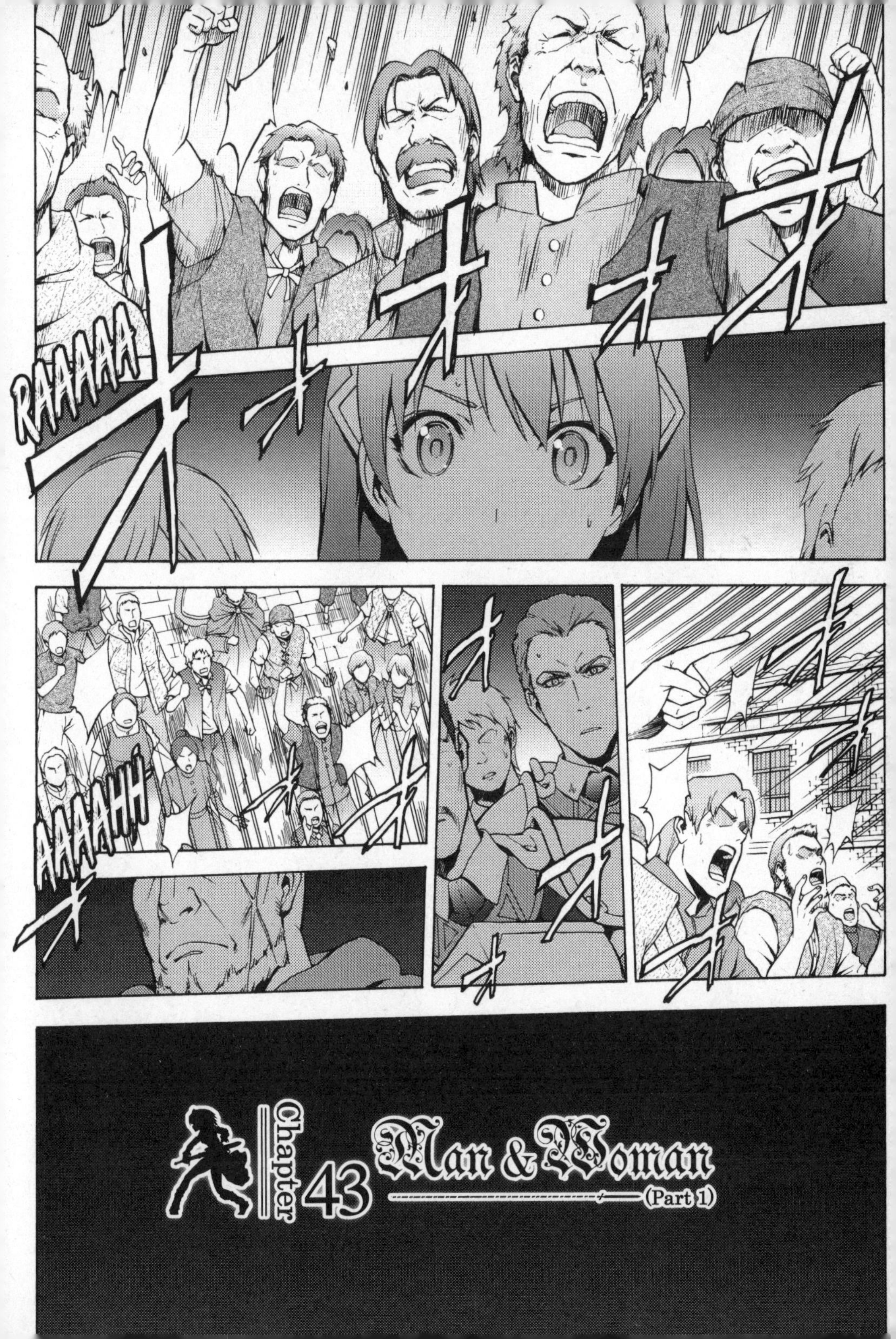
RAAAAA
AAAAHH

Chapter 43 Man & Woman (Part 1)

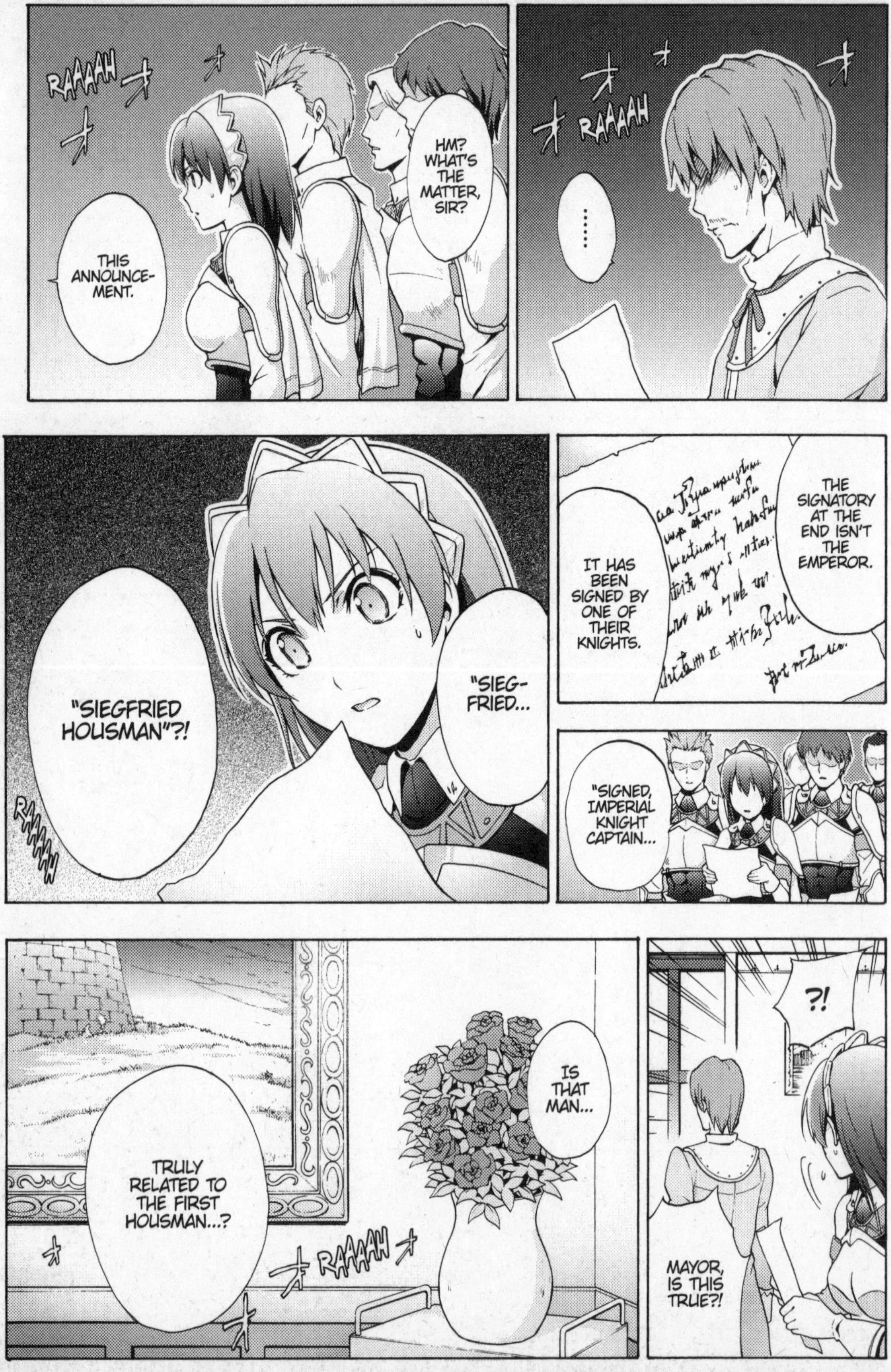
オ
オ
オ RAAAAH
......
RAAAAH オ
オ
HM? WHAT'S THE MATTER, SIR?
THIS ANNOUNCEMENT.
THE SIGNATORY AT THE END ISN'T THE EMPEROR.
IT HAS BEEN SIGNED BY ONE OF THEIR KNIGHTS.
"SIGNED, IMPERIAL KNIGHT CAPTAIN...
"SIEG-FRIED...
"SIEGFRIED HOUSMAN"?!
RAAAAH
?!
MAYOR, IS THIS TRUE?!
IS THAT MAN...
TRULY RELATED TO THE FIRST HOUSMAN...?
オ RAAAAH オ
オ

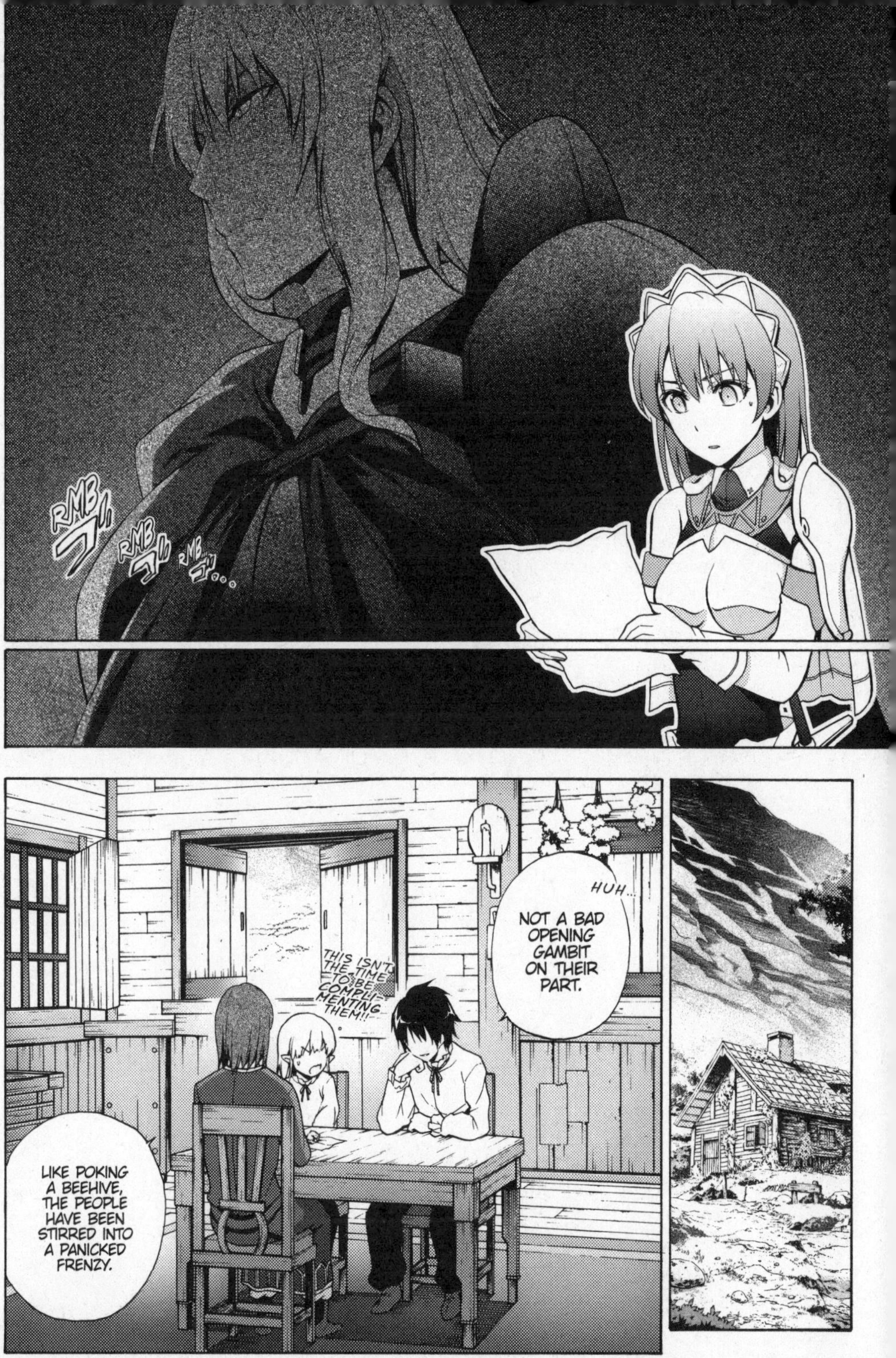
RMB
RMB
RMB...
HUH...
NOT A BAD OPENING GAMBIT ON THEIR PART.
THIS ISN'T THE TIME TO BE COMPLI-MENTING THEM!!
LIKE POKING A BEEHIVE, THE PEOPLE HAVE BEEN STIRRED INTO A PANICKED FRENZY.

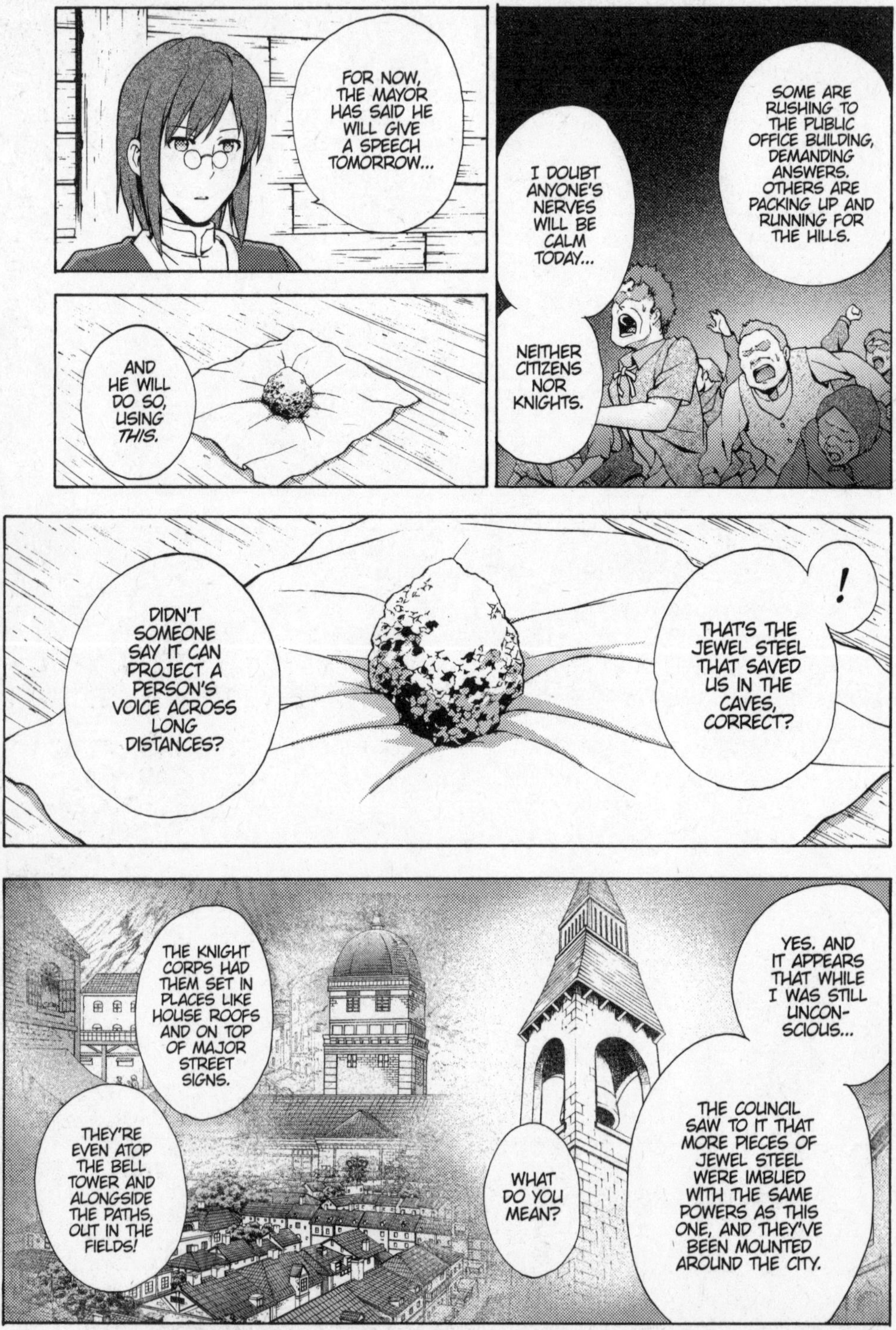
SOME ARE RUSHING TO THE PUBLIC OFFICE BUILDING, DEMANDING ANSWERS. OTHERS ARE PACKING UP AND RUNNING FOR THE HILLS.
I DOUBT ANYONE'S NERVES WILL BE CALM TODAY...
NEITHER CITIZENS NOR KNIGHTS.
FOR NOW, THE MAYOR HAS SAID HE WILL GIVE A SPEECH TOMORROW...
AND HE WILL DO SO, USING *THIS.*
!
THAT'S THE JEWEL STEEL THAT SAVED US IN THE CAVES, CORRECT?
DIDN'T SOMEONE SAY IT CAN PROJECT A PERSON'S VOICE ACROSS LONG DISTANCES?
YES. AND IT APPEARS THAT WHILE I WAS STILL UNCON-SCIOUS...
THE COUNCIL SAW TO IT THAT MORE PIECES OF JEWEL STEEL WERE IMBUED WITH THE SAME POWERS AS THIS ONE, AND THEY'VE BEEN MOUNTED AROUND THE CITY.
WHAT DO YOU MEAN?
THE KNIGHT CORPS HAD THEM SET IN PLACES LIKE HOUSE ROOFS AND ON TOP OF MAJOR STREET SIGNS.
THEY'RE EVEN ATOP THE BELL TOWER AND ALONGSIDE THE PATHS, OUT IN THE FIELDS!

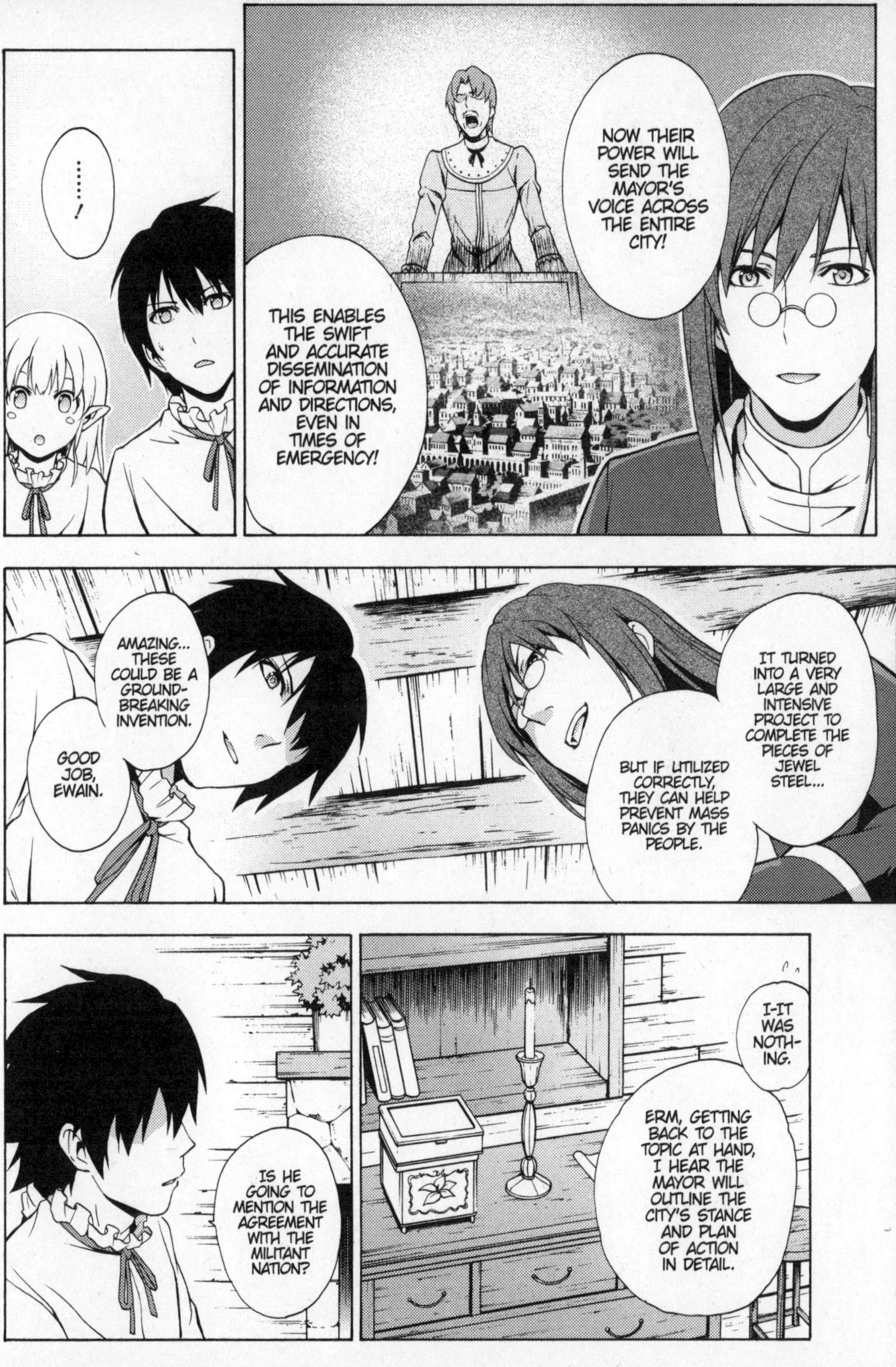
NOW THEIR POWER WILL SEND THE MAYOR'S VOICE ACROSS THE ENTIRE CITY!
THIS ENABLES THE SWIFT AND ACCURATE DISSEMINATION OF INFORMATION AND DIRECTIONS, EVEN IN TIMES OF EMERGENCY!
......!
IT TURNED INTO A VERY LARGE AND INTENSIVE PROJECT TO COMPLETE THE PIECES OF JEWEL STEEL...
BUT IF UTILIZED CORRECTLY, THEY CAN HELP PREVENT MASS PANICS BY THE PEOPLE.
AMAZING... THESE COULD BE A GROUND-BREAKING INVENTION.
GOOD JOB, EWAIN.
I-IT WAS NOTH-ING.
ERM, GETTING BACK TO THE TOPIC AT HAND, I HEAR THE MAYOR WILL OUTLINE THE CITY'S STANCE AND PLAN OF ACTION IN DETAIL.
IS HE GOING TO MENTION THE AGREEMENT WITH THE MILITANT NATION?

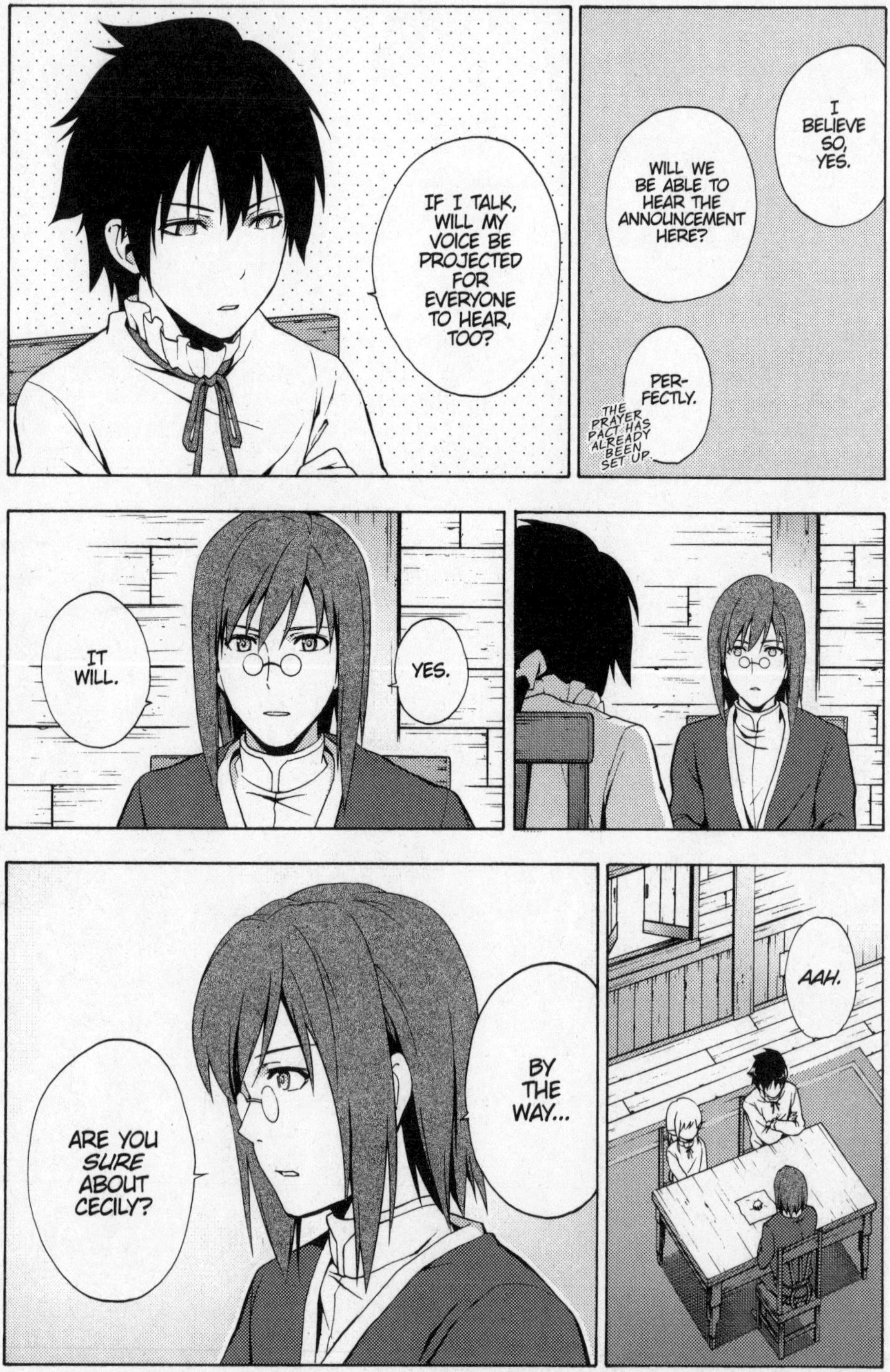
I BELIEVE SO, YES.
WILL WE BE ABLE TO HEAR THE ANNOUNCEMENT HERE?
PER-FECTLY.
THE PRAYER PACT HAS ALREADY BEEN SET UP.
IF I TALK, WILL MY VOICE BE PROJECTED FOR EVERYONE TO HEAR, TOO?
YES.
IT WILL.
AAH.
BY THE WAY...
ARE YOU SURE ABOUT CECILY?

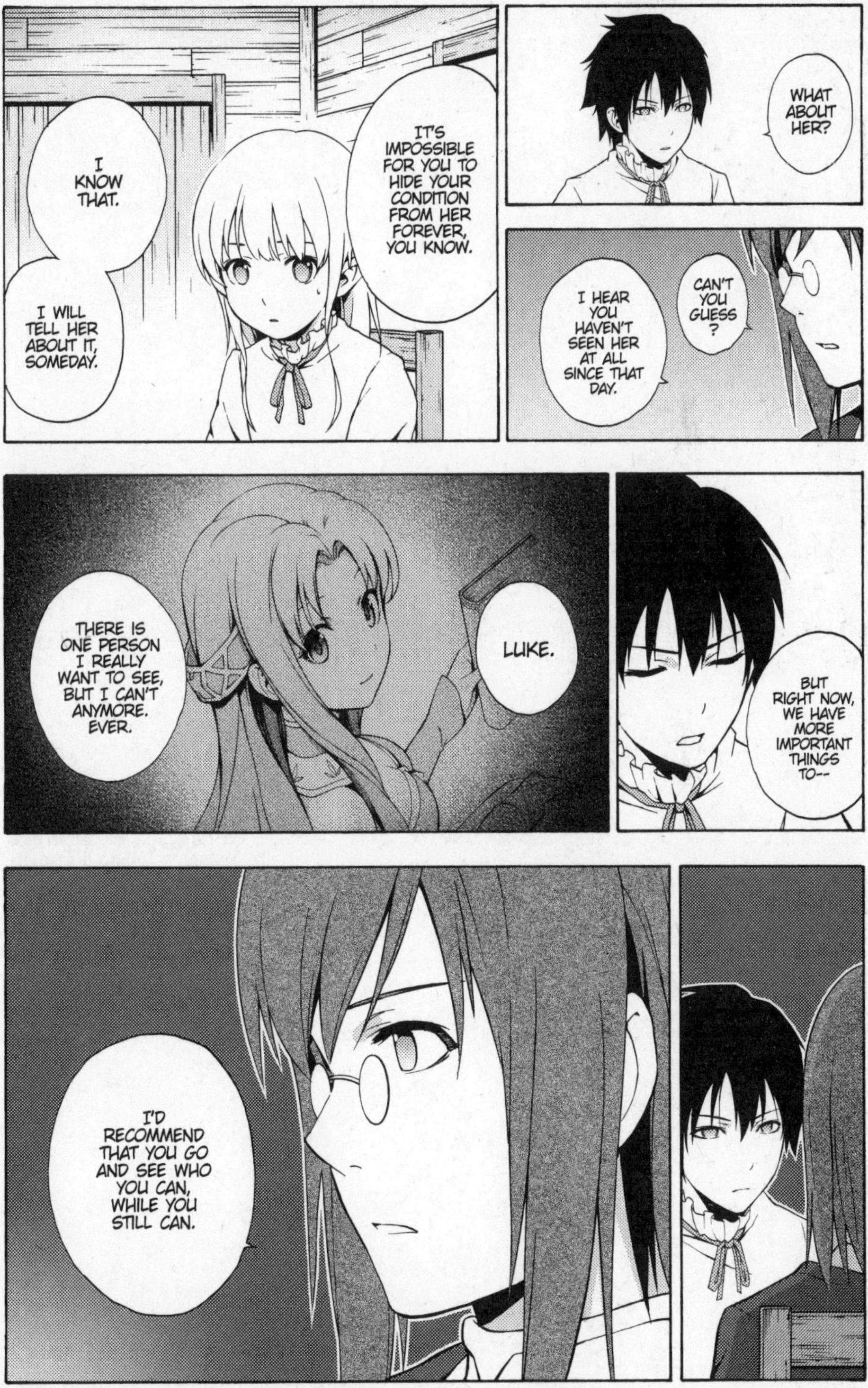
WHAT ABOUT HER?
CAN'T YOU GUESS?
I HEAR YOU HAVEN'T SEEN HER AT ALL SINCE THAT DAY.
IT'S IMPOSSIBLE FOR YOU TO HIDE YOUR CONDITION FROM HER FOREVER, YOU KNOW.
I KNOW THAT.
I WILL TELL HER ABOUT IT, SOMEDAY.
BUT RIGHT NOW, WE HAVE MORE IMPORTANT THINGS TO--
LUKE.
THERE IS ONE PERSON I REALLY WANT TO SEE, BUT I CAN'T ANYMORE. EVER.
I'D RECOMMEND THAT YOU GO AND SEE WHO YOU CAN, WHILE YOU STILL CAN.

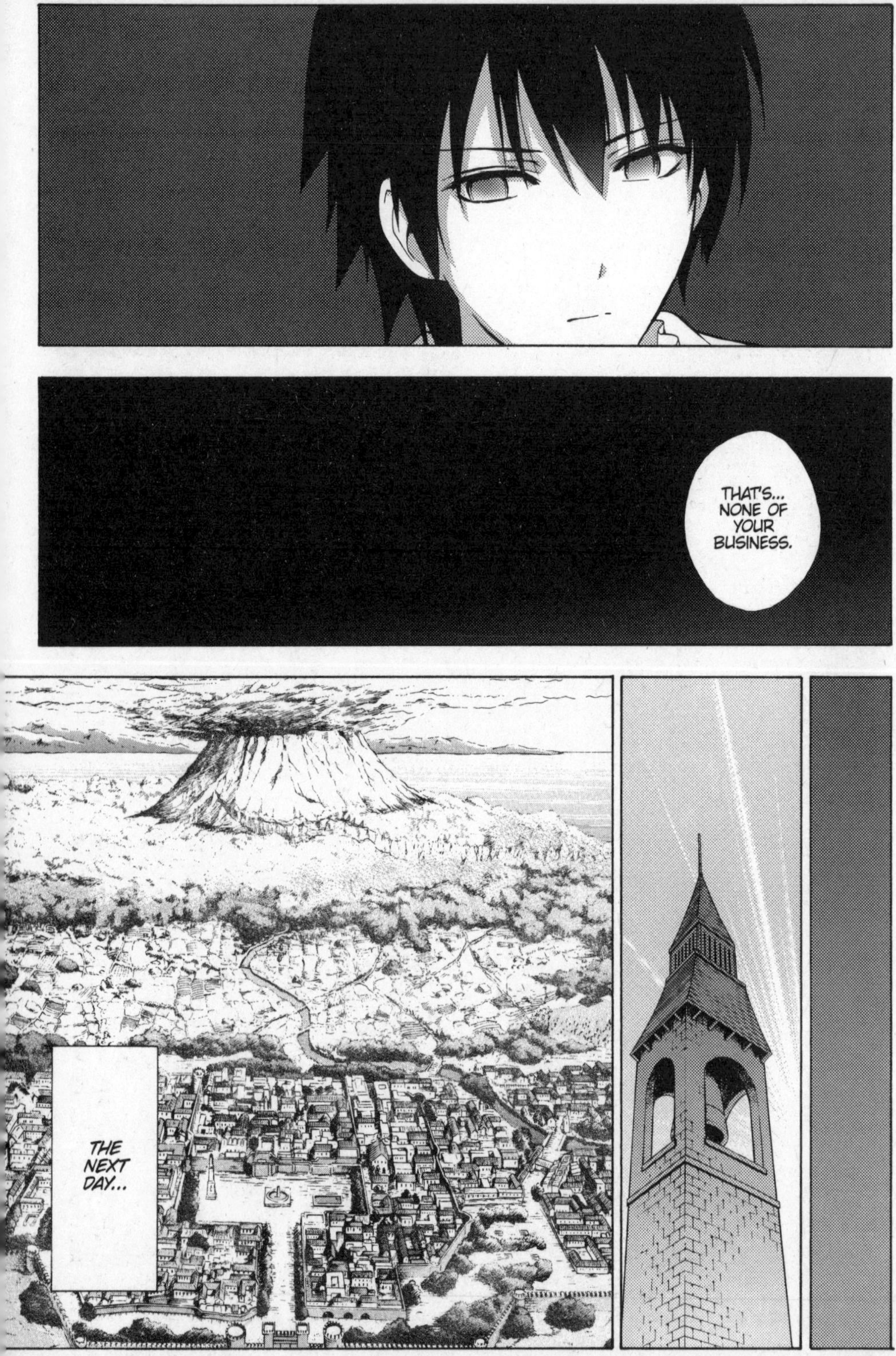
THAT'S... NONE OF YOUR BUSINESS.
THE NEXT DAY...

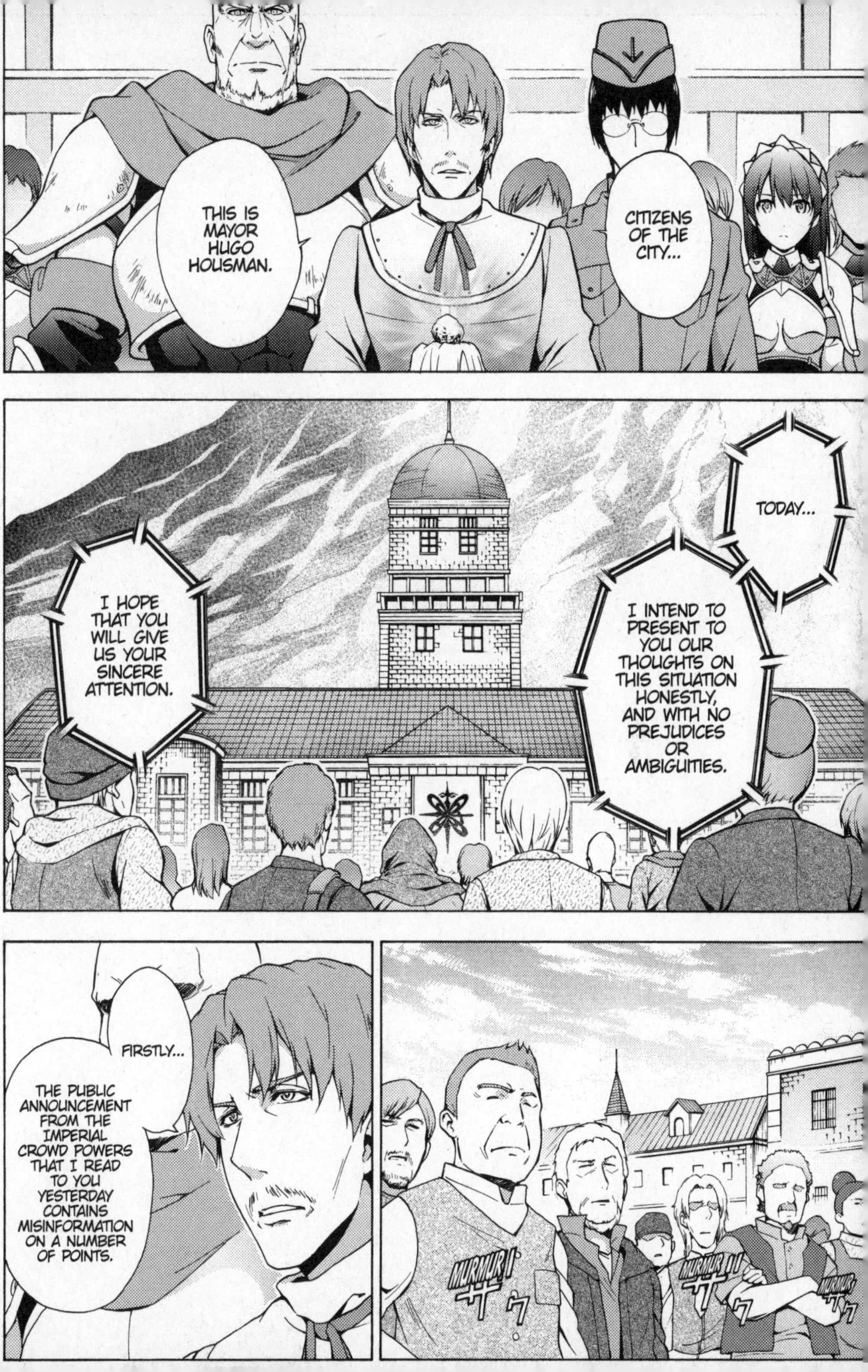
CITIZENS OF THE CITY...
THIS IS MAYOR HUGO HOUSMAN.
TODAY...
I INTEND TO PRESENT TO YOU OUR THOUGHTS ON THIS SITUATION HONESTLY, AND WITH NO PREJUDICES OR AMBIGUITIES.
I HOPE THAT YOU WILL GIVE US YOUR SINCERE ATTENTION.
MURMUR
MURMUR
MURMUR
FIRSTLY...
THE PUBLIC ANNOUNCEMENT FROM THE IMPERIAL CROWD POWERS THAT I READ TO YOU YESTERDAY CONTAINS MISINFORMATION ON A NUMBER OF POINTS.

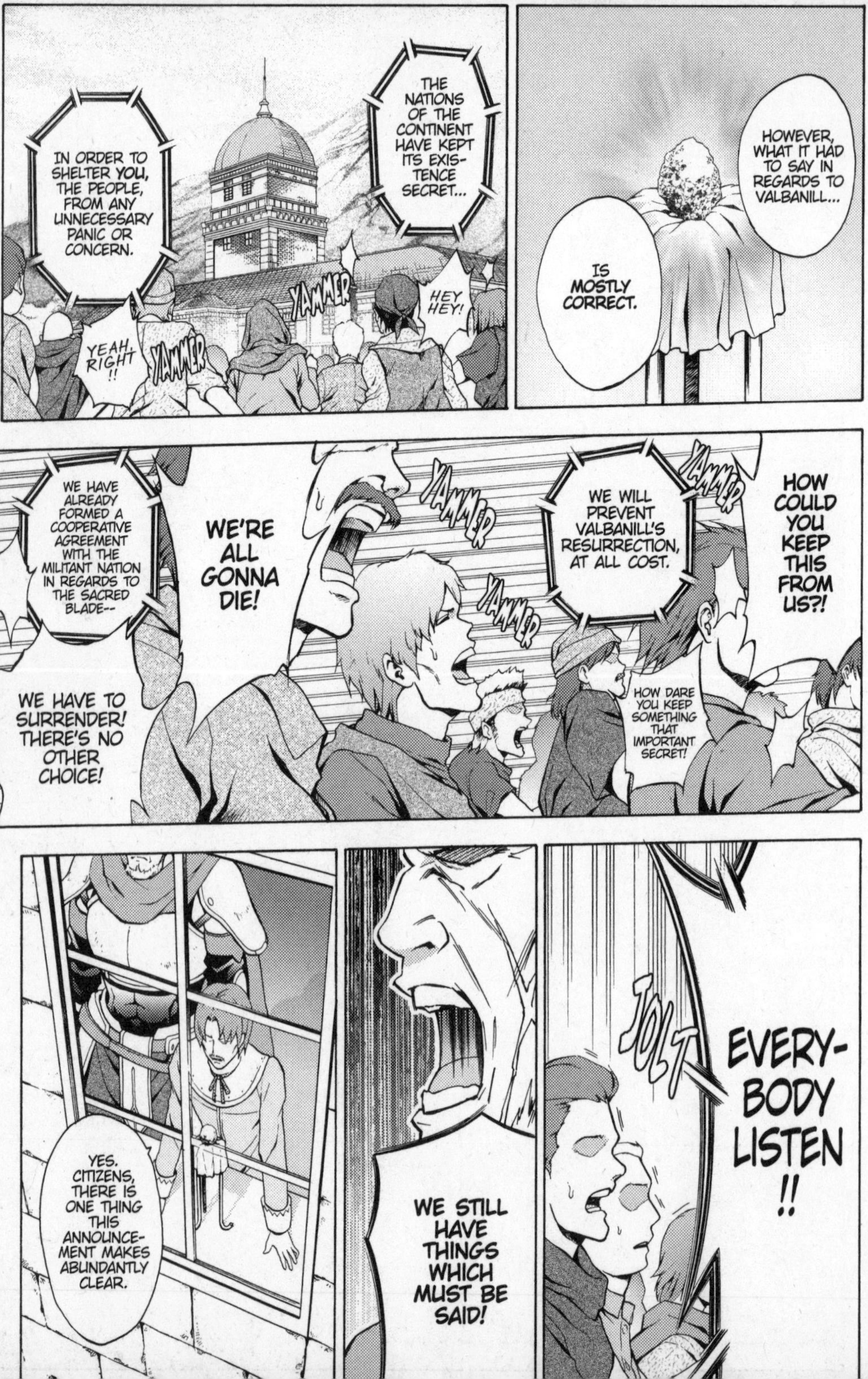
HOWEVER, WHAT IT HAD TO SAY IN REGARDS TO VALBANILL...
IS MOSTLY CORRECT.
THE NATIONS OF THE CONTINENT HAVE KEPT ITS EXISTENCE SECRET...
HEY HEY!
YAMMER
IN ORDER TO SHELTER YOU, THE PEOPLE, FROM ANY UNNECESSARY PANIC OR CONCERN.
YAMMER
YEAH, RIGHT!!
HOW COULD YOU KEEP THIS FROM US?!
YAMMER
WE WILL PREVENT VALBANILL'S RESURRECTION, AT ALL COST.
YAMMER
HOW DARE YOU KEEP SOMETHING THAT IMPORTANT SECRET!
YAMMER
WE'RE ALL GONNA DIE!
WE HAVE ALREADY FORMED A COOPERATIVE AGREEMENT WITH THE MILITANT NATION IN REGARDS TO THE SACRED BLADE--
WE HAVE TO SURRENDER! THERE'S NO OTHER CHOICE!
JOLT
EVERYBODY LISTEN!!
WE STILL HAVE THINGS WHICH MUST BE SAID!
YES. CITIZENS, THERE IS ONE THING THIS ANNOUNCEMENT MAKES ABUNDANTLY CLEAR.

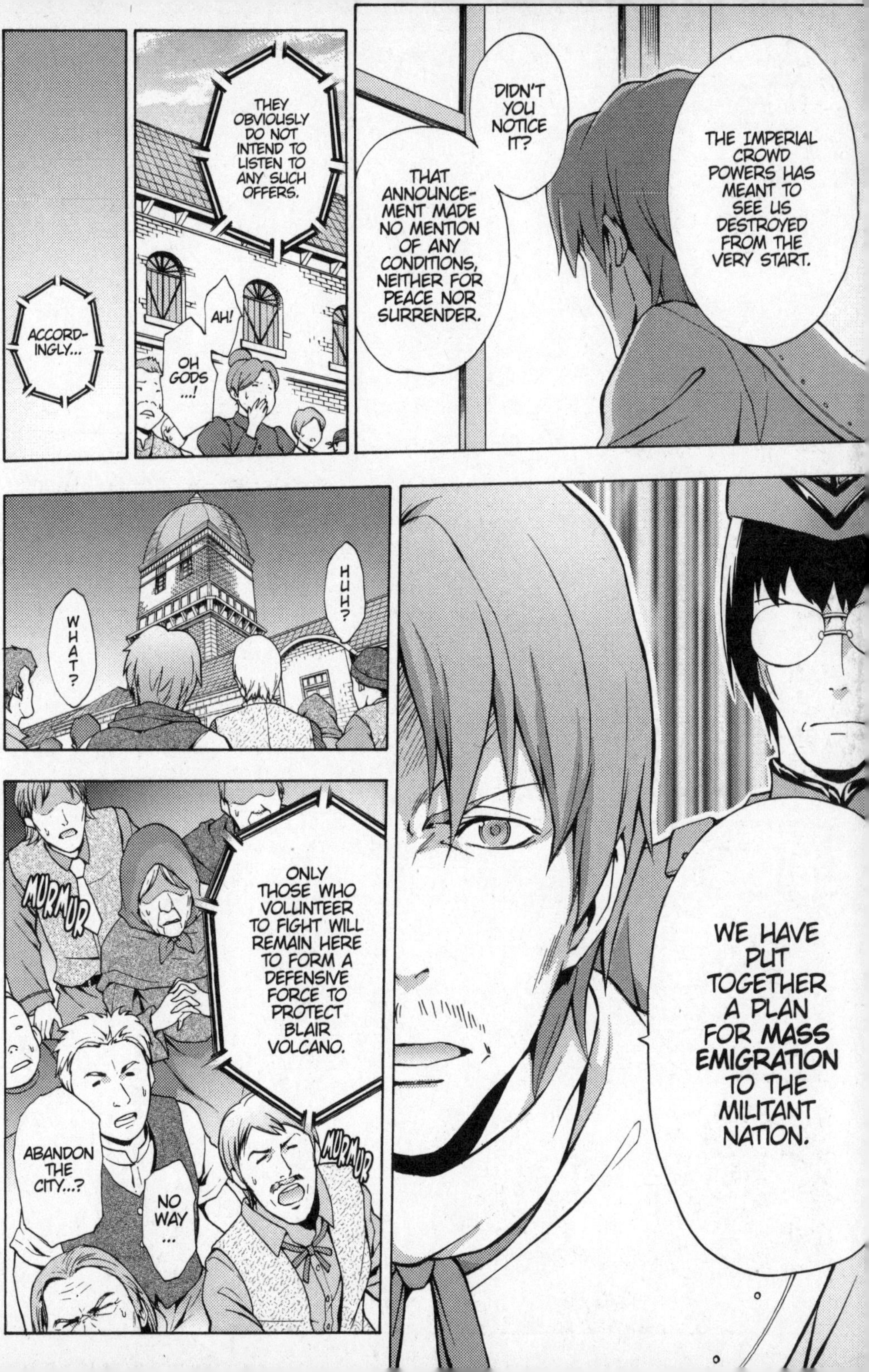
THE IMPERIAL CROWD POWERS HAS MEANT TO SEE US DESTROYED FROM THE VERY START.
DIDN'T YOU NOTICE IT?
THAT ANNOUNCEMENT MADE NO MENTION OF ANY CONDITIONS, NEITHER FOR PEACE NOR SURRENDER.
THEY OBVIOUSLY DO NOT INTEND TO LISTEN TO ANY SUCH OFFERS.
AH!
OH GODS ...!
ACCORDINGLY...
WE HAVE PUT TOGETHER A PLAN FOR MASS EMIGRATION TO THE MILITANT NATION.
HUH?
WHAT?
ONLY THOSE WHO VOLUNTEER TO FIGHT WILL REMAIN HERE TO FORM A DEFENSIVE FORCE TO PROTECT BLAIR VOLCANO.
MURMUR
MURMUR
ABANDON THE CITY...?
NO WAY ...

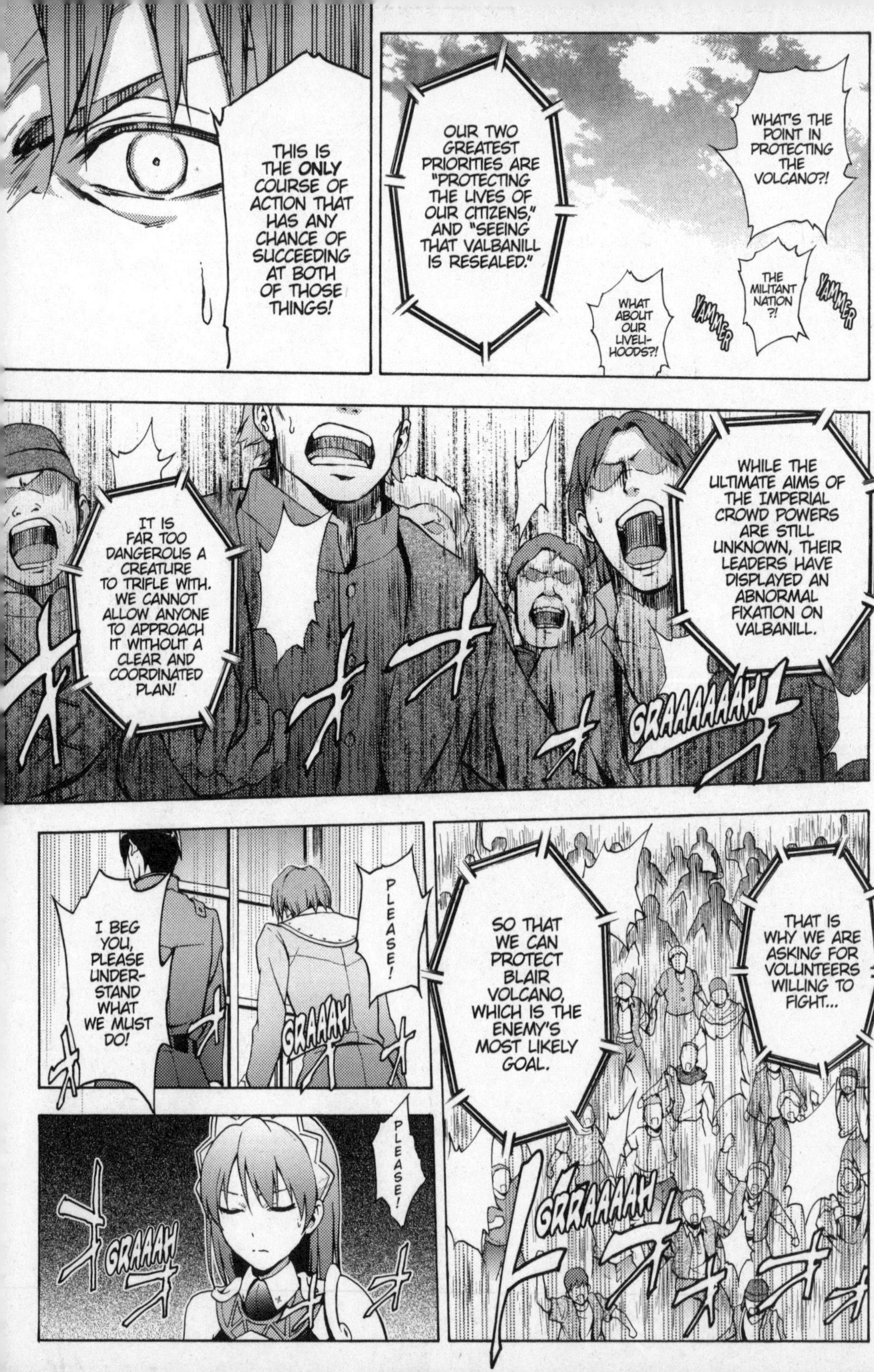
WHAT'S THE POINT IN PROTECTING THE VOLCANO?!
YAMMER
THE MILITANT NATION?!
YAMMER
WHAT ABOUT OUR LIVELI-HOODS?!
OUR TWO GREATEST PRIORITIES ARE "PROTECTING THE LIVES OF OUR CITIZENS," AND "SEEING THAT VALBANILL IS RESEALED."
THIS IS THE ONLY COURSE OF ACTION THAT HAS ANY CHANCE OF SUCCEEDING AT BOTH OF THOSE THINGS!
WHILE THE ULTIMATE AIMS OF THE IMPERIAL CROWD POWERS ARE STILL UNKNOWN, THEIR LEADERS HAVE DISPLAYED AN ABNORMAL FIXATION ON VALBANILL.
GRAAAAAAH
IT IS FAR TOO DANGEROUS A CREATURE TO TRIFLE WITH. WE CANNOT ALLOW ANYONE TO APPROACH IT WITHOUT A CLEAR AND COORDINATED PLAN!
THAT IS WHY WE ARE ASKING FOR VOLUNTEERS WILLING TO FIGHT...
SO THAT WE CAN PROTECT BLAIR VOLCANO, WHICH IS THE ENEMY'S MOST LIKELY GOAL.
GRRAAAAAH
PLEASE!
I BEG YOU, PLEASE UNDER-STAND WHAT WE MUST DO!
GRAAAH
PLEASE!
GRAAAH

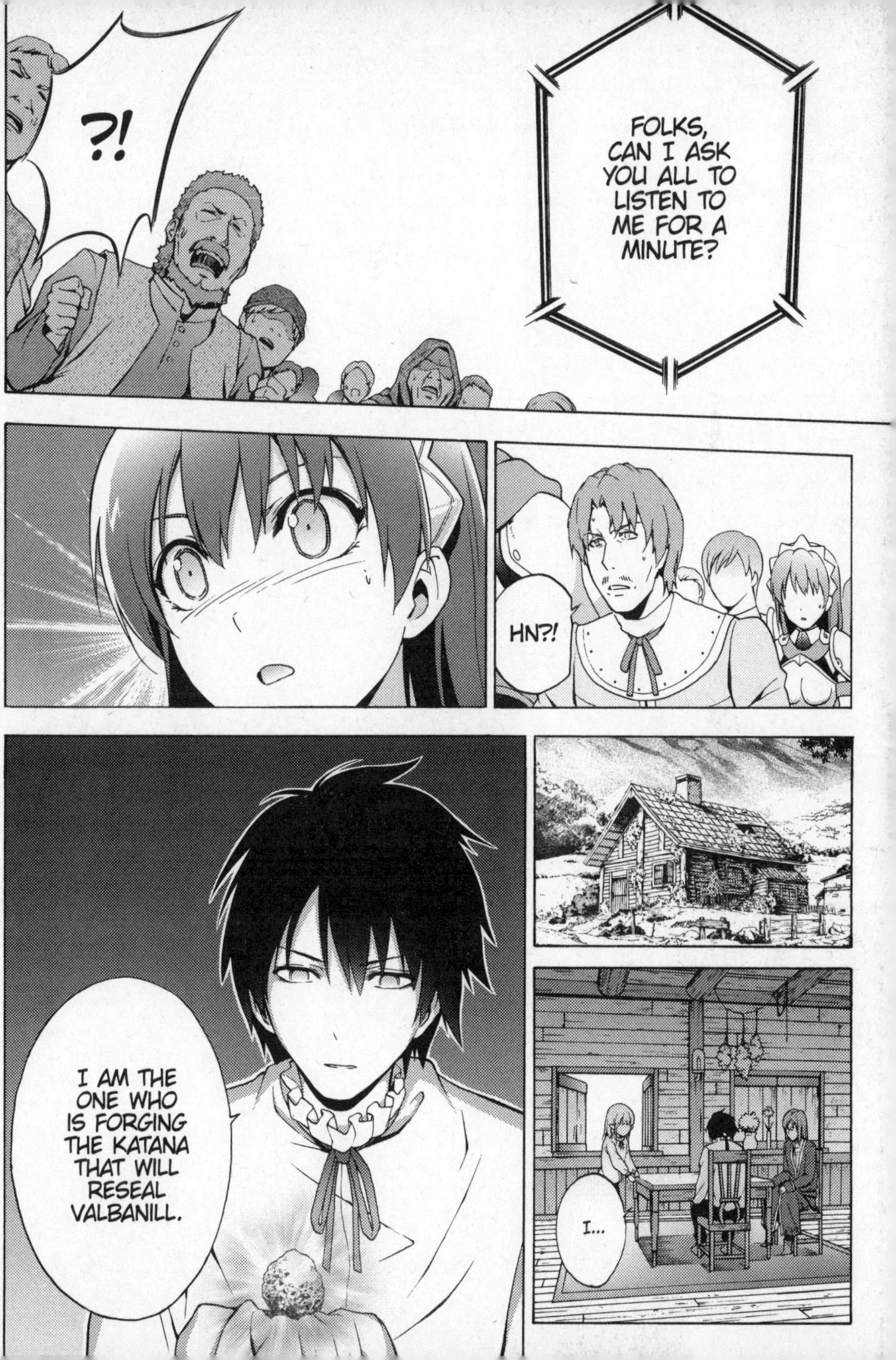
FOLKS, CAN I ASK YOU ALL TO LISTEN TO ME FOR A MINUTE?
?!
HN?!
I...
I AM THE ONE WHO IS FORGING THE KATANA THAT WILL RESEAL VALBANILL.

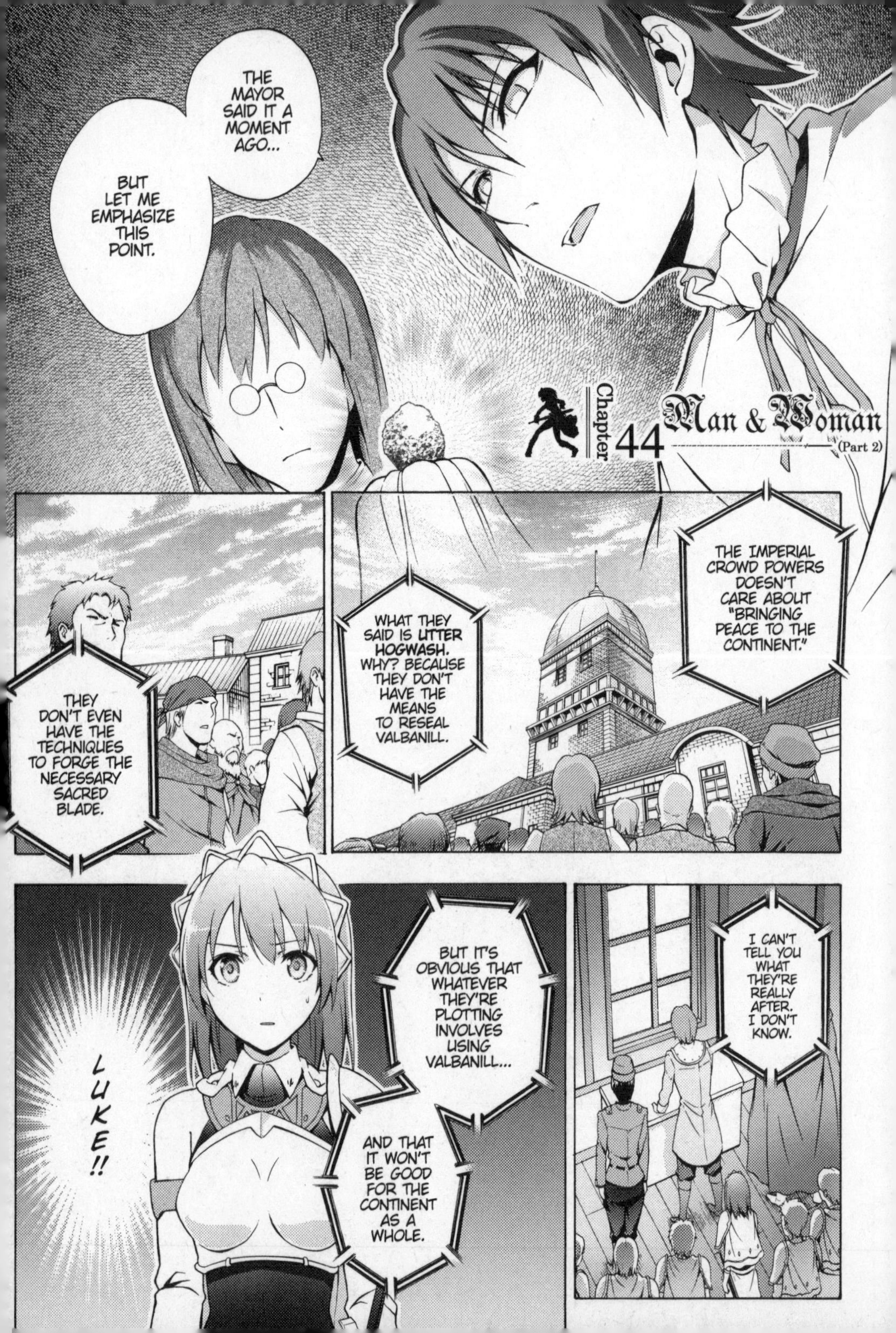
THE MAYOR SAID IT A MOMENT AGO...
BUT LET ME EMPHASIZE THIS POINT.
Chapter 44
Man & Woman (Part 2)
THE IMPERIAL CROWD POWERS DOESN'T CARE ABOUT "BRINGING PEACE TO THE CONTINENT."
WHAT THEY SAID IS UTTER HOGWASH. WHY? BECAUSE THEY DON'T HAVE THE MEANS TO RESEAL VALBANILL.
THEY DON'T EVEN HAVE THE TECHNIQUES TO FORGE THE NECESSARY SACRED BLADE.
I CAN'T TELL YOU WHAT THEY'RE REALLY AFTER. I DON'T KNOW.
BUT IT'S OBVIOUS THAT WHATEVER THEY'RE PLOTTING INVOLVES USING VALBANILL...
AND THAT IT WON'T BE GOOD FOR THE CONTINENT AS A WHOLE.
LUKE!!

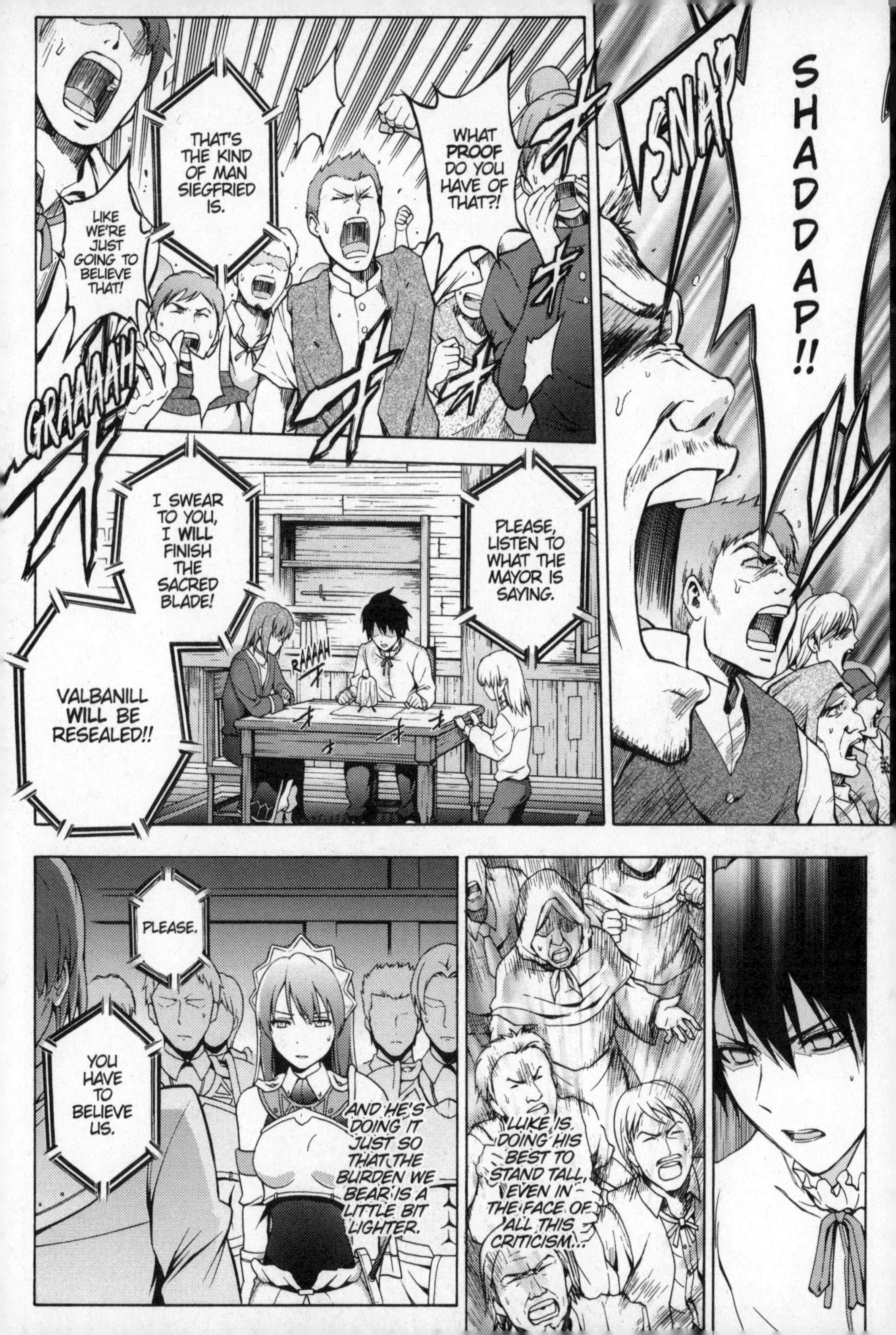
SNAP
SHADDAP!!
WHAT PROOF DO YOU HAVE OF THAT?!
THAT'S THE KIND OF MAN SIEGFRIED IS.
LIKE WE'RE JUST GOING TO BELIEVE THAT!
GRAAAAAH
PLEASE, LISTEN TO WHAT THE MAYOR IS SAYING.
RAAAAH
I SWEAR TO YOU, I WILL FINISH THE SACRED BLADE!
VALBANILL WILL BE RESEALED!!
LUKE IS DOING HIS BEST TO STAND TALL, EVEN IN THE FACE OF ALL THIS CRITICISM...
AND HE'S DOING IT JUST SO THAT THE BURDEN WE BEAR IS A LITTLE BIT LIGHTER.
PLEASE.
YOU HAVE TO BELIEVE US.

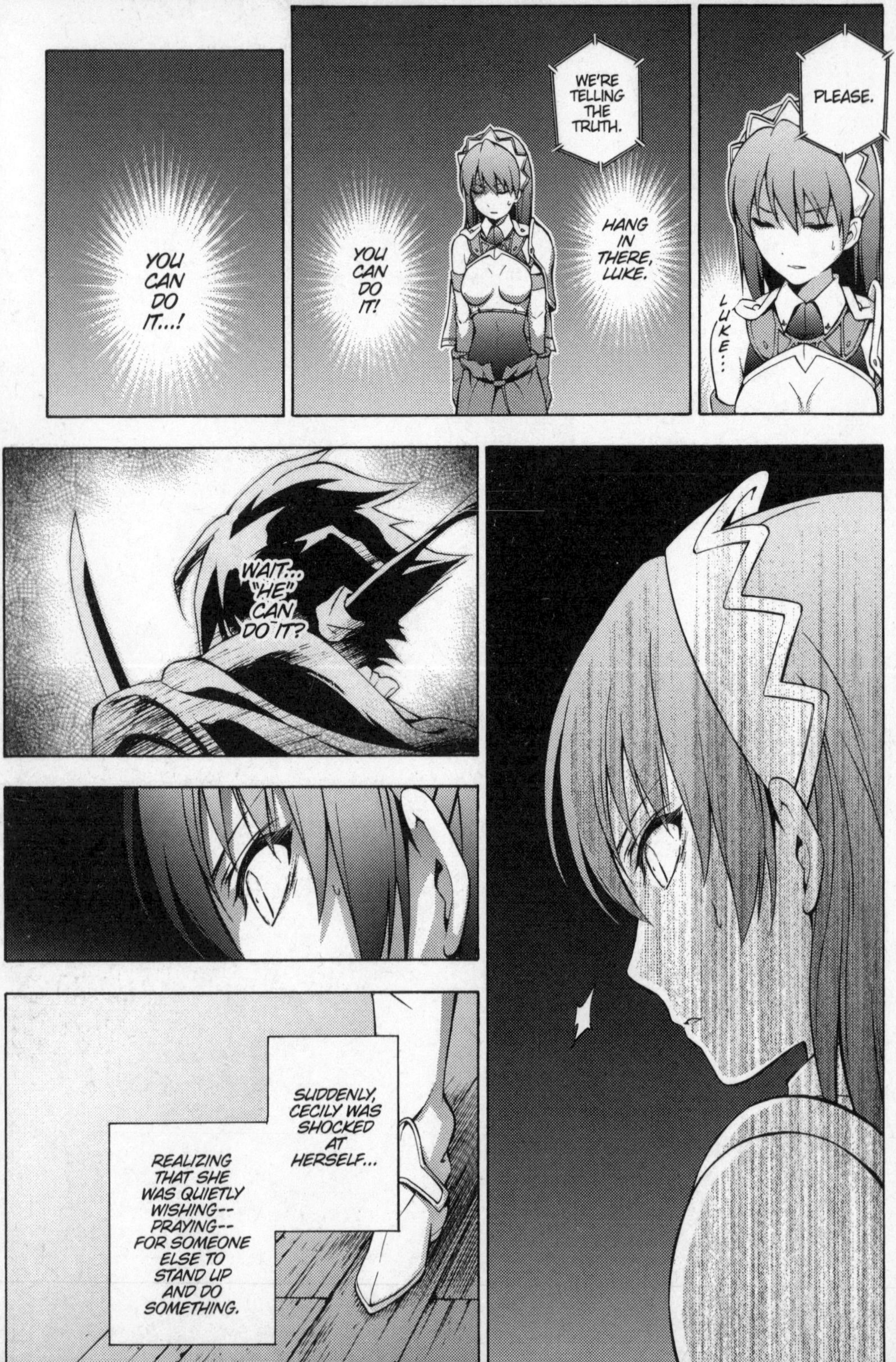
PLEASE.
LUKE...
WE'RE TELLING THE TRUTH.
HANG IN THERE, LUKE.
YOU CAN DO IT!
YOU CAN DO IT...!
WAIT... "HE" CAN DO IT?
SUDDENLY, CECILY WAS SHOCKED AT HERSELF...
REALIZING THAT SHE WAS QUIETLY WISHING-- PRAYING-- FOR SOMEONE ELSE TO STAND UP AND DO SOMETHING.

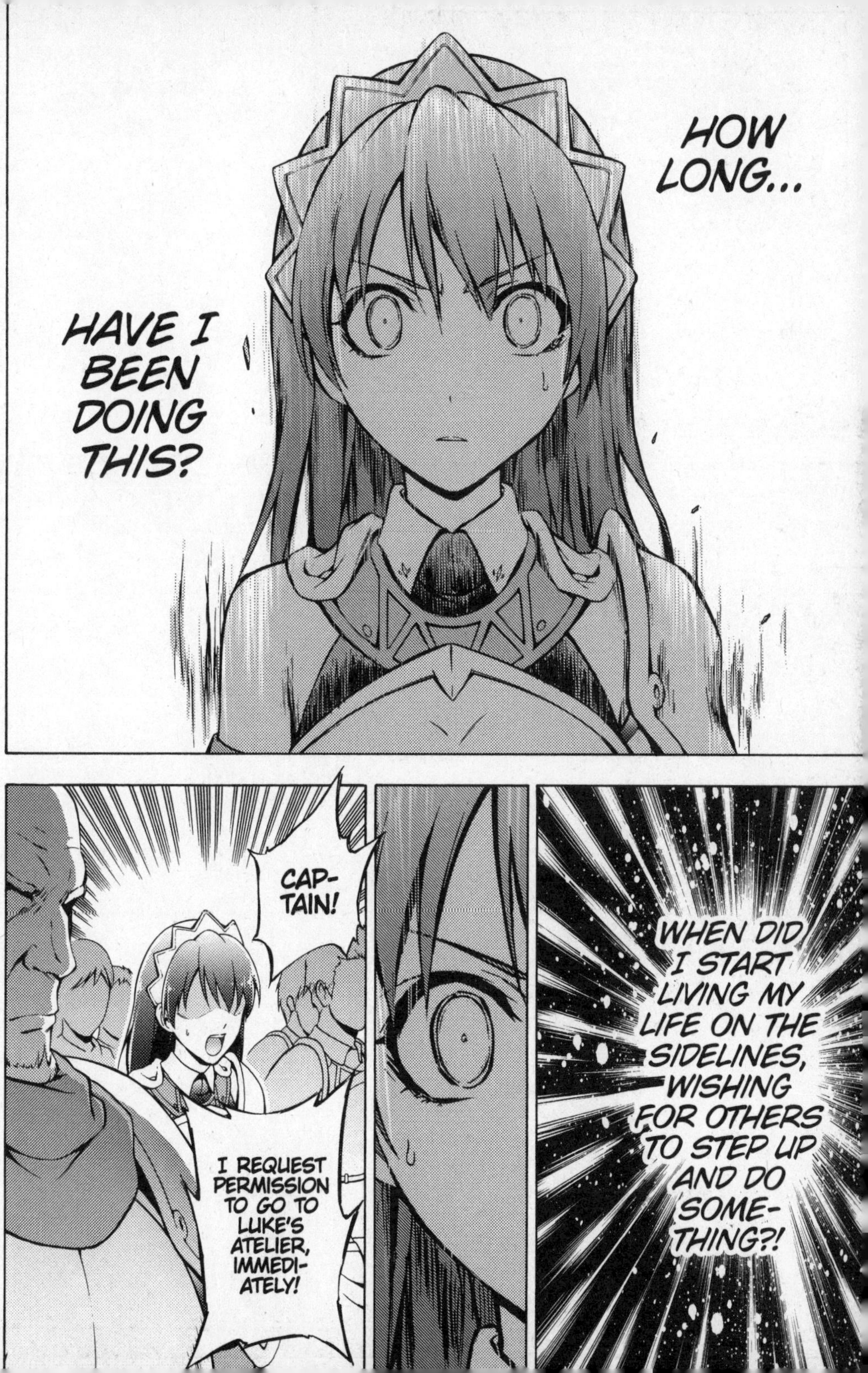
HOW LONG...
HAVE I BEEN DOING THIS?
WHEN DID I START LIVING MY LIFE ON THE SIDELINES, WISHING FOR OTHERS TO STEP UP AND DO SOME-THING?!
CAP-TAIN!
I REQUEST PERMISSION TO GO TO LUKE'S ATELIER, IMMEDI-ATELY!

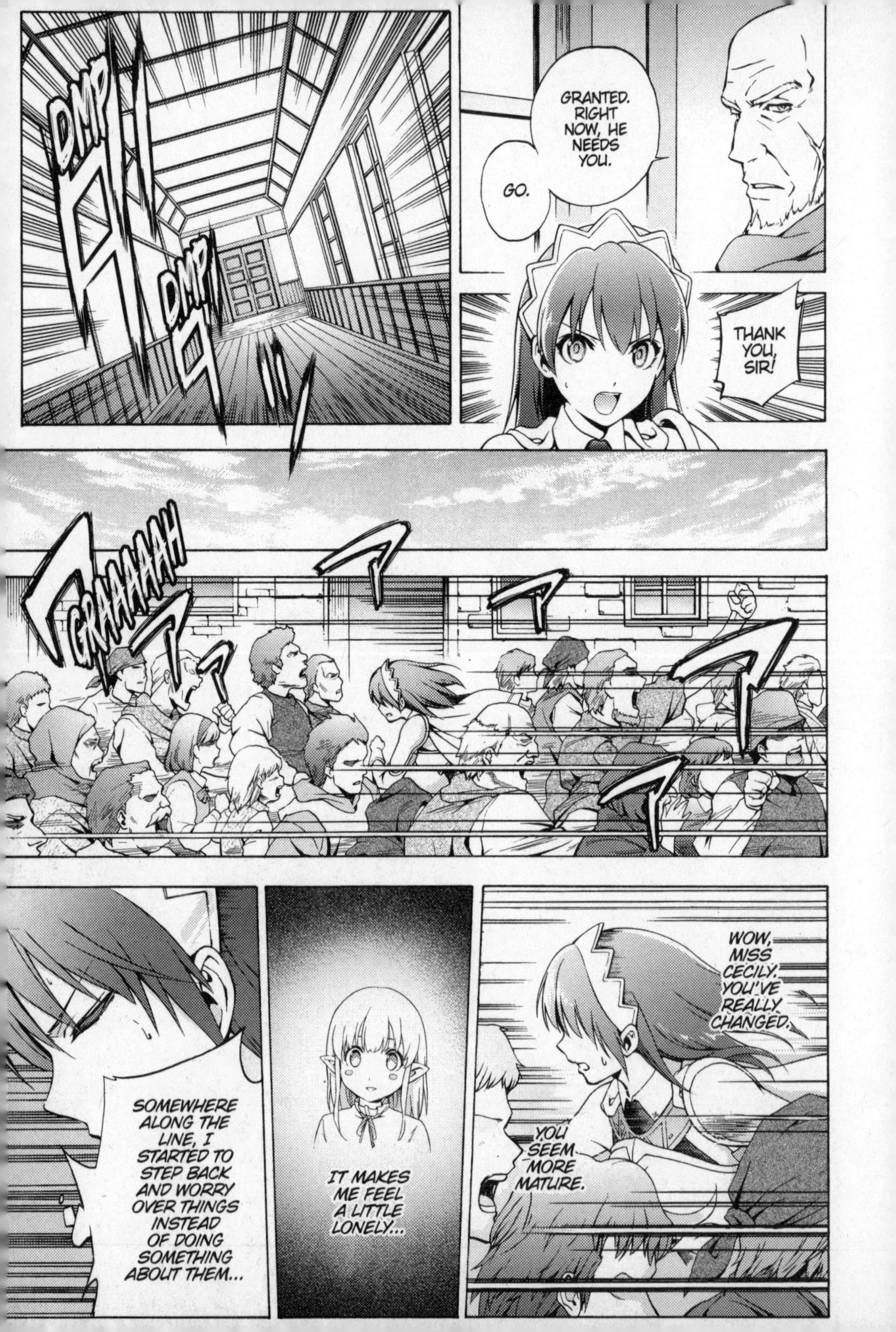
GRANTED. RIGHT NOW, HE NEEDS YOU.
GO.
THANK YOU, SIR!
DMP
DMP
GRAAAAAH
WOW, MISS CECILY. YOU'VE REALLY CHANGED.
YOU SEEM MORE MATURE.
IT MAKES ME FEEL A LITTLE LONELY...
SOMEWHERE ALONG THE LINE, I STARTED TO STEP BACK AND WORRY OVER THINGS INSTEAD OF DOING SOMETHING ABOUT THEM...

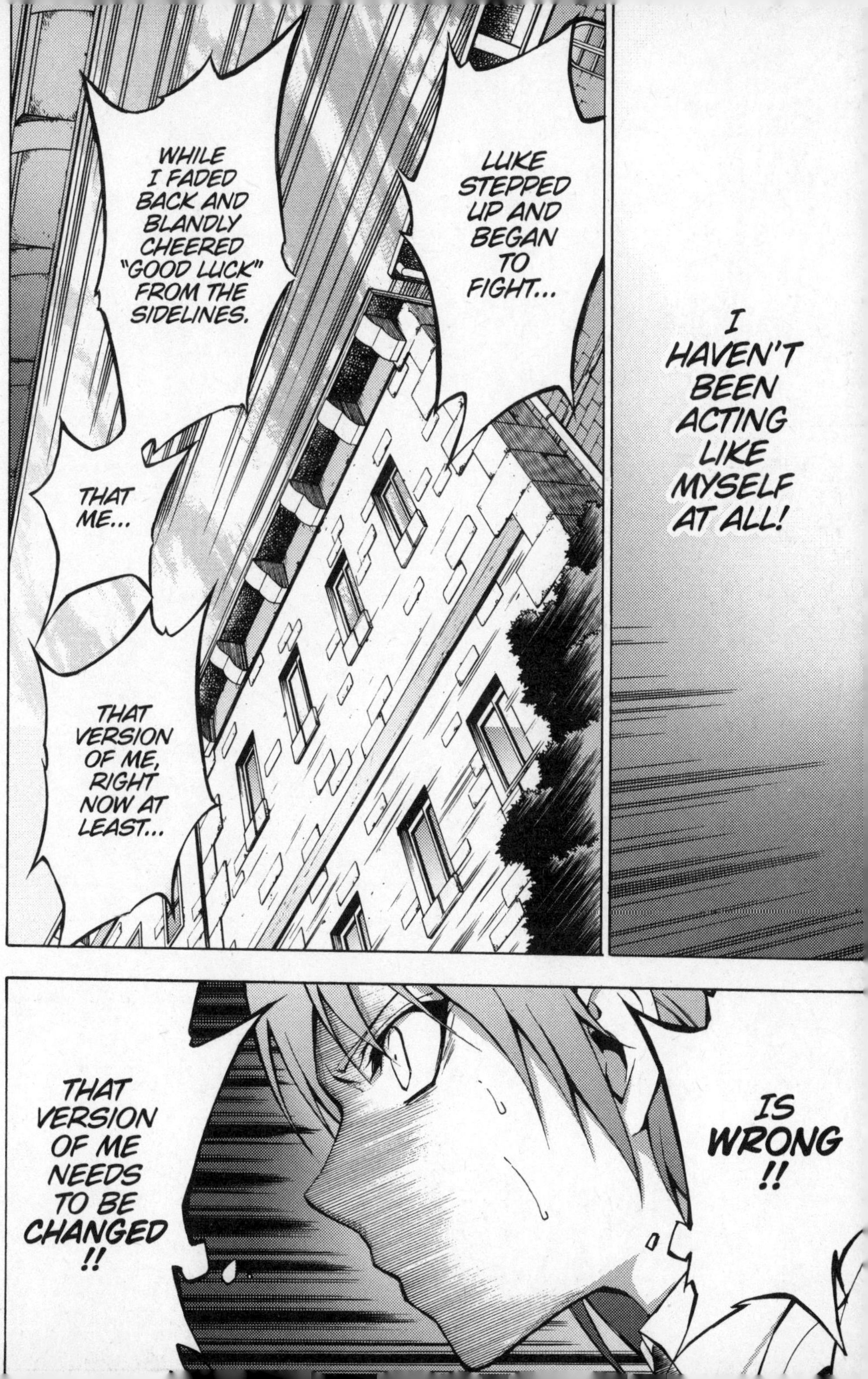
I HAVEN'T BEEN ACTING LIKE MYSELF AT ALL!
LUKE STEPPED UP AND BEGAN TO FIGHT...
WHILE I FADED BACK AND BLANDLY CHEERED "GOOD LUCK" FROM THE SIDELINES.
THAT ME...
THAT VERSION OF ME, RIGHT NOW AT LEAST...
IS WRONG!!
THAT VERSION OF ME NEEDS TO BE CHANGED!!

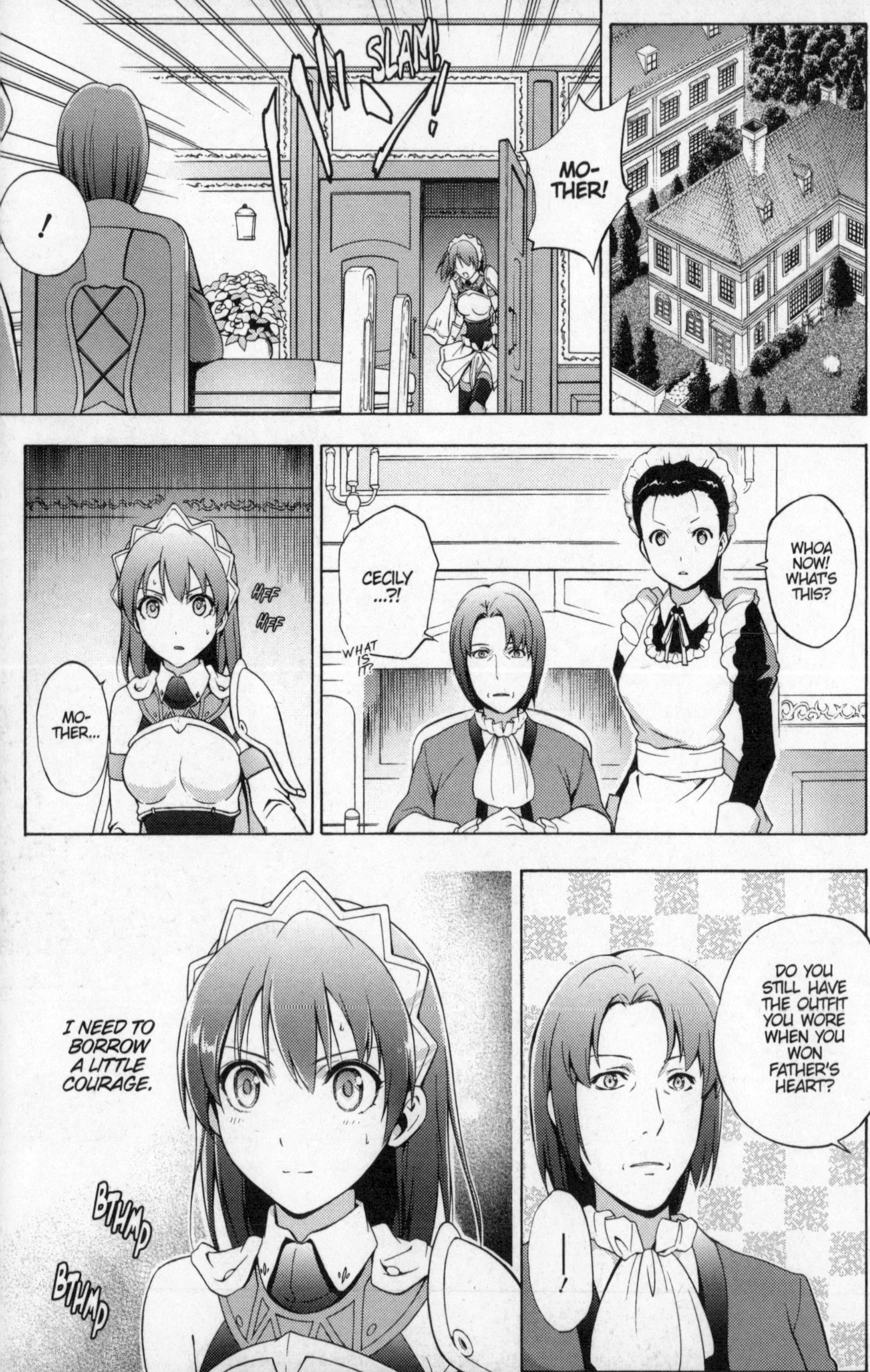
MO-
THER!
SLAM!
!
WHOA NOW! WHAT'S THIS?
CECILY ...?!
WHAT IS IT?
HFF
HFF
MO-
THER...
DO YOU STILL HAVE THE OUTFIT YOU WORE WHEN YOU WON FATHER'S HEART?
!
I NEED TO BORROW A LITTLE COURAGE.
BTHMP
BTHMP

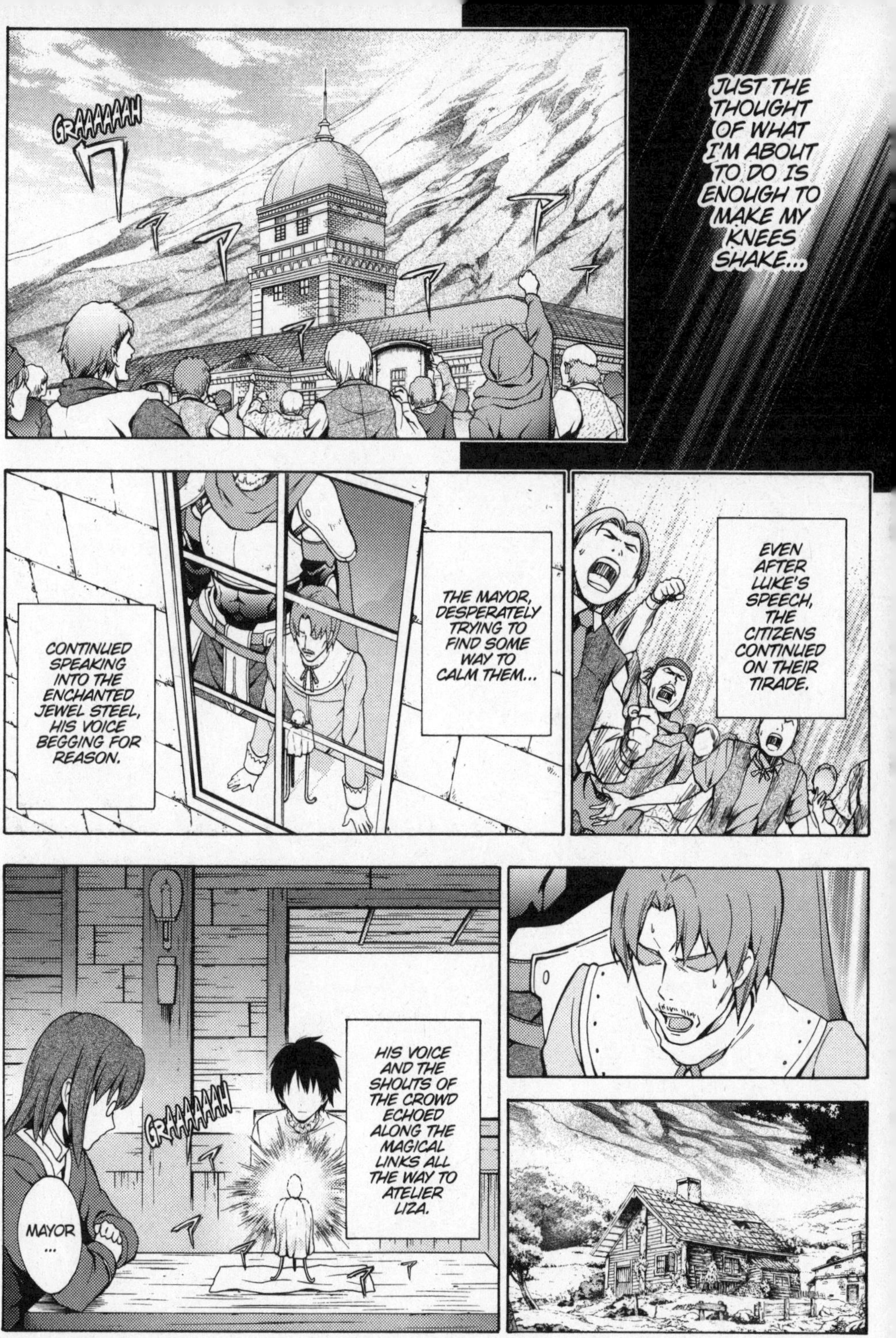
JUST THE THOUGHT OF WHAT I'M ABOUT TO DO IS ENOUGH TO MAKE MY KNEES SHAKE...
GRAAAAAAH
EVEN AFTER LUKE'S SPEECH, THE CITIZENS CONTINUED ON THEIR TIRADE.
THE MAYOR, DESPERATELY TRYING TO FIND SOME WAY TO CALM THEM...
CONTINUED SPEAKING INTO THE ENCHANTED JEWEL STEEL, HIS VOICE BEGGING FOR REASON.
HIS VOICE AND THE SHOUTS OF THE CROWD ECHOED ALONG THE MAGICAL LINKS ALL THE WAY TO ATELIER LIZA.
GRAAAAAAH
MAYOR ...

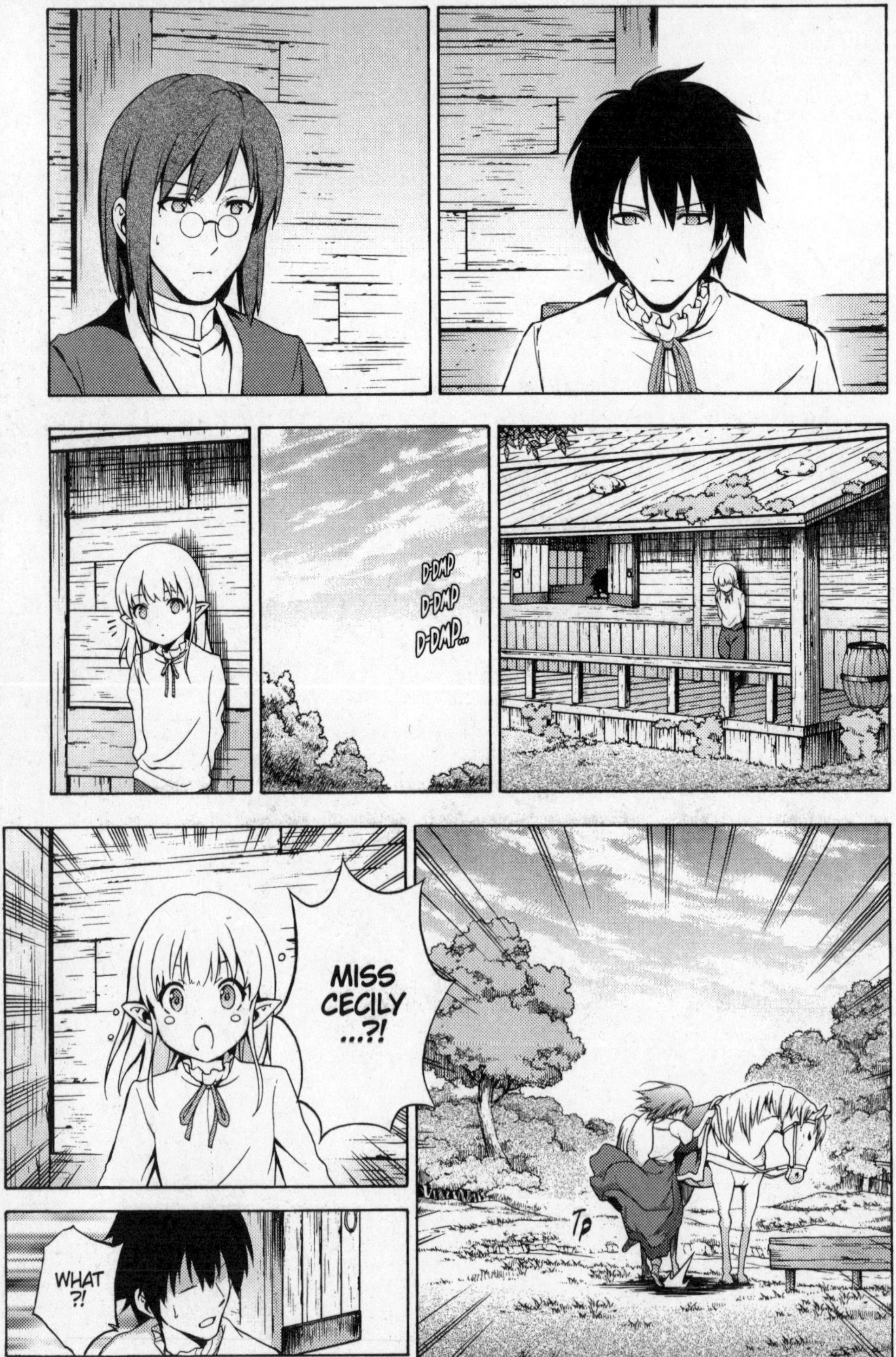
D-DMP
D-DMP
D-DMP...
Tp
MISS CECILY ...?!
WHAT ?!

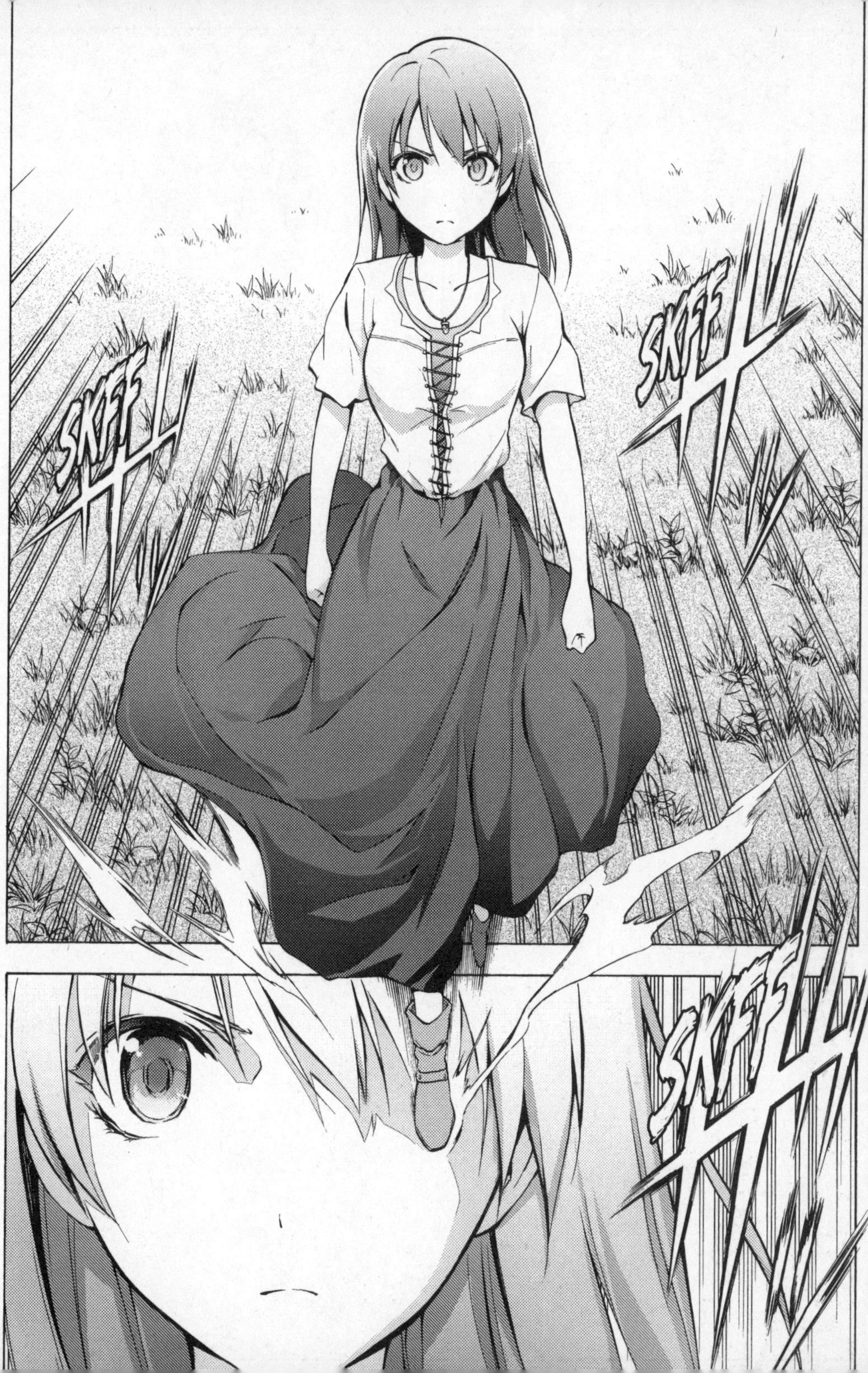
SKIFF
SKIFF
SKIFF

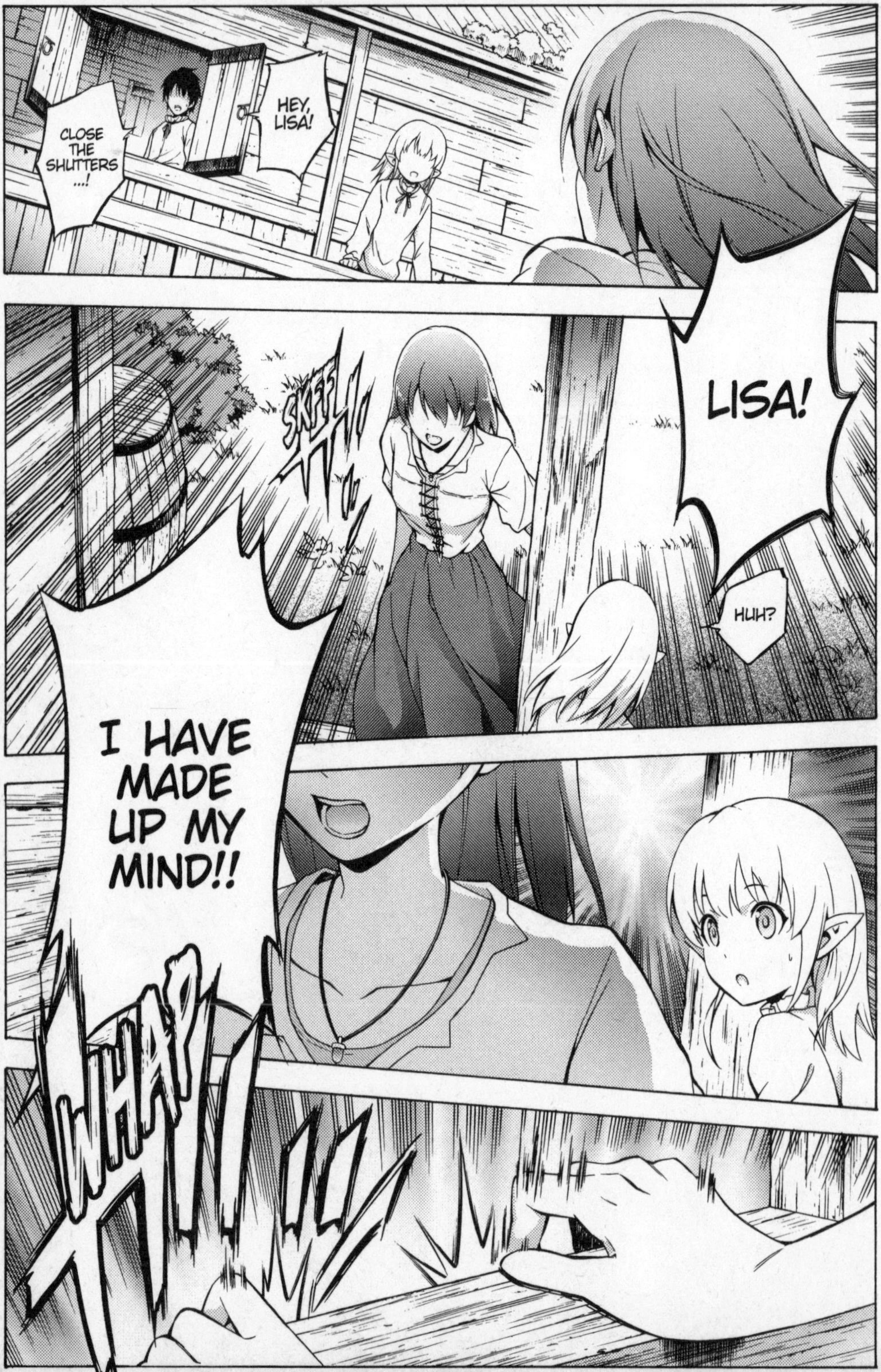

HEY, LISA!
CLOSE THE SHUTTERS ...!
LISA!
SKIFF
HUH?
I HAVE MADE UP MY MIND!!
WHAP

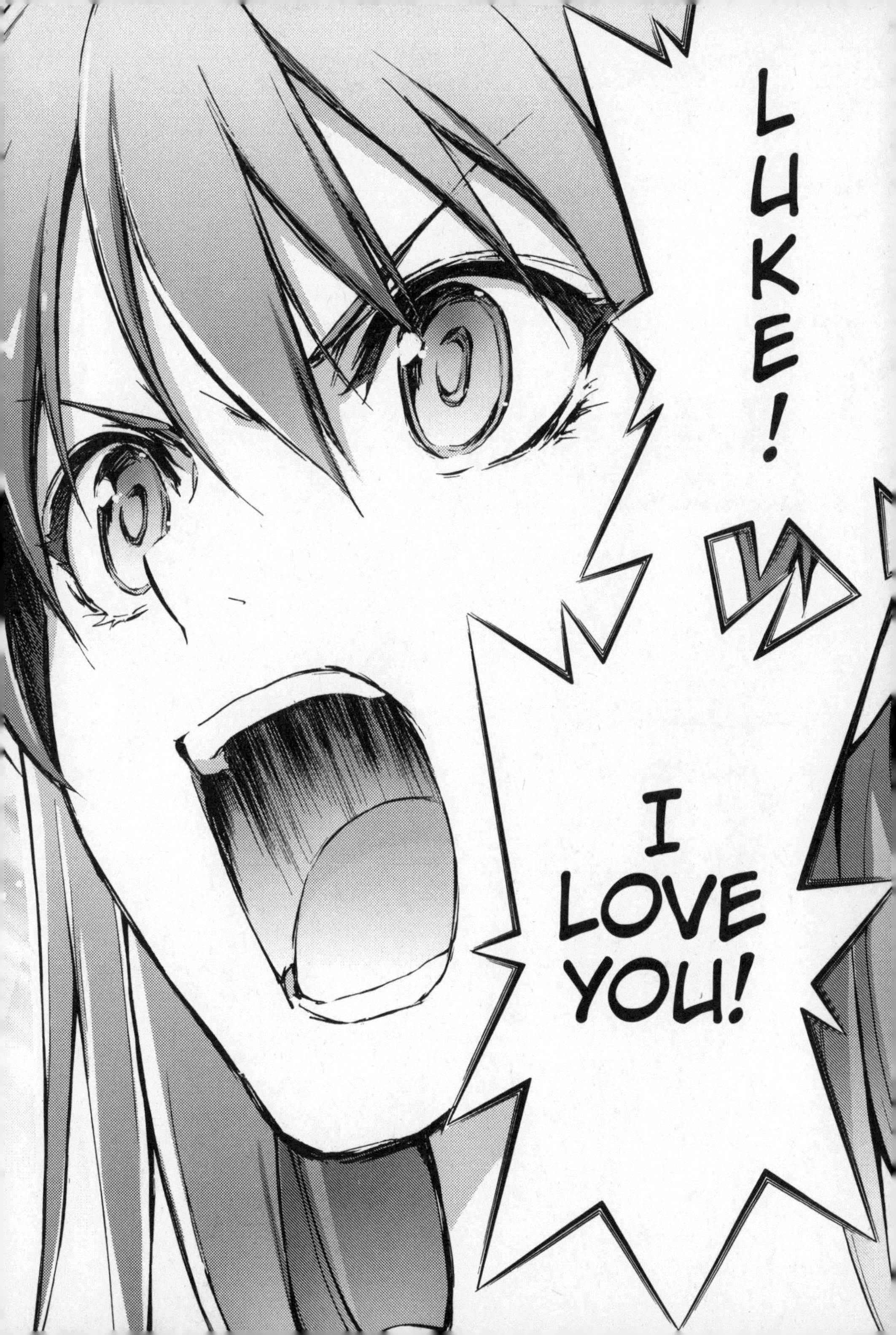
LUKE!
I LOVE YOU!

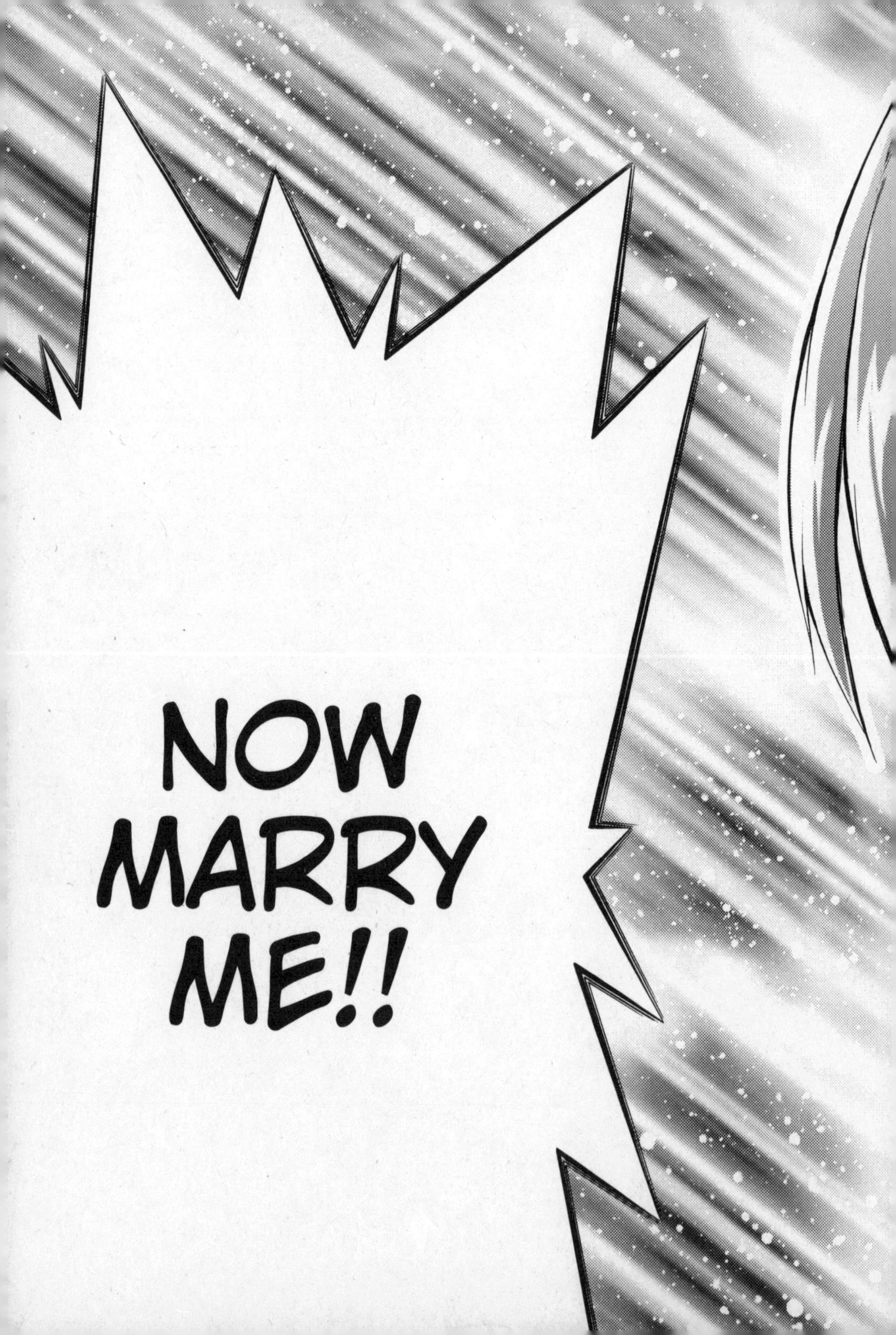
NOW MARRY ME!!

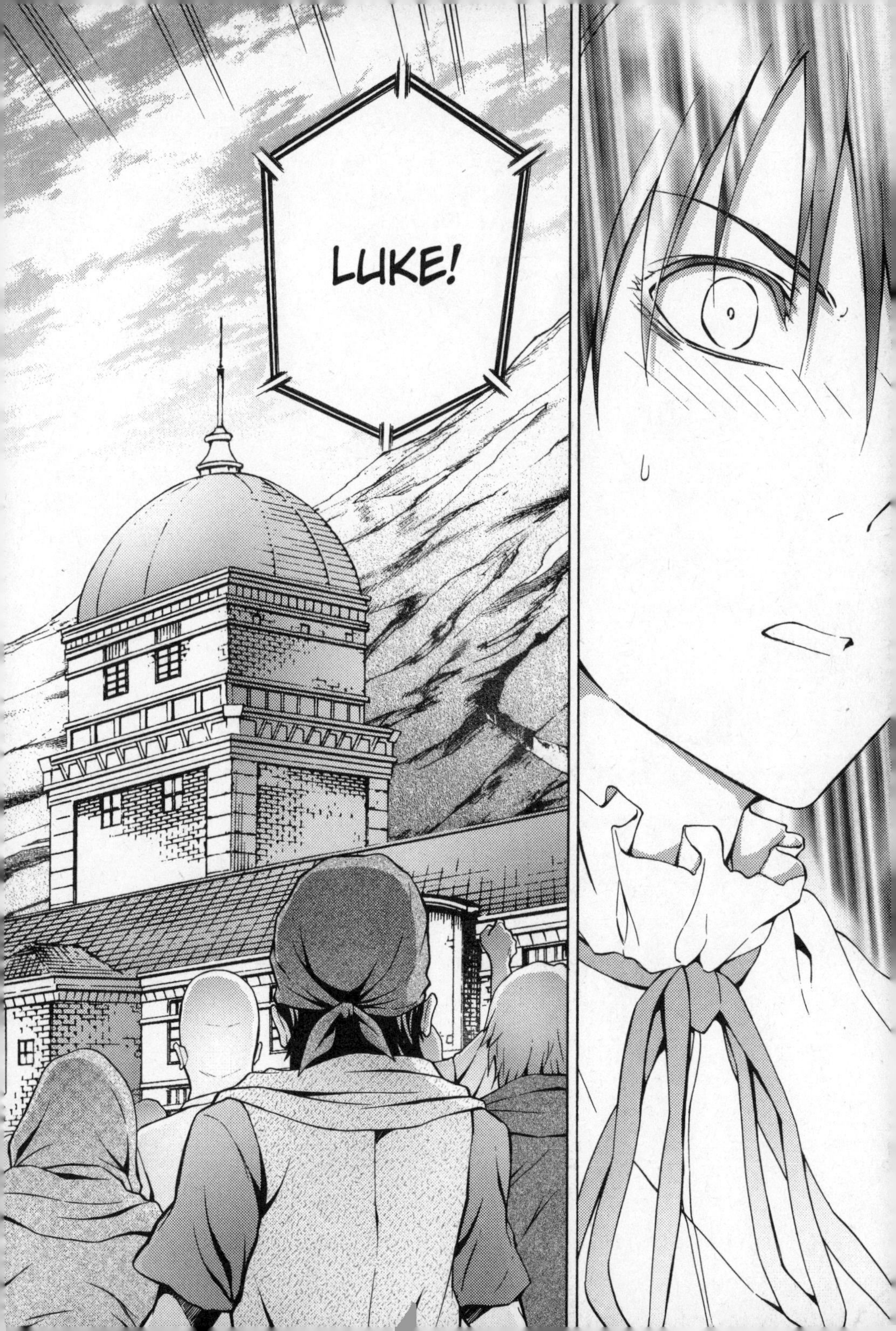
LUKE!

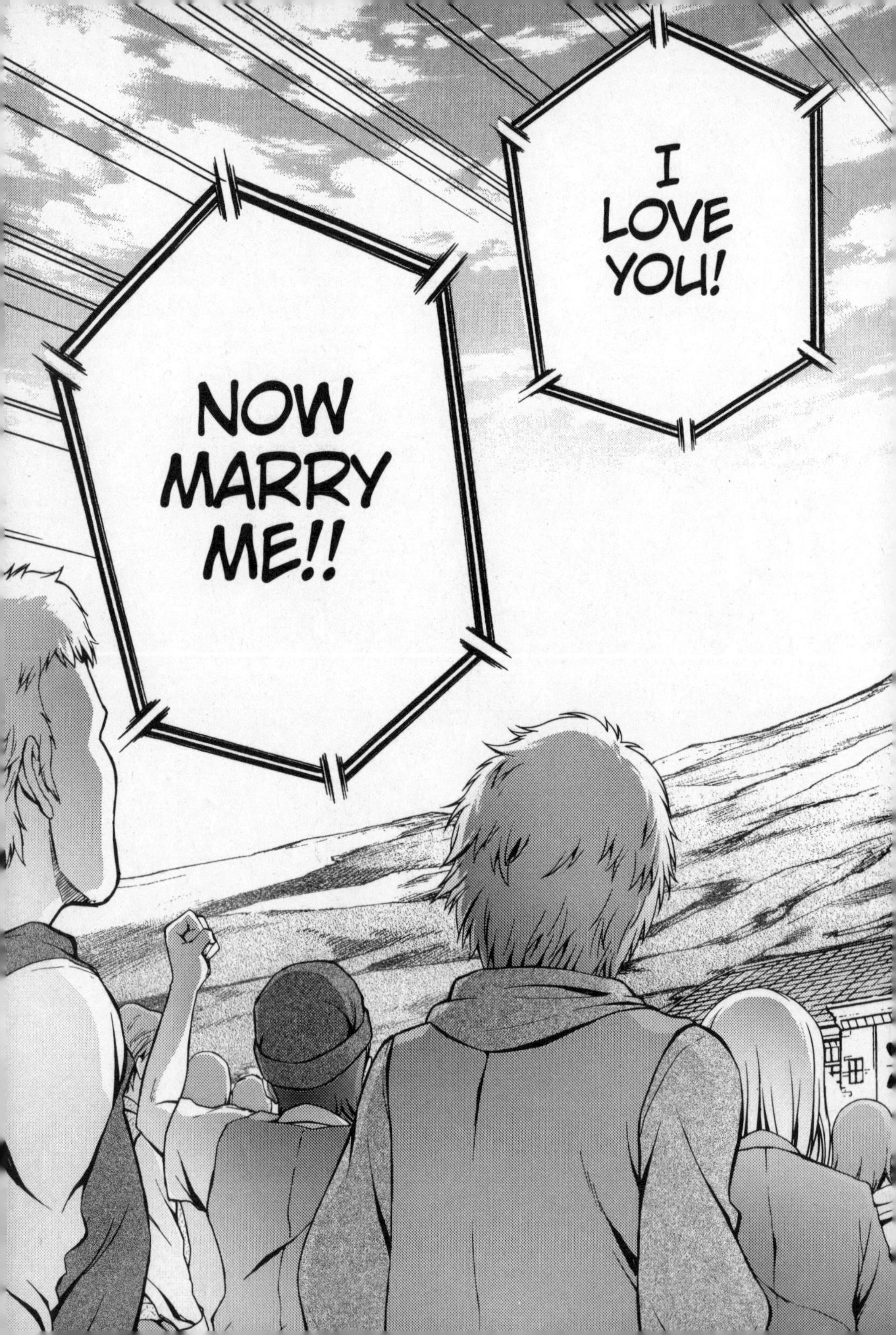
I LOVE YOU!
NOW MARRY ME!!

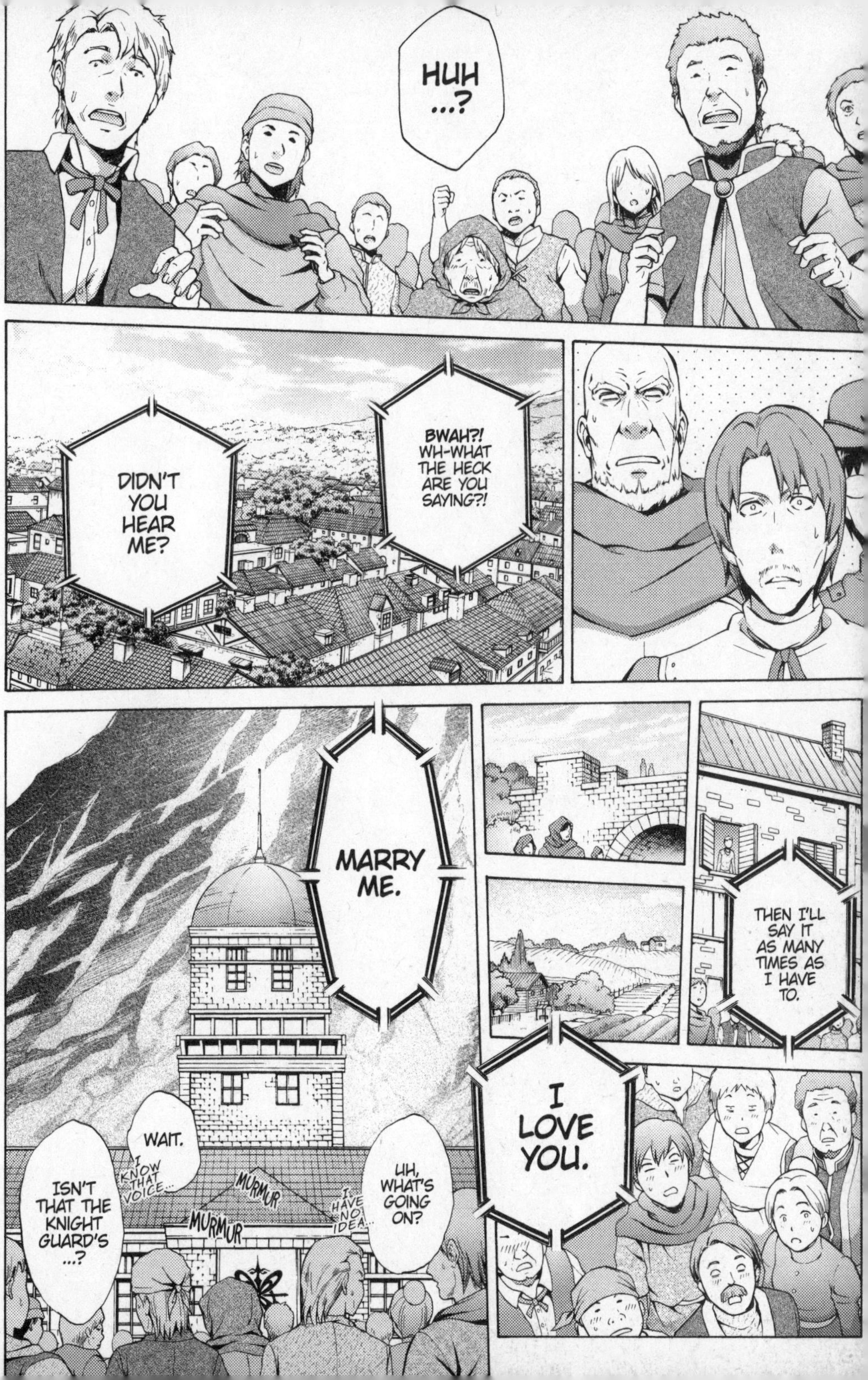
HUH ...?
BWAH?! WH-WHAT THE HECK ARE YOU SAYING?!
DIDN'T YOU HEAR ME?
THEN I'LL SAY IT AS MANY TIMES AS I HAVE TO.
I LOVE YOU.
MARRY ME.
UH, WHAT'S GOING ON?
I HAVE NO IDEA...
MURMUR
WAIT.
I KNOW THAT VOICE...
MURMUR
ISN'T THAT THE KNIGHT GUARD'S ...?

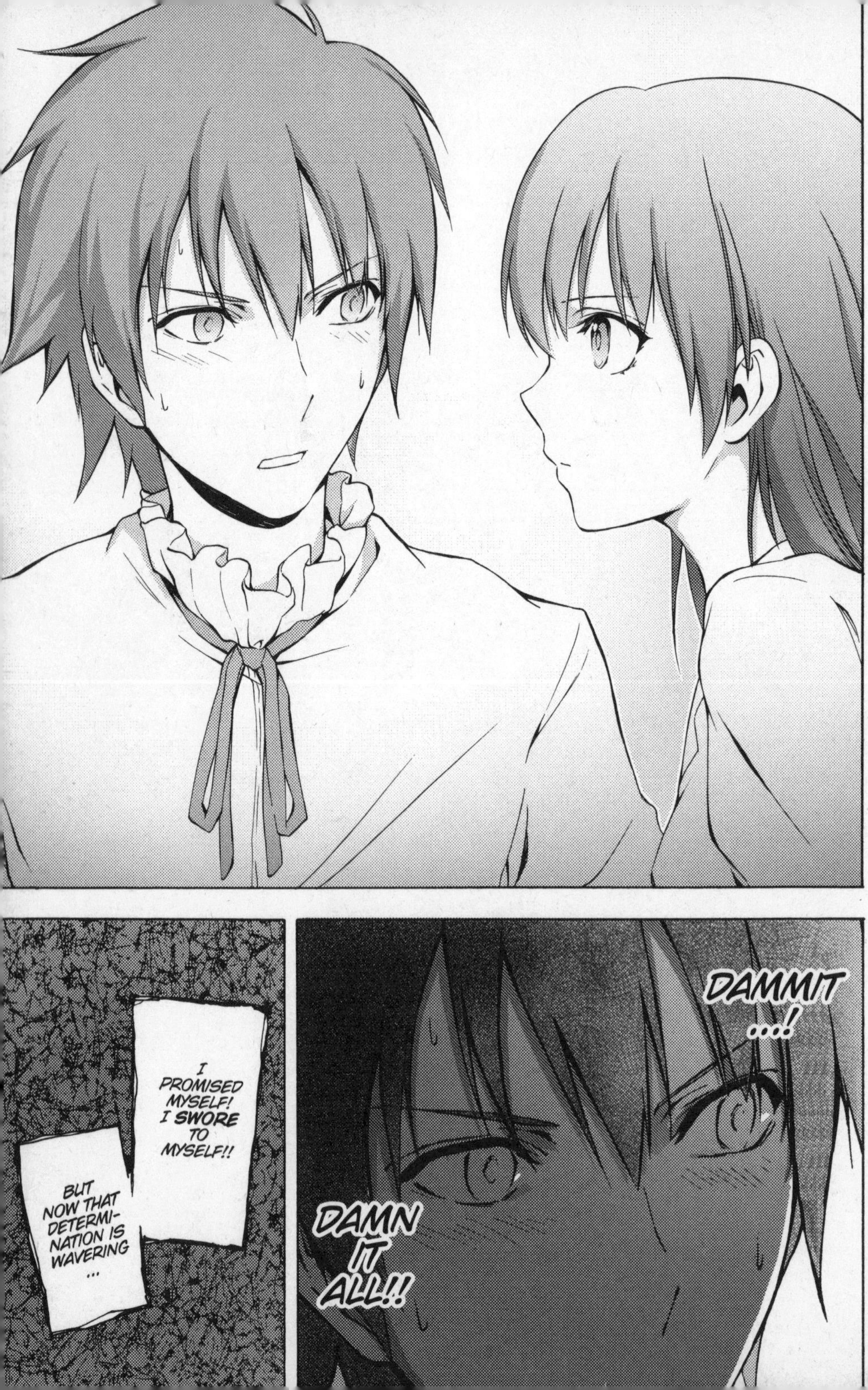
DAMMIT ...!
DAMN IT ALL!!
I PROMISED MYSELF! I SWORE TO MYSELF!!
BUT NOW THAT DETERMINATION IS WAVERING ...

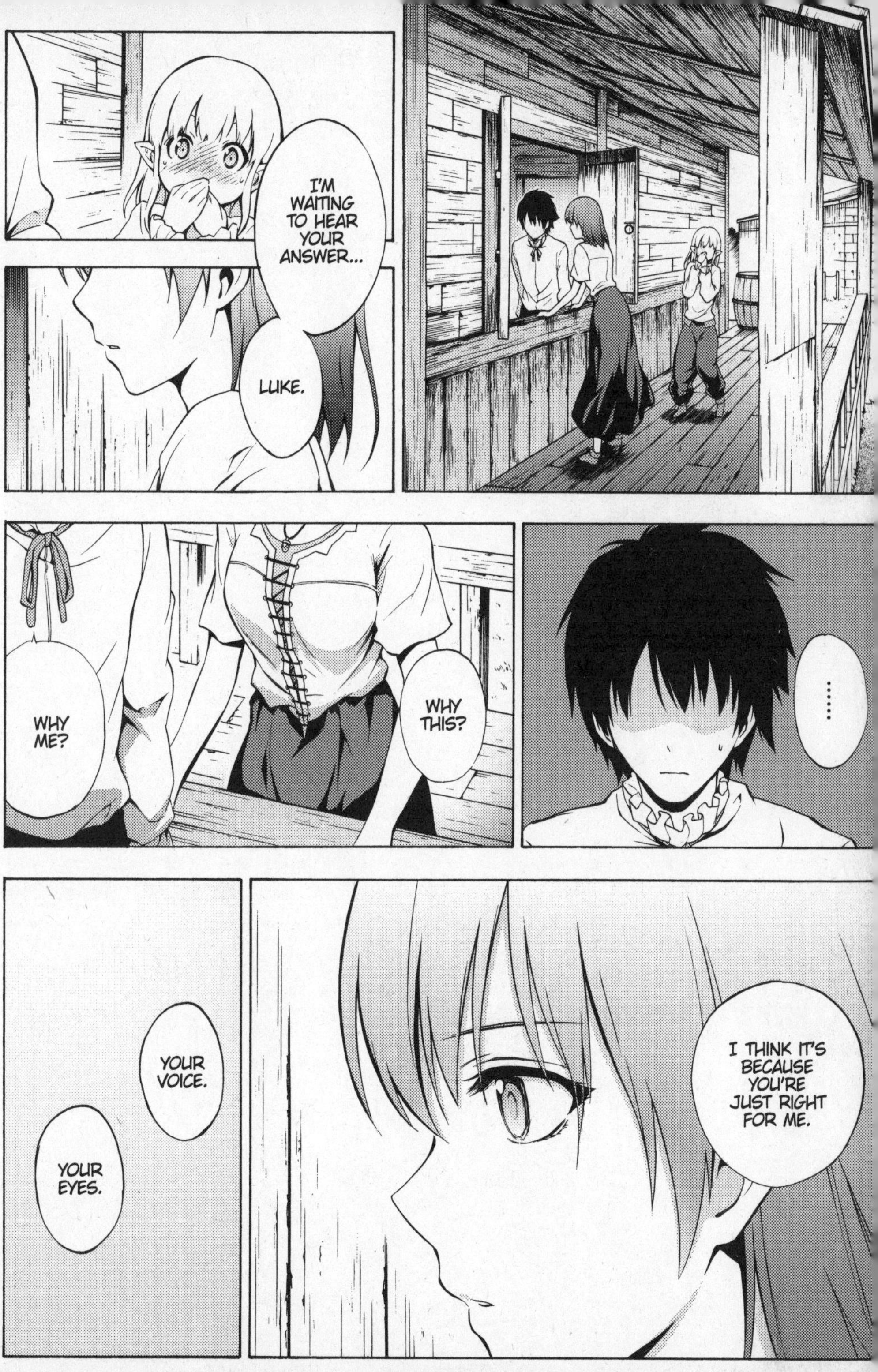
I'M WAITING TO HEAR YOUR ANSWER...
LUKE.
......
WHY THIS?
WHY ME?
I THINK IT'S BECAUSE YOU'RE JUST RIGHT FOR ME.
YOUR VOICE.
YOUR EYES.

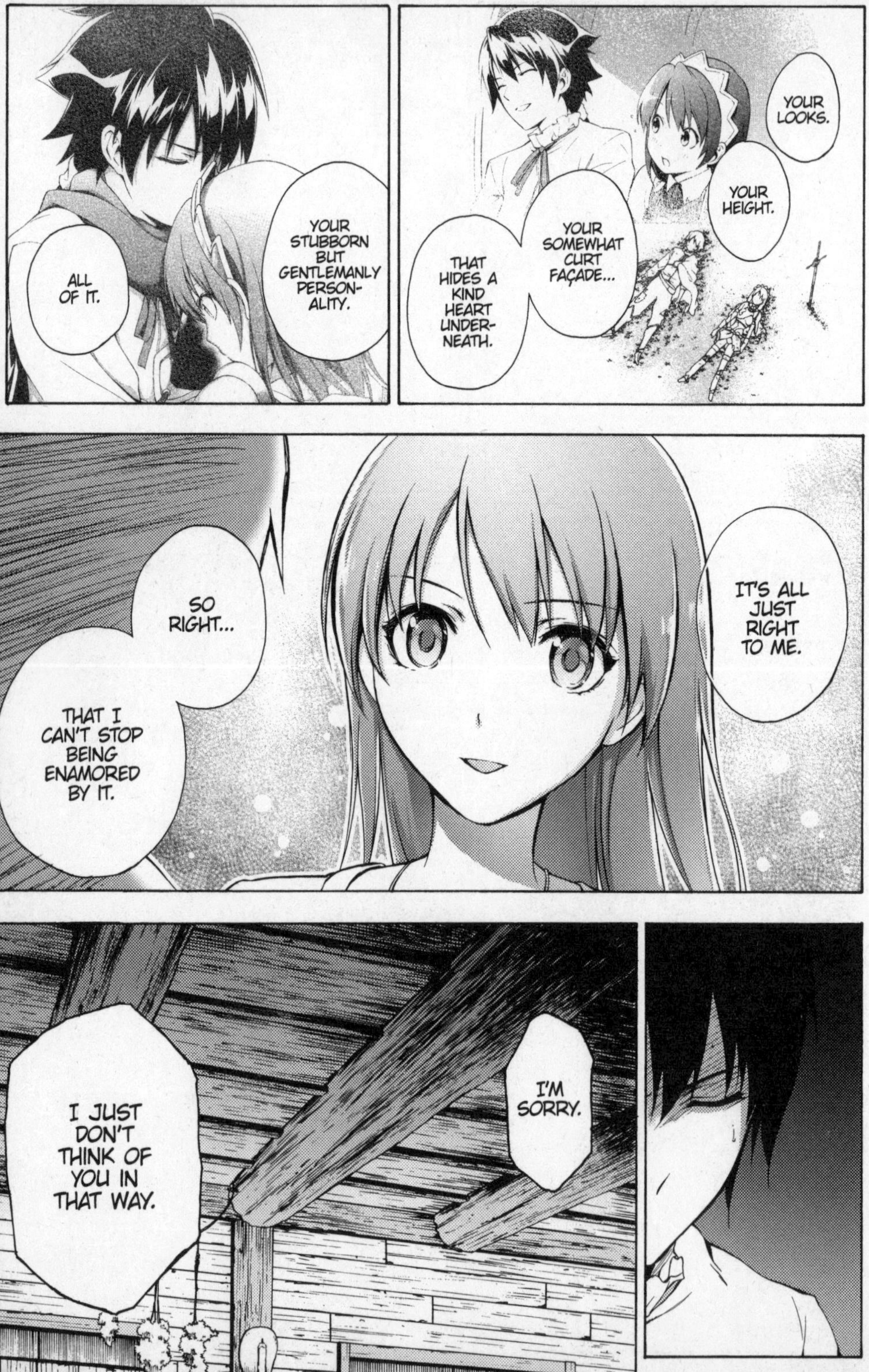
YOUR LOOKS.
YOUR HEIGHT.
YOUR SOMEWHAT CURT FAÇADE...
THAT HIDES A KIND HEART UNDER-NEATH.
YOUR STUBBORN BUT GENTLEMANLY PERSON-ALITY.
ALL OF IT.
IT'S ALL JUST RIGHT TO ME.
SO RIGHT...
THAT I CAN'T STOP BEING ENAMORED BY IT.
I'M SORRY.
I JUST DON'T THINK OF YOU IN THAT WAY.

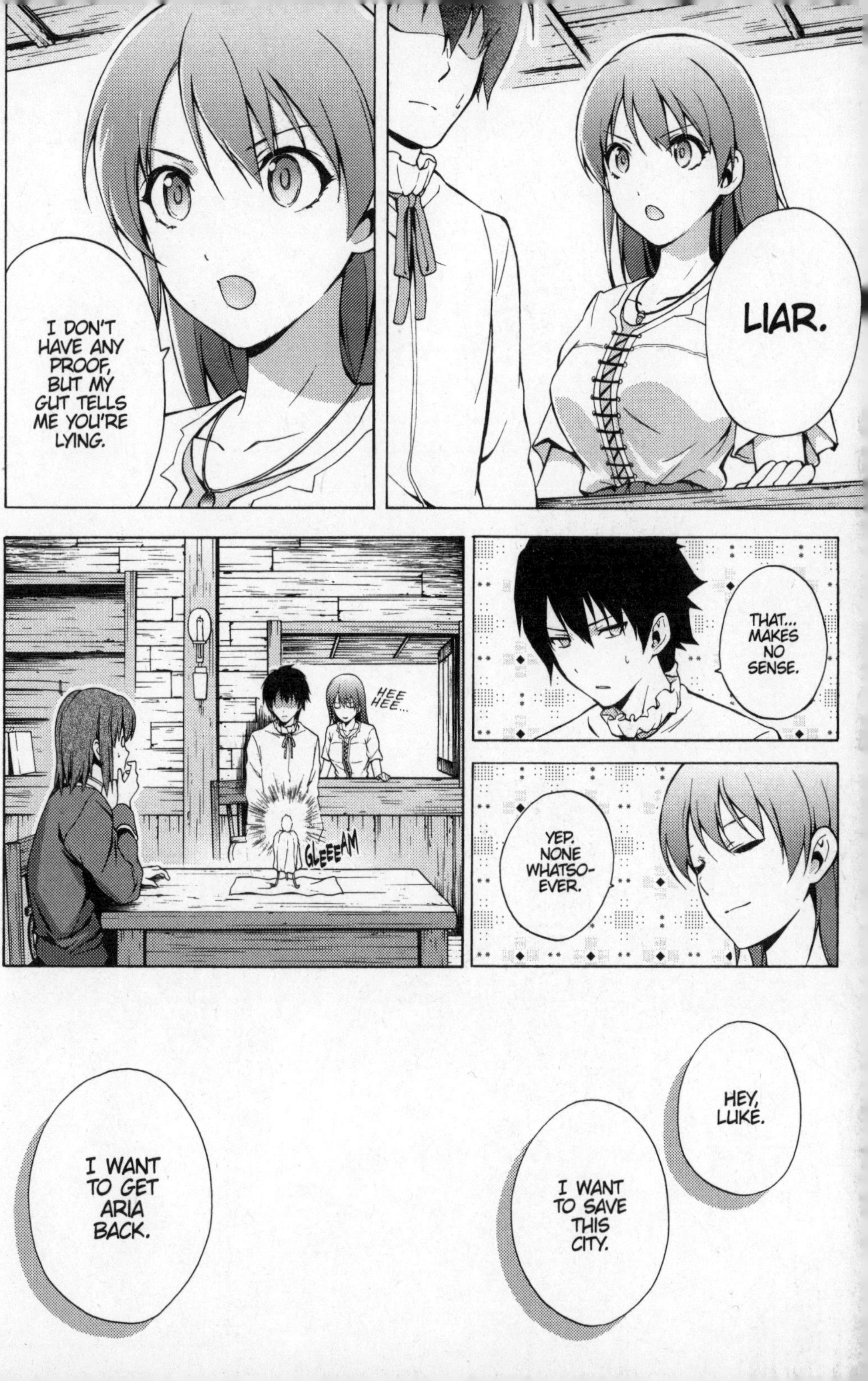
LIAR.
I DON'T HAVE ANY PROOF, BUT MY GUT TELLS ME YOU'RE LYING.
THAT... MAKES NO SENSE.
YEP. NONE WHATSO- EVER.
HEE HEE...
GLEEEAM
HEY, LUKE.
I WANT TO SAVE THIS CITY.
I WANT TO GET ARIA BACK.

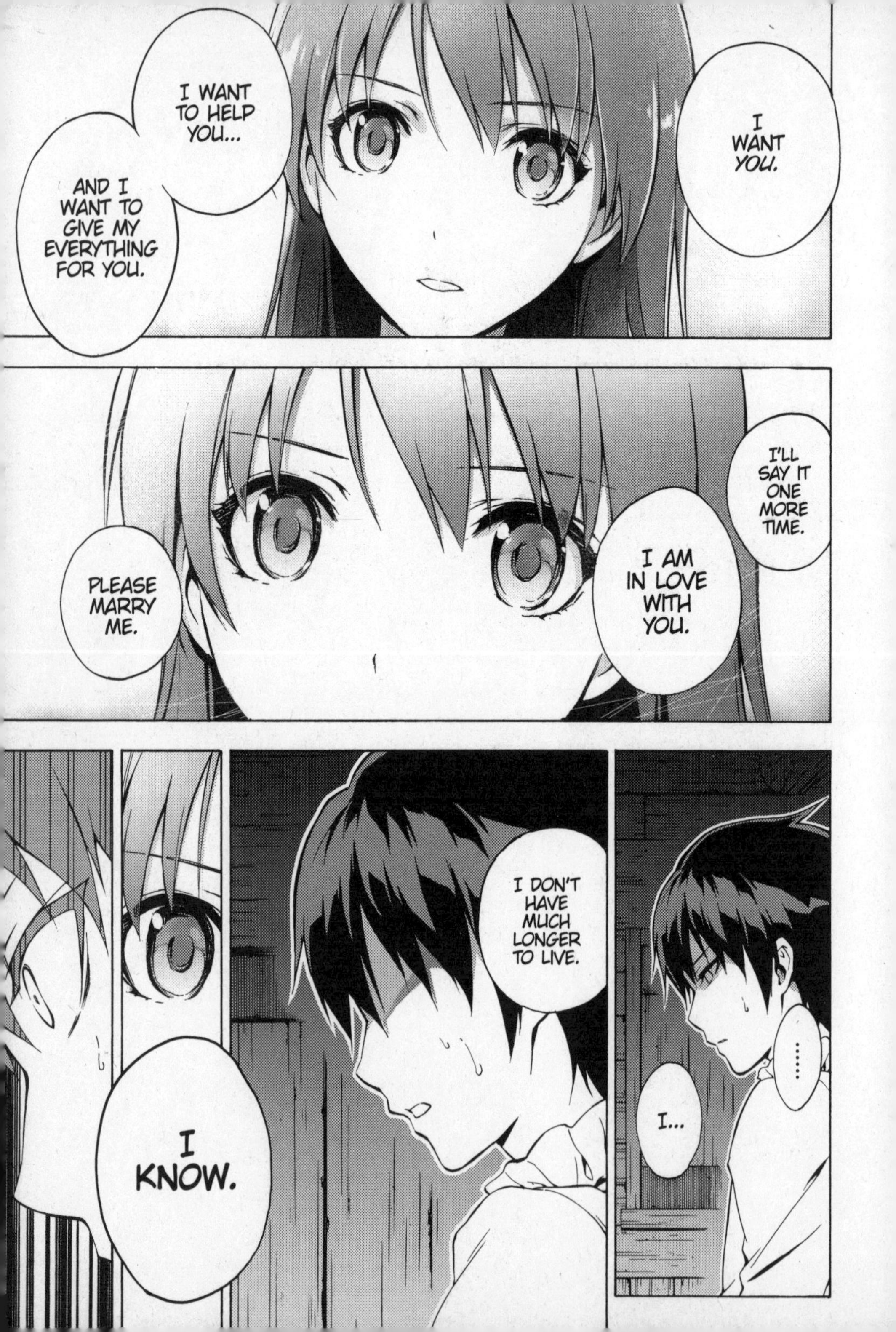
I WANT YOU.
I WANT TO HELP YOU...
AND I WANT TO GIVE MY EVERYTHING FOR YOU.
I'LL SAY IT ONE MORE TIME.
I AM IN LOVE WITH YOU.
PLEASE MARRY ME.
......
I...
I DON'T HAVE MUCH LONGER TO LIVE.
I KNOW.

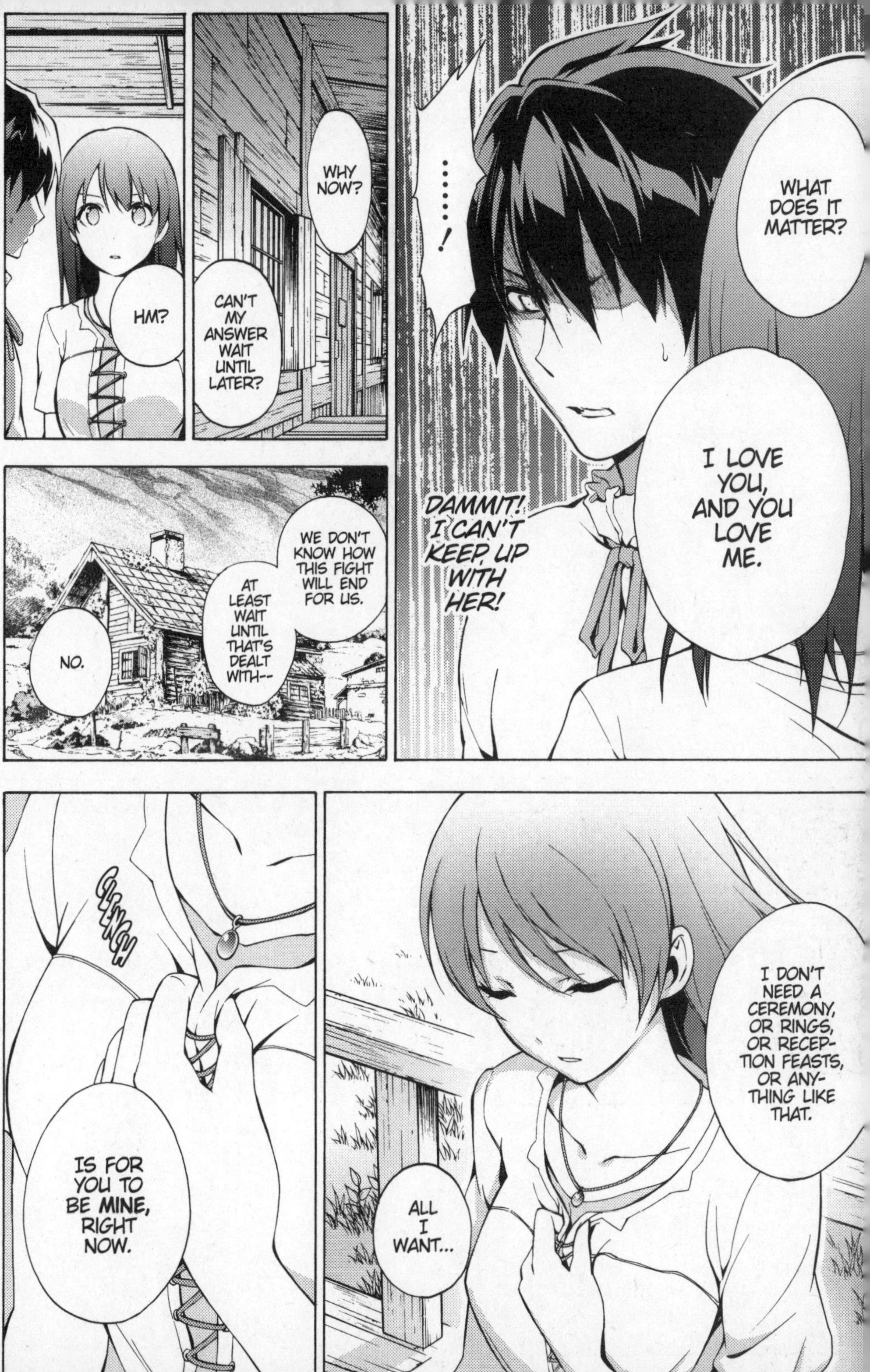
......!
WHAT DOES IT MATTER?
I LOVE YOU, AND YOU LOVE ME.
DAMMIT! I CAN'T KEEP UP WITH HER!
WHY NOW?
CAN'T MY ANSWER WAIT UNTIL LATER?
HM?
WE DON'T KNOW HOW THIS FIGHT WILL END FOR US.
AT LEAST WAIT UNTIL THAT'S DEALT WITH--
NO.
I DON'T NEED A CEREMONY, OR RINGS, OR RECEPTION FEASTS, OR ANYTHING LIKE THAT.
ALL I WANT...
CLENCH
IS FOR YOU TO BE MINE, RIGHT NOW.

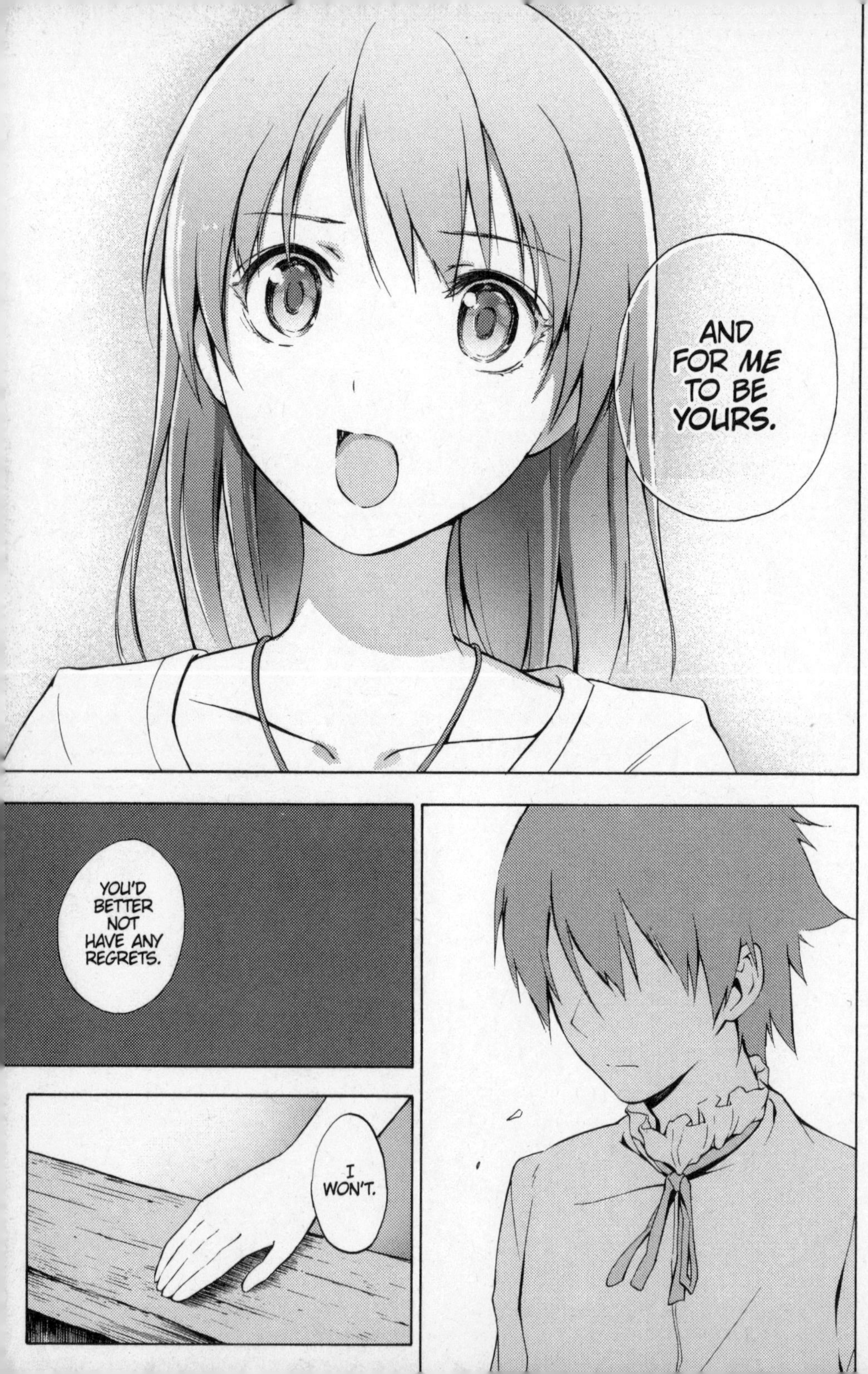
AND FOR ME TO BE YOURS.
YOU'D BETTER NOT HAVE ANY REGRETS.
I WON'T.

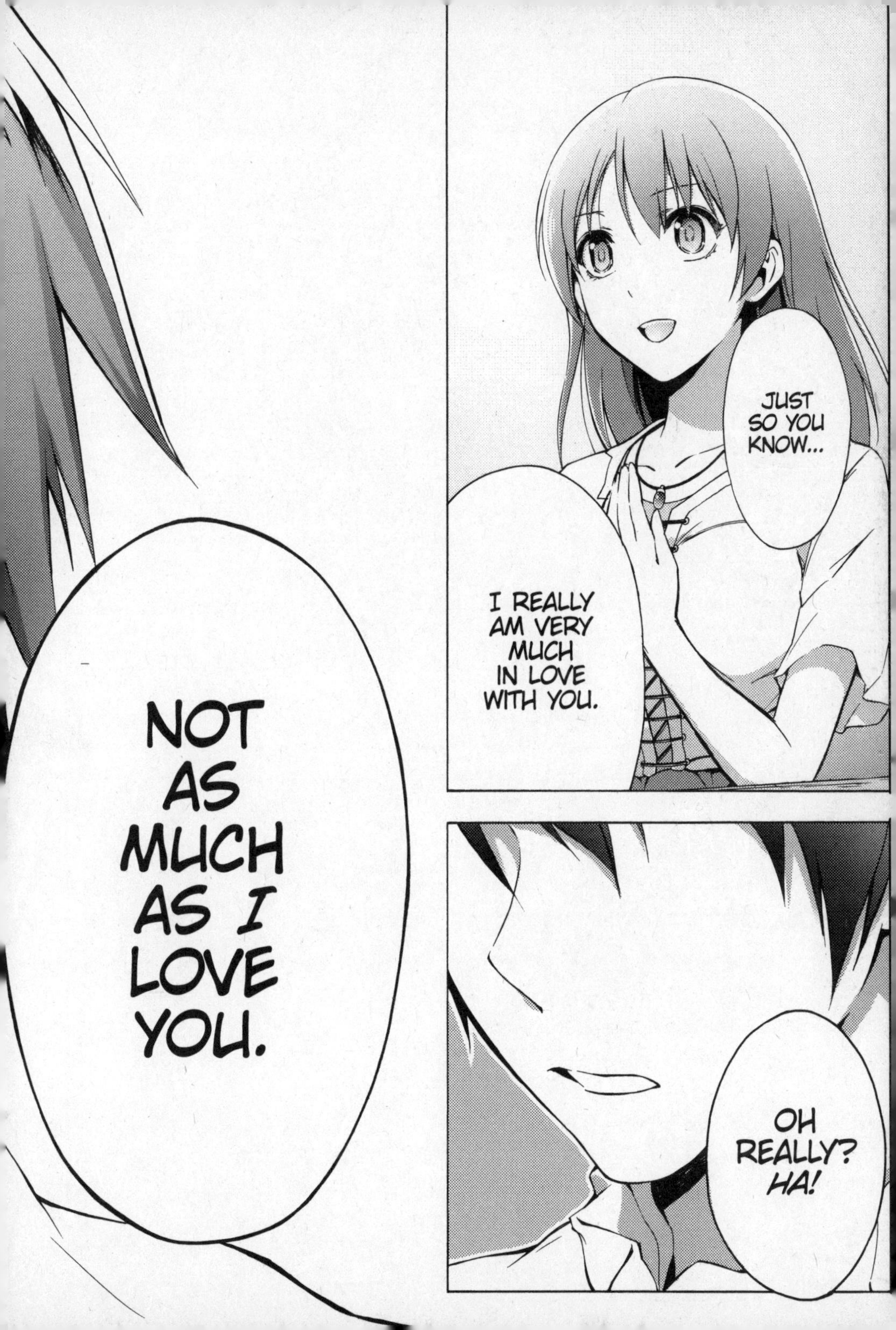
JUST SO YOU KNOW...
I REALLY AM VERY MUCH IN LOVE WITH YOU.
OH REALLY? *HA!*
NOT AS MUCH AS I LOVE YOU.

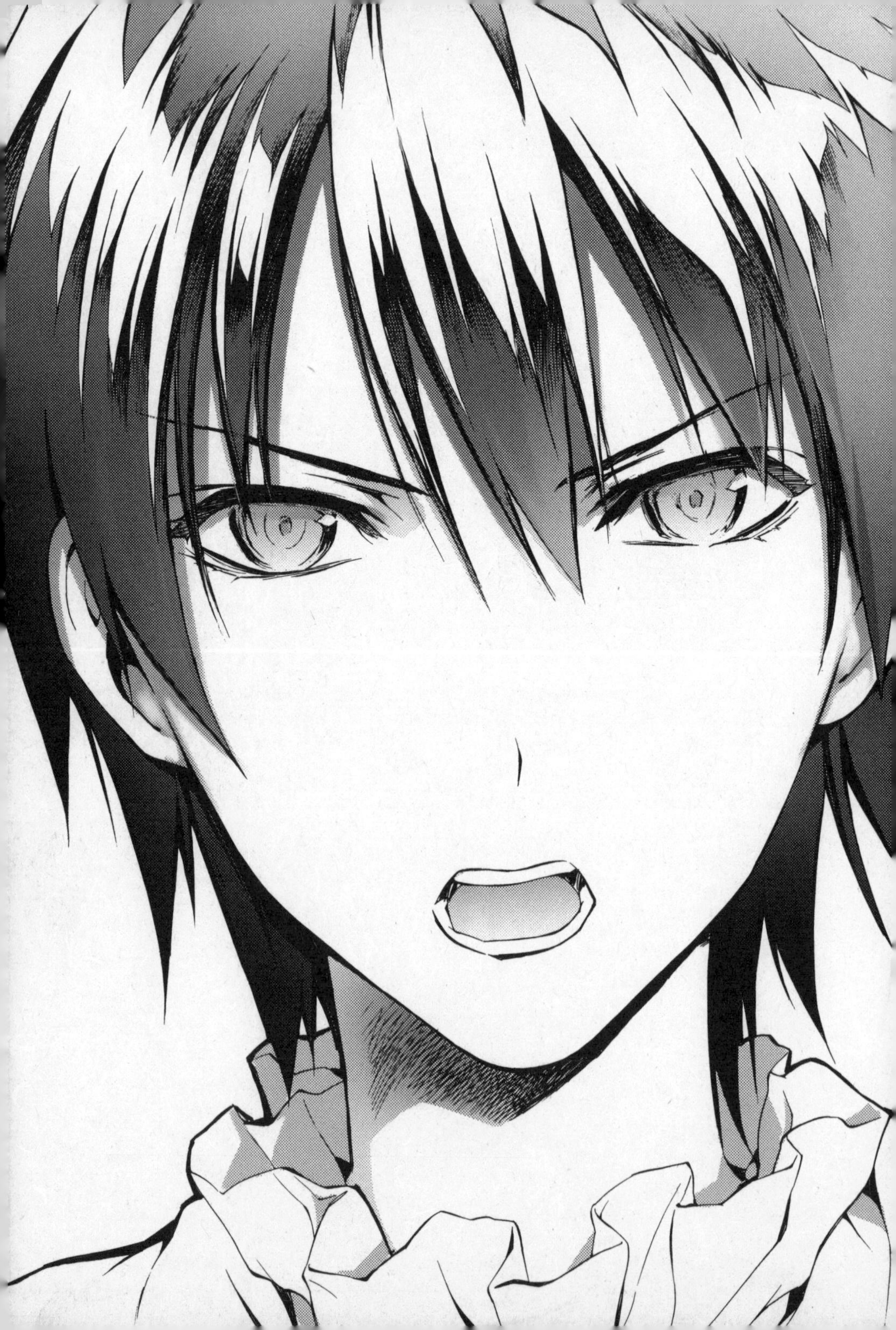

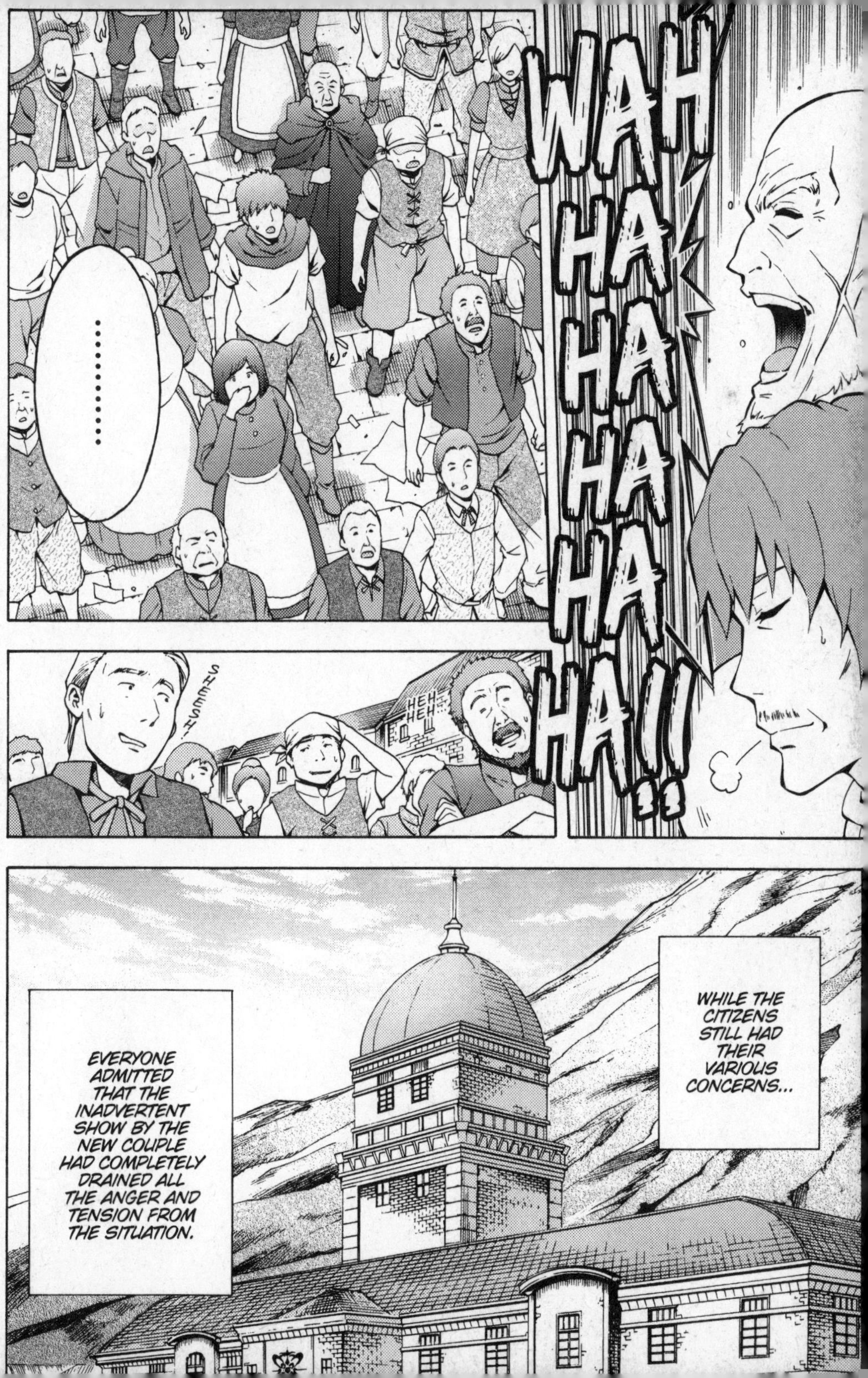
WAH HA HA HA HA HA HA!!
......
SHEESH!
HEH HEH
WHILE THE CITIZENS STILL HAD THEIR VARIOUS CONCERNS...
EVERYONE ADMITTED THAT THE INADVERTENT SHOW BY THE NEW COUPLE HAD COMPLETELY DRAINED ALL THE ANGER AND TENSION FROM THE SITUATION.

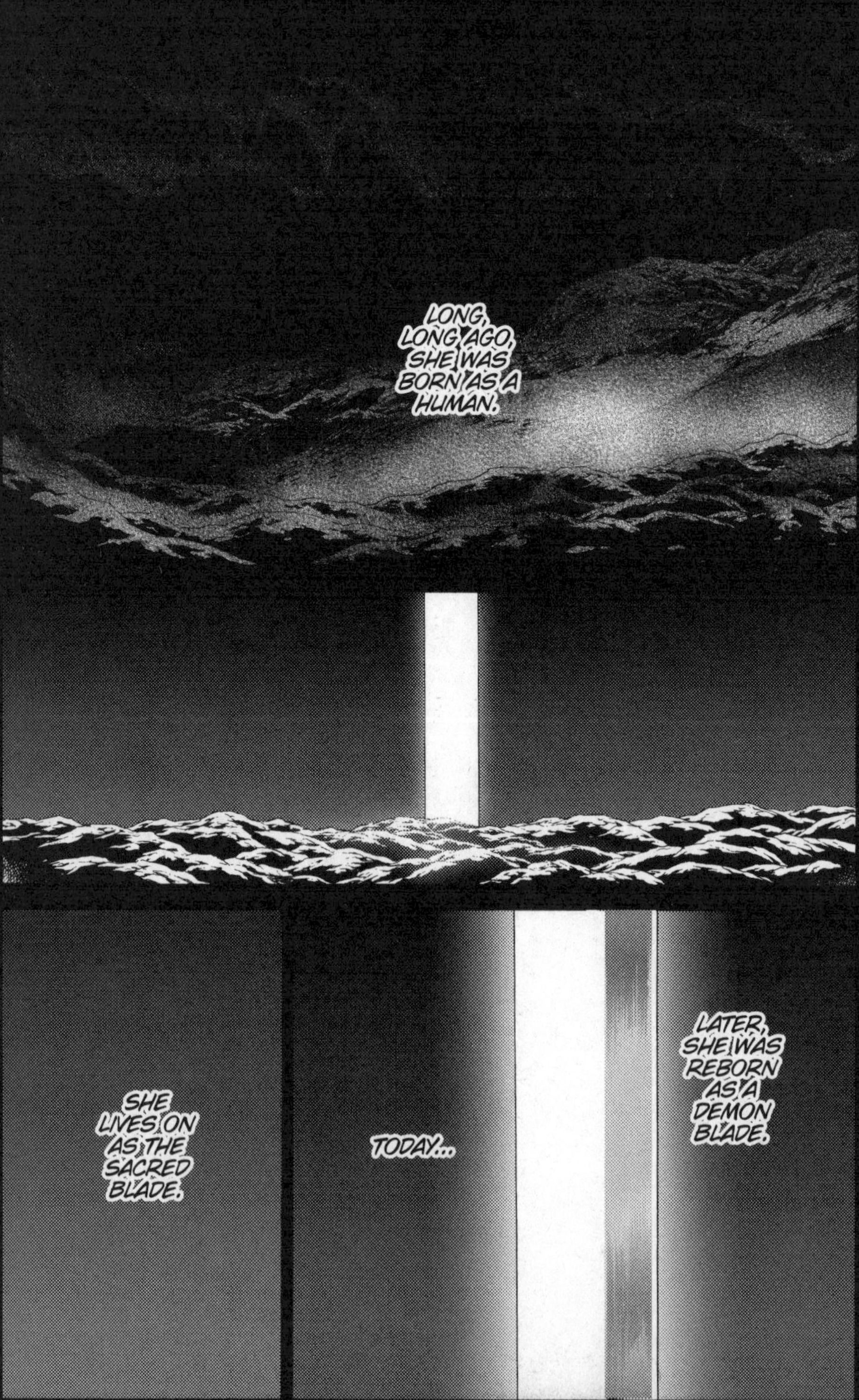
LONG, LONG AGO, SHE WAS BORN AS A HUMAN.
LATER, SHE WAS REBORN AS A DEMON BLADE.
TODAY...
SHE LIVES ON AS THE SACRED BLADE.

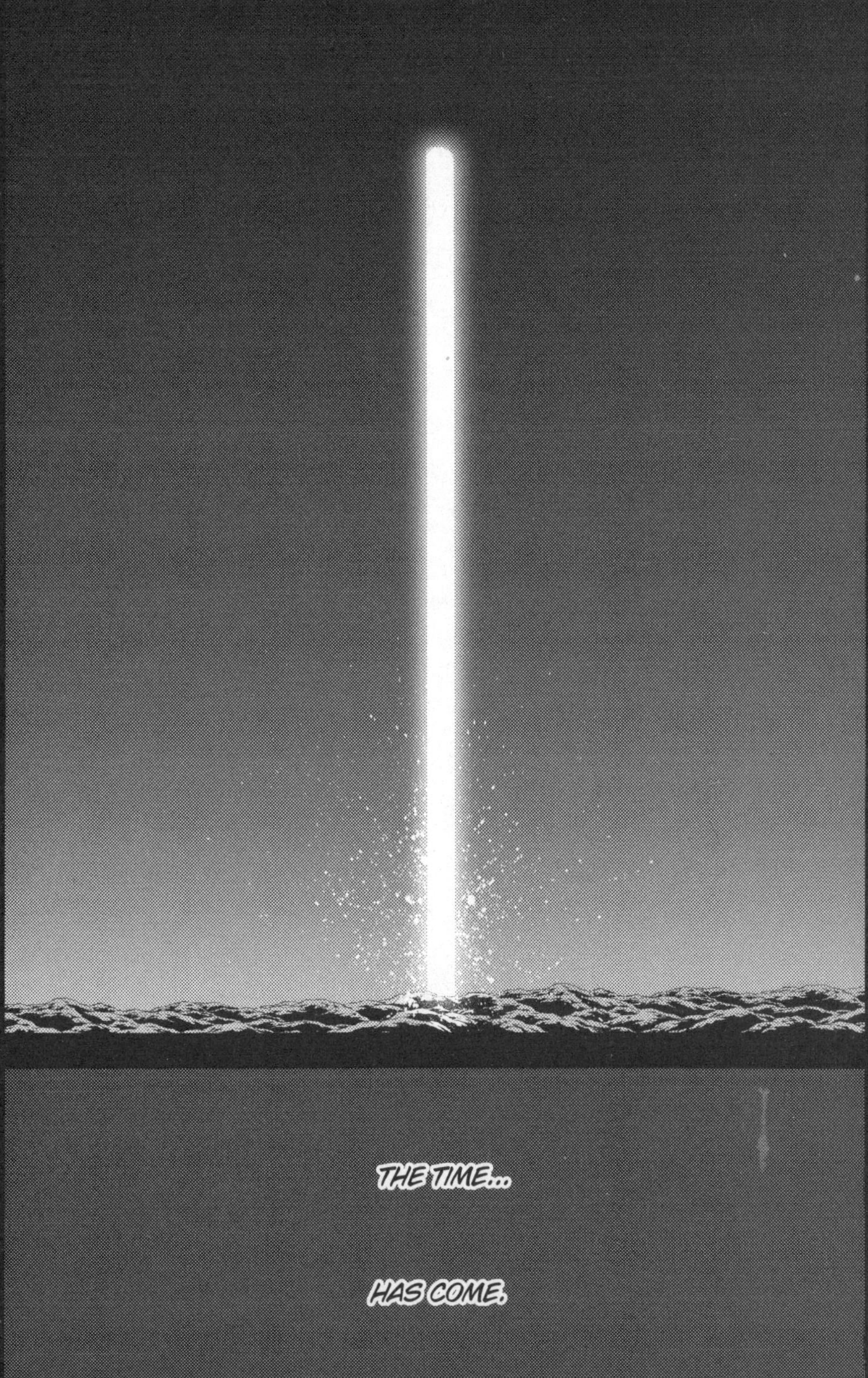
THE TIME...
HAS COME.

To be continued...

The Sacred Blacksmith

聖剣の刀鍛冶

アトリエ 工房リーザ

atelier Liza BRANCH OFFICE I

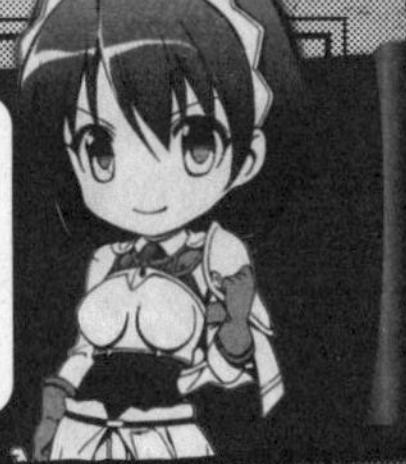

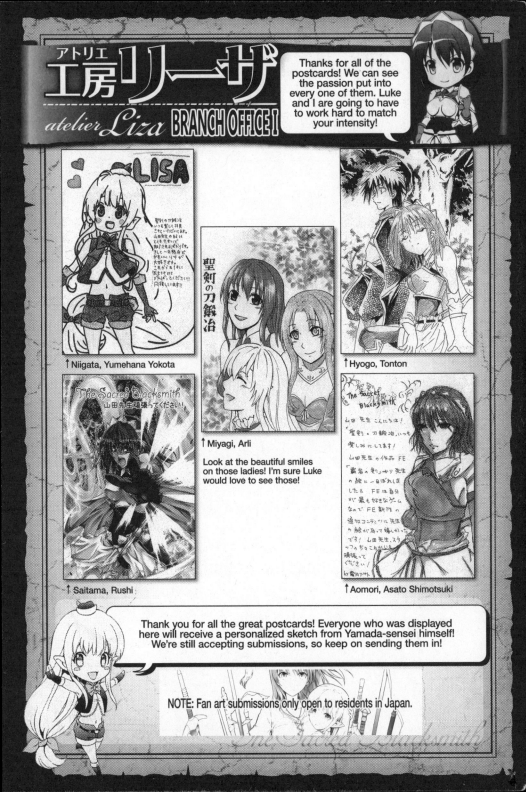

Thanks for all of the postcards! We can see the passion put into every one of them. Luke and I are going to have to work hard to match your intensity!

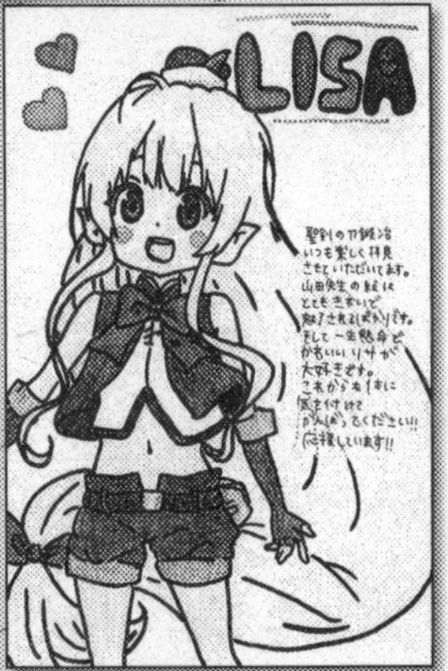
LISA

↑ Niigata, Yumehana Yokota

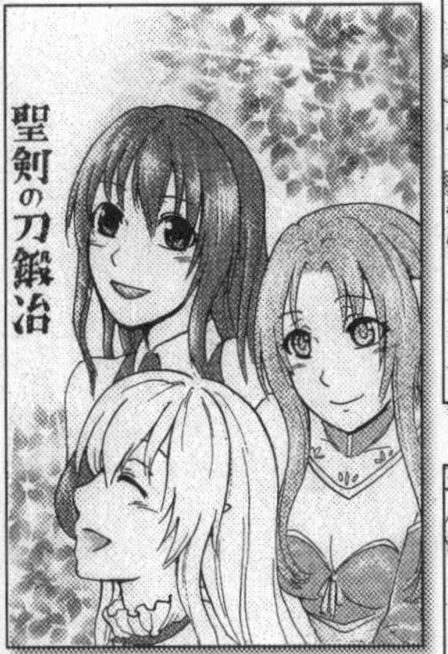
聖剣の刀鍛冶

↑ Miyagi, Arli

Look at the beautiful smiles on those ladies! I'm sure Luke would love to see those!

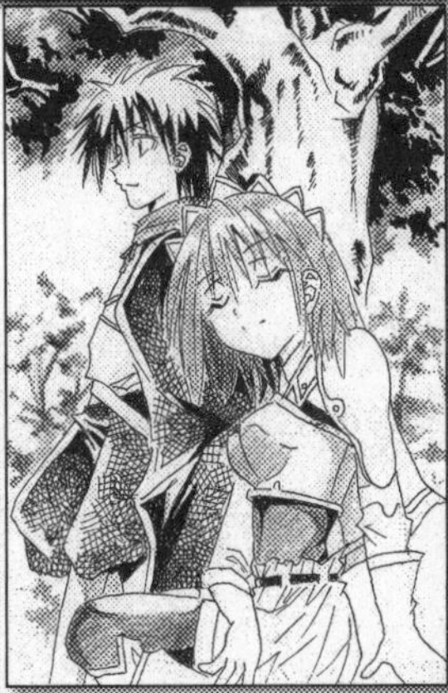

↑ Hyogo, Tonton

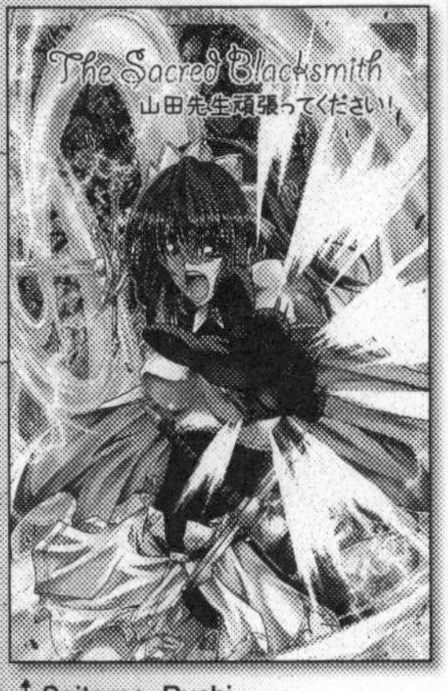
The Sacred Blacksmith
山田先生頑張ってください!

↑ Saitama, Rushi

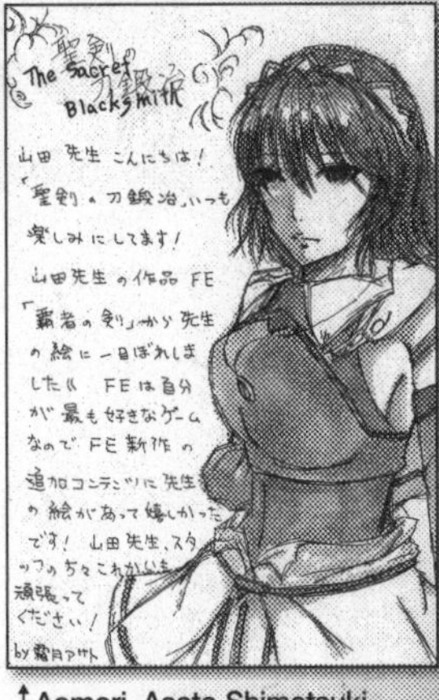
聖剣の刀鍛冶
The Sacred Blacksmith
山田先生こんにちは!
「聖剣の刀鍛冶」いつも楽しみにしてます!
by 霜月アサト

↑ Aomori, Asato Shimotsuki

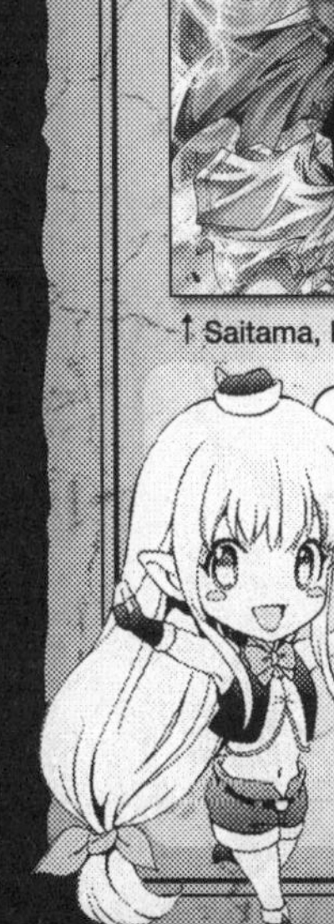

Thank you for all the great postcards! Everyone who was displayed here will receive a personalized sketch from Yamada-sensei himself! We're still accepting submissions, so keep on sending them in!

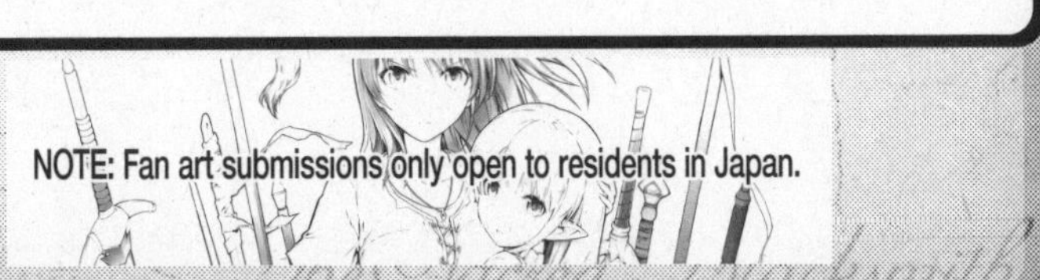

NOTE: Fan art submissions only open to residents in Japan.

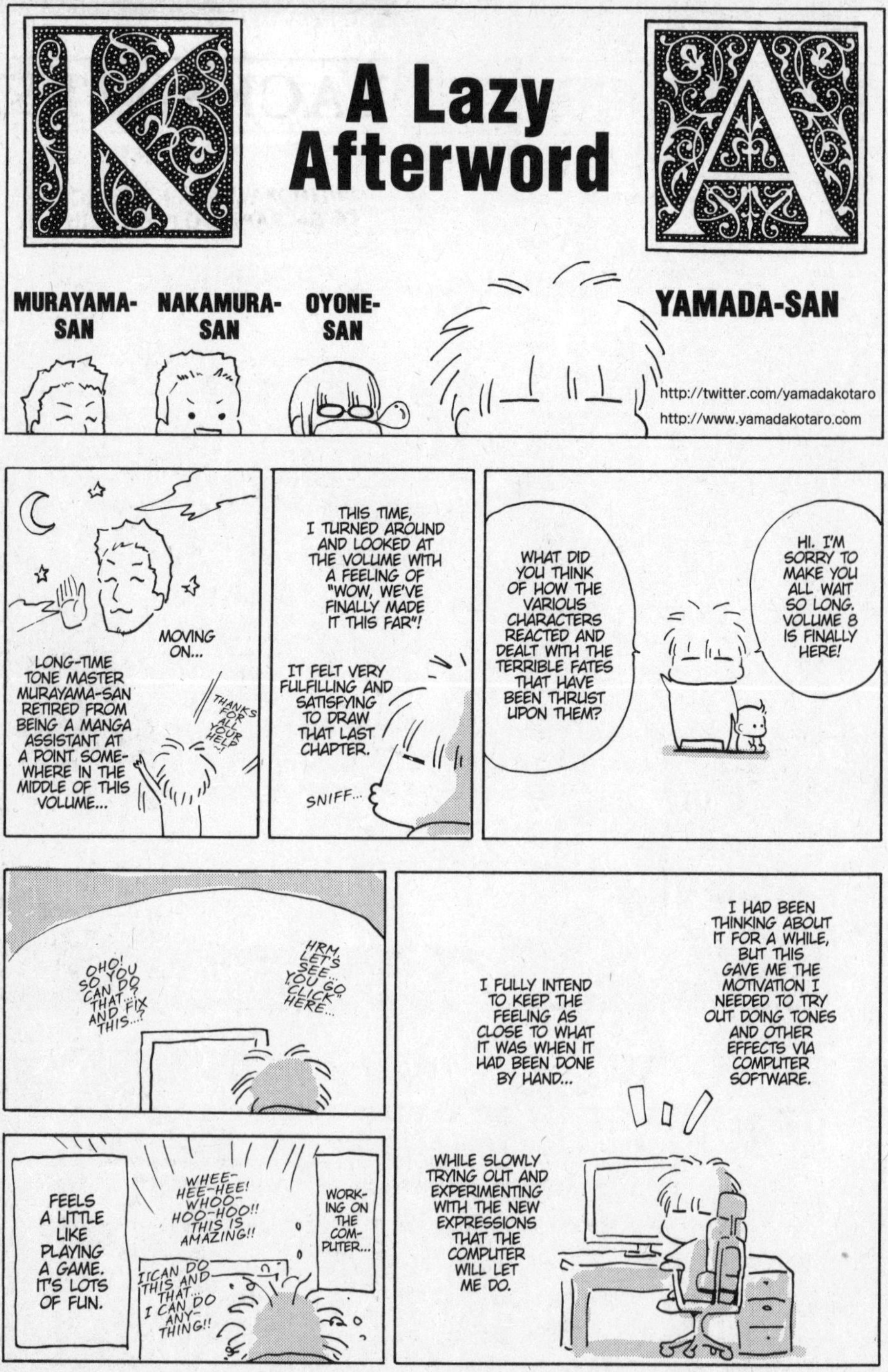
A Lazy Afterword
YAMADA-SAN
http://twitter.com/yamadakotaro
http://www.yamadakotaro.com
OYONE-SAN
NAKAMURA-SAN
MURAYAMA-SAN
HI. I'M SORRY TO MAKE YOU ALL WAIT SO LONG. VOLUME 8 IS FINALLY HERE!
WHAT DID YOU THINK OF HOW THE VARIOUS CHARACTERS REACTED AND DEALT WITH THE TERRIBLE FATES THAT HAVE BEEN THRUST UPON THEM?
THIS TIME, I TURNED AROUND AND LOOKED AT THE VOLUME WITH A FEELING OF "WOW, WE'VE FINALLY MADE IT THIS FAR"!
IT FELT VERY FULFILLING AND SATISFYING TO DRAW THAT LAST CHAPTER.
SNIFF...
MOVING ON...
LONG-TIME TONE MASTER MURAYAMA-SAN RETIRED FROM BEING A MANGA ASSISTANT AT A POINT SOMEWHERE IN THE MIDDLE OF THIS VOLUME...
THANKS FOR ALL YOUR HELP~!
I HAD BEEN THINKING ABOUT IT FOR A WHILE, BUT THIS GAVE ME THE MOTIVATION I NEEDED TO TRY OUT DOING TONES AND OTHER EFFECTS VIA COMPUTER SOFTWARE.
I FULLY INTEND TO KEEP THE FEELING AS CLOSE TO WHAT IT WAS WHEN IT HAD BEEN DONE BY HAND...
WHILE SLOWLY TRYING OUT AND EXPERIMENTING WITH THE NEW EXPRESSIONS THAT THE COMPUTER WILL LET ME DO.
HRM, LET'S SEE... YOU GO "CLICK" HERE...
OHO! SO YOU CAN DO THAT...? AND FIX THIS...?
WORKING ON THE COMPUTER...
WHEE-HEE-HEE! WHOO-HOO-HOO!! THIS IS AMAZING!!
I CAN DO THIS AND THAT... I CAN DO ANYTHING!!
FEELS A LITTLE LIKE PLAYING A GAME. IT'S LOTS OF FUN.

SEVEN SEAS ENTERTAI[NMENT]

THE SACRED B[LACKSMITH]

art by **KOTARO YAMADA** / story by **ISAO MIURA**
Original Character Designs by **LUNA**

VOLUME 8

TRANSLATION
Adrienne Beck

ADAPTATION
Janet Houck

LETTERING
Roland Amago

LAYOUT
Bambi Eloriaga-Amago

COVER DESIGN
Nicky Lim

PROOFREADER
Shanti Whitesides

ASSISTANT EDITOR
Lissa Pattillo

MANAGING EDITOR
Adam Arnold

PUBLISHER
Jason DeAngelis

THE SACRED BLACKSMITH VOL. 8
©2013 Kotaro Yamada, ©2013 Isao Miura
Edited by MEDIA FACTORY.
First published in Japan in 2012 by KADOKAWA CORPORATION, Tokyo.
English translation rights reserved by Seven Seas Entertainment, LLC.
under the license from KADOKAWA CORPORATION, Tokyo.

Seven Seas books may be purchased in bulk for educational, business, or
promotional use. For information on bulk purchases, please contact Macmillan
Corporate & Premium Sales Department at 1-800-221-7945 (ext 5442)
or write specialmarkets@macmillan.com.

Seven Seas and the Seven Seas logo are trademarks of
Seven Seas Entertainment, LLC. All rights reserved.

ISBN: 978-1-626921-62-7

Printed in Canada

First Printing: July 2015

10 9 8 7 6 5 4 3 2 1

FOLLOW US ONLINE: *www.gomanga.com*

READING DIRECTIONS

This book reads from *right to left*, Japanese style.
If this is your first time reading manga, you start
reading from the top right panel on each page and
take it from there. If you get lost, just follow the
numbered diagram here. It may seem backwards at
first, but you'll get the hang of it! Have fun!!

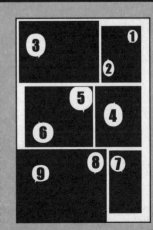